The Cambridge Companion to Brahms

This companion gives a comprehensive view of the German
composer Johannes Brahms (1833–97). Twelve chapters by leading
scholars and musicians provide systematic coverage of the
composer's life and works. Their essays represent the latest research
and reflect changing attitudes towards a composer whose public
image has long been out of date.

The first part of the book contains three chapters on Brahms's
early life in Hamburg and on the middle and later years in Vienna.
The central section considers the musical works in all genres, while
the last part of the book offers personal accounts and responses from
a conductor (Roger Norrington), a composer (Hugh Wood) and an
editor of Brahms's original manuscripts (Robert Pascall).

The volume as a whole is an important addition to Brahms
scholarship and provides indispensable information for all
enthusiasts and students of Brahms's music.

Michael Musgrave is Emeritus Professor of Music at Goldsmiths
College, University of London. He is author of *The Musical Life of
the Crystal Palace*, *The Music of Brahms*, and *Brahms: A German
Requiem* in the series Cambridge Music Handbooks.

Cambridge Companions to Music

Composers

The Cambridge Companion to Bach
Edited by John Butt
0 521 45350 X (hardback)
0 521 58780 8 (paperback)

The Cambridge Companion to Berg
Edited by Anthony Pople
0 521 56374 7 (hardback)
0 521 56489 1 (paperback)

The Cambridge Companion to Brahms
Edited by Michael Musgrave
0 521 48129 5 (hardback)
0 521 48581 9 (paperback)

The Cambridge Companion to Chopin
Edited by Jim Samson
0 521 47752 2 (paperback)

The Cambridge Companion to Handel
Edited by Donald Burrows
0 521 45425 5 (hardback)
0 521 45613 4 (paperback)

The Cambridge Companion to Schubert
Edited by Christopher Gibbs
0 521 48229 1 (hardback)
0 521 48424 3 (paperback)

The Cambridge Companion to

BRAHMS

EDITED BY
Michael Musgrave

CAMBRIDGE
UNIVERSITY PRESS

PUBLISHED BY THE PRESS SYNDICATE OF THE UNIVERSITY OF CAMBRIDGE
The Pitt Building, Trumpington Street, Cambridge CB2 1RP, United Kingdom

CAMBRIDGE UNIVERSITY PRESS
The Edinburgh Building, Cambridge CB2 2RU, United Kingdom http://www.cup.cam.ac.uk
40 West 20th Street, New York, NY 10011–4211, USA http://www.cup.org
10 Stamford Road, Oakleigh, Melbourne 3166, Australia

First published 1999

Printed in the United Kingdom at the University Press, Cambridge

Typeset in Adobe Minion 10.75/14 pt, in QuarkXpress™ [SE]

A catalogue record for this book is available from the British Library

Library of Congress cataloguing in publication data
The Cambridge Companion to Brahms / edited by Michael Musgrave.
        p.   cm. –
Includes work list, bibliographical references, and index.
ISBN 0 521 48129 5 (hardback) – ISBN 0 521 48581 9 (paperback)
1. Brahms, Johannes, 1833–1897 – Criticism and interpretation.
I. Musgrave, Michael, 1942–   .
ML410.B8C36   1998
780′.92–dc21   98–3057   CIP
[B]

ISBN 0 521 48129 5 hardback
ISBN 0 521 48581 9 paperback

Contents

Illustrations

Acknowledgements

Music examples are reproduced by kind permission of the copyright owners. Ex. 8.1: Ludwig Doblinger (B. Herzmansky) KG, Vienna (c. 1984); Ex. 9.10b, G. Schirmer Inc., New York; Exx. 8.4b, 8.6a, 8.7a, 8.7b, Peters Edition Limited, London (Peters Editions Nos. 3672, 2082). All other examples in score are taken from the *Johannes Brahms Sämtliche Werke*, 1926–8, published by Breitkopf & Härtel, Wiesbaden. All newly engraved examples are by Brian Fairtile, New York City. Illustrations and plates are by courtesy of and with thanks to the following institutions: Plate 1.1 and 1.2, Brahms Institut, Lübeck; Plate 11.1, Pierpont Morgan Library, New York; Plate 11.2, Brahms Institut, Lübeck; Plate 11.3, Gesellschaft der Musikfreunde, Vienna; Plate 12.1, Bildarchiv, Österreichische Nationalbibliothek, Vienna; Plate 12.2, Gesellschaft der Musikfreunde, Vienna. The jacket image is by courtesy of the Portrait Gallery of the Royal College of Music, London, with thanks.

Particular thanks are expressed to Morna Flaum for assistance with typing and to Daniel Grieco for assistance with translations; to Edward Roesner and Virginia Hancock; and to Lucy Carolan for her most painstaking and helpful editing of the text. Finally, I am indebted to my contributors for their patience during the preparation of this book, and I thank Roger Norrington especially for his kind hospitality during the preparation of his chapter.

Michael Musgrave

Contributors

Kurt Hofmann has assembled since the 1950s the largest private collection of Brahms material, which has formed the main part of the Brahms-Institut at Lübeck, of which he is Director with Renate Hofmann. His research has resulted in publications, many of them standard works of reference, including the editing of the reminiscences of Richard Heuberger and Richard Barth, a study of the first editions (*Die Erstdrucke der Werke von Johannes Brahms*, Tutzing, 1975), a detailed calendar of Brahms's life (*Johannes Brahms: Zeittafel zu Leben und Werk*, with Renate Hofmann, Tutzing, 1983), a revised listing of Brahms's library (*Die Bibliothek von Johannes Brahms*, Hamburg, 1974), and studies of Brahms's connections with Hamburg and Baden Baden. Professor Hofmann is an editor of the *Johannes Brahms Briefwechsel: Neue Folge*, which has continued the original, sixteen-volume, series of *Briefwechsel*.

Leon Botstein is editor of *The Musical Quarterly*, conductor of the American Symphony Orchestra and President of Bard College, New York, where he has pioneered annual festivals devoted to individual composers, including, in 1990, Brahms. His Brahms writings include articles on concert life, science and music in Brahms's Vienna, and on Brahms and nineteenth-century painting. He is editor of and contributor to *The Compleat Brahms*, forthcoming from Schirmer in 1999. As a conductor he has performed little-known nineteenth- and twentieth-century orchestral and choral works. His recordings include performances of works by Joachim and Schubert, in orchestrations by Joachim, Mottl and Webern, and Brahms's Serenade in D, in both its published version and a reconstructed version as a nonet.

John Rink is Reader in Music at Royal Holloway, University of London. His fields of specialism are performance studies, theory and analysis, and nineteenth-century studies. He is the author of *Chopin: The Piano Concertos* (1997), joint editor, with Jim Samson, of *Chopin Studies 2* (1994) and editor of *The Practice of Performance: Studies in Musical Interpretation* (1995), all published by Cambridge University Press. Dr Rink is Project Director and one of three series editors of *The Complete Chopin – A New Critical Edition* (Peters Edition).

David Brodbeck is Associate Professor and Chair of the Department of Music at the University of Pittsburgh. He is former President of the American Brahms Society and edits the series of *Brahms Studies* published by the University of Nebraska Press. He has contributed essays to *Brahms Studies: Analytical and Historical Studies* (Oxford University Press, 1990), *Mendelssohn Studies* (Cambridge University Press, 1992), *Brahms and His World* and *Mendelssohn and His World* (both Princeton University Press) and *Schubert: Critical and Analytical Studies* (University of Nebraska Press), as well as to the periodicals *19th-Century Music* and *Journal of Musicology*. He is author of *Brahms: Symphony No. 1* (Cambridge University Press, 1997).

Kofi Agawu is Professor of Music at Princeton University, having previously taught at King's College London, Cornell University and Yale University. He is the author of *Playing with Signs: A Semiotic Interpretation of Classical Music* (Princeton University Press, 1991) and of many analytical articles, including 'Theory and Practice in the Analysis of the Nineteenth-Century German Lied' in the journal *Music Analysis*, 1992. His study *African Rhythm: A Northern Ewe Perspective* was published by Cambridge University Press in 1995.

Malcolm MacDonald is the editor of *Tempo*, the quarterly magazine of modern music. He lives in Gloucestershire as a freelance writer on music. As 'Calum MacDonald' he has broadcast and contributed to many periodicals on a wide range of subjects, especially twentieth-century music. His books include the volume *Schoenberg* in the *Master Musicians* series, a three-volume study of the music of the English composer Havergal Brian and a major study of the life and works of Brahms in the expanded *Master Musicians* format in 1990. He is currently completing a book on the music of Varèse.

Daniel Beller-McKenna earned his Ph.D. from Harvard University in 1994 and has taught at the University of South Carolina and the University of New Hampshire, where he is Assistant Professor of Music History. His essays on Brahms's vocal and orchestral music have appeared in the *Journal of Musicology*, *19th Century Music*, *The New York Times*, and various anthologies of Brahms studies. He is currently writing a book on the intersection of religious music and nationalism in Brahms's music. He is also preparing a series of essays on John Lennon and the Beatles, the first of which will appear in *Music & Letters* (1999). Beller-McKenna is Vice President of the American Brahms Society and a member of the American Musicological Society Council.

Roger Norrington founded and conducted The Schütz Choir of London in 1962 and The London Classical Players in 1980. A leading pioneer in the performance of music using original instruments and playing styles, he has presented a number of extended weekend 'Experiences' on London's South Bank and abroad devoted to major composers; these have included, in 1992, 'The Brahms Experience', centring on a performance of *A German Requiem*. His wide catalogue of recordings includes – in addition to the symphonies of Brahms, the *German Requiem* and other choral and orchestral works – the complete symphonies of Beethoven, symphonies by Schubert, Schumann and Bruckner, overtures of the early romantic period, and operas of Mozart (*The Magic Flute* and *Don Giovanni*). Sir Roger received his knighthood in 1997.

Robert Pascall is Professor of Music and Head of the Music Department at the University of Wales, Bangor, and Professor Emeritus of the University of Nottingham. He is president of the Society for Music Analysis, Chair of the Editorial Board of the journal *Music Analysis*, Vice Chair of the new *Johannes Brahms Gesamtausgabe*, and Corresponding Director of the American Brahms Society. He has published on Brahms and his contemporaries, on nineteenth-century music history and on Franz Schmidt; his edition of Brahms's First Symphony for the *Johannes Brahms Gesamtausgabe* inaugurated the edition in 1996, and he will edit all four symphonies.

Hugh Wood is a composer who has worked at Cambridge for twenty years as

University Lecturer in Music and as Director of Studies in Music at Churchill College, of which he is a Fellow. He studied composition with Iain Hamilton and then with Mátyás Seiber. He has written much chamber music, including four string quartets; a vocal-orchestral piece *Scenes from Comus* (with which he made his *Prom* debut in 1965); concertos for cello, for violin and for piano, and a chamber concerto; a chamber-orchestral song cycle to poems of Pablo Neruda; a cantata; and a symphony. He has also written about fifty songs, including four sets to poems by Robert Graves.

Michael Musgrave is Emeritus Professor of Music at Goldsmiths College, University of London and lives and works in New York City. The focus of his research is German and English music of the nineteenth century, on which he has written and broadcast widely. His books include *The Music of Brahms* (1985, rev. edn Oxford University Press, 1994), *The Musical Life of the Crystal Palace* (Cambridge University Press, 1995), *Brahms: A German Requiem* (Cambridge University Press, 1996). He is editor of the Brahms Serenades Opp. 11 and 16 for the new *Johannes Brahms Gesamtausgabe* and a contributor to the forthcoming edition of *The New Grove Dictionary of Music and Musicians* and the *New Dictionary of National Biography*. He is a member of the Advisory Board of *Music Analysis*.

Chronology

1833	Brahms born 7 May, in Hamburg, son of Johann Jacob Brahms and Christiane Nissen.	Mendelssohn: *Italian Symphony*; Marschner: *Hans Heiling*. Borodin born.
1834		Liszt: *Harmonies poétiques et religieuses*; Berlioz: *Harold in Italy*. First issue of *Neue Zeitschrift für Musik* published in Leipzig.
1835	Birth of younger brother Fritz, 26 March.	Donizetti: *Lucia di Lammermoor*, Naples; Schumann: *Carnaval*. Mendelssohn appointed conductor of the Leipzig Gewandhaus Orchestra. Bellini dies, Saint-Saëns born.
1836		Glinka: *A Life for the Tsar*, St Petersburg; Meyerbeer: *Les Huguenots*, Paris.
1837		Berlioz: *Grande messe des morts*; Liszt: *24 grandes Etudes*. Field and Hummel die. Balakirev born.
1838	Family moves to 38 Ulricusstrasse.	Schumann: *Kinderszenen* and *Kreisleriana*. Bizet and Bruch born.
1839	Begins lessons with his father. Attends the *Privatschule* of Heinrich Voss, Dammthorwall.	Berlioz: *Roméo et Juliette* Symphony. Musorgsky born.
1840	Begins piano lessons with Otto Cossel.	Schumann marries Clara Wieck and composes over a hundred songs. Paganini dies.
1841	The family moves to Dammthorwall 29.	Schumann's symphonic year. Chabrier and Dvořák born.
1842	A great fire destroys much of Hamburg (8 May) Attends *Bürgerschule*.	Wagner: *Rienzi*, Dresden; Verdi: *Nabucco*, Milan; Glinka: *Ruslan and Ludmilla*, St Petersburg. Schumann: Piano Quintet and other chamber works. Mendelssohn: *Scottish Symphony*. Boito, Massenet, Sullivan born; Cherubini dies.
1843	First appearance as pianist. Offer of an American tour.	Wagner: *Flying Dutchman*, Dresden; Berlioz: *Treatise on Orchestration*. Opening of the Leipzig Conservatoire. Grieg, Heinrich von Herzogenberg born.
1844		Mendelssohn: Violin Concerto; Nietzsche, Rimsky-Korsakov born. Liszt at Weimar.

1845	Now entirely Marxsen's pupil.	Wagner: *Tannhäuser*; Schumann: Piano Concerto. Fauré born.
1846		Berlioz: *The Damnation of Faust*, Paris; Schumann: Second Symphony in C. Mendelssohn: *Elijah*, Birmingham. Ignaz Brüll born.
1847	Summer at Winsen, near Hamburg.	Mendelssohn dies.
1848	Hears Joachim play the Beethoven Violin Concerto in Hamburg.	Donizetti dies. Duparc, Parry born.
1849	Second solo concert.	Berlioz: Te Deum; Meyerbeer: *Le Prophète*. Chopin, Kalkbrenner, Nicolai, Johann Strauss I die.
1850	Fails to meet the Schumanns when they visit Hamburg. Composes songs and first chamber music.	Schumann: *Rhenish Symphony*; Liszt's first symphonic poem. Fibich, Henschel born.
1851	Scherzo in E♭ minor, which he plays to Henry Litolff.	Verdi: *Rigoletto*; Liszt begins issuing *Hungarian Rhapsodies*. Lortzing, Spontini die. D'Indy born. First volume of the Leipzig Bach Gesellschaft Edition published.
1852	Sonata in F♯ minor [later Op. 2] and more songs.	
1853	Sonata in C major [later op 1]. Concert tour with Reményi: meets Joachim in Hannover, Liszt and his circle at Weimar; Rhineland walking tour; meets Hiller and Reinecke at Cologne and the Schumanns at Düsseldorf. Schumann hails Brahms in the *Neue Zeitschrift für Musik*. Meets Berlioz, David, Moscheles in Leipzig. Opp. 1, 2, 6 published. First public performance in Leipzig (Op. 1, Op. 4).	Liszt: Piano Sonata, *Festklänge*; Schumann: Violin Concerto.
1854	Meets Bülow in Leipzig. Opp. 2, 4, 5 published.Travels to Düsseldorf to be with Clara after Schumann's attempted suicide. Works on a two-piano sonata in D minor, later orchestrated as a 'symphony'.	Liszt: *Faust Symphony, Orpheus*; Wagner: *Das Rheingold*; Berlioz: *L'Enfance du Christ*, 1850–4; Humperdinck, Janáček born.
1855	Lives in Düsseldorf. Concert tours with Clara and Joachim. Trio Op. 8 given in Danzig.	Chausson, Liadov, Röntgen born.
1856	Works on a Mass in canonic form; Sonata/Symphony in D minor converted into the D minor Piano Concerto (Op. 15); first version of the Piano Quartet in C minor (Op. 60) in C♯ minor. Counterpoint exchange with Joachim.	Liszt: *Dante Symphony*; Wagner: *Die Walküre*. Schumann dies; Martucci, Sinding, Taneiev born.

Lives in Hamburg until spring. Lives in
Bonn to be near dying Schumann. Visits
Detmold in Autumn. Subscribes to the
Bach Gesellschaft edition. First Brahms
performance in England (Clara plays
'Sarabande and Gavotte' at Hanover
Square Rooms).

1857 Composition and teaching in Hamburg.   Czerny and Glinka die; Elgar,
Second visit to Detmold. Appointed to   Leoncavallo born.
conduct and teach piano at the Detmold
court, position obtained though Clara
Schumann.

1858 Works at Hamburg on Piano Concerto.   Wagner: *Wesendonck Lieder*; Joachim:
Serenade (Op. 11) begun as octet or nonet. *Concerto in the Hungarian Manner*;
Folk-song arrangements. *Ave Maria* Op.   Berlioz: *Les Troyens*. Chrysander
12 and *Begräbnisgesang* Op. 13 composed.   founds the Handel Gesellschaft
Becomes greatly attached to Agathe von   Edition. Reubke dies; Puccini, Hans
Siebold. Second autumn at Detmold.   Rott, Ethel Smyth born.

1859 Secret engagement to Agathe von Siebold   Wagner: *Tristan und Isolde*;
broken off. Piano Concerto Op. 15   Verdi: *Un Ballo in Maschera*.
premiered in Hannover; Serenade Op. 11,   Spohr dies, Forster born.
'for small orchestra', premiered in
Hamburg. Founds the Hamburg
Frauenchor.

1860 Leaves Detmold for Hamburg. Serenade   Albeniz, Charpentier, Mahler,
No. 2 in A premiered in Hamburg   Paderewski, Rezniček born.
(Brahms); Serenade No. 1 in D 'for full
orchestra' premiered in Hannover
(Joachim). String Sextet Op. 18 premiered
in Hannover. The 'Manifesto' against the
New Germans published prematurely by
the Berlin *Echo*.

1861 Mainly in Hamburg and in the summer at   Marschner dies; Arensky, Chaminade,
Hamm, on the outskirts. First performance   McDowell born.
of the Handel Variations Op. 24 and the
Piano Quartet in G minor Op. 25

1862 Spring in Hamburg. Works on the   Verdi: *La Forza del Destino*: Otto von
Magelonelieder, String Quintet in F minor Bismarck made minister-president of
and C minor Symphony begun. Travels to   Prussia; Halévy dies; Debussy, Delius
Vienna (8 September) and remains till   born.
spring, meeting many musicians.
Successful performances, including the
first performance of Op. 26. Julius
Stockhausen appointed to conduct
Hamburg Philharmonic Orchestra.

1863 Spring/summer in Hamburg. Appointed   Mascagni, Pierné born.
conductor of the Wiener Singakademie for
1863–4. Travels to Vienna in August,
remains until Spring. First performance of
the *Paganini Variations* and Horn Trio.

1864 Summer in Lichtental with Clara Schumann. Meets her circle. Returns to Vienna for the winter.

Offenbach: *La Belle Hélène*. Meyerbeer dies; Richard Strauss born.

1865 Death of his mother in Hamburg. Summer in Lichtenthal, concert tours during the autumn and winter.

Liszt: *Missa Choralis.* Dukas, Magnard, Glazunov, Nielsen, Sibelius born.

1866 Continuing tour includes Oldenburg and Switzerland, with Joachim; completes *Ein deutsches Requiem* at Karlsruhe, Winterthur, Zurich and Lichtenthal. Returns to Vienna in November.

Liszt: *Christus;* Smetana: *The Bartered Bride;* Bruckner: Symphony 1 and Mass in E minor. Busoni, Satie born.

1867 Concert tours of Austrian provinces in spring and autumn; summer walking tour with his father and Josef Gänsbacher; returns to Vienna in November. Partial performance of *Ein deutsches Requiem* in Vienna (mvts 1–3).

Verdi: *Don Carlos;* Wagner: *Die Meistersinger.* Marx: *Das Kapital.* Sechter dies; Granados, Koechlin born.

1868 Tours of Germany and Denmark with Stockhausen; first important Brahms performance in France (Op. 34 in Paris); first performance of *Ein deutsches Requiem* in Bremen; June/July in Bonn; concerts in the Autumn with Clara and Stockhausen.

Bruch: Violin Concerto No. 1. Berwald, Rossini die.

1869 First performace of *Rinaldo* Op. 50 in Vienna; final version of the *Requiem* in Leipzig; concerts in Vienna and Budapest with Stockhausen; summer in Lichtental. From now based on Vienna.

Joachim becomes first Director of the Berlin *Hochschule für Musik.* Berlioz, Dargomizhsky, Loewe die; Pfitzner, Roussel born.

1870 First performance of *Alto Rhapsody;* attends *Das Rheingold* and *Die Walküre* in Munich.

Franco-Prussian War. Mercadante dies; Léhar, Novak born.

1871 First performance of first part of the *Triumphlied;* summer at Lichtenthal; first performance of the *Schicksalslied;* in December moves to Karlsgasse 4, thereafter his permanent home.

Verdi: *Aida.* Establishment of German Empire under Wilhelm 1. Auber, Thalberg die. Zemlinsky born.

1872 Death of his father in Hamburg. First performance of the complete *Triumphlied* in Karlsruhe; summer in Lichtenthal; becomes artistic director of the Gesellschaft der Musikfreunde.

Bizet: *L'Arlésienne.* Skriabin, Vaughan Williams born.

1873 Summer in Tutzing. Attends Schumann Festival under Joachim at Bonn in August.

Bruckner: Symphony No. 3; Dvořák: Symphony 3. Rachmaninov, Reger born.

1874 Summer near Zurich. Meets J. V. Widmann. Awarded Order of Maximilian by King Ludwig of Bavaria. Visits Leipzig

Bruckner: Symphony No. 4; Musorgsky: *Boris Godunov;* Smetana: *Vltava;* Verdi: Requiem. Franz and Munich, meets the Herzogenbergs and Philipp Spitta.

Schmidt born. Cornelius dies; Holst, Ives, Franz Schmidt, Schoenberg, Suk born.

1875 Resigns from the Gesellschaft. Works to complete the First Symphony at Heidelberg and near Zurich. Becomes a member of the music committee for the award of grants from the Austrian Government. Approves an award to Dvořák, whose music he is now coming to know and admire.

Bizet: *Carmen*; Goldmark, *Die Königin von Saba*; Tchaikovsky: Piano Concerto No. 1. Sterndale Bennett, Bizet die; Hahn, Ravel, Tovey born.

1876 Visits to Holland, Mannheim, Coblenz; summer at Sassnitz, Isle of Rügen where completes First Symphony. First performance of First Symphony at Karlsruhe (Dessoff). The beginning of his estrangement from Hermann Levi.

Bruckner: Symphony No. 5; Tchaikovsky: *Swan Lake*; first complete *Ring* cycle at Bayreuth; Goetz dies; Falla, Wolf-Ferrari, Ruggles born.

1877 Summer in Pörtschach and Lichtenthal. First performance of Second Symphony in Vienna (Richter).

Saint-Saëns: *Samson et Dalila*; Dvořák: *Symphonic Variations*. Dohnányi, Karg Elert born.

1878 First Italian holiday in April with Billroth. Brahms finds a new supporter in Hans von Bülow.

Tchaikovsky: Violin Concerto, Symphony No. 4; Dvořák: *Slavonic Dances*. Schreker born.

1879 Awarded an honorary doctorate by Breslau University. Summer in Pörtschach. Concert tour of Hungary, Transylvania and Poland with Joachim. First performance of the Violin Concerto (Joachim).

Bruckner: String Quintet; Franck: Piano Quintet. Jensen dies; Bridge, Ireland, Respighi born.

1880 Attends the unveiling of the Schumann Monument in Bonn; concert tour of the Rhine. First summer residence at Ischl, where he meets Johann Strauss II. Serious rift with Joachim over his suit for divorce from his wife Amalie.

Mahler: *Das klagende Lied*; Dvořák: Symphony No. 6. Bloch, Medtner born; Offenbach dies.

1881 Tours in Holland and Hungary where he meets Liszt again through Bülow. Spring holiday in Italy with Billroth and Nottebohm. Summer in Pressbaum near Vienna. Rehearses the Second Piano Concerto at Meiningen.

Bruckner: Symphony No. 6. Bartók, Enescu, Miaskovsky born; Musorgsky dies.

1882 Tours Germany and Holland with the Second Piano Concerto. Summer in Ischl. Late summer in Italy with Billroth, Brüll, Simrock. Graz in November with the dying Gustav Nottebohm.

Wagner: *Parsifal*. Kodaly, Malipiero, Grainger, Stravinsky, Szymanowski born; Raff dies.

1883 Summer in Wiesbaden, where he forms a close attachment to Hermine Spies.

Dvořák: *Scherzo Capriccioso*, Casella, Hauer, Varèse, Webern born; Wagner dies.

1884	Spring in Italy, summer in Mürzzuschlag. Winter tour as pianist and accompanist for Spies in Hamburg, Bremen and Oldenburg.	Mahler: *Lieder eines fahrenden Gesellen*; Debussy: *L'Enfant Prodigue*. Smetana dies.
1885	Summer at Mürzzuschlag. Premieres the Fourth Symphony at Meiningen, where he meets the young Richard Strauss. Subsequently tours with the work in Holland.	Franck: *Variations Symphoniques*; Dvořák, Symphony No. 7; Berg born; Hiller dies.
1886	Summer in Hofstetten near Thun. Elected Honorary President of the Wiener Tonkünstler-Verein. Visits Meiningen in October.	Goldmark, *Merlin*; Franck: Violin Sonata. Liszt dies.
1887	Spring holiday in Italy with Simrock and Theodor Kirchner, Summer at Thun.	Goldmark: *Ländliche Hochzeit* Symphony; Verdi: *Otello*; Bruckner: Symphony No. 8. Borodin dies. C. F. Pohl, archivist of the *Gesellschaft der Musikfreunde*, dies; succeeded by Eusebius Mandyczewski; Marxsen dies.
1888	Meets Tchaikovsky and Grieg in Leipzig. Spring in Italy with Widmann. Summer in Thun.	Franck: Symphony in D minor; Tchaikovsky: Symphony No. 5. Alkan dies.
1889	Awarded the freedom of the city of Hamburg. Order of Leopold conferred by Franz Josef. Summer in Ischl.	Dvořák: Symphony No. 8; Mahler: Symphony No. 1; R. Strauss: *Don Juan; Tod und Verklärung*; Henselt dies.
1890	Spring holiday in Italy with Widmann. Summer in Ischl. Meets Alice Barbi. Plans his will.	Wolf: *Spanisches Liederbuch*; Fauré: Requiem. Franck, Gade die; Martin born.
1891	Hears Mühlfeld play at Meiningen. Visits Berlin in the Spring. Makes Will. Friendship with Adolf Menzel. Attends Mahler's performance of *Don Giovanni* in Prague.	Wolf: *Italienisches Liederbuch*; Rachmaninov: Piano Concerto No. 1.
1892	Spring in Italy. Summer in Ischl. Death of Elisabet von Herzogenberg and of his sister Elise.	Nielsen: Symphony No. 1; Sibelius: *Kullervo* and *En Saga*; Dvořák: Te Deum. Lalo dies; Honegger, Milhaud born.
1893	Spring holiday in Italy and Sicily. Summer in Ischl. Work on the collected edition of Schumann's works. Hermine Spies dies.	Tchaikovsky: Symphony No. 6; Dvořák: Symphony No. 9; Verdi: *Falstaff.* Gounod, Tchaikovsky die; Haba born. Strauss: *Guntram*
1894	Summer in Ischl. Publishes the *Deutsche Volkslieder* in seven volumes. Offered but refuses conductorship of the Hamburg Philharmonic. Accompanies Alice Barbi at her final concert. Billroth dies.	Debussy: *L'Après-midi d'un faune*. Bülow, Chabrier, Rubinstein, Spitta die. Fauré: *La Bonne Chanson*. Mahler: Symphony No. 2;
1895	Tours German cities with Mühlfeld, performing the Clarinet Sonatas. Summer	Rachmaninov: Symphony No. 1; Dvořák: Cello Concerto;

in Ischl. Visits Clara in Frankfurt,   Hindemith, Orff born.
conducts in Zurich.

1896 Last public appearance as conductor.   Mahler: Symphony No. 3; Strauss: *Also*
      Conducts both piano concertos with   *sprach Zarathustra*; Puccini: *La Bohème*.
      d'Albert in Berlin. Attends Clara   Bruckner, Clara Schumann, Ambroise
      Schumann's funeral in Bonn. Summer in   Thomas die.
      Ischl. Deterioration of health. Goes to
      Karslbad to take the waters. Attends
      Bruckner's funeral.

1897 Last public appearance at a concert.   Cowell, Korngold born.
      Revises his will. Rapid decline in health
      and appearance. Death on 3 April of
      cancer of the liver. Public funeral 6 April.

Preface

Brahms in perspective

The last decades of the twentieth century have seen a striking increase in scholarly interest in the music of the nineteenth century. As this era moves yet further into the distance, it has been a fresh experience to find its repertory – long better known to concert audiences than that of any other period – viewed in a new setting, now that its social, political and creative backgrounds have been more fully revealed. In this new perspective, few images of composers have changed as much as that of Brahms. It has not been merely a matter of filling in the gaps of knowledge, or even of exploding certain myths. New examinations of his music have revealed just how much the received view of its significance was based on what it was *taken* to represent in the historical picture of the nineteenth century, rather than on its actual substance. With changing fashion after Brahms's death, an image full of stereotypes became even more firmly entrenched by neglect. For example, that of Brahms 'The Absolutist Composer', the implacable opponent of Wagner, whose own failure to write an opera indicated a lack of interest in drama and literature. And, growing from this, the all-encompassing view of Brahms 'The Conservative', in the light of his preference for instrumental forms in an age of increasing programmaticism. In few cases can the perception and evaluation of a composer's achievement have been so inadequate to the reality as with Brahms; in few cases can such oversimplified epithets – first the 'epigone' of Schumann; later, more durably, of Beethoven – have been so glibly applied.

There were of course good reasons for this failure to gain his measure. Brahms cultivated a classical profile in a romantic era, systematically mastering genre after genre in an age where specialism was the tendency. He commands an extraordinary historical position in the sheer range of the music he produced (though it does not extend to opera, it includes some highly dramatic vocal music). Few composers can be represented as typically in such accessible pieces as the 'Wiegenlied', the Hungarian Dances or the *Liebeslieder* waltzes, and yet also in complex fugues and variations, types of works which generally appeal to completely different audiences. And even to critics surveying the whole output, Brahms gives a different message – appearing to some as a sonorous Romantic, to others, a musical ascetic out of his historical time. Of course, Brahms sought to synthesise the many dimensions of his music and did so magnificently. But that very integration, the richness arising from – for example – the fusion of lyricism and complex counterpoint, has remained a problem for many listeners. For all the revision in attitudes towards his contemporaries, Brahms has continued to be difficult to categorise – hence the convenience of the catch-all label 'Conservative', which avoids the issue. And as with the music, so with the life: inherited images of a deprived childhood have continued to colour our views of Brahms's mature personality, to leave him as something of a mystery as a social being.

The sense of distance is perhaps the more remarkable in the light of Brahms's actual closeness to us in historical time and personal circumstance. Had he lived just a few years longer into the twentieth century (he was only sixty-three at his death), we would surely view him differently. As it is, those who remember him personally were still broadcasting their memories in the early years of the LP record after the Second World War. As a self-made man in an age of bourgeois culture, with all his lack of sentimentality about music and his religious scepticism, he seems much closer to our world than to those (only twenty years or so older) to whom he is so often related: Wagner, Liszt, Schumann, Mendelssohn.

Of course, there was always a narrow line of professional knowledge and admiration on the part of younger composers in the Austro-German tradition that kept alive a respect for Brahms's technical achievements as a composer. This manifested itself most openly in Schoenberg's famous essay 'Brahms the Progressive' (first broadcast in the centenary year of 1933, then published in revised form in 1950), which did more than any other text to place Brahms in a position of historical continuity. But Schoenberg saw Brahms as a 'progressive' essentially because of the Brahmsian principles he made his own: he was legitimising his often problematic music in claiming Brahms as his mentor. From the technical standpoint, Schoenberg's was always a one-sided view of Brahms, as was his view of the future. And Schoenberg' s successors would essentially grant Brahms's greatness despite rather than because of the full character of his musical personality: acknowledging the technical dimension, whilst passing with reserve over the expressive substance.

The situation is very different now. It is Brahms's place as a pioneer in reclaiming the past – a past much more distant than that explored by any other composer-contemporaries in this historicising era – that is now of interest. Of all composers of the nineteenth century, he seems central to modern outlooks in his lifelong concerns with the performance and editing of earlier music and its absorption into his own. Historical reference has become a new index of 'meaning' in modern composition, just as notions of abstract 'unity' and 'structure' were the shibboleths of Modernism. In tracing the continuity, Brahms now seems the most tangible link between the musical past and present. No longer an 'anti-Pope' (as he himself ruefully put it) to the great aesthetic innovator and 'progressive' of the century, Wagner, he now stands on an equal footing, relevant to late twentieth-century listeners as one of music's most powerful intelligences.

The aim of this book is to reflect changing attitudes in a range of essays written partly by established Brahms specialists and partly (especially in discussion of the music) by scholars coming to the music from different backgrounds. The book's three sections deal with his life, with his works and finally with the personal views offered by musicians with some special involvement with the music.

In Part I, Kurt Hofmann places Brahms's difficult early years in Hamburg in a completely fresh perspective with the help of new documentation. Here the familiar picture of the abused young prodigy forced to work in a low-life setting is significantly revised in the light of his family background and the life of the professional musician. Brahms's gradual estrangement from Hamburg and his earlier years of association with Vienna are the subject of my own essay, which sees this as a period of slow and difficult transition as he continued to attempt to establish himself as an independent composer from 1862 to 1875. Once established, however, Brahms became the most important musical figure in the city and released the major orchestral works by which he is best known to concert audiences. Viewing these compositions from a sociological rather than a purely musical standpoint, Leon Botstein offers new views of both Brahms's motivation for composing them and the political dimension of their performance and reception (so prominent a feature of Brahms's mature years in the city).

Part II covers the full range of Brahms's output. John Rink explores the three distinctive chronological and stylistic phases of Brahms's piano music in the light of the integrity of musical thought and technique which characterises his output, to reveal the brilliant resolution of striking tensions and dichotomies of style. Kofi Agawu shares an interest in the dynamic process which interacts with the larger form, pursuing the creative tensions between 'architectural' and 'logical' form at the heart of Brahms's style through identifying strategic moments in the symphonies. For all the familiarity of Brahms's orchestral work in the concert hall, his instrumental output was overwhelmingly devoted to chamber music, which exercised great influence on the younger generation. Its deep relationship with the past on the one hand and its profound originality on the other are explored in David Brodbeck's discussion of representative works from the entire output. A major additional theme, however, is their extra-musical dimension: reflecting recent emphases of scholarship, he seeks to uncover unsuspected biographical connections that help to erode the absolutist view of Brahms the composer. Malcolm MacDonald's discussion of the four concertos also blends the structural dimension – here the symphonic element as feeding the complex individuality of the works – while also emphasising the poetic and extra-musical aspect more than tradition has generally allowed. With the discussion of texted works, the issue of meaning in relation to form can be seen from the opposite position: that of the role of structure in communicating expression. Brahms's large and varied output of choral music, of both small and large proportions, accompanied and unaccompanied, is the least known part of his oeuvre. Yet, as Daniel Beller-McKenna reveals, the works inter-relate closely with those of other genres and have the added dimension of a frequently overt link to musical history or social context. Form and expression interact at a more intimate level in the vast output of solo songs with piano; my own discussion of them argues for a higher esteem of Brahms's ambitions and achievements through formal and stylistic subtleties in a wide range of examples.

In Part III, the discourse of biography and analysis is set aside for more personal responses to Brahms today. Roger Norrington approaches the music from the standpoint of a conductor seeking to realise the score in an historically informed light, using instruments and performing styles of the period. Facing similar issues from another perspective, Robert Pascall draws on the experience of editing the scores themselves for the new *Johannes Brahms Gesamtausgabe*, with the fullest reference to all the now available evidence, to clarify how Brahms produced them and the kinds of problems which attend their realisation. Finally, Hugh Wood places Brahms in the ultimate perspective for the present day, in responding as a composer himself, providing a further context for many of the preceding themes in the book: Brahms's personality, the nature of his achievement, how we relate to him in historical time, the values he enshrines and what they mean today.

PART I

Stages of creative development and reception

1 Brahms the Hamburg musician 1833–1862

KURT HOFMANN

Family background

Brahms's family associations with North Germany were long and deep. His forebears on his mother's side came from Schleswig-Holstein. They can be traced to Itzehoe, Tondem, Leck and Flensburg, and included school teachers, pastors and aldermen, several of whom belonged to the Schleswig-Holstein minor nobility: one of the most famous of them, the engraver Melchior Lorch (1527–86, the creator of the so-called 'Elbekarte' which bears his name), was also a prominent portrait painter. Research on the mother's side reveals a line traceable to connections with the Swedish king Gustav Wasa (1496–1560). Brahms's maternal grandfather, Peter Radeloff Nissen, migrated from Itzehoe to Hamburg, where, on 4 July 1789, Brahms's mother, Johanna Henrica Christiane Brahms, was born. The forebears on the paternal side led from Heide in Holstein, the birthplace of Brahms's father, Johann Jacob, to Brunsbüttel and further over the Elbe back to Lower Saxony, to the area between the Elbe and the Weser. It was from there that Peter Brahms, Brahms's great-grandfather, migrated to Holstein around 1750. His son Johann came from Brunsbüttel via Meldorf to Wöhrden, a suburb of Heide. His first-born son, Peter Hinrich, Brahms's uncle, later occupied the house that still exists today as the Heide *Brahmshaus*, (now in the possession of the Schleswig-Holstein *Brahms Gesellschaft*). In another, strongly built house in the market place in Heide, Brahms's father, Johann Jacob, was born. The paternal forebears were chiefly craftsmen and minor tradesmen.

The family name Brahms or Brahmst is fairly well disseminated in North Germany. The variants Bramst, Braamst, Brahm, even Bramst and Brambst are to be found in the seventeenth century in church registers in the vicinity of Cuxhaven (Lower Saxony). These variants are dialect forms, reflecting the spelling given to the officiating minister at the time of a birth or death: personal documentation did not then exist. There is therefore no conclusive identity to the family name; it is a question of ancient versions copied down at the time of christening, a practice which has still not completely disappeared from North Germany and especially Ostfriesland: an interpretation of the name as derived from *Bram*, the golden-yellow gorse bush of the area, as suggested by Max Kalbeck, is one possibility.[1] The name 'Brahmst' stood on Brahms's father's nameplate. The young Johannes often deleted the 't' at the end, explaining to Richard Heuberger as late as 1893 that 'gradually I got my father to give up the "t"'.[2] In Hamburg, Johann Jacob had had 'a description of the coat of arms and lineage of the name Brahms' drawn up by Kettnich's 'Wappen-Comptoir' ('Heraldic Depository') in Berlin.[3] The four-sided large-format documentation – which Brahms himself carefully preserved – relates the noble descent of the 'von Brahms' family to the middle of the seventeenth century, its origins supposedly in the 'Brahmins of India', who had travelled to Holland. The 'genealogical coat of arms' belonging to it hung in the living room of the Brahms family.[4]

Johann Jacob Brahms devoted five years to the study of music in Meldorf, Heide and Wesselburen. He mastered the violin, viola, cello, flute and flügelhorn, but later his main instrument was the double bass. Thus equipped, he came to Hamburg with his letter of apprenticeship at the beginning of 1826. He first played as a wind and string player in places of entertainment in the Hamburger Berg district, in what was known from 1833 as the 'Vorstadt St Pauli' (St Pauli Suburb), and as a street musician in the city's little alleys and courtyards. These offered the only possibilities for such music-making within the Hamburg city limits. After he had become acquainted with Johanna Henrica Christiane Nissen, later to be his wife, in 1829 and had found lodgings in her home, Ulricusstrasse 37, this solid, vigorous and industrious man looked out for his best prospects. Upon swearing the civic oath ('Bürgereid') in Low German on 21 May 1830, he was made a citizen of Hamburg. This was a requirement for marriage and any professional activity, and might even lead to the acquisition of landed property.

In order to categorise the social position of the Brahms family, it must be related to issues of cost and income in the so-called Hamburg 'lower class'. Rental costs for accommodation make a good starting point. The average annual rental for a 'modest' worker's dwelling – possessing a kitchen-cum-living room with a fireplace and a bedroom, the so-called 'alcove', in which a double bed was customary – amounted in 1842 (that is, before the great fire of Hamburg), to around 60 Hamburg marks; 'better' accommodation, with stoves and a living-room and two alcoves cost at that time around 84 marks annually. Half of the apartments of Hamburg in the Old and New Towns cost less than 100 marks annually. As a result of the Hamburg fire, which destroyed 1,749 houses, not only did the supply of accommodation for the lower classes decrease, but the cost of rent rose, especially for newly built houses, which now were mostly built with only four storeys. However, housing supply diminished not only because of the

Hamburg fire, but also owing to the steady increase in the existing population. A glance at the population statistics indicates this unequivocally. For example, though Hamburg already had 115,862 inhabitants in 1848, this number had risen in four years to 123,299, an increase of just under 6½ per cent that almost amounted to a population explosion.

In 1848, the annual income of a bricklayer was 498 marks for an eleven-hour day, six days a week, that of a carpenter (a joiner) 518 marks – to take only the highest earners among the lower classes. In 1848, a family of five had to pay 218 marks to cover the barest necessities of life, according to the calculations of the Hamburg poorhouse. If one adds to these essentials heating, lighting, clothing and schooling, at least 500 marks were required to cover the necessary commitments. And a quarter of the income had to be set aside for the rental. Rising rental costs meant less money for the essentials. This left child labour as the only possibility for improving income: the 13–14-year-olds earned 2–3 marks a week as drudges, that is, between 104 and 156 marks a year. If essential expenses exceeded income, cheaper accommodation had to be found; and this meant coming down in the world. The average family lived, therefore, from hand to mouth, and could be classed as the 'potentially poor'.

To return to the Hamburg Bürger Johann Jacob, however, one must distinguish between the lower middle class, which was qualified for the most general trades, and the middle class proper, whose members were required to have a considerable business. Since Brahms's father had applied to the Hamburg civil militia ('Bürgerwehr') as a 'musician' ('Musicus'), acquiring the rights of a free citizen was a costly affair. Johann Jacob had to show that he was in possession of uniform, weapon and movable property. On top of this, he had to pay at least 74 marks, a sum which approximated to a year's rent. It is already clear from this that Johann Jacob's social position at this time was on the borderline between the middle class and lower class, in the so-called 'Stand der kleinen Leute'.

On 26 May 1830 he became a 'Musicus' (musician) and a member of the 2nd Infantry Battalion of the Hamburg Bürgerwehr. Later, from 1837 until the Bürgerwehr's subsequent dissolution in 1867, he was a flügelhornist in the 2nd Jäger company. His monthly pay in 1867 amounted to 24 Hamburg marks. On his discharge he received the 'silver medal for good service' and a two-thirds pension as 'Oberjäger' (lit. 'leading hunter') for the rest of his life. The 'Instructions for the Members of the Music Corps of the *Bürger Militär*' dated 3 June 1839, which Johann Jacob was given, were carefully preserved by his son. On 9 June 1830, Johann Jacob married Johanna Henrica Christiane Nissen, seventeen years his senior. His social rise can be dated from this point. On 31 May

1831 he became one of the founder members of the Hamburger Musikverein by the 1840s he was considered to be one of the best double bass players in Hamburg). Beginning – from 1831 – as a deputy for the second violinist, he was from 1840 a regular member of the sextet of the Hamburg Alsterpavillon, which well-to-do Hamburgers liked to frequent. The earnings for each individual engagement were between 3 and 5 marks. His annual income in 1840 was somewhere between 804 and 1,002 marks. This total came jointly from his pay as a member of the civil militia and the earnings as double bassist of the Alsterpavillon sextet. Later we also have to add the income from his activity as a member of the Stadttheater, as a member of the orchestra of the Philharmonic concerts, and as organiser and active participant in chamber music evenings. Altogether, therefore, Johann Jacob had a very healthy annual income, as is indirectly to be confirmed from the last letter of Brahms's mother to her son (between 26 and 30 January 1865),[5] which reports quite astonishing outgoings and income: for example, that the father's income in 1864 was 1,800 marks. That the money sometimes did not suffice had less to do with the father's income than with his bursts of spending, in which he could only have indulged, however, if sufficient money were left over after the covering of all expenses. Accordingly, one cannot properly speak of poor circumstances in the parental home. If the statistics of the year 1867 testify that 20 per cent of Hamburgers lived in 'good' economic circumstances, we may conclude that Johann Jacob Brahms had already lived for around twenty years in this way. As for his social position, we can align it with that of Brahms's first teacher Otto Cossel.

One might compare him with the fathers of several other important composers, such as the father (and grandfather) of Beethoven, and the fathers of Carl Maria von Weber, Cherubini and Richard Strauss. Enterprising, calculating (except where his own finances were concerned), free-spirited and with an earthy sense of humour, this musician (who always spoke Low German) pursued no higher goal in life than to live it to the full and with the greatest enjoyment. He still enjoyed dancing in later years, and still played in the convivial *Lokals*, many of which later – though not, it should be noted, in the period of the son's youth – fell into disrepute. The achievement of his father, who had risen from the rank of rural petit bourgeois to that of a respected Bürger, a music teacher even, was always admired by the son: this was his role model.

The young married couple lived from Martinmas 1830 (11 November) in the Cordes Hof building, Bäckerbreitergang, where, on 11 February 1831, Brahms's elder sister Wilhelmine Louise Elisabeth (known as Elise) was born. In autumn 1831, again at Martinmas, the family of three took rooms on the first floor, left, in the back courtyard of

Schlüters Hof, Speckgang 24 (later Speckstrasse 60). Here, in a small room, Johannes Brahms was born on Tuesday 7 May 1833. Since the publication of Kalbeck's biography, the Brahms literature has made the seemingly ineradicable mistake of describing the living conditions of the Brahms family as poor and as determined by the worsening of their finances.[6] The portrayal of the birthplace as being in 'one of the most disreputable, narrow and darkest alleys in the notorious *Gängeviertel*', and as 'harbouring rabble of all kinds in its murkiest shadows' in the Brahms literature rests on the impressions first received by Kalbeck during his stay in Hamburg (though Alfred von Ehrmann still describes it so in 1933).[7] But this was the period around 1901. These were impressions of that time, which had nothing to do with Brahms's early years in the era of sailing ships. In Brahms's youth Hamburg was still a small city: parts of it belonged to Denmark or to the Kingdom of Hannover. Hamburg was still outside the German customs zone. At that time, in the epoch before the industrial revolution, the Hamburg *Neustadt* was not yet threatened by the extension of the harbour and the redevelopment of the city. The *Gängeviertel* arose through the disposition of smaller paths (*Gänge*) which had been laid out between the single small gardens inside the Hamburg city walls. In the seventeenth century, half-timbered houses were built on these little plots of land, which could only be reached through the prescribed *Gänge*. These houses were as a rule clean, indeed partly tended in the Dutch manner (with clean white curtains and flowering plants), and interspersed with trees and gardens. The inhabitants of the *Neustadt* ('New Town', so called since 1626) were predominantly middle-class people, minor tradesmen and respected artisans. Accommodation in the environs of the Stadttheater in the Dammthorstrasse and of the many other cultural establishments, was in great demand by musicians, singers, actors and other theatre people. The social classes were very mixed. Brahms's second teacher Eduard Marxsen, the most famous music pedagogue of his time in Hamburg, lived in the so-called 'Caffamacherreihe' near the Stadttheater, after the Hamburg fire of May 1842. He actually lived next to a widow who placed her rooms at the disposal of 'girls' in order to improve her income. This was also the case in the Dammthorwall, where, at No. 29, stood the house we can properly designate the 'Brahms House'. For it was here that young Johannes grew up and lived from his ninth until his seventeenth full year. From this house he went out for the first time into the public world of music, and it was here, as he later famously told Joseph Viktor Widmann, that 'the most beautiful *Lieder* came to me before dawn when I was cleaning my boots'.[8] The fact that the Brahms family changed their accommodation a total of eight times between 1830 and 1864 has nothing to do with their supposedly poor circumstances. An examination of each separate address in the census report drawn up at that time by the Hamburg civil militia results in a quite different conclusion: the apartments became bigger and more expensive.

The following list of the Brahms family homes between 1830 and 1864 differs from that to be drawn from Kalbeck's account and underlines the social rise of the father and the family.[9]

Period	Address	Annual rent
M 1830 – M 1831	Bäckerbreitergang 78 II, Cordes Hof	70 Hamburg marks
M 1831 – M 1833	Speckgang 24, Schlüters Hof	72 Hamburg marks
M 1833 – M 1836	Ulricusstrasse 15	108 Hamburg marks
M 1836 – M 1838	1. Erichstrasse above No. 7 Hamburger Berg, St Pauli Vorstadt	not known
1838? (according to Brahms's mother)	Schaarmarkt (hitherto never noted)	
M 1838 – M 1841	Ulricussstrasse above No. 38	90 Hamburg marks
M 1841 – S 1850	Dammthorwall 29	250 Hamburg marks up to May 1842; 300 marks after the city fire
S 1850 – S 1852	Kurze Mühren 13 I (new building after the fire)	225 Hamburg marks
S 1852 – S 1857	Lilienstrasse 7 I (where Clara Schumann lived in April 1855 with the Brahms family)	156 Hamburg marks
S 1857 – June 1864	Neustädter Hohe Fuhlentwiete 74 II	400 Hamburg marks

(M = Martinmas/November; S = Spring)

Contrary to general custom, the father had published a birth announcement in the *Wöchentlichen Nachrichten* on 8 May, so overjoyed was he at the birth of a son. The baptism was celebrated on 26 May in the great St Michaeliskirche. The two godfathers were his grandfather Johann Brahms from Heide and his uncle Philip Detmering (whose marriage to Brahms's aunt Christina Friederica (née Nissen) produced two sons, Heinrich and Christian). The third godparent was a Katharina Margaretha Stäcker (of whom we know no more). The family lived in the house of Brahms's birth for only six months before they moved to a bigger apartment at Ulricusstrasse 15, where the third son Friedrich, called Fritz, was born on 26 March 1835. At that time and even beyond the turn of the century, it was customary in Hamburg to move house regularly, because the landlord had to cover the cost of renovation.

The little flaxen-haired, blue-eyed 'Jehann' or 'Hannes', as he was called, was a small, delicate, pallid, dreamy but also playful boy. Like his sister, he suffered until puberty from nervous headaches. The father soon noticed that the child, whilst playing with his lead soldiers or with beans, immediately took notice when he practised his instrument. The genius manifested itself when the father realised that Brahms could effortlessly repeat correctly all the melodies that he heard: the child had absolute pitch. He discovered for himself a system of notation even before his father gave him music lessons. Brahms learnt to play the violin, was instructed in the fundamentals of cello playing, and the natural horn became one of his favourite instruments. At an early stage he received piano lessons from a colleague of his father. Kalbeck's assertion that there was no piano in the family home because of their meagre circumstances is not true. Elise Giesemann, a youthful friend from his time at Winsen (1847 and 1851), later wrote to Brahms, specifically recalling a piano 'which [stood] in your room' – obviously the family living room.[10] From 1839 Brahms went to an elementary school, and from 1842 to 1848 attended a good 'Bürgerschule'. Here he even learnt foreign languages. 'I read French quite well', he vouchsafed to his publisher Fritz Simrock as late as 1893.[11] There exists one Christmas greeting to his parents written in French, as well as an autograph two-sided letter composed in French to the French pianist Caroline de Serres of April 1889.[12] Nothing comparable is known of his skills in English. He could certainly read English but he never mastered the spoken language. School attendance was at that time voluntary and must obviously have been regarded as essential by the parents; the cost was in the region of 15 to 20 marks quarterly. That this expense was considered feasible for all three children is further indication of the secure social position of the Brahms family.

At the end of 1840 Brahms started piano lessons with Otto Friedrich Willibald Cossel (1813–65).

Cossel, taught by Eduard Marxsen, was considered an excellent teacher. Brahms placed great faith in him and continued to respect his memory in later years, commenting even in June 1896 to Richard Heuberger, 'you would hardly get a better grounding today than I received from my first teacher Cossel'.[13] Cossel had introduced Brahms to the essentials of the piano literature. His thesis that the pianist should be able to express through his fingers what he felt in his heart was absorbed by Brahms, as friends could see for themselves when he played for his intimate circle. Thus Joseph Joachim, in his first description of the young Brahms, wrote to his friend Gisela von Arnim on 20 October 1854 that he 'already makes music quite divinely, I have never heard piano playing (apart from that of Liszt) that satisfied me so completely.'[14] Among Cossel's papers (many of which were destroyed in the Second World War) are to be found several manuscripts and printed editions which bear

witness to the young musician's hours of study. These are (1) a page with a
Study 'Allegro' written out by Cossel with the comment 'when passing the
thumb under, the elbow must remain quite still'; (2) fugue No. 4 from J. S.
Bach's *Well-Tempered Clavier* BWV 849 written out by Cossel, with
fingerings in his hand and also that of Brahms; in addition, Cossel has
written out another study, of sixteen bars in 3/4, on the empty verso (3)
the 'Gavotte by J. C. von Gluck' (*sic*) in a single printed sheet by the
Hamburg publisher Johann August Böhme (c. 1842); (4) 'Momens musi-
cals' by Franz Schubert (D. 780, Nos. 4–6), published by the Vienna publisher Diabelli in a reprint of c. 1830; (5) 'Deutsche Tänze und Ecossaisen'
by Franz Schubert in a reprint by Böhme.[15] The fugue by Bach provides
the most certain indication of when Brahms first became involved with
his music, though in a largely technical way, as the numerous fingerings
confirm. The Schubert publication confirms that the young Brahms was
already drawing near to the art of the Viennese masters, and the 'Gavotte
of Gluck' certainly became one of his favourite pieces; this publication was
doubtless the starting point for his own later arrangement of the piece 'for
Frau Clara Schumann' (McCorkle, *Werkverzeichnis*, Anhang 1 N. 2), and
the preoccupation with this dance form may also have contributed to the
origins of his own Gavottes (McCorkle WoO 3). Though Cossel first gave
instruction in finger exercises and studies, Brahms later took on works by
Czerny, Clementi, Cramer, Hummel and Kalkbrenner. This and other
piano music he also practised in the family house on the Dammthorwall.
Brahms must have immediately made quick progress in piano playing,
since one can reasonably conclude that regular practice was not possible
in the family home owing to the cramped living conditions, and out of
consideration for his mother and sister, who had to work there.[16]

Study with Marxsen and first public appearances

In 1843 the ten-year-old *Wunderkind* had his first public success before an
invited audience. He played an Etude by Henri Herz and also the piano
part in Beethoven's Wind Quintet Op. 16, and in a Mozart piano quartet.
As a result of this appearance, an offer was made by an impresario to let
the young Brahms appear in America. Otto Cossel could only restrain the
eager father by ensuring that Brahms would study wholly with Eduard
Marxsen, Hamburg's leading teacher, who had previously resisted taking
sole responsibility. After a long period of reflection, Marxsen took over
the instruction around 1845. Brahms 's brother Fritz was likewise taught
by Cossel and later by Marxsen. Through Marxsen, Brahms came to know
the works of Beethoven, and, thirsty for knowledge, studied in Marxsen's

extensive library. There still survives a copy of Schindler's Beethoven biography of 1840 with the autograph signature of Eduard Marxsen and the visible evidence of the young Brahms's extensive reading: numerous turned-down page corners and distinctive markings can be identified in the volume, which Brahms probably borrowed from the teacher.[17] Marxsen's instruction was devoted to the classics; Brahms did not get to know either Chopin or Schumann, let alone Liszt's transcriptions. Instruction in theory and composition only followed later when Marxsen recognised the youth's creative strength. Marxsen often spoke of this period on later occasions, as when he wrote to Hermann Levi in 1873:

> restless eagerness and application awakened my interest more and more, and the manifestly rapid progress strengthened my opinion that an extraordinary God-given talent was here to be developed. I even taught him without any financial return for the necessary period. From the beginning of the studies, a clear- and deep-thinking spirit was apparent, and yet later on original creation became difficult for him and required a real amount of encouragement on my side. We also busied ourselves with the study of form. None the less the talent quickly developed, in my opinion more beautifully and significantly, even though at that time he had not yet produced a great work. When Mendelssohn's death was announced [in 1847] I observed to a friend from the deepest conviction 'a master of art is departed, a greater blooms in Brahms.'[18] Consequently he progressed with even greater speed to create outstanding songs and instrumental music, which later appeared in print.

In placing Marxsen's comments in perspective, however, one should note that this letter was written at a time when Brahms's renown as a composer was already established.

Marxsen's piano lessons lasted until 1847, the composition and theory lessons until 1848. Otto Cossel had already complained of Brahms in 1842 that 'it is a pity about him, he could be such a good player, but he will not stop his never-ending composing'.[19] Brahms later elaborated on this himself to J. V. Widmann: 'I composed, but only in secret and very early in the morning. All day I arranged marches for wind music and at night I sat at the keyboard in pubs.'[20] The twelve-year-old played a piano sonata in G minor to his youthful friend Luise Japha (later Langhans-Japha). This lost work must be his first known composition. In addition, Kalbeck notes that Brahms had composed at Christmas 1845 some 'Zwischenaktmusik' for the 'Theater Pittoresque', now lost, at the instigation of a Hamburg puppeteer in the Deichstrasse. That Brahms in later years was extremely disdainful of Marxsen's instruction, which he had at first praised to Louise Japha, can be explained by the reservations of his mother which emerge in her letters from the years 1854 and 1855. The parental home apparently had little faith in Brahms as a composer, thinking he would do better to give concerts and thereby ensure income for the essentials of life. [21] His mother was strengthened in her opinion by Marxsen, whom she had asked for advice concerning the matter. Marxsen too hardly believed Brahms to be capable of a freelance career as a composer, since he himself could not survive by composition. Brahms, who only a little earlier had been publicly promoted by Robert Schumann, no less, as the coming Messiah in his famous article 'New Paths', must have been severely affected by these attempts to make his own mind up for him. Moreover, his first works had already appeared in December 1853 from the leading Leipzig publisher Breitkopf & Härtel, establishing a degree of fame as a composer. Clara Schumann, who visited Brahms's parents' home in 1855, commented on this in her diary: 'It is so sad to me to see that they understand so little. The mother and sister can sense only that there is something extraordinary in him, but the father and brother cannot even do that.'[22] This remark certainly indicates the difficulty of the young Brahms's situation with his family. He depended entirely on his parents: they had enabled him to have a good education, but on the other hand they could not, or did not wish to, follow him into his world of the imagination. Marxsen's lessons had the goal of making him into an outstanding pianist. That was what the progressive studies and fundamental grounding in theory were for. Moreover, the development of Brahms the young pianist happened at a time when popular taste determined the content of programmes for anyone appearing in public. Salon pieces, fantasias and variations were popular, followed by folk music, especially music from the Scandinavian countries, and above all from Scandinavian artists such as Ole Bull and Jenny Lind, who performed in Hamburg. It was mainly this kind of music that the young Brahms came to know. This is reflected in the programme of his first appearance in a concert of the violinist Birgfeld on 20 November 1847: Brahms played the 'Norma Fantasy' of Sigismund Thalberg. The critics of the Hamburg paper *Freyschütz* of 27 November extolled the performance of the 'little virtuoso named J. Brahms', 'who not only displayed fine preparation, precision, clarity, strength and security, but has also acquired the spiritual, creative inclination and received excited and undivided applause on all sides'. On the day the criticism appeared, the little virtuoso was again to be heard. He played a duo for two pianos by Thalberg in a musical soiree together with the recitalist Therese Meyer. The Hamburg newspapers noted the young pianist 'Broms' or called him 'Bruhns' and attested to his exceptional talent and solid artistry. At the 'Memorial Celebration to honour the departed composer Felix Mendelssohn Bartholdy' which was given by the Philharmonic Society on 22 November 1847, the young Brahms also took part. He carefully preserved the programme with works of Beethoven, Cherubini, Mendelssohn and Graun.[23]

When Brahms commented to Widmann that 'at night he sat at the keyboard in pubs' it must not be assumed, as has been long believed, that these were 'notorious places'. Kalbeck's remark that 'to observe the picture of the unspoilt blondhaired, blue-eyed child and youth playing in unthinkably dreadful company has something deeply affecting about it' is simply false, and its facts have never been established.[24] Brahms never played in 'Tanzbordellen'. Unfortunately he portrayed himself in similar terms in his later years to Max Friedländer, as Robert Haven Schauffler has reported.[25] Of course, as a result of the location of his home in the Stadttheater district, he would have seen 'women of easy virtue' and their clients. He would have been shamed by these circumstances when he came to Düsseldorf and met Robert and Clara Schumann. But it is out of the question that he could have played for dancing in bordellos, for Paragraph 15 of the Hamburg statute of 1834, 'Regulation concerning Bordellos and Prostitution', specifies 'No landlords or girls should permit entry to young people under the age of twenty.' And under Paragraph 16 it even says that 'all dance music is forbidden in bordellos'. When Brahms commented on or alluded in later years to playing in sailors' taverns to Siegfried Ochs and Josef Victor Widmann (as well as Friedländer),[26] he was really appealing to the cult of the hero so prevalent in the nineteenth century: he could be certain that the people with whom he was in conversation would admire his rise as a genius from such a background all the more. In this endeavour, only Max Kalbeck exceeded him in portraying his youth, even having the presumption to assert that 'Brahms grasped every opportunity to strike up a tune for dancing with all ten fingers'.[27] Yet on the other hand, Kalbeck also quotes Luise Langhans-Japha as indicating that Brahms 'never recalled [to her] that he had to play dance music'.[28] Brahms's aversion to presenting himself openly remained with him throughout his life. By Brahms's time, the word *Kneipe* had acquired much better connotations than it had had in the eighteenth century, when it was still was used for all small and low-class taverns. Since the liberation wars of 1813, when the students took this word over for their collective meetings, it had already become a fashionable word for different kinds of *Gasthäuser* or inns, and the words *Wirtshaus* and *Schenke* were almost completely forced out of general usage. *Kneipe* now designated better eating places as well as simple *Wirtshäuser*.[29] The word does not indicate that Brahms played in sailors' taverns. The sailors generally ventured only into the suburb of St Pauli outside the city limits; Johann Jacob played there before 1830 and from 1836 to 1838 when Johannes was five years old, but never the son. A friend of Brahms's youth, the pianist Christian

Miller, saw him playing for a dance on one occasion in 1846. Adolf Steiner has described it thus: 'At that time Brahms played on Sundays in a summer inn in Bergedorf near Hamburg for a fee of two thalers for the whole afternoon. There the young Miller heard him for the first time and was so impressed with his playing that he took the opportunity to perform with him. On the next Sunday the young people walked together towards Bergedorf and regaled their unsuspecting guests with four-handed piano playing.'[30] The summer hostelry referred to must have been the Gasthof 'Zur schönen Aussicht' in Bergedorf bei Hamburg, or the Gasthof 'Stadt Hamburg', a late eighteenth-century half-timbered building opposite the church of St Peter and St Paul, which still exists today.

The well-known anecdote according to which Brahms played for 'Twee Daler und duhn' (*Plattdeutsch* for 'Zwei Thaler und zu trinken, so viel er will': 'Two thalers and as much to drink as you want')[31] has even been connected quite erroneously with the 'Kneipen' in the harbour; this completely overlooks the fact that it referred to only one event in the private house of the Hamburg piano maker Schröder in the Grosser Burstah. According to Miller's report, Brahms earned two thalers in an afternoon or evening for his performance. One can readily assess the value of the income, since the value of a thaler at that time was 2 marks 8 schillings in Hamburg currency. Brahms therefore earned 5 marks for an afternoon. In comparison, it is worth noting that a week's wages for a printer was 9 marks and 13⅓ schillings, and that of a lithographer between 12 and 15 marks.[32] If one takes the average annual rent of 1848, namely 84 marks, as a further comparison, it is clear that from his fourteenth year Brahms was well rewarded for his activity as a pianist. Christian Otterer, who was a violist colleague of Johann Jacob in the orchestra of the Hamburg Stadttheater and a member of the Sextet in the Alsterpavillon – he lived at Dammthorwall 35, thus only a few houses away from the Brahms family house at Dammthorwall 29 – tells of Brahms's youth: 'With the best will in the world, I cannot remember that Brahms played in *Lokals* when he was still a young child; I was with his father every day at that time and would have known if it had been the case. Jacob was a quiet and upright man and held Johannes arduously to his studies, removing him as far as possible from general notice.'[33] Most conclusive, however, is the fact that an authentic witness, the wife of Otto Cossel, energetically refutes Kalbeck's assertion: 'It cannot be true, my husband never said such a thing when speaking of Johannes's childhood; and if he had known of it he would never have let it happen.'[34] Brahms therefore played in modest venues, though sometimes at more exalted ones, and certainly in no case before the age of thirteen. His earnings were not for family essentials. The mother opened a bank account for her son. She reminded Johannes of it in April 1854: 'When you had had work from Cranz [a Hamburg publisher]for a time, which brought you in a considerable sum, do you remember how I took care that the money went into the bank?'[35] From the age of fourteen, Brahms gave his teacher Bode free piano lessons. Henny Wiepking recalls: 'He was already at school at seven o'clock in the morning. So the fourteen-year-old pupil turned into a teacher, and the thirty-year-old teacher into a pupil. Johannes sat at the piano and invented pretty variations to Bode's first simple exercises.'[36] The works studied favoured the taste of the time. Brahms's younger brother also studied piano with him. The only surviving evidence of this is a copy of Henri Herz's *Variations Brillantes pour le Piano-Forte sur le dernière Valse de C. M. von Weber* Op. 51, on which Brahms marked at the beginning of the Finale (on page 12) the reminder 'Fritz, pay attention'.[37]

Outside Hamburg

Brahms was to be found outside Hamburg for the first time in May 1847 at the town of Winsen an der Luhe. Here he spent treasured weeks in (1847, 1848 and 1851) at the invitation of Adolf Giesemann, an acquaintance of Johann Jacob, in order to give piano lessons to his daughter Elise, known as Lieschen, and to enjoy the fresh country air. Brahms's first English biographer Florence May received a thorough account of these times from Lieschen Giesemann.[38] Whenever they met and went around together, Brahms always carried a dummy keyboard with him. He never played with boys of his own age around the village, but read romances of chivalry with Lieschen and other like-minded young people, such as 'Die Geschichte der schönen Magelone und des Ritters Peter' ('The Story of the Beautiful Magelone and the Knight Peter'), which he later set to music as Op. 33 and first read at this time. Not far from Winsen lay the tiny hamlet of Hoopte behind the Elbe dyke. Here a small group came together in order to spend the afternoons. In the village inn there would be dancing and singing, but music-making was the most popular. It was not long before Brahms was the darling of the Hoopte public. They enjoyed his lively dance tunes and enthusiastically listened out for the difficult concert pieces he occasionally inserted into the proceedings. He also conducted a song, and did it so well that he was elected to the directorship of the male voice choir during his stay. Brahms went about the task earnestly and with discipline; he 'attacked the beat with great animation and scrupulously controlled the *pianos* and *fortes*, and likewise the necessary gradation of *rallentandos*'.[39] He composed several four-part songs for this society. One was a 'Waltz for Male Voice Choir' on the 'A B C'. It consisted of thirty-five bars in 2/4, with three bars' introduction for the letters A B C, then four eight-bar phrases for the remaining letters of the alphabet, first one after the other, then in syllables each made up of two letters, with the composed conclusion 'Winsen, eighteen-hundred and forty-seven', sung by full choir, slow and *fortissimo*. This and 'Des Postillons Morgenlied' to the words 'Vivat! und ins Horn ich stosse' by Hoffmann von Fallersleben number as the earliest works of Brahms with titles. When he stayed with the Giesemanns for the last time at Winsen in 1851, he wrote an 'Abschiedschor' together with two other works as a memento for Lieschen Giesemann, calligraphically decorating the title and adding a special dedication. The 'Abschiedschor für Männerquartett' carried the superscription 'Abschied von Winsen a.d. Luhe'. The text read:

> Farewell, farewell, ye friends honest and upright,
> Restlessly the artist is driven forward from joy to sorrow,
> And the heart's urgency is stilled by the sound of music,
> Farewell, farewell, remember me. Winsen a.d. Luhe 1851.

Brahms remembered these early works again in 1880, demanded them back from Elise and destroyed them. [40]

Brahms used the money which he earned from around 1847 through his teaching and playing almost entirely for his library. From 1850 onwards, he was very familiar with classical and romantic literature from around 1850. He read Cicero, Dante, Eichendorff, Klopstock, Lessing, Sophocles and Tasso. The works of Schiller and Goethe also naturally belonged to his reading material, which he obtained from a lending library. The youth's romantic enthusiasm found its nourishment in the works of E. T. A. Hoffmann, Heine, Novalis and Jean Paul. Following E. T. A. Hoffmann's fantasy creation Kapellmeister Kreisler, the young Brahms named himself 'Johannes Kreisler jun.' or 'Kreisler II', a name which even graces his first published works. One can hardly doubt Kalbeck's suggestion that Brahms kept one or two volumes of classical literature open on the stand instead of the music when he was invited to play for dances, his fingers automatically playing the keys.[41] His mother's attempts to bank his income are understandable when one knows what he passionately declared to Hedwig von Salomon on 5 December 1853: 'I spend all my money on books, books are my greatest enjoyment. I read as much as I could from childhood and have explored everything from the worst to the best without any guidance. I gulped down numerous chivalric tales as a child until *Die Räuber* came into my hands; I didn't know that it was written by a great poet; but I longed for more by this same Schiller and improved myself in this way.'[42] And he wrote of this lifelong passion to Clara Schumann in a letter of 27 August 1854: 'When I [earn] the next 10 louis d'ors, it will remain a hard battle to keep away from a bookshop.'[43] Through an inner drive combined with literary knowledge, he acquired such a degree of cultivation that he became one of the best-educated and best-read personalities of his time, whose opinions on literary questions were valued by such figures as the writers, historians and critics Gottfried Keller, J. V. Widmann, Wilhelm Lübke, Jacob Baechtold and Michael Bernays.

On 13 April 1848 Brahms was confirmed in the St Michaeliskirche, Hamburg, and in the same year his schooling ended. He had in his library the little Hamburg catechism with numerous seventeenth-century woodcuts, apparently a gift from his mother, as well as several Bibles which he kept for bibliophile as well as religious reasons. He later gave the well-thumbed catechism as a present to the choral conductor Julius Spengel.[44] On 21 September 1848, Brahms gave his first solo concert. He played the Adagio and Rondo from a Piano Concerto in A by Jacob Rosenhain, the 'Fantasia on Motives from Rossini's *William Tell*' for piano by Theodor Döhler, a Fugue by J. S. Bach, a Serenade for the Left Hand Alone by Marxsen, and a Study by Henri Herz. The programming again signifies the taste of the time. Whether the Bach fugue is the same as the one from the *Well Tempered Clavier* which he practised for Cossel cannot be decided. In this context it was more of a pianistic 'crowd-puller', which none the less is likely to have been put into the programme by the young Brahms rather than Eduard Marxsen. As a result of the political circumstances, there was no review of the concert. Europe was in uproar, and the revolutionary events in Hungary had brought numerous refugees to Hamburg. Among them was the violinist Eduard Hoffmann, known as Reményi. It seems that it was at this time that Brahms first heard Hungarian melodies, when the émigré musicians assembled to form anything from duos up to entire ensembles, in order to earn enough money from performances to sail to America.

With his own second concert on 14 April 1849, Brahms had a publicised success. He played Beethoven's *Waldstein* Sonata, Sigismund Thalberg's 'Don Juan Fantasia', an 'Air italienne' of E. Mayer and a 'Fantasia on a Favourite Waltz', his own composition. On 17 April 1849, the Hamburg newspaper *Freyschütz* reported: 'in the concert by J. Brahms, the young virtuoso gave the most beautiful demonstration of his artistic progress. The performance of the Beethoven sonata showed that he has been able to venture successfully into the study of the classics and does him honour in every respect. The demonstration of his own composition ("Fantasie for Piano") also revealed unusual talent . . . The concert therefore had a rich programme, and the beautiful salon in the Jenisches' house was so full that a large part of the audience could only find a seat in the anteroom.' The Hamburg *Correspondent* of 2 May gave a more comprehensive review, devoting more attention to Brahms's playing, as in the following extract: '[his playing] is easy and free, the attack generally clean and never overbearing at moments of strongest force, unlike so many present-day virtuosos with a mania for hammering the keys'. And of the Fantasia on an original composition, one reads: 'The wonderful gifts of creativity, idea and expression, appear to have been borrowed in full measure from Nature, and it will depend entirely on him and his diligence to bring them one day to outward perfection in the bright raiments of beauty.' One might therefore conclude from this reaction that Brahms could anticipate a great future as a pianist in Hamburg. Yet only a few concerts in which he participated are known to us: just three in 1849 and two in 1850. They show a continuing preference for Thalberg's variations and fantasias. His shyness about playing in public has been frequently attested. His nature, so resistant to contact, outwardly blunt, even coldly cynical, was probably the actual reason, however. That much has been indicated by many friends of his youth and later contemporaries.

Brahms began his first work for the Hamburg publisher Cranz in 1849. The only surviving arrangement from this time, the 'Souvenir de la Russie', which Cranz published under the collective pseudonym 'G. W. Marks' as Op. 151, was newly edited by me in 1971 with a lengthy foreword.[45] Research has long endeavoured to discover more about these arrangements, but has had to rely on pieces of circumstantial evidence. One such is the printed edition of 1847 of Carl Czerny's four-handed arrangement of Mozart's symphonies K. 173d A, 161d, 167a (Serenades, Finalmusik) and 186a. These symphonies still have their wrappers.[46] Two of these wrappers carry on the reverse side the publisher's advertising, as was customary at that time. These indicate the newest publications for piano duet, among which are editions by G. W. Marks. It is noteworthy that after the first listed G. W. Marks title, the 'Souvenir de la Russie' Op. 151, there follows directly a longer series of works: 'Op. 158. Trois Fantaisies for piano. No. 1, Robert le Diable, No. 2, Les Huguenots, No. 3, Le Prophète' and then 'Op. 160. Trois Fantaisies pour piano. No 1 La Fille du Régiment; No. 2, Lucia di Lammermoor; No. 3, Maria di Rohan'. This kind of collective presentation is an indication that Brahms can be taken as the author, particularly since other subsequent G. W. Marks arrangements without opus number refer to the 'Musikalischer Kinderfreund am Pianoforte' and the collected title 'Collection des Potpourris de meilleurs Opéra', whose arrangements cannot be connected with Brahms. The fact that the Mozart arrangements are not indicated in the Köchel Catalogue (7th edition, 1965), suggests that these arrangements have not been noted before by scholars. If one considers the kind of titles of works by G. W.

CONCERT-PROGRAMM

zur

fünfundzwanzigjährigen Hochzeitsfeier

des

Herrn Schröder und Frau

am 5. Juli 1851.

1. Aufforderung zum Tanz, von Weber, vorgetragen von Herrn Miller.
2. Lied von Gumbert, vorgetragen von Herrn Schörling.
3. Gesangs-Vortrag von Fräulein Ziegeler.
4. a. Lied-Duett von Karl Würth, für Piano und Violoncello.
   b. Ave Maria von Schubert, vorgetragen von Herrn d'Arien.

5. Trio von Karl Würth, vorgetragen von den Herren Gade, d'Arien und Brahms.
6. Ständchen von Schubert, vorgetragen von Herrn Schörling.
7. Schweizer-Bub von Pixis, vorgetragen von Fräulein Ziegeler.
8. Trio von Mendelssohn (erster Satz), vorgetragen von den Herren Miller, Gade und d'Arien.

Plate 1.1 Concert programme for the twenty-fifth wedding anniversary of Herr and Frau Schröder, 5 July 1851, showing the names of Brahms and Karl Würth

Marks and the time of the appearance of the Mozart arrangements, which must have been issued around 1850, it seems reasonable to connect Brahms with the G. W. Marks Fantasies Op. 158 and Op. 160. This is conceivable even according to the most prudent supposition, because the Fantasies Op. 160 include one on the opera *Lucia di Lammermoor* – and Brahms played Thalberg's *Variations on Lucia di Lammermoor* at this time. Quite possibly he was then inspired to write an original Fantasie. If Brahms edited his own original arrangements and transcriptions under the pseudonym G. W. Marks for the publisher Cranz, this indicates exactly the same secretive character trait that he displayed when, on 5 July 1851, he performed a 'Lied-Duet' (McCorkle, Anhang 2A Nr. 10) and a Piano Trio (McCorkle, Anhang 2A Nr. 6) at the silver wedding of the piano manufacturer Schröder under the pseudonym Karl Würth. The programme (see Plate 1.1) from his own collection has faint connecting lines, in his own hand, under the names of Brahms and Karl Würth. [47]

Brahms was also regularly active as a piano or song accompanist behind the scenes and on the stage of the Hamburg Thalia-Theater. In his collection of programmes there are two announcements from the

Plate 1.2 Extract from the programme at the Thalia-Theater, 9 September 1851, in which Brahms participated as accompanist

'Vereinigte Hamburger Theater'. One can conclude from this that on 30 May 1851 the young Brahms accompanied the 'Songs to be Performed' ('Vorkommende Gesänge') – Recitative and Aria from *Der Freischütz*, 'Österreichisches Lied' and a comic duet by Franz von Suppé – in the Thalia-Theater, and played the remaining music behind the scenes on the harmonium. Likewise on 9 September 1851 (see Plate 1.2), when the '36th Guest performance of 48 Young Dancers' took place in the Thalia-Theater: Brahms apparently undertook the off-stage accompaniment to the items 'Tarantella', 'Pas des Fleurs', and the 'Fahnen-Tanz'.[48]

At the beginning of the 1850s, Brahms apparently undertook his first tour, a fourteen-day concert tour with the so-called 'Konzertgesellschaft Molinario'. Brahms performed with two singers and a violinist all evening in Riegel's wine restaurant at the Klingenberg in Lübeck during the period of the Christmas market. No programme survives, yet if Brahms

accompanied his colleagues and also played some solo pieces, his repertory must surely have been that of the Hamburg concerts.

Brahms's principal activity around 1850 was piano tuition. Walter
Hübbe, to whose older brother Brahms gave lessons from 1851, reports:

> On 22 May my father noted in his calendar: "Today B had . . . the first piano
> lessons with Herr Brahms." The last piano lesson came very soon. My brother
> didn't make progress even after the last lesson and soon gave it up. Mostly,
> while he botched his way through his fingering exercises sitting on the right,
> Brahms sat resignedly on the left and improvised wonderfully ingenious
> accompaniments. Once, since there was no practice material, he wrote down
> a wonderful improvised study: unfortunately it no longer exists.' [49]

It is from Hübbe that the first characterisation of the young Brahms
originates:

> He was totally lacking in any outward impressiveness. There was something
> bashful, self-conscious and embarrassed about him. You might have
> compared him with a yet unfledged young eagle, which nevertheless you can
> see will eventually fly to the heights. His still noticeably high, bright and
> harsh voice contributed a lot to this external impression. It sounded like that
> of a prepubescent boy. I can still recall precisely how, after the first visit and
> the lesson, the lanky figure left the house with not-quite-firm steps, a rather
> ungainly posture and rather wobbly top hat, went out over the Wiese to the
> Stadtgraben along the Steintor. The malicious lads from the houses soon
> found a nickname for him. Using an expression from the 'Hamburger
> Ausruf' familiar to us through our grandfather, we usually called him
> 'Brahms-broom' ('Brahmbessen'). Despite that, we were silently inspired by
> some kind of reverent awe; for I, at least, realised that he had something
> about him quite different from the normal piano teacher.[50]

A lively impression of his piano teaching in Hamburg comes ten years
later from Minna Völckers.

> At the beginning of February in the year 1861, Brahms came to us on a
> Friday afternoon and I had to play to him. There were études by Stephen
> Heller and pieces from Bach's Inventions. When I was ready he said that he
> knew of only three teachers for me, Avé Lallemant, Grädener or his humble
> self, whereupon my highly delighted parents immediately invited 'his
> humble self' to take over the instruction. On the coming Tuesday I should
> have had my first lesson. But Brahms immediately decided that instead of
> practising for $\frac{3}{4}$ hours a day, as before, I should have two periods of $\frac{3}{4}$ hours
> practice. Previously practising, just like the whole lesson, had given me little
> pleasure. That all changed. Between Friday and Tuesday I had to learn a
> study by Cramer, a prelude from Bach's *Well-Tempered Clavier* and the first
> movement of a sonata by Beethoven. That seemed to me an insurmountable
> task. But it went much better than I imagined. In this first lesson I was given
> the fugue belonging to the prelude, another étude by Cramer and the second

movement of the sonata. I also had to get the daily studies of Czerny to work on, of which he gave me new ones each time. I had to play him scales every time. He was very exact with everything and placed special emphasis on a loose wrist. I was beside myself with excitement, the whole teaching was the opposite of what I had had previously. Brahms could not be bettered as a teacher. He was gentle and kind, without praising much. I quickly made big strides with him. He let me play a lot of Clementi, Mozart, Mendelssohn, Bach and turned up quite regularly at the same time.

The greatest reproach that I received from him during 1½ years of instruction was that he would occasionally say of a Bach fugue: 'you are playing that to me for the third time today', which shamed me deeply ... My weak side in playing was always my trills. Brahms was such a gifted teacher that after several exercises with him I could do them. I really wanted to play some of his compositions, but hesitated to say so to him. My mother did it for me. 'Yes', he said, 'the things are still too difficult, but I will play duets with her', and we had to work on his B♭ Sextet, which we immediately got down to in the next lesson. I had to play primo, and we went through it very exactly, and my family were also delighted by the fine music. None of us could ever understand the stupid twaddle that one so often heard about him, that his music was confused. Sometimes, if I asked him, he played fugues after the lesson, which I already had to hand[51]

However, it must be stressed that Brahms taught piano only very reluctantly, although he gained a regular income from it. 'You always hated it, and it brings in only a little – I mean for you, who can do so much more', his mother reminded him in a letter of 20 March 1855.[52]

The relationships in the family home certainly impressed themselves conclusively on the character of the young Brahms. The great age difference of the parents released marital tensions which were not hidden from the son, and even affected him directly. This is indicated indirectly in the last letter, mentioned above, from Christiane Brahms to her son, written in January 1865, several days before her death. It is an important document. On the one hand it illuminates the sad relationship in the parental home, on the other it also reveals the patriarchal dimension, and shows how little understanding Johann Jacob had for his son. Amongst other things she wrote:

it was very difficult for me in the house; in the last four years my good Elise stood by me faithfully, then we moved to the Kurze Mühren [in the period from early 1851 to early 1852, thus in Brahms's eighteenth and nineteenth years][;] your education lasted much too long for your father, he was often grumpy and constantly found fault. We both always used to sit together in the evenings, it seems to me as though it were now, I was probably a bit silent, and then you said, 'Ah mother, father is so peculiar, now you are too'. Then I had to say to you that father wanted you to do something to get on in

the world; he didn't want to feed you any longer. You became so upset, and
we both cried and went to bed late. And Elise lay in bed fighting for air, and
you called a doctor and she got an emetic. It was the middle of the night;
when you came back again, I made you a lovely cup of coffee. – Once I had to
write you an unpleasant letter to Düsseldorf. I always had to fight a great deal
with father's unsatisfied moods and Elise often noticed it and wept a lot.
How often he said: 'the children won't go anywhere, you'll see'. No matter
how much I argued with him, it didn't help. I suffered everything with
patience and always rejoiced over my good children, and thought that once
you were both independent, he would rejoice with me'.[53]

The words of the father, that Brahms 'should do something to get on
in the world' and 'the children [Johannes and Fritz] won't go anywhere,
you'll see', affected the sensitive Johannes deeply. The trauma of having
to prove to his father that he could achieve an elevated position in which
the father could take pride – as a composer, and not as a pianist – never
left Brahms, as can be seen from many remarks, even in the last period of
his life. The understandable longing to lift himself out of his modest
origins would certainly compensate for this, as did his wide reading,
which set him apart from the milieu of the family home. Brahms knew
and was convinced from the beginning that he was a composer, and consequently considered all other activities as routes that led him to this
goal.

The decade 1850–60, especially the first part, was to be the most
momentous in Brahms's life. From this period date his first published
works, his first extended tours outside Hamburg and his first
identification of professional goals involving an institutional position
outside Hamburg. The Scherzo Op. 4 belongs with the song 'Heimkehr'
Op. 7 No. 6 to 1851 as his earliest published works. The tour with Reményi
in 1853, first to Winsen, then other towns in the area, led in turn to the
meeting with the violinist Joseph Joachim in Hannover and with the
Schumanns in Düsseldorf: within only weeks the establishment of the
closest friendships in Brahms's life. Through Schumann Brahms's earliest
works came into print as Opp. 1–6, and within weeks of their meeting, his
article 'Neue Bahnen' broadcast Brahms's name to the musical world
through the *Neue Zeitschrift für Musik*. These friends had an incalculable
effect on his development. Joachim's and Schumann's music opened up
new style-worlds to him and set him new artistic goals and an awareness
of what life could be like in a cultured and musically dedicated environment, though this was more of a hindrance than a help, since he was
unknown to the larger public as either a composer or a pianist. After
Schumann's death in 1856, Clara became his artistic ideal and companion. Through her he obtained a position for three winters' teaching and

conducting at the court of Detmold (near Hannover). By the time he gave up the post he had identified even clearer goals in relation to practical performance, both as a professional and as a composer seeking to broaden his base from the requirements of his own instrument. Clara and Joachim willingly played his works, using their influence to programme them, and counselled him in technical issues and the building of a career. By its end, the decade would see Brahms with Joachim and others of like mind issuing a Declaration asserting their artistic values against those proposed by the so called New German School (which had no significant impact at the time and was not even recorded in Brahms's biography until Kalbeck included it after his death). By this time also has become apparent the sensitivity and defensiveness of Brahms's personality, prone on the one side to detachment, on the other to domineering behaviour, sarcasm and rudeness which would colour his social life throughout. He was accustomed to dismiss anything that did not measure up to his personal values with the remark 'Yes, that is all just Pimpenkram' (apparently a word devised by himself, to express that which is unimportant and insignificant).[54] His attitude soon became widely known among musicians.

Professional ambitions in Hamburg

Brahms's activity as director of the Hamburg Frauenchor was, as in Detmold, intended to serve purely personal goals in the testing of his conducting and compositional capacities. The choir itself came into being rather by chance, as a result of the musical provision for a wedding at which Brahms played the organ as a favour to his Hamburg colleague Carl Grädener, who conducted the music. After this, on 6 June 1859, twenty-eight young women again found themselves singing together, now *Volkslieder* and women's choruses at the house of the auctioneer Hermann Wagner, under the direction of Brahms himself. From the beginning, there were regular rehearsals which took place on one morning a week. Brahms rehearsed his works Opp. 12, 22, 27, 37 Nos. 1 and 2, 44, and numerous folk-song arrangements for women's choir with his 'little vocal republic'. It must be stressed that these rehearsals took place completely away from the glare of publicity. In fact, the Frauenchor, which numbered up to forty members, appeared only three times publicly under Brahms's direction, and then only as members of the 'Damen Chor', not as the 'Hamburg Frauenchor', the name which appears as the society's insignia, and in the well-known 'Avertimento' devised by Brahms. Indeed, it was in a concert of Carl Grädener's Academy (founded in 1851) on 2 December 1859 that Brahms conducted his *Ave Maria* for female voices and orchestra Op. 12 and the *Begräbnisgesang* for chorus and orchestra Op. 13 for the first time, also performing the Schumann Piano Concerto.[55]

Brahms's compositions were well spoken of in the press. Of special significance for the composer were the reviews in the *Hamburg Wochenblatt* of 10 December 1859 and the popular weekly *Der Nachbar* of 11 December 1859. It was these two papers – and not the great dailies – that took Brahms up. Copies are to be found among his papers and are here republished for the first time. The *Hamburger Wochenblatt* of 10 December even allowed two reviews of a performance to appear.[56] In the first, the reviewer asserted immediately of the *Ave Maria* that its 'simple clarity and inwardness recalled the old masters,' whilst the *Begräbnisgesang* 'was rendered with such simple beauty and impressive character that it was difficult for it to avoid making a strong impression on the listener'. In the review 'by another reporter', the *Begräbnisgesang* already appears to represent a vision of the much later *Deutsches Requiem*. The reviewer elaborates the view that the two compositions belong in 'character to a much earlier period than Handel's' and even

> give an indication of how richly our young, profoundly endowed countryman has been impressed by the deep and inward old German music without losing his individuality. The 'Song at the Graveside' belongs to the most gripping things that we have heard for a long time. Simple and without pretension, like a grieving dialogue, intoned from the deepest voices with the omission of the sopranos and without introducing the full instrumental accompaniment, comes the exhortation 'Now let us bury the dead one'; then the previously single voices gather themselves together with the rich accompaniment of woodwind, brass and timpani for the first burial song: 'He is from Earth and to earth will return.' Yet already the deep sorrow is mixed with more joyful expression, uplifted through the transition from minor to major: 'his work, sorrows and suffering have come to a good end'. And while the remaining voices continue with this, there suddenly enters a heavenly, consoling promise, the soprano's pledge taking away earthly sorrow: 'his soul lives eternally in God', to which the remaining voices consent while part of the instrumental accompaniment, going into triple rhythm, drives the funeral procession unstoppably towards its goal. Then the mourners part with the words 'Now we let him sleep and we go our ways' etc., at which point the single choir enters again in the minor. Herr Brahms has given much more in his unusually successful setting than might have been expected from the modest title of the felicitously chosen old German song: it is no mere 'Funeral *Song*', but rather a serious funeral *celebration*, composed with humanly elevated art and full of dramatic strength, truly dedicated to transfigure earthly sorrow into eternal joy and hope, and certainly unforgettable in retrospect to anyone who has heard or sung it. –

Not less significant is Brahms's 'Ave Maria'. Here too female choir alone is employed, but certainly in a rich four-part setting, with a proper understanding of the poetry in the old German Marian service. Specially impressive in the design is the unison with which the women treat the actual prayer 'Sancta Maria, ora pro nobis'.

The (likewise unnamed) reporter of the *Nachbar* exalts the whole character of the concert and expresses the opinion that

> this time, however, something new and even truly gratifying arrived. This was the compositions of Herr Johannes Brahms, his 'Ave Maria', and above all his wonderfully beautiful *Begräbißgesang* to the old hymn 'Nun lasst uns den Leib begraben' to the original text by Michael Weisse, a priest of the Bohemian Brotherhood, who edited a songbook with German translations of songs by Huss and others in 1531. One could not avoid the impression, whether one was a connoisseur or not, that one of the great old masters had risen up to compose for all time and for all hearts. The simple power and mighty artlessness with which this death and resurrection song streams into a believing community cannot be described further but will just have be heard and experienced. That the young master belongs to our Hamburg is a source of further joy and hope.

The two critics confirm what Brahms meant when he said to Clara Schumann, 'Actually something of a cult is already developing with me in Hamburg; but that can hardly be a bad thing, I think. At least I always write happily, and the sounds inside me feel as if they must come out as something heavenly with time.'[57]

The Frauenchor appeared for a second time in Hamburg in a concert given by Clara Schumann on 15 January 1861. One notes that the programme only indicates 'with the valued participation of a DAMEN CHOR'. Brahms conducted first performances of the Songs for Womens' Voices with Two Horns and Harp Op. 17, complete, and the Songs for Women's Voices Op. 44 No. 1 'Minnelied' and Op. 44 No. 2 'Bräutigam' in this concert. It was repeated several days later in Altona, in the Bürger-Vereins-Saal. The *Hamburger Correspondent* noted concisely: 'A varied Andante by Schumann [he means the Op. 46 Variations for Two Pianos] provided opportunities for the talented local composer and exceptional pianist Herr Johannes Brahms . . . to compete laudably with Frau Schumann. Six, for the most part very enjoyable, songs of his, written for amateurs, filled the intervals between the instrumental pieces . . .'[58] The third and last concert of the Hamburg Frauenchor took place on 16 November 1861 – again arranged through Clara Schumann. At its centre stood the first performance of Brahms's Piano Quartet in G minor. Clara Schumann played the piano part. The *Hamburger Nachrichten* remarked on it only briefly, however: 'His new quartet for piano and string instruments in manuscript and also six songs for women's choir [that is, some songs from Op. 44] further guaranteed through their content the high reputation of this esteemed artist.'[59]

During the period 1860–1 Brahms gave several concerts in Hamburg. On 10 February 1860, he played Schumann's Piano Concerto, and directed the first performance of his own second Serenade in A major Op. 16 at the 125th Philharmonic Concert.[60] Once again he had a great success, which found suitable expression in the press:

> Herr Johannes Brahms repeated the Schumann concerto in A minor with which he created a furore some time ago. On this occasion he did it on a piano from the exceptional firm of Baumgarten and Heins, and the beauties of Schumann's composition were illuminated for the listeners on renewed acquaintance even more clearly than earlier. Moreover, the first part of the evening brought a second Serenade for wind instruments from Brahms. Since we learnt to admire the young composer of the choral song 'Nun lasst uns den Leib begraben', his instrumental style has also become approachable to us. As a result, the newer serenade is much more concise and more skilfully prepared for the enjoyment of the moment than its predecessor, which we heard here. However, by his 'serenades' one must not imagine mere nocturnes, but rather whole scenes with changing moods, which this time come to a conclusion in an unruffled rondo that is not lacking in a popular quality. The reception that Herr Brahms was granted as both pianist and composer was a remarkably spirited one.[61]

The concert on 20 November 1860 deserves special note. In a soirée of chamber music Brahms played the piano part in works by Schumann, Bach, Schubert and Mozart. His fellow performers were intimates, young friends and colleagues, who have already been mentioned and, who partly through their reminiscences, have helped to illuminate Brahms's early years.[62] In the summer of 1860, Brahms completed his first String Sextet in B♭ Op. 18. He had already begun the composition in late autumn 1859 in Detmold. Kalbeck states that 'the sextet originally began at the eleventh bar'.[63] The instrumental parts, rediscovered in the year 1992, confirm this. The later-composed coda to the third movement also allows us to see the original conclusion to the scherzo. The parts give the first version complete and allow us a rare look into the composer's workshop.[64]

In April 1861, the baritone Julius Stockhausen, who had first appeared in a concert in Hamburg in March 1859, appeared with an innovation on the Hamburg concert podium. He sang complete song cycles for the first time: *Die Schöne Müllerin, An die ferne Geliebte* and *Dichterliebe*. Brahms accompanied him at the piano. Julius Stockhausen was equally known and loved in the concert salons of Paris, London, Leipzig, Vienna and Hamburg. This concert was also recalled by Walter Hübbe, who stressed the differing assessments of Stockhausen and Brahms by the public:

'Whoever can still recall how Stockhausen first began to perform entire song cycles in a concert here, beginning with Schubert's Müllerlieder, will surely also not have forgotten that Brahms was his accompanist – and truly with what mastery. Stockhausen himself naturally knew how to recognise Brahms's true worth, and it seemed to him unfair that he himself should take the lion's share of the applause. So he proved it: at the applause, he very obviously dragged the resisting Brahms along with him in front of the public to show how much he treasured him and wanted him to be celebrated as much as himself. However, Brahms looked really detached and ironical.'[65] Stockhausen sang Schumann's cycle *Dichterliebe* on 30 April 1861 and the happy Brahms noted to Clara Schumann on 2 May: 'Naturally we had a full hall and nothing passed without encore. The wonderful Schumann song cycle went tremendously, at least we felt really carried along by the enthusiasm of the listeners. Stockhausen and I have drunk in brotherhood in the songs.'[66] In May 1861 Brahms gave up the work with his Frauenchor and withdrew almost completely from the concert life of his native city. He took lodgings a short distance outside the city limits of Hamburg in the suburb of Hamm, at Schwarze Strasse 5. Here he composed or completed a series of early masterworks: the two piano quartets in G minor and A major; the *Variations and Fugue on a Theme of Handel,* the four-handed *Variations on a Theme of Schumann* and the first romances to Tieck's 'Magelone'. Brahms also began work here on his Piano Quintet, which was first composed as a string quintet. Brahms was also to work here in early 1862 on the first movement of his C minor symphony.

At the beginning of the 1860s the concerts of the Philharmonic Society in Hamburg began to decline in quality, in both artistic and material terms. Friedrich Wilhelm Grund, co-founder and director of the concerts, which had begun in 1828 jointly with the Hamburg Singakademie, was overtaxed after more than thirty years of activity. Attendance had declined noticeably, the standards of the concerts had fallen and new music was no longer given sufficient attention. So the members of the committee of the Philharmonic Society, who had guaranteed six annual concerts with their own money, sought a successor. In this, personality stood above everything. It was obvious that Hamburg could not afford to take risks: the long-term financial security of the concerts was at stake and artistic experiment was out of the question. Brahms's friend and supporter, Theodor Avé Lallemant, who was a member of the committee of the Philharmonic, planned at the beginning of 1862 to create the post of a second director of the Singakademie for Brahms. He confided this plan to Brahms in August 1862. It was obviously a private initiative which Avé must have communicated to the other members of the committee only after first discussing it with Brahms. Brahms therefore knew that he was in line not for the post of conductor of the Philharmonic Society, but (in the planned two-way division) for that of choirmaster of the Singakademie, which also included the duties of a repetiteur. This was Avé's plan alone. That the committee could not agree to the plan of paying the wages of a new second conductor as described is hardly surprising. For the Society it was only important to secure the future of the Philharmonic concerts, and it therefore needed a personality who possessed a unifying force and charisma: both towards the public and towards the musicians of the Society. These qualities were embodied in Julius Stockhausen, not in Johannes Brahms. So it came about that on 26 November 1862, Julius Stockhausen took up the invitation of the Philharmonic Society, Hamburg, to become the director of their concerts for the next season. We have come to know only a little from Stockhausen's notes and letters concerning the deliberations which led to this decision and concerning the conditions of his acceptance, since, remarkably, all the deliberations of the Philharmonic Society from the year 1862 no longer exist.[67] When Avé informed Brahms, who since September 1862 had had great success in Vienna as both pianist and composer, that Stockhausen had become conductor of the Philharmonic concerts, Brahms felt deeply wounded and communicated it directly to Clara Schumann,[68] who on her side now felt sick for Brahms and reacted emotionally against Hamburg, although she, as emerges from an unpublished letter from Stockhausen to her, had recommended him and not Brahms as conductor of the Philharmonic Society there: 'How it has come to pass that I have found an orchestra in Germany and been appointed to conduct it is still a mystery to me, a dream, and I thank you most, dear lady, for the chance, and give you my speediest and warmest thanks. Had you not come to Guebwiller, had you not played there with our sorry orchestra and then recommended me as one who had the right predisposition, perhaps I would not be a concert-director in Hamburg now.'[69] Stockhausen came to know just after his acceptance that Avé would have created a supplementary post for Brahms.

Stockhausen was convinced that Brahms was not cut out to be a conductor. 'He is not practical enough, not friendly with the orchestral musicians, first holding a grudge, then too patient! On the other hand, although he is so gifted (as I am not), he cannot be bothered to point out mistakes and would not have the patience to make something out of nothing.'[70] Stockhausen's insight is confirmed by Christian Otterer. Kalbeck noted the following from Otterer's assertions in his notebook from the Hamburg period concerning Brahms. 'Brahms inflexible as conductor, went straight through relentlessly, also in the performance, was not therefore so respected or liked. With Stockhausen the public and musicians were exceptionally contented. Justice requires it to be said that the Hamburgers had no reason to rue their decision to appoint him and not Brahms to the conductor's position.' We certainly look in vain for this passage in Kalbeck's biography: he never published it![71] Finally, the viewpoint from which alone the choice of the new conductor had been reached can be established from a letter from Avé Lallement to Stockhausen on 6 September 1863. Stockhausen wanted to bring Theodor Kirchner to Hamburg to enable him to earn a living there. Avé writes: 'I fear his [Kirchner's] whole personality will be a problem in Hamburg. He is very quiet and uncommunicative, completely so, just as Schumann was. Schumann would never have been a suitable personality for Hamburg, however often he was here. One admires the great composers, but – ... Do you think you would have such an enormously electrifying and stimulating effect if you didn't have this amazingly attractive personality? Brahms could not have created a domain for himself here, however much I begged him and helped him. Believe me, Brahms's personality was the real reason ... why else do you think everything comes to you?'[72]

In his innermost being, Brahms had had hopes – no doubt strengthened through Avé's personal intervention for him – for the position, since it signified a bourgeois existence and would have strengthed his position in relation to his father. With this position above all, he could have shown him that he had 'made something out of himself' after all. He could have stood in front of the orchestra in which his own father played double bass and could have repeated a scene similar to that noted at a rehearsal of the A major Serenade under Brahms's direction in 1861: 'It was touching when Brahms, who had had to interrupt the rehearsal because one of the basses had made a mistake, discovered his own father to be the miscreant and put the parent right with a soft reproach.'[73] Yet outwardly Brahms had never let it be known that he hoped to become conductor of the Philharmonic concerts. No more did he reveal his motives for setting off on what was to be a short visit to Vienna in September 1862 even before he knew the outcome of the decision, the consequences of which were to be fundamental to his future.

Translated by Michael Musgrave

2 Years of transition: Brahms and Vienna 1862–1875

MICHAEL MUSGRAVE

Brahms's first visit to Vienna towards the end of September 1862 is often taken as inaugurating the major professional change of his life: the move from provincial Hamburg, with its hard upbringing and limited opportunities, to the city of the classic masters, and his subsequent dominance of its musical life as their greatest successor. Yet the reality is otherwise. Brahms settled into Vienna only very slowly and it could not really be called his home for upwards of a decade. These years spanned a difficult transition in both professional and personal life as he sought a career path and a domestic identity. The fight to realise his artistic aims and ambitions, begun in Hamburg was to continue for long years. It was only when he finally became established as a financially independent composer in Vienna, by the mid-1870s, that he really found stability and routine for his composition; prior to this, a pattern emerged rather by default.

It is difficult to know what Brahms first expected of Vienna. He had several contacts in Hamburg who would have encouraged him to make what was still a long journey – for example the composer Carl Peter Grädener (1812–83) and Bertha Porubszky, a Viennese girl who had been a member of his choir – in addition to the wider circle of musicians who performed in Vienna, beginning with his intimates Clara Schumann and Joseph Joachim.[1] His first comments leave the issue open. He wrote shortly before leaving to his fellow composer Albert Dietrich, 'I am leaving on Monday for Vienna! I look forward to it as a child. Of course I do not know how long I shall stay. We will leave it open and I hope to meet you some time during the winter. Pray do not leave me quite without letters',[2] leaving Dietrich some business addresses rather than a private one or hotel. Doubtless he himself did not fully know the reasons for the journey, beyond a natural desire to know the city which had become the increasing focus of his musical values and commitments (he had apparently planned a trip earlier in the year).[3] Clear in retrospect, Brahms's destiny there was undoubtedly hidden from his full perception for years. For this reason it is appropriate to assess the situation he faced in 1862 from both points of view: on the one hand, the restraining claims of Hamburg – the assumptions of his upbringing, issues of family, friends and professional expectation; on the other, the attractions of Vienna – the opportunities for personal creative development, wider artistic contact and the promotion of his music which the Austrian capital offered.

The claims of Hamburg

Two connecting factors underpinned Brahms's attraction to Hamburg: his relationship with his family and his desire for a secure professional position and institutional status; to them can be added more generally a need to be close to his supporting circle of colleagues from the Schumann days still resident in the north and the Rhineland. He writes to Clara from Vienna in November 1862: 'you see, I am rather old-fashioned in most respects and in this among others: that I am not at all cosmopolitan, but cling to my native city as to a mother ... Now here, where I have so much reason for gratification, I feel, and always shall feel, that I am an outsider.'[4] His attachment was not only emotional. In 1862 the family income was still variable and, as in youth, Brahms's economic self-sufficiency through his professional earnings remained – at the very least – essential. He could not rely on his parents – indeed, he always felt the need to make additional contributions. When in the same month he wrote to tell his parents of first successes in Vienna, he was clearly homesick, immediately remembering family events and asking for a letter,[5] though his mother responded in her letter of 6 December that, given the many activities he had described, he was 'probably not homesick any longer'.[6] He returned to Hamburg on 5 May 1863 after about seven months in Vienna to share his thirtieth birthday with his parents at home; in the summer, in order to work on the cantata *Rinaldo*, he took lodgings in nearby Blankenese on the Elbe, where he soon met up with former members of his Frauenchor. He would probably have stayed in the city or the north in the next year to continue work, as he had no special reason to make the journey back to Vienna. He had already commented to his mother that, despite the interest from publishers in Vienna after his first concerts, 'much pleases me better in North Germany than Vienna and particularly the publishers', and that he would rather take a smaller fee to be published by them.[7] However, in June he received the invitation to conduct the choir of the Vienna Singakademie, the result of support from an influential group of musicians and friends he had made in the city. Brahms held the post from October 1863 to April 1864, and had returned to Vienna by the last week of August 1863 to prepare for it.

After the season, in the spring of 1864, Brahms again had no pressing reason to remain in Vienna. Indeed, circumstances were quickly to prevent it, for his support in Hamburg was soon to be required as a result of the worsening relations of his parents. The summer of 1863 had seen increased tensions between them as his mother, Christiane, had begun rapidly to age, their seventeen-year age difference now telling badly; Johann Jacob was still a vital and active fifty-seven and unminded to constrain his professional activities, especially since he had been invited that year by Stockhausen to play in the Philharmonic Orchestra and needed to practise undisturbed. The mother was deeply hurt by his robust attitude and Brahms sought to resolve their differences. But by the summer of 1864 it had become quite clear that separation was the only solution. Showing obvious professional sympathy for his father, though deeply devoted to his mother, Brahms took rooms for him in the Grosse Bleichen; his mother and sister, Elise, remained at home in the Fuhlentwiete before moving in November to a comfortable apartment with a garden in the Lange Reihe when the family home was given up. The younger brother, Fritz, took separate lodgings in the Theaterstrasse. The commitment to two homes naturally increased Brahms's family obligations, and he assumed financial responsibility for his mother and sister. He did not want to regard the break as permanent, and was still writing to his father in October 1864 in the hope that he would perhaps occupy the spare room kept in the Lange Reihe home for Brahms, in company with Brahms's books; he asked about all the practical arrangements, and for assurance that his mother was receiving an adequate part of what he gave his father.[8] Brahms was generous throughout. Indeed, Geiringer notes that Clara Schumann was even constrained to write to the father to point out the slender nature of Brahms's finances,[9] which throws an interesting light on what the father expected of his son. Even after Johann Jacob had remarried, and after his retirement in 1869, Brahms contributed to his support. On 2 February 1865, Christiane died. This loss, which affected Brahms deeply, did not lessen his family commitments, however: he continued to contribute to Elise's upkeep, even after she had married (Fritz became independent as a successful piano teacher).

His mother's death inaugurated a new phase of Brahms's life, one with no sure sense of professional context or direction, including a period of eighteen months without visiting Vienna. In the autumn of 1865 he undertook recitals in Switzerland and Germany, including performances in Detmold, Düsseldorf, Oldenburg and Hamburg. He spent an extensive part of 1866 in Karlsruhe, in various towns in Switzerland and in Baden Baden to complete *Ein deutsches Requiem*, not returning to Vienna until November 1866. In 1868 he embarked again on wide-ranging travels, including recitals with Stockhausen in North Germany and Denmark. He had taken a new interest in his father after his remarriage and accompanied him enthusiastically on a tour of Upper Austria in the summer of

1867, for a walking trip near Bonn in 1868 and to Switzerland in the same year. Yet whilst he travelled widely, either to give recitals or to find peace for extended composition (as in his summers at Baden Baden during 1864–72, where he took lodgings close to Clara's summer residence, shared meals with her family and became part of her rich cultural circle there), Brahms kept a room at his father's homes (he moved on his remarriage in 1866) until 1869, and regularly returned. In 1868, for example, he spent almost the whole of May in Hamburg after the Bremen premiere of the *Requiem*, and his tours drew him to the region in February, March and November of that year: every visit to the north involved a visit home. Not until 30 April 1869 did he ask his father to stop reserving his room.[10]

On the professional front, the conductorship of the Philharmonic Orchestra of his native city had been Brahms's great goal long before he went to Vienna and remained so long after. Though of humble background, the proud son of the city and of a solid Hamburg musician had complete belief in his suitability for the post, soon to be vacant on the retirement of its co-founder F. W. Grund. His interests were being promoted by his friend the teacher and musical antiquarian Theodor Avé Lallemant, who was on the committee. It appears, however, that a decision had already been taken, but not announced, in favour of Julius Stockhausen, one of the greatest baritone singers of the period, and already Brahms's close recital partner. Brahms obviously had his suspicions that this appointment would be made and Avé probably gave him some inkling. He asks his parents in his letter of November 1862, 'Does Avé often go to see you? Has he told you anything in particular about Stockhausen?'[11] Stockhausen's appointment was, if not a total surprise, a shock none the less. Brahms never forgave Hamburg for passing him over, though he bore Stockhausen no lasting grudge for it.[12] Joachim was clearly disappointed, writing to Avé (who had been a member of the committee) of Brahms's sterling qualities for the position, 'It is precisely as a man upon whom one can rely that I regard Johannes so highly, with his gifts and his will! There is nothing that he cannot undertake and, with his earnestness, overcome!', though he also alluded to Brahms's 'asperity of nature', which Joachim had hoped the position would help to alleviate.[13] And Brahms had to grit his teeth again as soon as 1867, when the situation repeated itself on Stockhausen's resignation: the society appointed the Berlin musician Julius von Bernuth (who would then remain for years, presiding over declining standards, and become outpaced by younger conductors).[14]

So, when offered the position in 1894, Brahms's coolly eloquent reply scarcely obscures the bitterness he had felt in facing up to the professional wrench consequent on these early disappointments: 'it was long before I got used to the idea of going along other paths. If things had gone according to my wishes I would perhaps celebrate an anniversary with you today; but in that case you would still have to look around for a younger, capable talent. May you find him now, and may he serve you as faithfully as would have . . . your respectful and obedient servant, J. Brahms.'[15] His ambitions were entirely natural and reasonable. As first a practical musician – a pianist, organist and conductor, who earned little from his extended compositions until the great success of *Ein deutsches Requiem* in the late 1860s – his models in professional life were those of his contemporaries and seniors who performed as well as composed. Joachim was court music director at Hannover from 1853 to 1868; Albert Dietrich was Hofkapellmeister at Oldenburg from 1861; Otto Julius Grimm was conductor of the Cäcilienverein in Münster, Westphalia from 1857 and later director of the Music Academy from 1878; even Robert Schumann spent his last years from 1850 as city music director in Düsseldorf, where Brahms first met him.

If Brahms was angered over the Hamburg situation, nor was he happy with many aspects of Viennese musical life when he first arrived and for some time after, as has been intimated. In December 1864 he observed: 'it is really hardly pleasant here. Hellmesberger and [Ferdinand] Laub [a famous violinist and quartet leader, and Hellmesberger's chief rival] are at each other's throats. Herbeck drowns himself and the public in music; and then there is Dessoff! Though one may be, as I am, quite unconcerned with all this music-making, one is obliged to breathe the atmosphere and unable to escape it; for all that it does not always smell sweet.'[16] Brahms continued to entertain hopes in the north throughout the decade. The letter asking his father to stop reserving his room, shows how events had finally drawn their own conclusions for him, yet there is still a sad resignation regarding his hoped-for career in Hamburg: 'after all, I cannot wish to settle in Hamburg, even if I visit you for shorter or longer periods, we can hardly for that reason keep two rooms empty all the year round . . . besides what should I do in Hamburg? Apart from you there is no one I want to see. You know well enough how little, if any, respect I get out of the place. In short, I realise at last that I must have some sort of home somewhere, so that I think that I shall try to make myself more comfortable in Vienna next autumn.'[17] His leading local supporters, his teacher Marxsen and the great Handel scholar Chrysander (who lived nearby at Bergedorf), had both made clear to him earlier their reserve about the city's attitude to him. Chrysander wrote in 1869 in hope of his visit: 'of course, I know only too well that no particular musical treat awaits you, but rather the hidden enmity of small-minded men, who, alas, are influential enough to see that nothing of importance can happen in

Hamburg'. And Marxsen, after a performance of the *Requiem* in the city, comments that 'the artists of Hamburg, your so-called intimate friends, were one and all conspicuous by their absence!!!' [18]

A peripatetic musician

Without a professional position, it made little difference to Brahms's income whether he lived in Vienna or Hamburg. He was insufficiently committed to piano teaching to find any great advantage in Viennese pupils over Hamburg ones, though he could certainly have developed a large and fashionable practice with his early contacts and reputation. And his recitals as soloist and as chamber musician, involving extended tours, took place of necessity over a much wider terrain, though his favourite partners, Joachim and Stockhausen, were still in the north. Brahms took little pleasure in piano teaching. None the less he was always a conscientious and responsible teacher with clear ideas on technique and practising. His playing was altogether a different matter: here he was very variable. Though a pianist with a prodigious technique and a mastery of the classical and much romantic literature as well as of the great demands of his own music (his skills in the execution of which had been recognised unreservedly by Schumann and were agreed by all who heard him), Brahms was rarely at ease as a public soloist and needed the response of a warm audience, or of his colleagues in chamber music. He was invariably well received and quickly gained a major reputation, though he was never considered as polished as his great contemporaries, his importance lying rather in interpretation.

From the perspective of Brahms's frequently peripatetic life, one can see the vital importance of the position with the Vienna Singakademie in 1863–4. It gave him a high public profile and provided a professional platform for his ground-breaking performances of early repertory. What he had begun to do in the obscurity of Detmold, and largely privately with his own choir in Hamburg, was now given a stage in a major musical city, and with it much of what he imagined he wanted professionally. Even though the Singakademie was in the shadow of the larger and very much more prestigious Singverein of the Gesellschaft der Musikfreunde, his programmes aroused interest and curiosity (and a little antagonism by some). The Vienna Singakademie had been founded as recently as 1858 to focus on early church music and unaccompanied singing. It gave three or four concerts annually and one oratorio. But Brahms might never have put down these roots after his first year 1862–3: the appointment was only narrowly approved. Despite Brahms's tight circle of supporters, there was severe competition between those who championed the Viennese Franz Krenn, who had taken over during the illness of the conductor F. Stegmayer (whose death then caused the vacancy), and those who wanted a younger man such as Brahms to revive the society's flagging fortunes. Chief of these were Josef Gänsbacher, a prominent singer, with a surgeon, Dr Scholz, a merchant, Herr Adolf Schulz, and a Viennese insurance official, Herr Flatz. Gänsbacher won over Krenn's supporters, headed by Prince Constantin Czartoryski, by a majority of one.[19] Brahms made a great impression. Though technical faults were revealed in his conducting and there were some performance problems (and though his pioneering programmes, including unknown works of the Baroque and Renaissance, were not always widely enjoyed or well received by critics), his commitment to thorough rehearsals and his deeply musical performances were widely appreciated and he was offered a three-year contract. Though he first intended to accept it, by the end of the summer his resolution failed and he resigned; he could not face the administration, the commitment and the needless exposure to unsympathetic critics. Indeed, in a letter to the critic Eduard Hanslick (with whom he had quickly established a rapport) he intimated how easily for these reasons he might have refused the position in the first place. Yet it served his creative needs at the time.

As a result of circumstances personal and professional, therefore, Brahms was wont to describe himself for much of the period as a 'vagabond'. [20] Having lived at home until he was almost thirty and destined to live in the same lodgings for the last twenty-five years of his life, Brahms lived in seven or more residences during the much shorter period 1862–71. They were as follows:

Autumn 1862: Leopoldstadt: Novaragasse 39; Novaragasse 55
Winter 1862 – 3: Czerningasse 7
Autumn 1863 – 1865: Deutsches Haus 1, Singerstrasse 7
December 1867 – early 1868: Postgasse 6
1869: Hotel Zum Kronprinzen at the Aspern Brücke
1870: Ungarngasse 2.
1871: Hotel Zum Kronprinzen at the Aspern Brücke

On 27 December 1871 he took the lodgings at Haus Wien, 4, Karlsgasse, which he would then keep; first two rooms, then later three.[21]

The attractions of Vienna

For all Brahms's links to Northern Germany and personal contacts with Hamburg, every year that passed after 1862 weakened them in some crucial way. In domestic terms, the death of his mother and the remarriage of his father soon after took off much of the emotional pressure. His father now had a happy marriage and moved to new lodgings in the Anscharplatz in the Valentinskamp district. Brahms got on well with his stepmother, Karoline Schnack, and continued to do so after his father's death (only five years later, in 1872), contributing to her upkeep until her death in 1892, and to that of her son. Brahms now had an increasingly superficial relationship with his sister, and none with his brother. In addition to the blows to his institutional ambitions in Hamburg in 1862 and 1867, this period also saw changes in the personal and professional lives of his contemporaries, who became married, began families, and sought new jobs and promotion. Joachim, for example had married in 1863 and become a father in 1864; in 1867 he resigned from the Hannover position on the abdication of the King of Hannover, and moved to Berlin to head the new Hochschule für Musik. Clara Schumann, having moved to Berlin from Düsseldorf in 1857, now took a home in Baden Baden from 1863 to 1873. Brahms's letters show how much these changes affected him. But he too was steadily growing in success, if not as he had imagined it: he had also to look to his own professional interests and move on with his life.

The success in Vienna in 1862–4 had given him confidence and contacts. Despite the problems already noted, he had made a major impression in a major city and had entered into mainstream institutional life. When he had first arrived he had found a very welcome response from fellow musicians: all the channels had been quickly made open to him, and he had taken advantage as pianist and composer. In addition to the Court Opera, Vienna's chief institutions were first the Gesellschaft der Musikfreunde, founded in 1812, with its Singverein (founded by Johann Herbeck in 1858) and its Conservatoire; and secondly the Philharmonic Society, founded in 1842, which used the orchestra of the Court Opera. When Brahms first arrived in Vienna, the artistic director of the Gesellschaft was Herbeck, who in 1859 had created an independent orchestra for the organisation (which had been formerly reliant, like the Philharmonic Orchestra, on that of the Opera); he was thus one of the most influential figures in Viennese music. At this time, the Gesellschaft and the Philharmonic Society had came to represent the liberal and conservative spirits of classical music respectively, though Otto Dessoff, as conductor of the Philharmonic (and of the Opera) since 1860, did seek to perform new works, for example the Schumann symphonies. The staff of the Conservatoire included its Director and head of violin, Joseph Hellmesberger, the pianist Julius Epstein as head of piano, the scholar and composer Gustav Nottebohm as professor of counterpoint, the organist Rudolf Bibl, organist of the Cathedral and later of the Imperial Chapel, and also Dessoff, who taught conducting. Hellmesberger, son of the great violinist and conductor Georg Hellmesberger (the contemporary of Schubert), dominated Viennese music. He was concert-master of the Opera (and therefore leader of the Philharmonic Orchestra), a former artistic director of the Gesellschaft (1851–9), leader of the only resident and celebrated professional quartet in Vienna, and an accomplished virtuoso player.

Immediately upon his arrival, Brahms made contact with the Conservatoire, calling on Julius Epstein, who already knew his published works. Epstein immediately went to Hellmesberger and a rehearsal of Brahms's piano quartets Opp. 25 and 26 was arranged, Hellmesberger expressing unreserved enthusiasm for the music and declaring of Brahms 'this is Beethoven's heir'. Epstein recalls that Brahms played the quartets 'with members of the Hellmesberger Quartet (Hellmesberger, Döbyal, Röver) at my house in the Schülerstrasse in the first place . . .We were all delighted and carried away.'[22] Hellmesberger immediately put the works into his coming season. On 16 November 1862, Op. 25 was given with Beethoven's Op. 131 and the Mendelssohn Eb Quartet in the Vereinsaal of the Gesellschaft, a major event arousing the interest of publishers and critics. The event immediately focused attention on Brahms and a circle of admirers began to form, persuading him to embark on a concert of his own, which took place in the Vereinsaal on 29 November and included the Op. 26 Quartet and solos by Brahms: the Handel Variations Op. 24, Schumann's Fantasie in C and Bach's F major organ Toccata in Brahms's arrangement. Brahms's music cannot be said to have been warmly received, but his playing went down very well indeed, and projected a much better sense of his musicianship to his audience. Though the reviews were not entirely without reservation, Hanslick especially noting his reticence in expression (a feature long known in his circle), the positive aspects were so great that Brahms immediately gained a favourable reputation. Selmar Bagge commented in the *Deutsche Musikzeitung* that 'we have to bestow high praise not only on the enormous technical attainment, but also on a performance instinct with musical genius, on a treatment of the instrument as fascinating as it was original'.[23] Later the Vienna correspondent of the *Leipziger Signale* was equally impressed: 'Brahms's playing is always attractive and convincing. His rendering of Bach's Chromatic Fantasia and of Beethoven's Variations was of the highest interest.'[24] The interest remained, as can be seen in the review by Karl Eduard Schelle of *Die Presse* of his concert of 17 March 1867: 'At last a pianist who entirely takes hold of one . . . one only needs to hear the first few chords to be convinced that Herr Brahms is a player of quite extraordinary stamp.'[25] On 7 December 1862, Herbeck gave Vienna its first performance of the D major Serenade at the second Gesellschaft concert.

Thus within three weeks Brahms had appeared as a chamber, piano and orchestral composer, as solo pianist in his own music and that of others, and had become the focus of interest and support. This core support was to be crucial when his music experienced the inevitable resistance from less sympathetic orchestral players, as happened in the following year, when Dessoff prepared the Second Serenade for performance with the Philharmonic on 8 March 1863. During the rehearsals there was dissension among the players, some of whom refused to continue. At this point, Dessoff threatened to resign, as did Hellmesberger as leader, and the first flute, Doppler. This quelled the rebellion and obviously represented an important moment in the establishment of his music in Vienna.[26] Apart from the immediate circle of performing musicians concerned with his work, Vienna offered many other contacts. He soon met Karl Goldmark, the city's most notable composer, resident since the age of eighteen, and now thirty and rising in fame. Brahms would retain a frequent, if not always relaxed relationship with him over many years. The composer Peter Cornelius (now resident) and the leading pianist Carl Tausig, both devotees of Liszt and Wagner, were soon in his company and through them he came into Wagner's circle when the composer visited Vienna in late 1862 and early 1863 to rehearse his works. During this time he laid the foundations of many later relationships with the artistic community.[27]

Yet for all the openings that Vienna offered in the fields of performance and composition, it is likely that the strongest attraction lay in its less public musical resources. The other things he could ultimately do without, but unique library resources, enabling him to study early scores and even the manuscripts of his esteemed composers, as well as books in all fields, could not be duplicated to the same extent elsewhere. The attraction seems implicit in his first reactions, as when he wrote to Schubring 'we have in particular the sacred memory of the great musicians, whose lives and works are brought daily to our minds'.[28] He quickly made a close friendship with Gustav Nottebohm, the senior resident scholar, whose knowledge of Beethoven and Schubert was unparalleled and who possessed many priceless items, with the theorist Simon Sechter, who wrote a canon for him,[29] and with Carl Ferdinand Pohl, librarian of the Gesellschaft archives. His friendship with the publisher J. P. Gotthard brought him into contact with a different aspect of historical study: the rediscovery of the unpublished music of Schubert and the plans for its publication. Spina, who had taken over the business of Diabelli, also took over unknown works which he was able to publish for the first time, including the Octet, the C major Quintet, and the B minor symphony.

With these contacts, and with his impact the following year as conductor of the Singakademie, Brahms had in a mere eighteen months laid very

firm foundations in Vienna as an outstanding pianist, a historically pioneering conductor and an idealistic composer of striking historical
orientation. He was now steadily to build on these in the ensuing years of
intermittent residence in the city. One signal moment was the renewed
contact in 1867 with the great surgeon Theodor Billroth, whom he had
met in the musical circle of Zurich the previous year, and who had now
been called to the professorship of medicine in the University. With
Eduard Hanslick, Billroth would become Brahms's closest musical and
cultural companion over the following years and his house the location of
numerous early private performances of Brahms's new works, in which he
participated as amateur violist. With the appearance of *Ein deutsches
Requiem*, enthusiastically reviewed in Bremen, if not in Vienna, Brahms
gained a reputation as a composer which began to match his fame as a
pianist. His many influential supporters saw him duly appointed as artistic director of the Gesellschaft itself in 1872, in succession to Anton
Rubinstein: an extraordinary transition in status over the ten years since
his narrowly achieved appointment to the far less prestigious
Singakademie. He again emphasised early music in programme planning,
performing many Baroque works, yet also included modern works by his
contemporaries, and by himself. He completely reformed the rehearsal
methods and his period as conductor, though brief (1872–5), is an
admired one in the annals of the Society. But his old reservations
remained as to the practicalities of the job (which included the hiring of
performers and choice of programme) and he decided to resign in 1875,
to be succeeded by Herbeck, who had been lobbying to return. Brahms's
relations with the Society remained cordial, and he was given honorary
membership and invitations to sit on its committees, symbolising the vast
influence he now commanded. This was to be his last institutional position and signals the beginning of his mature period as an independent
composer, playing only his own music. The First Symphony appeared in
the following year. Brahms still got offers of musical directorships, but
was less and less inclined to bother with them, claiming his desire to stay
in Vienna as his excuse. The 'stranger' of 1862 was now fully at home.

With all the professional advantages it offered, Vienna also provided
Brahms with an entirely different personal environment. Initially he
found living in Vienna intimidating, remarking that 'a big city is a desert
to one dangling in the air as I do'.[30] But he also took keen enjoyment in
aspects of its life. Before returning to Hamburg in May 1863, he had
delayed in order to go on a trip in the surrounding area, and he quickly
developed an enthusiasm for the amusement park, the Prater, where he
could hear performances of the Hungarian *Csárdás*.[31] In personal terms,
he was also free of family scrutiny in relationships with women, though

the patterns he had already set in avoiding commitment were quickly reinforced. After his brief engagement to Agathe von Siebold in 1859, he had many infatuations and was doubtless specially attracted by Viennese women, as Geiringer suggests, but he entered into no significant relationships that rivalled the permanent emotional attachment to Clara Schumann.[32] Even when she advised him in a motherly way to seek a wife and make a family life,[33] he never seems seriously to have taken her advice.

The creative reality

Brahms's failure to settle either professionally or personally during the period up to the Gesellschaft appointment and his tendency to remain on the edge of things finds its real context only in the realm of his compositional ambition. Had he possessed less talent he would doubtless have come to terms with practical issues more readily. But institutions took his energies and demanded more of him than he was able to give. The indecision and desperate need for privacy for much of the time betoken his great preoccupations: that he kept his plans and progress from even his closest circle reflects the size of the task he had set himself. His ambition went far beyond theirs, even that of Joachim, who was a gifted composer when Brahms first met him and whose works he greatly admired. The first symphonies of notable contemporaries such as Bruckner, Bruch and Dvořák, were first attempts that were regarded by them as such; their mature styles formed slowly and came to fruition in later works. Brahms's willingness to wait until middle age to complete a first symphony worthy of Beethoven (as well as the greatest symphonists since) gives, despite its routine familiarity in the history of nineteenth-century music, an extraordinary insight into his ambitions. Moreover, this commitment to producing complex and original first works in traditional genres dominates the earlier phase of our period equally. The years 1858–65, especially, were of enormous struggle and self-challenge.

The protracted birth of the First Symphony Op. 68 exactly spans the period of this chapter. Begun when Brahms was known to a very small public – its origins were vouchsafed only to Dietrich and Clara (not even directly to Joachim) – it was completed when he had risen to the very top of Vienna's musical life. Its style reflects these momentous years of change. Beginning, after the slow introduction, with an Allegro in Beethoven scherzo rhythm (the last of a series of C minor scherzi, and completed by 1862), it progresses through two inner movements of very individual character to a finale which is entirely different, and strikingly original in form; it is possible that the finale was under serious consideration only from 1868. The struggle to conceive and execute such a seminal work hardly melded with a conventional professional life. The Piano Quartet Op. 60 shows the reverse side of this struggle. It was not destined to be a comparable success or lead anywhere: rather, it was completed over nineteen years (1855–74) after its companions Opp. 25 and 26, begun later, had been long known. It took a change of key from C♯ minor to C minor and the addition of two later movements as movements 3 and 4 to complete a work of very different emotional character, almost autobiographical in its dynamic profile from tragic struggle to relieved acquiescence. Though the third of the C minor works, the String Quartet Op. 51 No. 1, is known only from the period 1865–73, the idiom of its first movement, at least, places it with the first movement of Op. 68, and the very original form of the outer movements suggests years of thought. The three chamber works composed in the first phase of this period (1860–5) were also slow to reach completion. The great Piano Quintet Op. 34 completed in 1864 began life in 1862 at Hamm bei Hamburg as a string quintet, being reworked later as a two-piano sonata before assuming its ideal form for piano and strings. Though the problem was with medium (a late example of the problem which afflicted the evolution of Op. 11 and Op. 15), it seems unlikely that the reworking did not involve recomposition. With the String Sextet Op. 36 and the Cello Sonata Op. 38 the issues were again formal. Three movements of Op. 38 were completed in 1862 at Munster-am-Stein and Hamm, and the finale not until 1865 at Lichtenthal. The failure to complete the work as first begun (Brahms omitted the original slow movement from the published version) may relate to the problems of matching the planned movements 1–3 to the predominantly fugal finale; the resulting scheme, with a neo-classical minuet and an atmospheric trio as the middle movement, is highly original. Though the delay with Op. 36 was less – movements 1–3 completed in 1864, the finale the following year – the fact that the theme of the slow movement was composed in 1855 again suggests a decade or so of interaction with the material.[34]

Similar observations can be made of the major choral works. The largest-scale of them, *Ein deutsches Requiem*, gives every evidence of a long gestation. We know that the material of the funeral march derived from the two-piano sonata/symphony of 1854: indeed, it seems very likely that movements 1–3 all significantly predated the final working period of 1865–6. Nos. 1–2 are linked by chorale prelude style and thematic substance, while the orchestral material of the first part of No. 3, in D minor, could easily come from the symphonic source. Movements 4, 6 and 7 are – like No. 5, which we know was completed last – rather different in idiom and must date from later. The next most complex works, the Motets

Op. 29 and 74, are also deeply embedded in the earlier period; published in 1864, Op. 29 No. 1 dates from c. 1860 and Op. 29 No. 2 from 1856, both steeped in contrapuntal device. Yet even the Motets Op. 74, published in 1876, go back earlier. The second (from the same school of strict Bachian working as Op. 29 No. 1), appears to have predated 1870 and is probably from much earlier; the first – the jewel of the group, Op. 74 No. 1, draws much of its material from the so-called 'Canonic Mass' of 1856. Again, the earlier material is crucially transformed formally to make the mature masterpiece, with its new opening question 'Warum [?]'. Quite apart from other works in these genres which may have been discarded, there was another whole sphere of creative interest with which Brahms was pre-occupied, namely dramatic music. Throughout the 1860s he considered operatic composition and continued to do so for years thereafter inter-mittently. Only the dramatic cantata *Rinaldo* tells us what such a work might have been like. By the time Brahms had added the final chorus in 1868, having completed most of the music in 1863, he had found a new dramatic style in the baritone solo writing of the *Requiem*. The first two sections of the *Alto Rhapsody* show even more strikingly the individuality of the dramatic style Brahms had developed by the end of the decade, and it continued to be reflected in the smaller confines of his *Lieder* for years after.

The period following the completion of the *Requiem* and *Rinaldo* in 1868 and of much chamber music a few years earlier represented a release for Brahms. A number of large-scale works suggest a new relaxation and ease in these media. In the choral sphere, the *Alto Rhapsody* has a flexibility and fluidity that seems more spontaneous than the *Requiem*, less hard-won, and the work was completed much more quickly. If the *Triumphlied* is an occasional work for national celebration with obvious imitation of Handelian oratorio style, it still possesses a very spontaneous quality, and was much more popular than the *Requiem* when first per-formed; and the *Schicksalslied* explores a sustained and individual mood which also seems more spontaneous in conception. In the orchestral sphere, the *Variations on a Theme of Haydn* reflect Viennese influence and associations: the theme was given to Brahms by C. F. Pohl in 1870 and Brahms completed the distinctly neo-classical composition in 1873. Closely tied to it in key and structure is the String Quartet Op. 67 in B♭. It follows the same structural principle of recalling the opening of the work at the end of a final variation movement, and the outer movements are again very neo-classical in idiom, breathing an entirely different air from that of the weighty and lengthy earlier chamber and orchestral composi-tions. Two other works belong between these two phases. The Horn Trio Op. 40 of 1865 lives largely in a musical world dictated by the romantic

associations of the *Waldhorn* (requiring traditional hand-horn technique) which Brahms specified for its performance: especially the
hunting-horn idiom of the scherzo and finale, the opening theme, and the
introspective chorale-like figure of the slow movement. Though credited
with the same period of working as its companion in C minor (begun in
the 1860s), the A minor String Quartet Op. 51 No. 2 seems to belong to a
later stylistic phase, with its dance-like qualities in the third and fourth
movements (compare the finale with the *Neue Liebeslieder* waltz No.14)
and the lyricism and flexibility of phrasing of movements 1 and 2.

It is only in Brahms's smaller-scale works, more easily written, more
conveniently performed, that some sense of the outer life, not least of the
association with Vienna, becomes tangible. His own instrument, the
piano, shows this first. Soon after his arrival he wrote the *Variations on a
Theme of Paganini (Studies)*, adapting his strict variation methods to the
needs of a virtuoso. If the form and principles are similar, the manner is
without precedent, with modern keyboard figuration drawn from Liszt
and Schumann standing in stark contrast to the studied transformation
of Baroque idioms and extraordinary rigour and thoroughness of the
Handel Variations. The inspiration was the technique of Carl Tausig.
More specific to Vienna were the Waltzes for piano duo Op. 39 of 1865.
They have many stylistic sources, but express a new lightness of mood and
pleasure in harmonic resource within the narrowest confines that shows a
new interest in small forms. Indeed Eduard Hanslick (the work's dedicatee) immediately noted the change of style in reviewing it. Though the
themes of the first set of Hungarian Dances of 1865 were apparently
derived from Brahms's first contacts with Eduard Reményi in 1852 and
1853, the contact with the outdoor performances of the *Csárdás* in Vienna
from 1862 must have had some effect on the composition, and the second
set, to original themes by Brahms, parallels the waltzes in its harmonic
and formal richness within the prescribed dance form. An intimate relation exists between the convivial idiom of the Waltzes for piano duo op. 39
(only subsequently arranged by Brahms as solos) and the vocal music:
Op. 39 No. 10 also appears in a version for vocal quartet. Brahms's waltz
style received greater exposure through the two sets of *Liebeslieder*
Waltzes Op. 52 to texts by Daumer, later followed owing to popular
demand by a set of *Neue Liebeslieder* Op. 65, ending with a coda to text by
Goethe. Here the Viennese association is unmistakable in No. 6 with its
text 'Am Donaustrande da steht ein Haus'. A popular idiom with Viennese
associations also appears in the solo songs. Brahms wrote the famous
'Wiegenlied' Op. 49 No. 4 as a counterpoint or variation on the Viennese
popular song by Alexander Baumann concealed in his accompaniment
and dedicated it to the Fabers, including in the published score the

dedication 'An B. F. in Wien . . .'[35] Extra-musical aspects are not only Viennese, however. Thoughts of Hamburg appear in the wistful vocal quartet 'An die Heimat' Op. 64 No. 1, which was begun in December 1863, his second Christmas in Vienna (which he spent with the Fabers), and which is an emotional expression of his homeward sentiments. The work was not published until 1874, with two other quartets. It is also possible that the group of three songs titled 'Heimweh' Op. 63 Nos. 7–9 to texts by the North German poet Klaus Groth are, in their longing for home and childhood, autobiographical.

The mirror image of Brahms's struggles as a composer is to be found in the reaction of critics. They showed him just what he had denied himself in pursuing his lofty artistic goals in the avoidance of easily absorbed music, and in offering constant challenge to the listener. This is nowhere clearer than in Vienna with its wide range of critical reactions and polemical atmosphere. At the extremes stood Eduard Hanslick, music critic of the new liberal daily the *Neue Freie Presse* since its foundation in 1856, and Rudolf Hirsch, of the conservative *Wiener Zeitung*, with others in between and changing their views according to the work concerned. Although Hanslick, had followed Brahms's career with interest since meeting him in 1856, he was not at first enthusiastic about the first performance in Vienna of the Piano Quartet Op. 26. By comparison with the Handel Variations, the impression made was 'by no means as favourable. For us the themes are insignificant. Brahms has a tendency to favour themes whose contrapuntal viability is far greater than their essential inner content. The themes of the Quartet sound dry and prosaic.'[36] The conservative Beethoven and Schumann follower Selmar Bagge, writing in the *Deutsche Musikzeitung*, was more enthusiastic and continued after leaving Vienna and writing for the *Allgemeine Musikalische Zeitung* in Leipzig. He found the Intermezzo of Op. 25 in the earlier concert 'charming', but, like Hanslick, found the 'melodic invention not significant, the character of the whole monotonous. The four instruments are constantly occupied, not in the nature of chamber music with individual voices, but only serving the *Klangwirkung*.'[37]

Another contributor to the *DMZ*, Hermann Deiters (later to be a close friend of Brahms and his first biographer), embraced the earnestness as an important feature, considering that in the Op. 25 Quartet, after a period of lengthy study, Brahms had come 'to the full expression of his artistic individuality'.[38] In the Vienna dailies, Brahms also found a keen supporter in Ludwig Speidel, a colleague of Hanslick on the *Neue Freie Presse* (though he soon became an enemy for personal reasons). He responded to Herbeck's performance of Op. 11 in December 1862 alluding to its reception: 'the serenade, a fine, interesting and intellectual work, deserved warmer acknowledgement'.[39] The Vienna correspondent of the *Neue Zeitschrift für Musik* was equally enthusiastic. 'It is fresh and rich in themes of which nearly every one is pervaded by a rare grace and a brightness of tone which are becoming every day more unusual. The score convincingly exhibits, moreover, one of the most prominent sides of Brahms's musical individuality. I would call this a power of refashioning, in the best spirit of the present day, the contrapuntal forms of canon and fugue.... Brahms succeeds in ... reconsecrating and carrying on the spiritual treasure inherited from Bach, Beethoven and Schumann, in the light of modernity'.[40]

Although Brahms continued generally to beget varied reactions, with reservations from Schelle and hostility from Hirsch, Hanslick grew warmer to Brahms's music, finding the Serenade more accessible than the tough piano quartets. 'If any of the young composers has the right not to be ignored, it is Brahms. He has shown himself in each of his lately performed works as an independent, original individuality, a finely organised, true, musical nature, as an artist ripening towards mastership by means of unwearied conscious endeavour.'[41] As a major work for chorus and orchestra, *Ein deutsches Requiem* was a test of developing Viennese reactions to Brahms. Herbeck was probably wise to restrict it to only three movements when it was first given in Vienna on 1 December 1867: the botched performance of movement 3 on this occasion gave the opportunity for easy criticism by Schelle and Hirsch. Hanslick alone recognised the level of the achievement, 'one of the ripest fruits in the domain of sacred music', reacting sharply to the disturbances made by an opposing group as 'a requiem for the good manners of our concert rooms'. [42]

Elsewhere, in many major cities, reviews long remained negative. In Cologne, despite the Gürzenich conductor Ferdinand Hiller's support, the serenade was found to be 'too lengthy and its themes too "naive" for his elaborate treatment of them'.[43] In Leipzig, he remained unwelcome to the highly conservative critic of the *Signale* Eduard Bernsdorff; even when the First Symphony was recognized on all sides in 1876, the latter wrote disparagingly of the support of Brahms's faction in underpinning its success when first done at the Gewandhaus.[44] The enthusiastic responses to the first performance of the *Requiem* in Bremen, which made Brahms's international name, were very unusual – clearly a tribute to a local composer and the attention brought to the city and the region. In smaller centres where his colleagues held sway Brahms could expect a warmer response from critics and audience. Albert Dietrich's enthusiasm for the First Serenade in Oldenburg resulted in good reviews for his performance.[45] In Karslruhe in 1865 when Brahms played the First Piano concerto under the court director Hermann Levi at the first subscription concert, the work was given for the first time with every sign of approval, Brahms commenting ironically 'the public, it seemed, had hardly any ill-humour'.[46]

In addition, considerable interest was shown in his technical processes. For example, Adolf Schubring wrote extensive early analyses of Brahms as a Schumann follower in *Neue Zeitschrift für Musik*, identifying the thematic dimension that was to be of such interest to later composers.[47] Thus there were effectively two audiences for his music: on the one hand, the specialist musical one that recognised its quality and what it represented in terms of new modes of expression and technical mastery of traditional means; on the other, many critics and the general audience, who needed longer to grasp it – or to come to believe that they should.

Critical responses had a natural effect on Brahms's instincts in promoting his music. He came to lean on trusted supporters and to relate closely to those interested in his work, rather than offering it to prestigious strangers. The circumstances which gave Vienna the first performances of the piano quartets Opp. 25 and 26 when he had only just arrived may be partly ascribed to coincidence; subsequently, however, his friends and contacts in Vienna served him well and there were more early performances there than anywhere else: the first performance of the String Quartet Op. 51 No. 1 (with the Hellmesberger Quartet), early performances of the Serenade Op. 16 (Dessoff and the Philharmonic), and the String Quartet Op. 67 (the Hellmesberger Quartet), the third of the Serenade Op. 11 (Herbeck, Gesellschaft der Musikfreunde), as well as first performances with Brahms himself at the piano – of Op. 34B (the Piano Quintet in its two-piano version) with Tausig, of the Piano Quartet Op. 60 (with the Hellmesberger Quartet). An early performance of the *Triumphlied* Op. 55 under Brahms at the Gesellschaft in 1872 gives a rare example of his using an institutional position to present an extensive new work (he had only performed his folksong arrangements at the Singakademie); the choices anticipate the reception he could expect, thanks to patriotic sentiment in the first case and musical accessibility in the second. In fact, he could have had a first performance of the First Symphony itself in Vienna had he wished. Herbeck, on hearing of its completion from Dessoff, immediately asked Brahms if the world premiere could be given in Vienna. Yet, as Otto Biba comments, 'Brahms, cautious as ever, thought it too risky to have his long awaited first symphony played for the first time to a Viennese audience; he wanted to have it tried out in smaller cities before presenting it in Vienna.'[48] Brahms's reaction shows the continuing importance of the kind of early support that Dessoff had given with the difficult rehearsals of the Op. 16 Serenade in 1863, and he wrote warmly to Dessoff in exactly the same terms later: 'it was always my cherished and secret wish to have the thing done in a small city by a good friend, a good conductor and a good orchestra'.[49]

Other performances also relate to his circle of supporters. Dessoff's predecessor at Karlsruhe, Hermann Levi, gave the first complete performance of the *Triumphlied* Op. 55, Brahms having previously given the *Schicksalslied*; Brahms and Dessoff gave the first complete performance of the *Neue Liebeslieder* Waltzes Op. 65 in Karlsruhe. Friends at Zurich gave the first performance of the Trio Op. 40 (Hegar and Gläss), and also a second performance of the *Alto Rhapsody* Op. 53, and Brahms also gave the first performance of the Paganini variations Op. 35 there. Joachim's presence in Berlin from Autumn 1868 accounted for the first performance of the String Quartets Op. 51 No. 2 and Op. 67, an early performance of the string quartet Op. 51 No. 1 and also several early performances of the Sextet Op. 18. In Oldenburg, Dietrich gave the Op. 11 Serenade its second and later performances. In Bremen, close to Oldenburg and Hamburg, the sympathetic C. M. Reinthaler, organist of the Cathedral and conductor of the Singverein since 1858, helped with the preparation of the first complete performance of the *Requiem* (in six movements), conducted by Brahms, and conducted the second performance himself, as well as early performances of Opp. 53 and 54. In Hamburg itself, Joachim had earlier given the first performance of the Op. 11 Serenade in 1859 and Brahms of the Op. 16 Serenade in 1860. Brahms's friendship with Pauline Viardot Garcia, a close friend of Clara Schumann, whom he met in her Baden circle in 1864, partly accounts for her giving the first performance of the *Alto Rhapsody*, conducted by the music director Ernst Nauman in Jena in March 1870; however, it had previously been done privately by Levi at Karlsruhe. Though Leipzig was not sympathetic to Brahms till the 1870s, and he long remained sensitive to its hostile reception of the First Piano Concerto in 1859, later supporters helped him here too. The personnel of the first performance of the Piano Quintet Op. 34 are not known, but the Cello Sonata Op. 38 was given its Leipzig premiere by Karl Reinecke and Hegar in 1871. Reinecke had previously given the first performance of the seven-movement *Requiem* in February 1869.

Brahms knew that the essence of his art was understood by some of the best musicians. But what they could not provide was the enthusiasm of a wider audience and a frequency of performance that would satisfy his self-image as an independent professional composer. What satisfaction he did gain would not have been possible without the support of sympathetic publishers. Though the young Brahms had quickly been provided with a publisher on Schumann's recommendation in 1853, the subsequent development of his music after Schumann's death had made publishers wary. Breitkopf & Härtel were slow to respond to the two orchestral serenades, eventually taking only the D major, and refused to take the controversial Piano Concerto in D minor Op. 15. It was the interest of the Winterthur publisher Melchior Rieter Biedermann that saw many of the works of the period into print, notably the Piano Quintet Op. 34, *Ein deutsches Requiem* and the smaller choral works. But the interest of the young Fritz Simrock, soon to take over his father's firm, would be the longer-lasting. With the exception of Op. 34, he took all the chamber music and orchestral music from the Second Serenade on. Brahms worked easily with him, and his new and difficult music soon got into the public domain. It is unlikely that any other publisher would have given him better investment or support.

With this backing, Brahms could afford to wait until he felt artistically ready to release his major works in orchestral form – and did so, settling after the appearance of the First Symphony in 1876 into a life of financial independence such as few great composers of his tradition had known before. How real was his image of a bourgeois professional and personal existence, which emerges from his repeated interest in music director-ships, and in the attractions of family life based around a regular post, for much of the period, we can never really know. But by the time his greatest compositional successes arrived, a pattern of independent personal life had been established. And his fame had taken him well beyond an institutional context into an arena of musical and social politics in which he would now be a central figure.

3 Brahms and his audience: the later Viennese years 1875–1897

LEON BOTSTEIN

Music in the public sphere: Brahms and the spectre of Wagnerism

The writing of music history frequently gains its primary impetus from that which we regard in our own time as great music: those works through which we have chosen to define the essential achievement and identity of a composer. Working backwards, so to speak, from a retrospective evaluation of an entire corpus of music, we distort biography and history to fit our judgements, justifying our own tastes through the medium of scholarly historical explanation. In the case of Johannes Brahms, his popularity and renown are now most often associated with his orchestral music. Therefore, among the most carefully scrutinised aspects of his evolution as a composer is his presumedly difficult and sustained struggle with the task of writing a symphony.[1] His first explicit public foray into this genre was completed relatively late in his career. The C minor Symphony was finished and first performed in 1876. Brahms was already well established and world famous. His substantial early reputation throughout Europe obviously did not derive from his work as a composer of symphonies. His most spectacular success before the completion of Op. 68 was achieved with *Ein deutsches Requiem* in 1868 and (with the added fifth movement) in 1869. The prominent Berlin critic Louis Ehlert, who considered himself a fair-minded but not uncritical Brahms enthusiast, had little doubt, writing in 1880, that the symphonic form was not, and would likely never be, Brahms's *forte*. To the contrary, Ehlert expressed considerable disappointment in the Second Symphony and was somewhat cool towards the First. For Ehlert, Brahms stood out as a composer of choral music and chamber music and as a master of the song form. In the end, the First Sextet, the Piano Quintet, the *Schicksalslied*, and the Handel Variations were the truly original and first-class works of Brahms.[2]

Since 1945 (if not before), owing to the overwhelming dominance in the twentieth century of symphony orchestra concerts in defining taste and reputation, our image of Brahms has become focused on the highly visible place the four symphonies, the two piano concertos, the Violin

Concerto, the Double Concerto and the smaller orchestral works possess in the repertoire.[3] By 1950, Brahms's orchestral music had achieved second place in popularity, after the works of Beethoven, within the concert programmes of American orchestras. Hans von Bülow's famous quips about Brahms's First Symphony as Beethoven's Tenth and about the three 'B's' became serious realities. The early nineteenth century had succeeded in reviving the reputation of Bach and had elevated Beethoven to the rank of the seminal genius of modern times. As far as symphonic music was concerned, despite the scepticism of many of Brahms's contemporaries, his achievements with orchestral music ultimately catapulted him into becoming the third 'B'.

If any period in Brahms's life can be viewed as being dominated by the composition of orchestral music, the last twenty-five years of his life qualify as such. Not only were all four symphonies written during this time, but so too were the Violin Concerto, the Second Piano Concerto, the Double Concerto, the *Tragic Overture*, and the *Academic Festival Overture*. With the exception of the First Piano Concerto and the two serenades, the canonic Brahms orchestral repertoire dates from after the mid-1870s. The earliest of the well-known orchestral pieces, the orchestral version of the Haydn Variations, dates from 1874.

In the extensive biographical literature on Brahms, great significance has been placed on the composer's resolve to come to terms, through composition, publication and performance, with his ambition to master traditional large-scale instrumental forms. It was not until 1873 that Brahms finally published two string quartets, Op. 51; although he had previously written more than twenty quartets, none of them seemed to him worthy of publication or performance. Siegfried Kross's recent biographical study identifies the second half of Brahms's creative life as being defined by his successful arrival in the 1870s on a path started much earlier towards the string quartet and symphony.[4] Brahms's seemingly unusually long journey towards these forms has been explained by the use of two major strategies alongside one another: the evolution of his work has been subjected on the one hand to a mixture of sophisticated psychological interpretation and on the other to elegant formal analysis.[5]

There are, however, other ways to illuminate the sequence of events in Brahms's output as a composer that draw on the realities of musical life between 1860 and 1880 well beyond the scope of biography. By the early 1870s, major shifts in the political significance and social character of musical culture were becoming apparent.[6] Despite our penchant for concentrating almost exclusively on the psychological illuminations of an artist's creative process augmented by detailed, close analyses of musical texts to argue for a coherent narrative regarding the development of a composer's technique and aesthetic ambitions, the fact remains that Brahms – like many of the legendary predecessors he so admired, including Haydn, Mozart and Beethoven – responded to practical realities. Our own attachment to the image of the genuine artist as motivated, so to speak, by some construct we invent of inner necessity and inspiration should not blind us to the fact that Brahms was eager to be successful financially and socially as a composer, in a quite simple and straightforward manner. In 1875 he not only stepped down as director of the concerts of the Gesellschaft der Musikfreunde, but he also gave up any residual ambitions he might have once harboured for a permanent position as either a performer or a teacher. In his final years he was appropriately proud of his financial success as a composer and musician who had lived well for more than two decades, primarily as a result of royalites. From 1875 on, he supplemented his income from composition by a not-too-strenuous regimen of concert-giving.

Although Brahms moved to Vienna in the early 1860s with the encouragement of Bertha Faber, it took him many years to feel entirely at home in that city and to be free from serious bouts of homesickness for Hamburg. Only in 1871 did he move into the building on the Karlsgasse where he was to remain until his death. An avid, if not fanatical, reader and collector of books and manuscripts, Brahms decided finally in 1877, fifteen years after he first arrived in Vienna, to move the bulk of his personal library from Hamburg to Vienna.[7] The emergence into the public arena of Brahms the symphonist and master of the orchestra coincided almost exactly with his decision to remain in Vienna and assume a role as a leading and permanent participant in the cultural life of the Habsburg Imperial capital.

This symmetry in events is no mere coincidence. The leading musical institution in Vienna was the Gesellschaft, the Society for the Friends of Music, whose concerts and activities remained the centrepiece of the city's public musical culture throughout Brahms's life. Although Brahms had his difficulties with the Society and stepped down in 1875 in part because of a complex and awkward rivalry with the handsome and dashing darling of the local musical public, Johann Ritter von Herbeck (whose talents as a musician were not universally admired), after 1875 the Society continued to be the institutional anchor and focus of Brahms's life in Vienna.[8] He was a member of the governing board of directors of the Gesellschaft for decades. He took a keen interest in its affairs, particularly in the archive, the library and the conservatoire. In his will he left the Society his library and manuscripts. Even Theophil von Hansen's neo-classical design for the new home of the Gesellschaft, opened in 1870, not to speak of the iconography of its decorative elements and the historical reference evoked by its interior spaces, mirrored many of Brahms's basic aesthetic convictions.[9]

Although Brahms never taught at the Conservatoire (which in Brahms's lifetime remained a private academy, not a state institution, owned and operated by the Gesellschaft), from the mid-1870s until the end of his life he cast a long, albeit indirect, shadow over the education of musicians in Vienna through his influence on the curriculum of the Conservatoire, and his relations with its faculty. From the mid 1870s on, he maintained contact with most of the prominent composers residing in the city. In 1886 he accepted the honorary chairmanship of Vienna's Society of Composers. The director of the Vienna Conservatoire, the violinist Josef Hellmesberger, with whom Brahms made his debut in Vienna in 1862, was a close associate. Brahms's circle of friends also included Julius Epstein, Robert Fuchs, Anton Door and Josef Gänsbacher, all of whom taught at the Conservatoire. Brahms was also on excellent terms with Johann Strauss Jun., Karl Goldmark and Ignaz Brüll, all highly visible composers in the city, as well as with Carl Ferdinand Pohl and Eusebius Mandyczewski, prominent music historians in Vienna, who, in succession, were employed by the Society. And of course Brahms was also associated with Eduard Hanslick (who held the first chair in music history at the University), Richard Heuberger and Max Kalbeck, all of whom were influential voices in the Viennese critical press during the last decades of Brahms's life. Even the illustrious critic and historian August Wilhelm Ambros, who died in 1876 in Vienna, was a Brahms supporter. Last but not least, Brahms kept up with colleagues in the second city of the Empire, Budapest, with, among others, the composer Robert Volkmann, the violinist Jeno Hubay, the cellist David Popper and Hans Koessler, the composer who would later become one of Béla Bartók's teachers.

Brahms was not a passive member of the Gesellschaft board, and his views were well known, which in part was why its students in the 1870s, including Hugo Wolf and some of his classmates (Gustav Mahler among them), developed hostile or, at best, ambivalent feelings about Brahms. Wolf's vicious attacks in the *Salonblatt* during the mid-1880s were an extreme reflection of the conviction among the young that Brahms represented a conservative, anti-Wagnerian, and – more to the point – anti-Brucknerian influence, powerful not so much in the critical press as indirectly in helping to shape the attitudes of leading pedagogues and colleagues. Brahms sat on juries in Vienna that awarded stipends and prizes.[10] Although Bruckner had been chosen to succeed the theorist Simon Sechter as a member of the faculty, strictly speaking he was not a teacher of composition. Brahms much preferred Fuchs, who did teach composition. Madness often clarifies the 'obvious'. Mahler's close and gifted young friend Hans Rott was institutionalised after a paranoid episode, during which he sought to prevent someone from lighting a cigar on a train he was travelling on because he believed that Brahms had planted a bomb; Brahms wanted to kill him because he challenged, by his talent, Brahms's prejudices regarding how music ought to be.[11]

Brahms emerged in the 1870s as the defender of high academic standards for musical training. His notoriously abrupt and unkind views of the work of many contemporaries marked him as a conservative and traditionalist within the musical world of Vienna. That local image of conservatism was not tempered by Brahms's enthusiastic embrace of Viennese popular music – not only the works of Johann Strauss Jun., but the urban folk music of his day. Wagnerians of Mahler's generation shared Brahms's attraction to seemingly authentic old rural folk traditions, but they were ideologically far less sympathetic to the urban popular and salon genres associated with the modern cosmopolitan life of post-1875 Vienna. This sort of music seemed to pander too clearly to ephemeral bourgeois fashion. Composers in this genre (one thinks, for example, of Richard Heuberger's 1898 hit *Der Opernball*) were said to lack ideals and were too content with mere popularity and commercial success.

The symphonic era of Brahms's career coincided with his assumption of a tacit but dominant public role in helping to shape the direction of musical tastes and the education of a new generation in Vienna. For example, in 1896 Brahms helped the Wiener Tonkünstlerverein support prizes with his own funds for new works written for chamber ensembles, including winds and brass.[12] The fact that Brahms held no salaried post should not prevent us from appreciating the enormous weight of his influence. The Brahms of the 1880s and 90s was a famous local personality, a powerfully public figure within a defined civic cultural context.

From the mid-1870s on, Brahms and the Viennese contemporaries with whom he associated were primarily preoccupied with the anxious perception that a precipitous decline in the standards of musical culture was under way. An obscure but useful coincidence of chrononology is the fact that Nietzsche's great essay 'On the Uses and Disadvantages of History for Life' was written in 1874, at the very moment that Brahms made his successful turn to the writing of symphonies. Nietzsche, despite his later severe and penetrating reversal on the question of Wagner, and unlike that other famous former Wagnerian who became a Brahms advocate, Hans von Bülow, never formed an entirely sympathetic view of Brahms.[13] Indeed, Nietzsche's trenchant description of his own age as 'over-saturated with history' fairly describes one of Brahms's salient qualities, precisely the characteristic that informed Brahms's form of cultural and historical pessimism. An obsessive preoccupation with history seemed to Nietzsche 'dangerous to life' because it 'implanted the belief, harmful at any time, in the old age of mankind, the belief that one is a late-comer and epigone; it leads an age into a dangerous mood of irony in regard to itself and subsequently into the even more dangerous mood of cynicism'.[14]

This description might aptly apply to Brahms's view of his personal place in history and the overall fate of his own historical era. Both seemed condemned to a recognition of their own 'lateness'.[15] The monumental achievements in the history of music weighed heavily on Brahms. The symphony was ultimately the most daunting legacy in terms of music of the past, the most public and far-reaching dimension of Beethoven's output. By the mid 1870s the legacy of Beethoven had been claimed in a radical manner by adherents of the New German School (through the claims of Liszt and Wagner). In their view, Beethoven's accomplishment demanded that a new generation create a distinctive music of the future that could match the grandeur and originality Beethoven had exhibited in his own historical era. Imitation of tradition, particularly Beethoven's symphonies, was a dead end and constituted a misreading of the true meaning of Beethoven.[16] Sceptics of this view, most of them admirers of Brahms, took their opinions on the musical past from Schumann. Schumann's legacy as a key figure in Brahms's musical development was to impart the perhaps more terrifying ambition to find ways to reconcile history and tradition with contemporaneity and originality. Mendelssohn and Schumann helped pioneer the nineteenth-century Bach revival, in part to circumvent the overwhelming dominance of Beethoven and find a way to use history against itself. They sought to find alternative historical precedents to which the music of Beethoven was not closely linked.

Brahms continued this line of endeavour – the reconstruction and realignment of the narrative of music history so that history and tradition could continue to serve as guides to the modern composer. In stark contrast, Wagner amalgamated music history, sorting through it so that a teleology emerged that justified his own innovations as the legitimate progressive culmination of a uniform and true logic of historical development. He believed in the necessity of progress in art and culture. Brahms reserved his enthusiasm for modernity and progress to science, scholarship and technology, not art. Brahms the historian was inspired by the impressive development of historical scholarship in his own time, not only in the field of music. He admired not only Philipp Spitta, but Theodor Mommsen and Jacob Burckhardt.[17] Therefore, Brahms the music historian concerned himself with more than Beethoven.

Particularly after the mid-1870s, he was deeply engaged as an amateur music historian, editor and collector of manuscripts, focusing on Schumann, Schubert, Haydn and Mozart.[18] In addition, his experiences as a choral conductor in the 1860s had led him to the Baroque and Renaissance masters. One of the criticisms levelled at Brahms by Society members in Vienna during his brief tenure in the early 1870s as conductor of the Gesellschaft concerts was his choice of repertoire – his introduction of works by Isaac and Cherubini, and his advocacy of less familiar works of Bach and Handel.[19] Even Hanslick was sceptical about the introduction of music from the Renaissance to contemporary listeners. Brahms's choices in terms of modern repertoire were viewed as equally conservative. They included Goldmark, Dietrich and Bruch. Schumann and Mendelssohn figured prominently in his programmes as well. All these choices were viewed not only as explicitly anti-Wagnerian, but as public demonstrations of the utility of the musical past for contemporary musical culture.[20]

Brahms's debut as a composer of a symphony in 1876 and his subsequent orchestral output represented not only the realisation of a composer's personal ambition: going public with symphonic and orchestral music constituted a public statement in response to a perceived need to challenge the Wagnerian appropriation of Beethoven and put forward a competitive example – in music – of how history could be respected, remain undistorted, and yet serve as a source of contemporary inspiration. Brahms's symphonic output from the mid-1870s represented an explicit attempt to seize initiative through music on a grand public scale in defence of normative musical standards perceived as being under siege: Wagner's success, after all, derived from the wide popularity and allure of his music. It was the music that gave credence to his ideas.[21]

By 1876 Wagner was at the height of both notoriety and fame, particularly in Vienna. Not only had he become the cause célèbre of a younger generation (including Wolf, Mahler, Rott and the music historian Guido Adler), but he had found adherents among Brahms's Viennese contemporaries, including Josef Standhartner, the prominent Viennese physician and patron of music (and fellow Gesellschaft board member), Hans Makart, Vienna's lionised painter (and rival of Brahms's friend Anselm Feuerbach) and of course Anton Bruckner. The 1871 Vienna premiere of *Die Meistersinger*, a work that, ironically, Brahms admired deeply (almost as much as Mozart's *Figaro*), was marred by open conflict between pro- and anti-Wagnerian groups.[22] Wagner harboured a profound sense of revenge towards Vienna. By his own account he had been poorly treated there in the 1860s. In 1875, one year before the completion of Brahms's First Symphony, Wagner returned to Vienna in unrivalled triumph, conducting orchestral performances of his music in the Gesellschaft's home, the Musikverein, to adoring audiences in packed houses. The magnitude of Wagner's success in the concert hall with orchestral excerpts could not have escaped Brahms.

There is little doubt that Brahms struggled to come to terms with the burden of being an heir to a glorious musical past in the wake of Wagnerism's rapid rise during the 1870s. Before the completion of the First Symphony the need for a counterattack through music on a large scale, written for the public concert stage (and not through published polemics, as had been tried by Brahms's close associates with disastrous results in the late 1850s), was evident to him. Brahms chose to perform Max Bruch's most successful large-scale work, the secular oratorio *Odysseus*, in 1875 in Vienna as part of the Gesellschaft concerts, knowing that the work had been conceived as a direct answer to Wagner. The appeal of *Odysseus* to Brahms (who was sympathetic but essentially cool to Bruch's achievements) lay in the fact that Bruch had chosen a classical epic subject equal to the mythic allure of the *Ring* and *Tristan*. Like Brahms in *Rinaldo*, Bruch, using the oratorio tradition, achieved the sense of drama through music and text, without employing the illusions of the theatre. Furthermore, Bruch fashioned the title role as a challenge to the character and sonority of Wotan. The immediate success of *Odysseus* with the public throughout Germany was seen as a victory in a struggle against Wagnerism.[23]

If the younger generation of Viennese composers and musicians after the mid-1870s saw Brahms as abrupt and arrogant, they misunderstood the extent to which he used history against himself, just as Nietzsche surmised. Josef Suk, the Czech composer and Dvořák's son-in-law, recounted how Brahms commented with irony, when seeing the young Suk's impressive quintet, that neither Suk nor Dvořák, and not even he himself, really knew how to write a quintet. Mozart did.[24] The symphonic legacy of Beethoven was imposing indeed; however, it did not, as some historians have assumed, deter composers after Beethoven from writing symphonies. Quite the contrary, the decades between the deaths of Beethoven and Schubert and the appearance of Brahms's First were filled with new symphonies, including, of course, those by Schumann and Mendelssohn. As Kross has recently pointed out, we too often forget the enormous number of symphonies written by now-forgotten but once highly regarded composers.[25] Walter Frisch, in order to defend the nearly singular character of Brahms's symphonic achievement, has taken particular pains, using analysis, to point out the weaknesses in the symphonies of Bruch, who properly merits scrutiny as the contemporary German composer writing in traditional genres most comparable to Brahms. Yet it is not clear that Bruch's symphonies or all the symphonies between Schumann and Brahms are as weak as we suspect. Our own criteria of musical greatness and what qualifies as sufficient for masterpiece status demand self-critical re-assessments, initially through modern performance and rehearing.[26] None the less, it is clear that what concerned Brahms was not the *death* of the symphony, if not after Beethoven, then after Schumann, but rather the poor quality of its quite flourishing life.

Contemporary musical culture needed great, lush and imposing large-scale music that was not Wagnerian. Brahms's decision to enter the public arena from the late 1870s on with – in quite rapid succession – four essays in the symphonic form can be understood as a polemical act not of self-aggrandisement, but one designed to argue that a popular and powerful historical model was not aesthetically moribund. One therefore did not have to follow Wagnerian fashion into the theatre or the murky and form-less regions of Lisztian symphonic tone poetry. Despite the success of the *Triumphlied*, particularly in the context of the tepid public reaction to *Rinaldo* in Vienna (the glowing critical reviews and analyses notwith-standing[27]), it became clear to Brahms that if he wished to capture the imagination of the contemporary concert-going public with music pos-sessed of a large-scale dramatic scope and sonority, his strongest suit would be with the frameworks and procedures of the symphony and the concerto. These forms of instrumental music constituted the repertoire without text or explicit poetic programme that had the most sustained and continuing history of greatness and popularity.

What concerned Brahms in the mid-1870s with respect to musical culture in Vienna was not the quality of Wagner's music. To the contrary, with the exception of Brahms's break with Hermann Levi over Levi's enthusiasm for Wagner, Brahms avoided participating in anti-Wagnerian polemics and did not shun those who respected Wagner the composer. Actually Brahms often expressed genuine admiration for the greatness of Wagner's music.[28] What troubled him was the influence of Wagner – both the man and the musician – on others, particularly the young. Furthermore, Wagner's narrative strategies – effective in stage music and music drama – did not work in instrumental music, as Liszt's music amply demonstrated.[29] The danger was that Wagnerian norms would replace those derived from Viennese classicism and pre-1848 musical romanticism. Furthermore, the argument that the models of Viennese classicism were dead and useless and that new modes of expression had to be invented was anathema to Brahms. In this regard, it is important to realise that among Brahms's circle in Vienna (and Zurich) were profes-sional and amateur classicists, including Theodor Gomperz, J. Viktor Widmann and one of Brahms's closest friends, the surgeon Theodor

Billroth.[30] Like Anselm Feuerbach, Brahms became enamoured of Italy and its Roman and Renaissance heritage. In his Karlsgasse apartment, alongside a bust of Beethoven, hung copies of Raphael and Leonardo. In the visual arts, Brahms admired Adolph Menzel, Arnold Böcklin and Max Klinger, all of whom reconciled a respect for the classical and Renaissance traditions and techniques of Italy with the development of a distinct individual style and originality. In imagery, composition and the use of the materials of painting, they seemed to him to furnish a parallel to what contemporary composers ought to do using the musical equivalents of the plastic arts of Greco-Roman antiquity and their subsequent evocation during the Renaissance: the musical forms of the late eighteenth and early nineteenth centuries. The extension of tradition and the potential vitality of neo-classicism were central to Brahms's agenda. Within the framework of classicism Brahms included the work of Mendelssohn and Schumann, who were themselves so crucial in elevating the legacy of Mozart, Haydn and Beethoven to classical status.

Standards of musicality: the Viennese debate

Brahms's focus on orchestral and symphonic music from the mid-1870s on therefore can be understood as being driven in part by political factors. At the heart of what we have come to understand imperfectly and inappropriately as a widespread Brahms– Wagner rivalry in the culture of German-speaking Europe during the last quarter of the nineteenth century lay a more narrowly defined but more urgent and pressing immediate issue of contemporary cultural politics located within Vienna. From Brahms's point of view (one echoed by both Hanslick and Billroth) the drift of musical taste, particularly in the direction of Wagner – apart from its larger unattractive political and cultural meanings – was a symptom of a decline in musicality and musical standards in Vienna, the community to which Brahms had decided to commit himself.[31] Ironically, Wagner himself was not viewed as lacking those very standards about which Brahms and his immediate Viennese circle were so concerned. The struggle was rather over the soul, so to speak, of the next generation of composers, performers and above all, amateurs and listeners.

The particular local controversies in which Brahms became engaged in Vienna in the 1870s concerning the state of musical culture, musical practice and musical education in the city had their own somewhat longer history that predated Wagner's popularity in Vienna. Owing to his work in Vienna in the 1860s as conductor and performer, Brahms had become intimately familiar with these controversies. By 1848 the Viennese elite had become accustomed to regarding musicality as a key defining a perhaps unique local virtue: a dimension of civic superiority without peer within Europe. Yet even among the Viennese, this local conceit of Vienna as the quintessential *Musikstadt* was being challenged by a younger generation inspired by the revolution and reaction of 1848 and 1849. Frustrated revolutionary hopes were quickly transferred from politics to culture.[32] In 1855, less than a decade before Brahms's debut in Vienna, the critic Selmar Bagge (a prize student of Simon Sechter's who worked first in Vienna but later wrote criticism primarily from Leipzig), who became a staunch admirer of Brahms while employed as an organist in Gumpendorf (near Vienna), wrote a scathing critique of the musical standards of Vienna's Society for the Friends of Music. Bagge's complaints included an attack on the level of amateur music-making in the Society (whose standards he found deplorable), the failure at the Conservatoire to teach serious ear-training and theory owing to an over-reliance on the piano, and a general inability in the Conservatoire either to teach first-class technique or to cultivate a serious aesthetic sensibility.[33]

By the time Brahms arrived in Vienna in the 1860s, the Gesellschaft, as result of local debate and criticism during the 1850s, was in the midst of a radical transformation from being a semi-private club, devoted to amateur music-making and governed by aristocratic amateurs, which also maintained a Conservatoire and gave concerts, to a public institution dedicated to the dissemination of musical culture led by professionals in whose public concerts professional musicians would predominate. Two amateur performing organisations of the Society, the Orchesterverein and the Singverein, were consonant with the original charter. Founded in 1812, the Gesellschaft represented an effort by Vienna's aristocratic and financial elite to pool resources in order to continue musical activities once sponsored by individuals as patrons in their own palatial homes. The Napoleonic invasions brought to an end an eighteenth-century tradition of private individual patronage of collective music-making – the use of large ensembles of voices and instruments. Between the 1830s and 1870, the Society maintained a public concert hall with about 500 seats. But by the time the new home of the Society, the famous Musikverein (designed to seat over 1,400), was opened in 1870, the Orchesterverein had receded from any major role in Vienna's public concert life. Amateur instrumentalists had almost entirely vanished from the stage. The Society's own public concerts were performed increasingly by professional musicians. Those few amateur instrumentalists who participated in the Society's public concerts after 1870 were exclusively in the upper string sections. During Brahms's tenure as director in the early 1870s, the winds, the brass, and the double-basses were all professionals and, more often than not, members of the Opera Orchestra, the leading instrumentalists in the city.[34]

The last stronghold of public amateur music-making in the 1860s in Vienna – and throughout the rest of the century – was the arena of choral singing. By the time Brahms first arrived in Vienna he was already an experienced choral conductor through his work in Detmold and Hamburg. During the 1860s, he was extremely critical of local standards. He took a dim view of Vienna's star choral conductor, Herbeck, whose performance of Handel's *Messiah* suffered not only from stylistic lapses with respect to appropriate performance practice but from an overall lack of quality. As a choral conductor at the Singakademie and later the Singverein, Brahms was known as an individual intent on raising the Viennese expectations regarding proper standards of performance. When Brahms took over the Society's concerts in 1872, he succeeded another popular figure for whom he had little respect, particularly as a composer, the great pianist Anton Rubinstein. From the moment of his arrival, Brahms was drawn to the cause of elevating the tastes and ambitions of the Gesellschaft, from its audiences to its amateur participants.

Throughout the period of Brahms's residency in Vienna, most leading local patrons and practitioners of music were associated with one or another of the many choral societies that flourished in the city. These included not only the Singverein and the newer Singakademie (which Brahms conducted in 1863–4) but also the very influential Wiener Männergesangverein and the Schubertbund. The two individuals most responsible for the successful campaign to raise funds for a new home for the Society were Nikolaus Dumba and Franz Egger, both of whom had close ties to these choral groups.[35] The most popular composer among Viennese amateurs during the early 1870s was Schubert. Throughout Brahms's years in Vienna the musical politics of the city could be mapped by the shifting local attitudes towards Schubert and his music. The Viennese followers of both Brahms and Bruckner claimed Schubert for themselves. By the mid-1890s the struggle over the interpretation of Schubert's achievement and reputation – in anticipation of the centenary of his birth – became a centrepiece of the strident political conflict between liberals and Christian Socialists that dominated that decade.[36]

At the root of the debate over musical standards during the 1860s and 70s in Vienna – a debate that continued throughout Brahms's lifetime – was a fundamental shift in the social composition of the musical public and the attendant habits of music-making and listening in the city. Some observers, like Bagge, believed that the new public for music lacked the fundamental training for high-quality music-making, in part because it was too dependent on the piano as the primary instrument of musical education. The city's leading piano manufacturer, Ludwig Bösendorfer, writing in 1898, decried the enormous growth in the popularity of the piano in Vienna in the decades after 1848 as a 'plague' that was inimical to the cultivation of true musicality. The popularity of the piano took a particularly dramatic step forward in the 1870s, in part due to industrial, commercial and technological innovations. In 1867 at the Paris Exposition, Steinway and Sons caused a sensation. They displayed a 'parlor grand' piano with overstringing and basic design features that included a metal plate and a mode of frame construction that lent the piano a strikingly rich sonority and the capacity to hold its tuning for much longer periods of time than had previously been believed possible. The piano had made steady progress towards mechanical reliability, pitch stability, improved actions and lower unit prices, which helped fuel its rapid rise in popularity between 1830 and 1870. The Steinway piano of the 1860s demonstrated the possibility of building full-sounding pianos for home use that required relatively little maintenance and produced a pleasing resonance. The Steinways explicitly chose not to exhibit at the Vienna Exposition of 1873. Instead, they arranged to have examples of their instruments made available outside the framework of the formal exhibits, much to the consternation of Bösendorfer. Indeed, the jury at the Vienna Exposition went out of its way to single out the Steinway. Among the enthusiasts for the new piano on the jury was none other than Eduard Hanslick. He was in good company. After all, Berlioz, Wagner and Liszt all embraced the technological improvements in the piano that came to Europe from America in the 1860s and 1870s.[37]

The innovations visible in the Steinway piano in 1873 were copied, approximated and imitated rapidly by most of the German and Austrian piano industry, including Friedrich Ehrbar, a friend of Brahms in whose small concert hall in Vienna many of Brahms's symphonic works were first heard privately in two- and four-hand piano arrangements. Although sales of pianos in Vienna had been growing in the 1860s, they flourished even more strikingly in the 1870s, despite the financial crash of 1873. Although Brahms and Bösendorfer were never close friends, they shared a common aesthetic prejudice with regard to the sound of the piano. Brahms's piano at home was a Viennese instrument, a Streicher, which had belonged to Schumann and which was, of course, constructed using a pre-Steinway system. Likewise, Bösendorfer, much to the financial detriment of his firm, resisted adopting many of the innovations in piano design because he preferred what he regarded as the sweeter, less metallic and more lyrical sound of the older Viennese tradition. Indeed, the new pianos sounded orchestral and symphonic; they evoked the sounds of the public concert hall and seemed no longer appropriate vehicles of domestic and intimate music-making.

At stake in the evolution of the modern piano and its introduction into Vienna was more than a debate about the aesthetics of piano sound. The new technology was linked with a new musical culture of listeners, a new industrial system of manufacture and a new form of commercial marketing (pioneered by William Steinway[38]) all at odds with Viennese guilds and artisan traditions. The modern piano stayed in tune longer; its more penetrating sound allowed for less discriminating listening and therefore appealed more to a broader public than to those with clear musical gifts. The more 'user-friendly' the modern keyboard instrument seemed, the more pessimists worried about the disappearance of a higher grade of musical literacy, the sort required for singing and playing string instruments – those indispensable components of the classical traditions of chamber music. The keyboard had long been an essential part of a domestic musical ensemble, an equal partner to the voice and the violin. It no doubt had also served as a vehicle for the individual playing to herself or himself. The modern piano sounded more like a device for the reproduction of the sound of the large ensembles of public music-making from a concert hall and less like an instrument of personal and domestic expression. In many respects Brahms was an enthusiastic observer of modernity, including the Edison phonograph and the photographic camera. But his sentimental attachment to the Streicher piano was symptomatic of his pessimism regarding the level of musical discrimination that the owners of the improved pianos were developing. Brahms never endorsed the fanatical defence of the Viennese tradition of piano construction to which Bösendorfer devoted his later years. None the less, Brahms was pleased to play the Bösendorfers (despite his friendship with Ehrbar, Bösendorfer's local rival) and was delighted that Bösendorfer supplied the Conservatoire with his pianos.

When Ehlert wrote in 1880 that Brahms 'doesn't write for the people but for a parterre of kings', he was not alluding to any particular affection on Brahms's part for the aristocratic and noble classes.[39] Before 1870 Brahms had consciously directed his music at the most sophisticated amateurs and the most literate musical public – an elite whose habits of listening were evocative of an earlier era. In the years between the mid-1850s and the mid-1870s, there seemed to be a sufficient public to appreciate and participate in chamber music and choral singing and therefore in the music Brahms chose to publish during those years. By the mid-1870s the survival of these patterns and habits of musical life seemed in doubt. As the evolution of the Society of Friends of Music itself revealed, after 1870 the public for music, which had been dominated by active amateurs who even dabbled in writing music (Ludwig Bösendorfer among them), was increasingly a passive audience inspired by public listening. Public performances – the hearing of works in groups in public spaces – generated the purchase of sheet music. In contrast, the buying of books continued as a result of the reading of written criticism, the advice of others, the reading of excerpts in journals and newspapers or mere chance – followed by browsing and borrowing. As literacy spread, so did the commerce of publishing. However, insofar as the sale of sheet music had once been partly the result of reading reviews of texts (not merely performances), the ability to sight-read printed music, word-of-mouth recommendation and browsing through libraries without prior public performance, by the 1870s musical commerce was increasingly dependent on the public event and the response to hearing professional performances.

Music education flourished in Vienna, but it revealed new characteristics. The seemingly debased levels of literacy were more widespread, and they made the dense musical argument of Brahms less and not more accessible, particularly without the memory of public performances by professionals. Vienna's musical culture became as dependent upon institutions of public music-making, both local and institutional – including the first examples of modern-style impresarios, concert managers and travelling ensembles (including full orchestras) – as it was on reading and playing music at home in the first instance, and reading about music through the medium of journalism. Brahms's music from the 1870s on reveals his keen awareness – drawn from his experiences in Vienna – of new challenges represented by the new public. That public was a growing cadre of listeners whose active skills of music-making were not as uniformly well-developed as those of the elite milieu to which Schumann and Mendelssohn had become accustomed in the 1840s. Ultimately it would be frequent performances of his symphonies, followed by reviews, that would drive the sale of the piano versions. These piano versions of the symphonies, in turn, would lead the concert-dependent public to Brahms's chamber music. The same pattern would become true for quartets and other chamber music as well. Public performances by leading ensembles would lead to the purchase of two- and four-hand piano versions. The modern piano in the contemporary home came to be used as a tool of reproduction. It could evoke the memory of public performance and anticipate its future experience.

Brahms's turn to music entirely dependent on public performance by professionals, particularly his use of a large orchestra, reflected a practical concession to the changing realities of musical life, not only in his adopted city but throughout Europe. It also reflected his desire to enter into an open struggle through his own music against the new music that adapted all too well to the new culture and was explicitly designed to capture the imaginations of music's expanded public. As Arnold Schoenberg, Brahms's most influential twentieth-century advocate, pointed out, Wagner's genius consisted in part of his brilliant expressive use of thematic repetition in combination with harmonic ingenuity.[40] Wagner had found a way of writing great music that in the end made for easy listening. Brahms knew very well how elegant and subtle Wagner's writing was, and he knew that its popularity rested not on its internal musical sophistication but on its uniquely magical, if not narcotic, musical surface. Wagner could keep the focus of the listener on a single line. The illusion that the surface – the narrative and ornament of sound in Wagner – could suffice remained undisturbed. Wagner therefore appealed to the untutored and tutored alike. In contrast, the surface of Brahms seemed to demand a journey into the musical interior and an engagement with the logic of musical composition. It is in this context, therefore, that the structure and orchestration of Brahms's symphonies can be understood. In his own way, Brahms sought to approximate Wagner's success, but only in terms of scale. The symphony, the concerto and the string quartet – the classical forms – despite the desultory character they had assumed at the hands of some of his contemporaries, possessed the potential for a principled response to the Wagnerian challenge. Spurred by a concern for the future of music, Brahms met the need of his day by producing brilliant alternatives for the listening public composed within the consciously chosen framework of tradition and history. He turned out to be right. The broad public was enchanted by the surface of Brahms's orchestral writing and the connoisseur dazzled and moved by the interior logic of his musical imagination.

The social context of Viennese musical politics

The transformation of musical culture in the city of Vienna during the period of Brahms's residency ran parallel with fundamental changes in the character of the city itself. The social and political changes well beyond the confines of the world of music that Brahms witnessed cannot be assumed to be entirely irrelevant to the evolution of his aesthetic ambitions. The 1870s are frequently regarded as watershed years in Brahms's life. The physical changes in his appearance alone tell a remarkable story. In 1878 he wrote to Bertha Faber that during the summer in Pörtschach he had grown a beard. Although he blamed the event on the lack of a barber, the decision to maintain a beard can be understood as a conscious choice to demarcate the boundary between youth and adulthood.[41] At the age of forty-three Brahms made his dramatic public appearance as a composer of the most impressive large-scale symphony, if not since Beethoven, then certainly since Schumann and Mendelssohn. The conscious assumption of the image of solidity and gravity mirrored an explicit intent to associate himself with a particular stratum of society. That stratum – the liberal elite of Vienna – experienced its heyday and most triumphant moment in the *Gründerzeit* era of the late 1860s and early 1870s. Brahms's assumption of a new appearance in the late 1870s can be construed, as will become immediately evident, as a politically significant sign of allegiance to a particular segment of Viennese society. Once again psychology and politics intersect in Brahms's biography. Indeed, Brahms's circle of friends and his intellectual and political alliances in Vienna offer insights into his personality and ambitions in the two decades after 1876.

Before embarking on an effort to describe Brahms's place in Viennese society in the last twenty-five years of his life, one might ask in what way Brahms's conscious transformation in his self-presentation can be understood as defining his own awareness of the changes in the social structure of his day and age. Again, thinking about Wagner reveals one answer. By assuming a clearly urban bourgeois appearance, Brahms went to great lengths to place a visible distance between his image of an artist's proper public persona and Wagner's. Brahms had no tolerance of either the pose of bohemianism or the explicitly anti-bourgeois aestheticism that would come to dominate Wahnfried and Wagner's inner circle, particularly in Wagner's last years in Venice. Wagner's Italy was not Brahms's, any more than Brahms's clothes – decidedly emblematic of a prosperous but yet frugal member of an urban middle class – could be mistaken for Wagner's idiosyncratic, not to say exotic, finery.

The young Brahms who left Hamburg, went on tour and met Joachim and Schumann in the 1850s, and who later went to Detmold and spent time in Hannover and Göttingen, was introduced to an elite cultural and social urban milieu that had its clear roots in the *Vormärz*. The years 1848–50 were decisive in the European nineteenth century. Wagner's association with Bakunin, his role in the Revolution of 1848, his flight from Dresden and his sojourn in Zurich can be usefully contrasted to Brahms's experiences during the same years. Like Wagner, Brahms also spent time in Zurich, a city with which he had a particular affinity and where he had life-long friends. It was Brahms who opened the Tonhalle in 1895, conducting a performance of his *Triumphlied*, and his friends there included Friedrich Hegar, Viktor Widmann, Arnold Böcklin, Gottfried Keller and Billroth (who, like Brahms, eventually moved to Vienna).[42] Brahms had a more distant, but none the less important, contact with the Zurich resident

Mathilde Wesendonck, who had inspired and protected Wagner; but Brahms was never a political refugee and had no political associations with radical or revolutionary movements. Although he, like Wagner, suffered from insecurity about his origins and formal education he never struggled with his own status as a bourgeois. In fact, he aspired to an ideal of middle-class respectability that Wagner despised and supplanted with a style of life perhaps, ironically, even more susceptible to scorn as essentially bourgeois, all appearances and disclaimers notwithstanding. Unlike Wagner, Brahms lacked grandiose social pretensions. He had little of Wagner's obsession with nobility and aristocratic privilege.

Brahms felt particularly comfortable in the highly cultivated intellectual and literary circles into which he was introduced by the Schumanns and Joachim. Insofar as one can speak loosely of a cultural 'establishment' in Europe before 1850, the influence of which extended beyond the Revolution of 1848, it was Wagner, not Brahms, who rebelled against it. The circles in which Brahms travelled and the individuals whom he befriended in the 1850s – Agathe von Siebold, Julius Grimm, Julius Stockhausen, Julius Allgeyer and Bettina von Arnim – were the best exemplars of a cultural milieu to whom the music of Mendelssohn and Schumann spoke with immediacy and in whose company both of these composers during their lifetime felt particularly at home. This milieu consisted of educated, cultured aristocrats who continued the pattern of patronage and activity associated with aristocrats of the late eighteenth century such as Baron van Swieten and the Viennese patrons and friends of Mozart and Beethoven. The individuals we meet in the accounts of Goethe in Weimar, particularly in the conversations that Eckermann recorded in the later 1820s, help round out the picture.

By the mid-century, a highly educated, musically active and intensely literate elite had evolved. The growth of the middle-class audience for high culture between 1815 and 1848 in German-speaking Europe was significant, and its habits extended and imitated the traditions of a particular segment of the aristocracy. The Society for the Friends of Music was remarkable in that it was founded as an organisation in which a cultivated older aristocracy and a 'second' society of well-to-do professionals, civil servants, bankers and merchants collaborated on behalf of music. Although the patronage of music in Vienna and throughout German-speaking Europe was increasingly dependent on new wealth gained through commerce and not through land, the tone continued to be set by the aristocracy. The same pattern can be observed in the Berlin of Abraham Mendelssohn and his children Fanny and Felix.

Only in the 1860s in Vienna did the cultural leadership shift from the older aristocracy to non-aristocrats and the more recently ennobled members of the 'second' society. Egger and Dumba, who greeted the Emperor at the opening of the Musikverein in 1870, were respectively a lawyer and an industrialist. They were representatives of the leaders of a new economic and social era. Their immediate predecessor as head of the Gesellschaft had been Prince Czartoryski, a member of the landed aristocracy. Brahms's physical transformation in 1878 was a symbolic recognition of the ascendancy of a middle-class elite. The pattern of Brahms's friendships continued to mirror his own idealised picture of the world to which he had been introduced in the 1850s. By the mid-1870s, the 'second society' of Vienna, made up of either recently ennobled individuals – a new aristocracy of wealth – or leading urban citizens without titles, was firmly in control. Brahms's friends included the Herzogenbergs, the Wittgenstein family, the Fabers, the Fellingers, Alice Barbi (who married an aristocrat), Josephine von Wertheimstein and Viktor Miller zu Aichholz: a mixture of professionals, civil servants, artists, writers, industrialists and academics.[43] With few exceptions, the high aristocracy in the later nineteenth century, having ceded the arena of culture, learning and art to a new elite of wealth, retreated to the confines of the Jockey Club and to non-intellectual habits decidedly in contrast to those of their predecessors of the late eighteenth and early nineteenth centuries.[44]

By the 1830s and 1840s, London and Paris had already developed a wider-ranging urban public for art music and literature. The evolution of concert life that we associate with the Crystal Palace in London after 1851 has its closest analogue in developments in Vienna that began only in the late 1860s.[45] A new kind of urban life took shape during the last decades of Brahms's life in Vienna. This can be demonstrated statistically. In 1850 Vienna had under 500,000 inhabitants, of whom nearly 60 per cent could be considered native to the city. In 1890 Vienna had become a metropolis of nearly 1,400,000, of whom only 35 per cent were native. Slightly under 60 per cent of the city in which Brahms lived in 1890 had immigrated there from within the Habsburg Empire. By the end of the century the membership rosters of Vienna's leading musical institutions mirrored this change.[46]

From the mid-1870s to Brahms's death in 1897, despite this enormous explosion in population, Vienna's concert life expanded quite slowly. Only in 1913 did the city build a new concert hall, the Konzerthaus.[47] Despite considerable public discussion from the 1880s to the 1890s, all efforts to create a new professional symphony orchestra for the city (apart from the Vienna Philharmonic, which gave only a select number of concerts each season) failed. Between 1870 and 1913, in addition to the Musikverein, only the Bösendorfersaal, with 500 seats, was opened as a new concert venue. Concerts were given in ballrooms and parks, but the demand for music exceeded the supply. In 1874 the Conservatoire in Vienna had 620 students; in the year of Brahms's death there were close to 900. In addition, several smaller conservatoires were founded in the city to accommodate the enormous pressure for musical instruction.[48]

The dramatic growth in Vienna's population occurred primarily after 1867, when the Habsburg monarchy was reorganised as the Dual Monarchy as a result of its defeat by the Prussians in 1866. The internal migration into Vienna included a very high percentage of Jews, among others. By the time of Brahms's death, Jews accounted for between 9 and 10 per cent of Vienna's population; in the inner city, in the first district, 11 per cent of the population was Jewish. By contrast, nearly 30 per cent of the enrolment in the Conservatoire was of Jewish origin.[49] Apart from Jews, the new migrants to the city included Moravians, Bohemians, Hungarians, Slovenes and Poles.

The Vienna Brahms encountered in 1862 seemed therefore more like Schubert's Vienna; the city in which he died was very different. Most dramatic was the constantly decreasing percentage of native German speakers, and among them native-born Viennese. The new inhabitants of Vienna were not only different in terms of social status but also far more diverse in terms of nationality and religion. The politics surrounding this dramatic social change were as radical as the demographic changes suggest. During the thirty-five years of Brahms's residency in the city, political liberalism experienced a steady and dramatic decline. As Richard Heuberger reported, in the 1890s Brahms was deeply disturbed by the rise of Christian Social political radicalism, which appealed to a nativist and angry community of artisans and shopkeepers. Led by Karl Lueger, a brilliant, attractive and dynamic modern-style urban politician, the Christian Social Party would eventually come to power by the end of the decade, in defiance of the wishes of the Emperor Franz Josef. Central to the platform of this new radicalism was anti-Semitism, an alliance with the Catholic Church and an anti-cosmopolitan ideology rife with a nostalgia for a pre-industrial Vienna.

The 1860s were a period of rapid economic development. When Brahms first arrived the city's walls were being torn down, and the open spaces separating the inner city from the outlying districts were being sytematically filled with monumental structures, elegant palaces and apartment buildings grouped around a new magnificent boulevard, the Ringstrasse.[50] Brahms lived through these changes. However, the economic boom came to a dramatic halt in 1873. In that year the high point of economic growth and liberal optimism had been reached and passed. What occurred in the 1860s and early 1870s can be compared to other periods of unregulated rapid acceleration, replete with overexpansion, excessive numbers of speculative ventures and an explosion of shaky new stock companies and investment schemes. Between 1 May and 9 May 1873, over two hundred Viennese companies declared bankruptcy. By the end of the year, over forty banks, six insurance companies a railroad company, and fifty-two industries were liquidated. The crash of 1873 coincided with what had been planned as the most dramatic display of industrial and social progress in the Empire and Vienna, the World Exposition of 1873. The year of the crash was followed not only by a sustained economic depression but by a cholera epidemic. The Viennese economy did not recover fully until the mid-1890s.[51]

The consequence of this sequence of boom and bust, accompanied as it was by constant demographic growth, was a massive political reorientation. The years from 1873 to 1893 marked the Habsburg Empire's sustained decline as a world power, its stabilisation as a client-state of the new Prussian-dominated German Empire, and the rapid rise of nationalism within the Empire among Czechs, Poles and Hungarians in particular. Nationalism, however, was not limited to the non-German populations of the Empire. By the final decades of Brahms's life, a powerful and visible pan-Germanism in Vienna had come into being, alongside the Germanocentric Christian Social movement, which argued for the dissolution of the Habsburg monarchy and an alliance between a German Austria and the German Empire. Christian Socialism benefited most from a Viennese politics of resentment that grew out of the debacle of 1873. Anti-Semitism thrived on the image of the Jew as the quintessential capitalist speculator and foreign exploiter. The local rage for Wagner, German chauvinism and political anti-Semitism were inextricably linked. At the same time, socialism, an underground movement, gained support among both intellectuals and the working classes of the city. The liberal elite, the very individuals who were in charge of the leading musical institutions, became increasingly beleaguered in their fight against the new politics and ideologies.

If Brahms owed the early years of his career to the support of a privileged group insulated from the modern realities of urbanisation and industrialisation, his loyalties in Vienna remained steadfastly allied with late nineteenth-century Viennese liberalism.[52] Brahms himself was an outsider in Vienna and remained so despite his prominence. He was a Protestant, a member of a minority smaller in number than the Jews, living in an overwhelmingly Catholic city. He was a north German who maintained a lifelong admiration for Bismarck. The *Triumphlied*, which was performed with great success in Vienna, can be considered a revealing transitional work in Brahms's development. Written for large-scale orchestra and chorus, it was an act of German patriotism still somewhat foreign to Viennese sensibilites in 1871. It is significant that Brahms never returned to this form of nationalist expression. By the end of the decade Brahms's patriotism could easily have been misread as sympathetic to a new breed of intolerant nationalist and racialist local politics. Even in 1871 Brahms was careful to express his pride in Wilhelm I's accomplishment through a religious text set to music designed to evoke a connection to the history of music through explicit references to Handel, Bach and Beethoven.

Brahms's reputation among the Viennese in the 1880s was seen as linked to the older liberal elite dating from the 1860s as well as to his identity as a cosmopolitan personality. Many of his closest friends were either Jews or of Jewish origin. Among them was Daniel Spitzer, the brilliant satirist. Brahms not only became the object of hostile invective and criticism cloaked in the language of musical aesthetics, as in the case of Hugo Wolf: barely below the surface of Wolf's diatribes lay the political overtones and consequences of a certain type of widespread Wagnerian enthusiasm that would flourish in Vienna in the 1880s. Vienna's Wagnerians saw themselves as defenders of German culture against a foreign cosmopolitanism. By the end of the 1880s Wagnerism and pan-Germanism and other species of German nationalism were closely allied with local anti-Semitism. Vienna's Ringtheater burned in 1881, killing hundreds of people. The extensive trial that followed led eventually to the institution of new safety regulations for public theatres. The Ringtheater had been the primary venue for much light opera and operetta. Its public was extensively Jewish, as was much of the public for music and theatre in late nineteenth-century Vienna. Richard Wagner was delighted by the disaster and joked about the possibility of yet another fire that would kill all the Jews at a performance of Lessing's *Nathan der Weise*, that emblematic work of religious toleration, a play that celebrated the character of Moses Mendelssohn. Brahms was shaken by the fire. Spitzer understood the extent to which Brahms was viewed by the Viennese anti-Semites as almost a Jew himself and poked fun at the idea that Brahms could be tarred by the brush of local anti-Semitism.[53]

By the late 1880s Brahms had become profoundly dismayed by the direction culture and politics were taking in his adopted home. This fact helps to explain his antipathy to Anton Bruckner. In contrast to Brahms, Bruckner had willingly become the darling of the Viennese right wing. He consented to be the honorary head of a new Wagner Society in Vienna whose by-laws explicitly excluded Jews from membership. In the 1890s Bruckner was hailed as the rightful successor to Schubert. In the context of Viennese politics, Schubert was celebrated as a symbol of native German talent and local Viennese authenticity. Bruckner, a devout

Catholic from Linz, seemed to be a modern counterpart in the expression of a distinct Austro-German voice in music. Furthermore, he was an avowed disciple of Wagner. Although many of his students and acolytes were of Jewish origin, Bruckner's reputation, despite the reservations of the liberal critical and pro-Brahmsian press, particularly Hanslick and Kalbeck, grew in part because he and his music seemed to provide an alternative voice, one more forward-looking aesthetically and more in tune with Vienna's peculiar brand of German nationalism. Bruckner the local hero was the antidote to Brahms. Brahms's antipathy was not only to the music, but to the man and the politics with which he was associated. Brahms's Schubert was a composer more the heir to Beethoven. His Schubert was the musician who was profoundly admired by Schumann and Mendelssohn – a giant of classicism and romanticism of international significance.[54]

In the cultural environment of late nineteenth-century Vienna, it was nearly impossible for Dvořák to gain a foothold as more than an exotic and gifted exponent of how Czech and Slavic elements could be integrated, albeit superficially, into the traditions of German music. That Brahms and Hanslick (who was of Jewish origin) fought an ongoing battle on Dvořák's behalf is one of the clearest pointers to Brahms's intolerance of the new ways of political thinking. In turn, Dvořák's refusal to accept Brahms's offer to bequeath him his fortune if he would relocate to Vienna reflects in part the Czech composer's assessment that the Vienna of the 1890s could not make a truly hospitable home; it also mirrored Brahms's naive hope in the sustainability of a world of music and culture that interpreted national identity in a more old-fashioned and benign manner. Brahms's embrace of folk music included not only German texts and melodies, but Hungarian, Turkish, Persian and Slavic ones as well. Brahms's lifelong special engagement with German folk-songs – from the Piano Sonata Op. 1 to the *Deutsche Volkslieder* from the 1890s – is comparable much more to Haydn's use of folk material and the mature Bartók's view of the essential shared roots of all so-called national folk musics than to the musical nationalism of the late nineteenth century.

The two sets of *Liebesliederwalzer*, Op. 52 from 1869 and Op. 65 from 1875, make this point poignantly. The texts are drawn from a wide range of ethnic and national sources. Yet the musical form is unmistakably Viennese. By 1875 the Ringstrasse was virtually complete. Its development had already triggered a local nostalgia for Alt-Wien, an idealised version of the city's past before 1848, a time that seemed more coherent, simpler and more attractive, before the city's expansion, new populations and new modern forms of commerce. With characteristic irony, Brahms poked fun at this species of local pride and nostalgia. Through music the shared condition and common humanity of all of God's peoples are revealed. The quite local – the Viennese waltz – and the universally intimate – the trials and tribulations all humans encounter in the name of love – are effortlessly reconciled in works of music that bridge the gap between popular and concert genres, making an implicit mockery of claims to uniqueness based on language, nationality and place of birth.

For the listener and scholar, the extra-musical contexts surrounding Brahms's life must be considered in relationship to the remarkable output of music intended for public performance that Brahms wrote in the late 1870s and throughout the 1880s. Despite the rage for Wagner beyond German-speaking Europe, which continued after Wagner's death in 1883, Brahms was all too aware how closely allied Wagner's music was to racialist nationalism. Among non-Germans, Wagner fuelled ideas parallel to the kind of Germanocentric arrogance he himself propagated. Consider the admission by Theodor Herzl, the Budapest-born Viennese writer who wrote for the same newspaper as Hanslick and Julius Korngold, the *Neue Freie Presse*, that one of his inspirations for his 1897 formulation of Jewish nationalism – Zionism – was the effect of hearing *Tannhäuser*.[55] For Brahms, music, as both public experience and private activity, if located in the traditions of the pre-1860 world, might very well help further a different outlook on life. In his view, music was part of an older conception of *Bildung*, in which music, literature and painting were capable of cultivating a sensibility and an expressive subtlety at odds with the vulgarities of modern mass intolerance and hatred.

One of the most powerful critical insights into Brahms's later symphonic music has been the claim that, despite the scale of the forces he used, the orchestral music never relinquishes its essential character as chamber music.[56] The aptness of this perception connects directly with Brahms's ideological project during his last decades of compositional productivity, insofar as one can argue that he had a coherent agenda. The connoisseurship required in the appreciation of chamber music – which in the late nineteenth century was still regarded as the highest form of music – was precisely that which he wished to encourage within the expanded new public he encountered in Vienna after 1876. When Brahms went on tour with Hans von Bülow's Meiningen Orchestra, conducting his Fourth Symphony, he knew he was reaching a still wider concert-going public – the very public Wagner had captured more than a decade earlier. Too often commentators have confused Brahms's aesthetic ambitions with Eduard Hanslick's philosophical arguments from 1854 on behalf of the aesthetics of 'absolute music'. This represents a misunderstanding. Although Brahms was deeply interested in musical aesthetics and read widely about them in literature and philosophy, he never subscribed to the kind of narrow formalist agenda we have come to associate with Hanslick.

Like Schumann and Mendelssohn, Brahms assumed that the impact of his music on his public needed to be emotional and to have content that was not strictly musical in character. That impact was associated with what he regarded as the significance and achievement of Viennese classicism – the music of Haydn, Mozart, Beethoven and Schubert. Secular music spoke to the inner sensibilities of individuals and confronted their powers of feeling and discrimination. Music celebrated the universality of human experience. Brahms maintained a profound and straightforward Protestant religiosity. He believed that his music, like that of Bach, could evoke among his contemporaries the sense of the grace of God and a proper humility and wonder at God's work in nature and in humanity.

Not surprisingly, among the attractions of Bülow's orchestra for Brahms was that its level of performance – the quality of the orchestra itself – set new standards well above even those of Hans Richter and the Vienna Philharmonic. Cultural standards, love of learning and humanism seemed unquestionably allied in Brahms's mind, as is most poignantly evident in his reminiscences left to us by his friends in his final years. His generosity at the end of his life to many members of the younger generation revealed his religiously based optimism, which was often buried beneath a penchant for melancholy and ironic pessmism.[57] The social, political and cultural realities he observed deepened this natural bent towards a critical and severe outlook. But amidst Brahms's flirtation with melancholy, he retained, to his last days, the simplicity of his youthful enthusiasms and his capacity for wonderment. An ideal of beauty and the lyrical – the search for a powerful simplicity of musical expression, transfigured by the clarity and sustained logic of musical form and development (qualities that Heinrich Schenker so valued in Brahms) – seemed to renew his faith in the necessity of art and the capacity for awe in the face of life's sufferings, joy, loss and contradiction.[58] Wisdom and pessimism, as well as affirmation and religious faith, are inextricably intertwined in Brahms's secular instrumental music of his last decades. These qualities are perhaps most apparent in the very last works – including the chorale preludes Op. 122, the Four Serious Songs Op. 121, and the chamber music for clarinet – music that reveals Brahms's faith and his debt to the past. Brahms's mature works sought to communicate hope without any falsification of the harsh complexities of life so that individuals in an endangered modern world might be inspired to combat the erosion of intimacy, imagination, culture, civility and civilisation.

PART II

The music: genre, structure and reference

4 Opposition and integration in the piano music

JOHN RINK

Brahms's works for solo piano can be neatly grouped according to the four periods typically discerned within his music. The Sonata Op. 1, Sonata Op. 2, Scherzo Op. 4, Sonata Op. 5, Schumann Variations Op. 9 and Ballades Op. 10 are early pieces, dating from 1851 to 1854; the larger variation sets – Op. 21, Op. 24, Op. 35 – and Waltzes Op. 39 fall within the 'first maturity' (1855–76); the *Klavierstücke* Op. 76 and Rhapsodies Op. 79 belong to the 'second maturity' (1876–90); while the last four sets, Opp. 116–19, form part of the late music (1890–6). In addition to these solo works, the two piano concertos date respectively from 1854–9 and 1878–81, and there are of course numerous chamber compositions with piano. But the focus in this chapter is on Brahms's solo piano music, in particular four works serving as cross-sections of the stylistic succession outlined above: the second movement from Op. 5, the *Variations and Fugue on a Theme of Handel* Op. 24, the Capriccio Op. 76 No. 5 and the Intermezzo Op. 118 No. 6.

My purpose in isolating these four is not only to complement the broad-brush approach taken by enough other authors to make such a survey redundant here,[1] but to explore the tension between what Denis Matthews calls 'a definite plurality in Brahms's musical makeup' (three principal phases, respectively architectural, contrapuntal and lyrical in nature, defined by the use of classical forms in the early sonatas, the rediscovery of Bach and Handel in the variation sets, and the pre-eminence of melody in the late miniatures)[2] and, in contrast, the stylistic unity or integrity apparent from the composer's very first works for piano through to his late music. As Matthews comments, Brahms's style 'was to change little in a lifetime. It was to undergo subtle refinements in technique, texture and harmony. But the vocabulary remained.'[3] In a similar vein, Michael Musgrave notes that in Brahms's *œuvre*, 'there are no sudden changes of manner, no phases dominated by specific genres. The process is one of continuous integration and re-absorption of principles to new ends, and it is characterized by long consideration, endless revision and ruthless self-criticism. Experiments are there in plenty, but they have to be unearthed.'[4]

This dichotomy between stylistic integrity and stylistic evolution is apparent in our case-study pieces, as are different sorts of opposition that lie at the very heart of Brahms's compositional dynamic. The inner compulsion of his music often derives from some manifestation of what might be termed the principle of opposition – whether an opposition between idioms (as in the second movement from Op. 5), between levels of intensity (as in the Handel Variations), between rhythm and metre (as in Op. 76 No. 5), or between motivic material and tonal structure (as in Op. 118 No. 6). Explicitly identified by some authors and alluded to by others,[5] this principle of opposition is part of what makes the music come alive in sound, or, more to the point, what enables it to make a cogent, coherent artistic statement from the complex forms and structures for which it and its creator are most commonly praised. Nevertheless, as we shall see by surveying the critical literature on each of the case-study pieces, the standard response is inclined to concentrate on 'architectural', or spatial, attributes rather than the music's process – a tendency challenged in Edward T. Cone's classic essay on 'reading' a Brahms intermezzo.[6] Although not without problems, Cone's tripartite model usefully distinguishes between a 'reading based on total or partial ignorance of the events narrated', a 'synoptic analysis [which] treats the story, not as a work of art that owes its effect to progress through time, but as an object abstracted or inferred from the work of art, a static art-object that can be contemplated timelessly', and, in contrast, the 'ideal reading', one which views musical works in a 'double trajectory', both forward through time and retrospectively, with an appreciation of the ongoing temporal course and the contextualising whole.[7] Cone's view that the second of these – 'synoptic and atemporal' in nature – does 'scant justice to our experience of hearing a composition in real time'[8] applies with uncanny relevance to much of the literature on Brahms, for whom (in Malcolm MacDonald's words) 'form was never a matter of abstract patterning, but the palpable articulation of the ebb and flow of feeling'.[9] It is ironic, therefore, that his exacting compositional method has so often inspired a formalistic critical reaction – one celebrating architecture rather than process. Without wishing to downplay the brilliance of his structural conceptions, I intend in this essay to identify some of what makes Brahms's music work not just in the abstract but 'in real time', at once providing evidence of the principle of opposition that drives and shapes the four case-study pieces and, by concentrating on a wide array of compositional parameters (form, tonality, dynamics, rhythm, metre and motivic structure), exemplifying the purposeful tensions between a seemingly integrated musical style and one which itself experienced temporal progression.

The vocal and the symphonic in Op. 5

> Sitting at the piano he began to disclose wonderful regions to us. We were
> drawn into even more enchanting spheres. Besides, he is a player of genius
> who can make of the piano an orchestra of lamenting and loudly jubilant
> voices. There were sonatas, veiled symphonies rather [*mehr verschleierte
> Sinfonien*]; songs the poetry of which would be understood even without
> words, although a profound vocal melody runs through them all; single
> piano pieces, some of them turbulent in spirit while graceful in form; again
> sonatas for violin and piano, string quartets, every work so different from
> the others that it seemed to stream from its own individual source.[10]

Robert Schumann's famous phrase 'veiled symphonies', from his
account of Brahms's visit to Düsseldorf in autumn 1853, can be interpreted in at least two ways: as an indication of the variegated timbral
palette, dense textures and instrumental characterisations of at least some
of the young composer's music, but also as a commentary on the essentially non-pianistic nature of certain aspects of his piano style. To suggest
that Schumann used the phrase censoriously would be ludicrous, but one
might infer from it that this was music really suited to an orchestral
medium, music therefore in disguise (*verschleiert*).

Some of the criticisms levelled at the early sonatas and other juvenilia
stem from this conflict between a tremendous compositional facility initially and most naturally exploited in piano and vocal repertoire, and a
straining after something greater – a musical utterance of truly symphonic dimensions. Brahms's symphonic inclinations would of course be
realised only later, first of all in the Piano Concerto Op. 15, but meanwhile
they may actually have succeeded in frustrating the flow of the solo piano
music. As early as 1862, Adolf Schubring remarked on 'the padded
counterpoint and the overloaded polyphony' that contribute to the
'failure' of Op. 5 (a work which fits Schumann's description of 'veiled
symphonies' better than any other, according to Musgrave[11]), as well as
the 'feebleness and stagnation' resulting from the first movement's
doggedly monomotivic construction.[12] Echoing Schubring, Walter Frisch
attributes the 'stiff, even clumsy' nature of the exposition to 'Brahms's
emphasis on transformation at the expense of development', concluding
that the 'movement is rescued from utter stagnation by the progression of
the shapes [that is, stable melodic *Gestalten*] toward what I have called
lyrical fufillment or apotheosis'.[13]

That same progression towards apotheosis occurs in the second movement, but effected by means of a remarkable change of idiom at the most
unexpected moment in an initially straightforward ternary design. This

Andante, along with the eventual fourth movement ('Intermezzo: Rückblick'), predated the other movements in the Sonata and is one of few instrumental works by Brahms explicitly linked to a literary text – the first three lines from C. O. Sternau's poem 'Junge Liebe'.[14] Although Brahms himself observed that these verses are 'perhaps necessary or pleasant for an appreciation of the Andante',[15] it may be that the slow movement was closely modelled on the poem as a whole (as George Bozarth has argued), such devices as 'melodic construction, texture, harmony, and variation procedure' creating 'tonal analogues which convey the mood, imagery, and meaning of the poem'.[16] Among the movement's most remarkable features is its rhapsodic coda, which follows a conventional ABA' succession in which the implied motion towards closure is thwarted at the last possible stage, opening into one of the most passionate outpourings in all of Brahms. Bozarth argues that 'on first perusal, the coda would seem merely to function as a "textless" post-lude, another grand apotheosis of a poet's love, as in the Op. 1 Andante', but its real 'story' can be understood by comparing it to a German folk-song 'Steh' ich in finst'rer Mitternacht', about a young soldier recalling an 'affectionate parting from his now distant beloved'.[17]

Without denying the elegance of Bozarth's interpretation, I would counter that the movement's force lies not so much in its extramusical associations as in the sudden, unforeseen abandonment of a vocal idiom (which may or may not correspond to the lovers in Sternau's poem) for a symphonic one, the apotheosis at the end thus assuming the role of instrumental commentary on the love scene unfolded within the ABA' stretch of the movement. There is good reason to suppose that such a function may have been intended by Brahms, given the similarity of two influential models. The first, Beethoven's *An die ferne Geliebte* (a cycle of six songs about another 'distant beloved'), introduces an exciting piano postlude to round off the sixth song's reprise of the opening music and to suggest a rapturous union of the two lovers, just as the piano postlude in the final number of Schumann's *Dichterliebe* extends a repeated piano passage from the end of Song 12 to express the sense of reconciliation that the protagonist himself has been unable to articulate verbally. In both cases, the narrative conclusion or commentary is instrumental, not verbal, in nature, just as the piano-as-poet 'speaks' in the last work, 'Der Dichter spricht', in Schumann's *Kinderszenen* (and, like the final postlude in *Dichterliebe*, employs a recitative style to do so).

If instrumental commentaries were therefore an established composi-tional device when Brahms came to write the Andante from Op. 5, the tremendous expressive crescendo at the end of this hitherto placid 'Nachtstück'[18] had perhaps no such precedent. To appreciate its impact

Example 4.1 Brahms, Sonata Op. 5, movement 2, bars 1–5 and 37–44

requires preliminary discussion of the movement as a whole. The main body, an ABA′ design moving through the keys of I, IV and I (respectively bars 1–36, 37–105 and 106–43, each section itself having a ternary construction),[19] uses a dialoguing of parts, usually soprano and tenor, presumably to represent the 'zwei Herzen' in Sternau's poem.[20] (See Example 4.1.) Although the music occasionally grows more animated (for instance, at bar 92's *f* and con passione), Brahms retains a calm, restrained mood virtually throughout, as when section B enters, Poco più lento, *pp* and 'Äußerst leise und zart'. A′ promises to conclude as section A did (Example 4.2 compares the two endings), until an important deviation occurs at bar 139: over a rhythmically disruptive neighbour-note figure in the left hand (triplet semiquavers subdivided into groups of two), an extended cadential progression employing the minor subdominant unexpectedly moves to V[7] of D♭ major (hitherto acting as IV), whereupon the anticipated close of the movement is withheld and the 'coda' – in fact, a fourth principal section, C – tentatively begins, Andante molto, espressivo, *ppp* and with una corda. Its key of D♭ major is the one in which the movement ends, in a most unorthodox manner, the conventional I–IV–I structure retrospectively interpretable as a large-scale V–I progression (in which the A♭ major of sections A and A′ acts as dominant to the D♭ major of sections B and, especially, C).[21]

However radical the sudden change of tonic might be, it is the new, expressively potent symphonic idiom prevailing from bar 144 onwards that most strikes the listener. The timpani-like pulsation on the pedal-note A♭ builds tension (despite Brahms's 'sempre *pp* possibile' marking in bar 157) until bar 164's 'molto pesante' eruption at *ff*, the thickened textures, driving triplet rhythm and questing harmonic motion explosively

Example 4.2 Brahms, Sonata Op. 5, movement 2, bars 32–7 and 137–48

pushing towards climax at bar 174, the true coda (Adagio) then taking over at bar 179 and dissipating the overwhelming accumulated tensions with a final reminiscence of the 'duet' theme from section A.

Elaine Sisman comments on Brahms's ability 'to create new ambiguities, and hence to impart new aesthetic meaning to the traditional gestures' of the 'closed forms' – variation, rondo, ternary. The last of these in particular establishes 'a set of firm expectations in the listener . . . Yet Brahms found his most intimate voice in this form, which he transformed with a profound change in the relationships among the expected three sections.'[22] In Op. 5 this transformation is achieved not only by the unconventional modulation to the previous subdominant, but also by the shift from a vocal medium to a symphonic one – a fundamental change of idiom intended to articulate the 'poetic' commentary. As Malcolm MacDonald observes, here and in other early works Brahms 'discovered how to make an orchestra speak through the medium of the keyboard',[23] and its significance in this slow movement derives from an essential opposition to the main body of the work – an opposition so stark, and underpinned by such an unusual key progression, that it would threaten to pull the music apart were the composer's powers of integration less assured than those of the young Brahms. Instead, the remarkable opposition paradoxically draws the movement into a unified statement far transcending in expressive effect the conventional ABA' succession promised early on, and in this regard it serves as a harbinger of much of the piano music that Brahms would write in his 'first maturity' and well beyond.

Continuity in flux: the Handel Variations as gesture

The literature on Brahms's Handel Variations is filled with ecstatic praise for this musical colossus: 'one of the most important piano works he ever created';[24] 'completest mastery of the Variation form';[25] 'great enrichment of keyboard idiom', 'highly individual' detail, 'strength of form';[26] 'miraculously balanced' freedom and 'adherence to the rules';[27] 'massive scale and exhaustive command of piano technique', 'dwarfs all his previous variation sets';[28] 'ranks with the half-dozen greatest sets of variations ever written', 'represents a rediscovery of the fundamental principles of the form'.[29] Musgrave notes that between Op. 21 and Op. 24 Brahms assiduously sought out 'more rigorous, complex and historical models', among others preludes, fugues, canons and the then obscure dance movements of the Baroque period. Yet 'his characteristic pianism – his chains of thirds and sixths and rigorous contrary motion which produce harsh and unstylistic dissonances' – still prevailed, in a juxtaposition of keyboard styles 'far removed from his earlier style with those more common in the time . . . achieving through his own natural feeling for them a mediation with his natural pianism'.[30]

Perhaps more than in any other work thus far, Brahms's mastery of structure is supremely evident, along with a vocabulary of pianistic textures and gestures the richness of which cannot be exhausted even in twenty-five variations or the monumental fugue at the end. It is not surprising, therefore, that considerable scholarly attention has been devoted

to the work's architectural properties, albeit sometimes at the expense of
the musical process (as suggested earlier). Heinrich Schenker, for
instance, individually analyses the theme, variations and fugue in his
lengthy study, virtually neglecting the sum of these parts (although in a
final section – 'Noch etwas zum Vortrag' – he does provide a dynamic
representation of the theme and then discusses articulation, agogic
shaping and so forth).[31] Others are content simply to identify the stylistic
characters of the successive 'movements' (inspired, for instance, by
Hungarian, music-box and harpsichord idioms), while a spatial representation of the whole is offered by Hans Meyer,[32] who advances the following roughly symmetrical model comprising four 'unified blocks'
divided by the pivotal thirteenth variation and counterbalanced by the
109-bar fugue:

Variations	1–8	9–12	13	14–17	18–25
	'strict'	'free'	'synthesis'	'strict'	'free'

An altogether different approach is taken by Jonathan Dunsby, who
observes that 'at some level of the structure . . . Brahms usually creates a
functional ambiguity, giving his music its typically elaborate and complex
character'. In Dunsby's study, 'cases of simple, ambiguous formation are
created by isolating the first two bars of each variation', which 'are ana-
lyzed as a complex of binary oppositions. A graphic model is formulated
for each type of ambiguous structure, and the results are tabulated to see
whether there is any pattern through the work.' His 'table of transformations' depicts 'categories of articulation, each one being a summary of the
structure', and reflects a binary/ternary ambiguity present at least at the
start of each variation. Over and above this unifying feature, says Dunsby,
'the reappearances of the *Aria*'s structure articulate the piece as a whole'.[33]

Although it succeeds in identifying at least one 'continuing element' in
the variations,[34] Dunsby's analysis hardly captures what MacDonald calls
'the grand sweep of the structure',[35] nor for that matter would the model
sketched in Edward Cone's essay 'On Derivation: Syntax and Rhetoric',[36]
which focuses on small-scale progression and succession in theme-and-
variation works rather than the broader gesture. In Op. 24 that sort of
gesture – which is naturally of vital importance to the performer of the
set, and what most listeners will apprehend first and foremost – could be
defined in many different ways, but I shall confine myself to investigating
Brahms's expression markings, particularly his dynamic indications, for
these clearly point to an underlying 'shape' in the work. Table 4.1
summarises the key relationships and principal expressive markings
in the twenty-five variations, the latter determined in most cases by
the indication at the start of each variation. Using this information,

Table 4.1 *Expression and tonality in Brahms, Handel Variations Op. 24, Variations 1–25*

Variation	Key	Dynamics and character	Articulation	Tempo
1	I	poco *f*		
2		*p* animato	legato	
3		*p* dolce		
4	↓	risoluto, *sf*/*f*	staccato	
5	i♭	*p*, espressivo		
6	↓	*p* sempre	legato	
7	I♮	*p*, con vivacità ◁ *f*		
8		*f*/*p*/*sf*/*p*		
9		*sf* ▷ *p*	legato	poco sostenuto
10		*f*, energico / *p*/ *pp*		
11		*p* dolce		
12	↓	*pp*, soave		
13	i♭	*f* espressivo		Largamente, ma non più
14	I♮	*sf*/*f*	sciolto	
15		*f*		
16		*p* ma marcato		
17		*p*		Più mosso
18		[*p*] grazioso		
19		*p*, vivace	leggiero	
20	↓	*p* ◁ ▷ ; espressivo	legato	
21	vi	*p* dolce; espressivo		
22	I	*p* (> > > >)		
23		*p* vivace ◁ *f*	staccato	
24		*p* ◁ *f*		
25	↓	*ff*		

Example 4.3 charts an intentionally simplistic graph of the varying levels of dynamic intensity,[37] revealing peaks at Variations 4, 8–10, 13–15 and, most profoundly, 23–5, which sweep in an accelerando of momentum towards the climactic fugue. What is especially striking in both Table 4.1 and Example 4.3, however, is the polarisation of soft and loud dynamic levels – *pp* and *p* versus *f* and *ff*, with practically nothing specified between these apart from occasional crescendo and decrescendo indications and the initial 'poco *f*'. This terracing of opposed dynamics, especially obvious in the back-and-forth swings of Variations 8–10 and 23ff., is possibly as Baroque in origin as the very theme, which carves a rather more incrementally fluctuating, give-and-take progression through registral space (see Example 4.4), played on the piano with minutely changing dynamic levels.

The conclusion of all this is that Brahms takes pains to control the intensity level throughout the twenty-five variations, maintaining a state of flux in the first half, and then keeping the temperature perceptibly low after the peak of Variations 13–15 until the massive 'crescendo' towards the fugue begins in Variation 23. We thus find a sensitivity to motion and

Example 4.3 Brahms, Handel Varations Op. 24, Variations 1–25: dynamic flux

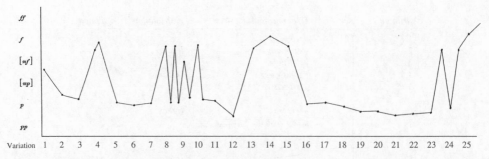

Example 4.4 Brahms, Handel Varations Op. 24, Aria: theme and and registral flux

momentum that complements – and possibly transcends in importance to the listener – the elegance of structure about which so many authors have (legitimately) enthused. What makes the music's course so powerful, however, is the opposition and indeed juxtaposition of dynamic maxima and minima, a throwback to the Baroque era but one that takes full advantage of the piano's equal capacity for microscopic nuance and almost brute force.

It is in the fugue that the tension between dynamic extremes is played out once and for all. MacDonald writes that in this 'astonishingly free' fugal conception,

> Brahms's primary objective seems to have been to reconcile the *linear* demands of fugal form with the harmonic capabilities of the contemporary piano. Accordingly his hard-acquired polyphonic skills, manifest in innumerable subtleties of inversion, augmentation, and stretto, perfectly accommodate themselves to an overwhelmingly pianistic texture ... The grand sweep of the structure, however, is never lost sight of: the immense cumulative power of this Fugue, gathered up in a chiming, pealing dominant pedal, issues in a coda of granitic splendour ...[38]

Musgrave reinforces this point: 'more Bachian than Handelian in its exhaustive wealth of contrapuntal device', the fugue uses

> diminution, augmentation, and stretto, building to the final peroration through a long dominant pedal with two distinct ideas above. But the pianism is an equal part of the conception, and in this, the most complex

example of Brahms's virtuoso style, the characteristic spacings in thirds, sixths, and the wide spans beween the hands are employed as never before. Indeed, the pianistic factor serves to create the great contrasts within the fugue, which transcends a conventional fugal movement to create a further set of variations, in which many of the previous textures are recalled in the context of the equally transformed fugal theme.[39]

If it is true, as Matthews claims, that 'the Brahms player needs to think orchestrally in order to draw the strongest contrasts from a mere keyboard',[40] then in the Handel Variations we find perhaps the pinnacle of Brahms's 'symphonic' piano style, a style which may well have constrained him in certain earlier works (by provoking 'padded counterpoint and overloaded polyphony') but which would here be employed to maximum musical effect. Even so, his success in Op. 24 suggests not so much an evolution as an actualisation of style, one which eventually would shape the keyboard 'miniatures' composed some fifteen years later, after a long hiatus during which he produced no solo piano music at all.

Two against three in the Capriccio Op. 76 No. 5

Perhaps more than any of Brahms's other solo piano works, the eight pieces in Op. 76 encapsulate the dichotomy identified earlier between a holistic compositional style and one experiencing continual change, occupying a central position (in Musgrave's words) 'between the character pieces of Brahms's youth and the rich flowering of the later period, the four sets published in 1892 and 1893. Yet, though they offer strong contrast to the large-scale variation works which preceded them in the second period, they actually draw much from them. Variation becomes an integral part of their exploration of characters and moods.'[41] As we shall see, this is particularly evident in the fifth work in the set, a quintessential example of the rhythmic and metrical opposition that was so vital a part of Brahms's compositional discourse.

As David Epstein has noted, temporal phenomena in music, not least those related to 'motion', are particularly difficult to conceptualise, hence the lack of a vocabulary to capture 'those seeming paradoxes and ambiguities of rhythm and metre' that Brahms excelled in and that often cause a 'disparity between how the music is heard and the way it is embodied in [the] score'. Nevertheless, says Epstein, in spite of its deepseated conflicts between metre and rhythm, Brahms's music 'in a fundamental sense is performance proof . . . its forward motion cannot be destroyed. Let the performer play the notes and the rhythms as they are

written and the music must move ... motion is built into the notes themselves, the inevitable product of their structure', which 'exerts its own
control'.[42]

Elsewhere I have questioned the validity of this hypothesis with regard
to Brahms's *Fantasien* Op. 116,[43] but in the case of Op. 76 No. 5 one would
be hard pressed to deny Epstein's point. The work is riddled with temporal clashes, yet despite these – or perhaps because of them – it manages not
only to cohere but to enact a drama of exceptional originality and fervour.
MacDonald writes that 'Brahms's characteristic love of cross-rhythm, 3/4
alternating with 6/8 and duplets playing against triplets, is on especially
lavish display in the ... powerful [Op. 76] No. 5, a Capriccio in C♯ minor in
an extended ternary form (with far-reaching variation of the basic
material) which derives its dark passion from the motive energy such
rhythmic ambiguities can supply.'[44]

Musgrave's extended description observes that

> Variation comes into much clearer focus in the remarkable C♯ minor
> Capriccio No. 5. Here the alternating form A B A B1 A1 A2 (coda) indicates
> the successive application of variation to two basic sections, the first a prime
> example of Brahmsian cross-rhythm, 3/4 and 6/8 existing simultaneously ...
> The two ideas are themselves rhythmically differentiated, the second
> building to very expansive pianism and modulating more widely. The
> repetition of A retains its original pattern for ten bars, after which it
> broadens to a lyrical cross-rhythmic passage 'poco tranquillo' ... The
> variation [that ensues] is now rhythmic, a radical variation which recalls the
> third movement of the Second Symphony. Rhythmic variation of A then
> follows including change of mode to major 'espress[ivo]', the piece ending
> with a further rhythmic transformation – phrases of five quavers which
> completely obscure the metre – to a powerful climax.[45]

My own analysis differs in certain details from Musgrave's, but what
the diagram in Example 4.5 reveals perhaps more clearly than any prose
description could is the fundamental tension between the chronological,
narrative flow of the music and the structure as a whole that embraces it –
a tension explicitly acknowledged in Cone's analytical model (see above)
and here thoroughly exploited by Brahms. Capitalising on the piano's
ability to layer textures 'contrapuntally',[46] he launches into the piece with
three different metrical schemes in operation at once: a melody suggesting 3/4, a bass in 6/8 and a sinuous tenor line which could be read either
way. (Example 4.6a offers an analytical reinterpretation of the passage.)
This multiplicity of organisational schemes is a foretaste of the fierce
battle fought throughout the work, in which the notated 6/8 metre eventually gives way to 2/4 in bars 78–111, following the violent jockeying

back and forth between the two in bars 69–77 (effected by the sequential statements of 'x' – see Example 4.5 – in bars 69–70, 73–4 and 77). The modulation from one metre to another in this way is extraordinary in and of itself, but the fact that the work's climax (in subsection a₃) occurs in the new metre and moreover in the parallel tonic, C♯ major (withheld until this point, and induced by the metrical displacement of the melody's E♯), makes it especially remarkable. Even more striking is the 'further rhythmic transformation' mentioned by Musgrave and broken down in Example 4.6b. The emergence of a new five-quaver group paying no real attention to the 6/8 notated in the score, with 5/8 implied in the lower parts and 3/4 - 1/8 in the upper (the start of each new phrase is almost like a syncopation, the full force of which can be projected in performance by means of a hiccup effect, that is, the tempo kept very steady indeed so that no 'bending' occurs), succeeds in initially suppressing expectations of metrical regularity, the sense of 5/8 disappearing with the extension to 5/8 + 1/8 in the lower systems and an at last untruncated 3/4 in the top line. This extension gives rise to the triplet implications of the left-hand octaves descending against the hemiola-like right-hand material, which in fact perpetuates the now well established 3/4 until the final sweep on the last beat of bar 115 – yet another momentum-generating extension. Here the right hand suddenly moves in triplets, while the left hand is both triple and duple in character, building terrific energy until the 'true' 6/8 metre is fully restored on the downbeat of bar 116, bringing the piece to a breathless close in just two bars.[47]

Brahms's control over this temporal battle is consummate: while allowing it to rage not only within individual bars (as in Example 4.6a and 4.6b; compare also bars 53ff.) but in the metrical plan as a whole (especially the 6/8 versus 2/4 opposition at the highest level of temporal organisation), he maintains order largely by means of the straightforward harmonic foundation shown at the bottom of Example 4.5. The three occurrences of section A, in the tonic C♯ minor (eventually, major), are punctuated by passages prolonging the dominant: first of all B₁, then C (in the minor dominant) and B₂. The smaller-scale i–V–i structures that emerge are seemingly contained within the ultimate progression through the climactic structural dominant in bars 103ff. to the tonic's return in the coda, which itself ends with an emphatic V⁷–i cadence (Example 4.6b).

Thus the relative simplicity of the tonal foundation counteracts the almost overwhelming metrical clashes in which Brahms revels, the piece embodying an opposition not just between duple and triple metres and subdivisions thereof (yet another manifestation of his seemingly insa-

Example 4.5 Brahms, Capriccio Op. 76 No. 5: metrical, formal and tonal structures

Notated time signature	$\frac{6}{8}$							$\begin{smallmatrix}2&6&2&6&2\\4&8&4&8&4\end{smallmatrix}$			$\frac{6}{8}$		
Bar	1	10	20	30	40	50	60	70	80	90	100	110	
Section	A_1		B_1		A_2		C		B_2		A_3	coda	
Subsection	a_1 a_2		$\underset{x}{\smile}$		a_1		$a_2{'}$		$\underset{x}{\smile}$		$a_1{'}$	a_3 = extension to climax	

Tonal structure

i ⟶ III→V — — — — —V i   i ⟶ v (v: i ⟶ III ⟶V) V— — — — —V i — — — — —I ⟶V#6/4 ⟶V#6/4—5 i⟶V→i
(sequences)   (sequences)   #   ♮

Example 4.6 Brahms, Capriccio Op. 76 No. 5

(a) Metrical implications in bars 1–4

(b) Metrical implications in bars 111–17

tiable appetite for two-against-three patternings) but between the de-stabilising temporal flow and the stabilising harmonic underpinnings, respectively centrifugal and centripetal in nature. For the listener or analyst to appreciate that opposition virtually requires an awareness of the 'double trajectory' described by Cone, that is, sensitivity to both the diachronic flow and the synchronic whole.[48]

None of this is meant to suggest that the tonal plan is static, rather that it is solidly built and able to withstand the assault of the temporal conflict above. A notably different situation arises, however, in the last of our case-

study pieces, Op. 118 No. 6, where the music's tonal foundations are threatened to the very core, this challenge caused in part by a motivic shape
whose pre-eminence virtually overwhelms all other structural aspects.

Music of the future: the 'progressive' Brahms

According to MacDonald, Brahms's last four sets of solo piano music,
Opp. 116–19, 'stand at the furthest possible remove from the rhetoric of
the early sonatas or the pugnacious challenge of the large-scale variation
sets. Though a few of them afford brief glimpses of the old fire and energy,
the predominant character is reflective, musing, deeply introspective, and
at the same time unfailingly exploratory of harmonic and textural effect,
of rhythmic ambiguity, of structural elision and wayward fantasy.'[49]
Nevertheless, just as Brahms's codas often serve a 'summarising' function
in individual works, as it were drawing together seemingly disparate ideas
from earlier on which in retrospect prove to be closely linked, certain
compositions within the four opuses do more than simply glance back at
previous stages within the solo piano output. Op. 118 No. 6 is one such
piece, rich in symphonic implications, masterful in its control of counterpoint, poised on the brink of instability through extreme expressive contrasts and a tonal scheme as unorthodox in its way as that of Op. 5's
second movement. What is perhaps more noteworthy, however, is the
Brahmsian legacy represented by this work, eventually taken up by such
composers as Arnold Schoenberg, whose serial technique was at least
partly inspired by the motivic working and in particular the 'developing
variation' at which Brahms excelled and which is an important agent
within Op. 118 No. 6.[50] Past and future are therefore united in this piece,
its apparently idiosyncratic audacities part and parcel of the piano style
practised for some fifty years, while paving the way for the revolution in
musical language to come. Certainly its expressive profundity has been
enthusiastically recognised by authors: 'perhaps the most signficant and
poetic of all the later pieces'; 'deeply introspective . . . rises to an intensity
not previously found'; 'high drama and pathos'; 'a movement portraying
the utmost grief and passion', in which Brahms's 'lesson' is 'the *production
of intensity of expression from the association of extremes*'.[51] Different
authors have emphasised the work's 'orchestral' qualities, some likening
the opening to a duet for oboe and harp, others clarinet and harp.[52]
MacDonald's description is one such example:

> The very opening, based on a wavering turn-figure, conjures up lonely
> clarinet and horn solos over harp arpeggios as profoundly plangent as those
> in the early 'An eine Äolsharfe' . . . Doubling in thirds (with the unmistakable

effect of flutes) only intensifies its bittersweet eloquence. A staccato, bitingly rhythmic music begins muttering in G♭ – an idea in Brahms's most irascible vein: it starts *sotto voce* and grows in decisiveness and vigour, with massive yet clipped chordal textures. But at the very moment of climax the 'dies irae' theme [from bars 1–4] is recalled, inextricably bound up with it, and this inspired work subsides into its former tragic monologue, dying out eventually in exquisite but bleak despair.[53]

Other authors have focused their attention on how the work's narrative course and underlying structure interrelate, one monitoring successive 'listening passes' to trace an evolving comprehension of the music, another attempting to devise 'continuity schemes' from the musical landscape as revealed through analysis.[54] In both cases, the work's profound 'mystery' is freely acknowledged – not surprisingly, for this is among Brahms's most inscrutable compositions. Like other late works (for instance, Op. 118 No. 1), it shuns a conventional tonal frame, only suggesting the tonic E♭ minor in the opening bars before a diminished seventh arpeggio in bars 3–4 *et seq.* diverts the harmonic setting to an implied B♭ minor, and it is not really until the cadential $^6_4$ in bar 71, after an extended developmental section reaching the work's climax, that the fate of E♭ minor as tonic is sealed once and for all.

Example 4.7 provides excerpts from the piece, showing first of all the opening articulation of the motive-cum-theme. As I have already suggested, this convoluted shape – obsessively intoning three pitches over and over again – controls the flow of compositional events to an extraordinary extent, exemplifying and as it were justifying Schoenberg's later celebration of Brahms's 'serial' technique. The four-bar pattern returns an octave lower in bars 5–8 with a similar but not identical accompaniment, and it is then developmentally worked in bars 8³–16, with overlapping fragments of varying lengths in canonic dialogue. Bars 17–20 (shown in the example) transpose the motivic melody to a definitive B♭ minor, the ensuing E♭ minor return of the opening at bar 21 sounding more like a subdominant than a tonic. After a varied repeat of bars 1–20, the music's character dramatically changes with new material that manages to escape the influence of the motivic theme for the first time in the piece. Here begins a more or less steady increase in activity and momentum, although the music initially stays close to the would-be tonic, B♭ minor, the emphatic cadential progression at bars 53ff. being deflected at the last minute to E♭ minor (see Example 4.7 and MacDonald's comments above). Ironically, it is the unexpected reappearance of the hitherto tonally destabilising main motive that achieves this deflection. The temperature rises even higher, transposed and enriched material from bars 49–52 energetically pushing towards a cadence

Example 4.7 Brahms, Intermezzo Op. 118 No. 6

(a) bars 1–5[1]

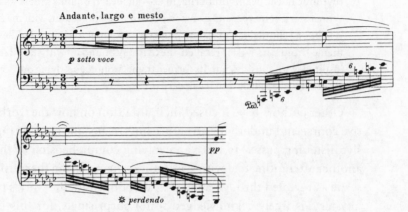

(b) bars 17–21[1]

(c) bars 53–5

(d) bars 59–62

(e) bars 81–6

promising finally to establish E♭ minor as tonic – but, at the height of the music's drama, this arrival is itself deflected, once again by the restatement in 59ff. of the motivic melody now reharmonised in an implied D♭ major (see Example 4.7), in one of the most impassioned and poignant passages in the composer's entire output. At this climactic moment we realise just how completely the shape eclipses all other structural considerations, its search for a stable identity still frustrated. Nevertheless, the music starts winding down with further developmental iterations of the motive, the successive Neapolitan settings (respectively suggesting B♭ minor and E♭ minor) in bars 66^3–70, beautifully evocative with their doublings in sixths and thirds, finally leading to the cadential $^6_4$ referred to above. Before this the music escapes from the insistent motivic shape for a few more bars (bars 41–52 and 55^2–9^1 are the only other passages in the piece making no explicit reference to it), until at last it enters in the context of E♭ minor, the passage shown in Example 4.7 concluding the work in a resigned state.[55]

To characterise Op. 118 No. 6 as a motive in search of a tonic would hardly do justice to the tremendous dramatic impulse generated by Brahms's incessant reharmonisations of the almost ubiquitous melodic shape. That this should be the case is both a testimony to Brahms's compositional genius[56] and an ironic rebuttal of some of the criticisms levelled at his early music, mentioned before in this chapter. Having initially noted the comparative stasis of certain 'monomotivic' compositions from the 1850s, putatively overburdened by their symphonic aspirations, we now encounter a particularly 'progressive' piece whose inner energies are activated and fully realised by an obsession with a single motive, the 'groundlessness' of which inspires a most unusual tonal plan. Moreover, Brahms's contrapuntal handling, especially deft when the doubled sixths and thirds enter over two successive Neapolitans, is magnificent, as is his ability to unite material at opposite ends of the expressive spectrum, alternately projecting bleak despair and (hollow?) triumph. Even more intriguing, however, is the way in which Brahms provides only the vaguest hints about what the work might 'mean', about the solution to the ineffable mystery that it poses. Although frustrating, the fact that its message will remain forever veiled and subject to speculation is of course part of the appeal of this and much of Brahms's other piano music, which thrives upon paradox and opposition almost to the point that its essential integrity is called into question.

5 Medium and meaning: new aspects of the chamber music

DAVID BRODBECK

In December 1890, in a letter to his publisher Fritz Simrock, the fifty-seven-year old Johannes Brahms announced his intention to retire from-composing: 'With this scrap bid farewell to notes of mine – because it really is time to stop'.[1] The 'scrap' in question was a part of the String Quintet in G major Op. 111, which the composer had completed during the previous summer. In February 1891, this new work appeared in print, together with a thorough revision made two years previously of the early Piano Trio in B major Op. 8, whose original version dated from 1854. The composer thus planned to make his valediction with two major chamber compositions which, like polished bookends, embraced the whole of his long and productive career.

Yet within only a few months of this letter Brahms was hard at work once more. In the summer of 1891, inspired by the skilful playing of Richard Mühlfeld, the principal clarinettist of the Meiningen Court Orchestra, he produced both the Trio in A minor for Piano, Clarinet and Violoncello Op. 114, and the Quintet in B minor for Clarinet and Strings Op. 115. Then, three years later, came still another pair of compositions featuring Mühlfeld's instrument – the two Sonatas for Piano and Clarinet, in F minor and Eb major, Op. 120. And it was only with these masterpieces of old age, finally, that Brahms concluded a lifetime's pre-occupation with chamber music.

Table 5.1 provides basic information concerning this legacy of twenty-five full-scale published works (including the two versions of Op. 8); entries will be found there for nearly every significant genre, with or without piano, from duo sonatas to string sextets. But full as it is, this inventory is by no means exhaustive of Brahms's activity in the field. Many other pieces, and not only youthful ones, were left unfinished or unpublished. In his famous essay 'Neue Bahnen' (October 1853) Schumann speaks already of 'sonatas for violin and piano, quartets for strings' (though only one of each can be accounted for); and we know of at least one piece from Brahms's high maturity, the first movement of a projected Piano Trio in Eb, conceived at the same time as the opening Allegro of the Piano Trio in C major Op. 87, that did not see the light of day. Some surviving works of his youth were never published in his life-

Table 5.1. *Works published in Brahms's lifetime*

Work	Date of composition	Original publication	vol. no. in JBSW[a]
Early period			
Piano Trio in B Op. 8	Jan. 1854	Leipzig Breitkopf & Härtel, 1854	IX:1
First maturity			
String Sextet in B♭ Op. 18	Summer 1860	Bonn: N. Simrock, 1862	VII: 1
Piano Quartet in G minor Op. 25	Autumn 1861	Bonn: N. Simrock, 1863	VIII: 2
Piano Quartet in A major Op. 26	Autumn 1861	Bonn: N. Simrock, 1863	VIII:3
Piano Quintet in F minor Op. 34	Aug. 1862 (String Quintet); rev. 1864	Leipzig and Winterthur: J. Rieter Biedermann, 1865	VIII: 1
String Sextet in G Op. 36	i, ii, and iii Sept. 1864; iv May 1865	Bonn: N. Simrock, 1866	VII:2
Sonata in E minor for Piano and Violoncello Op. 38	i, ii, and iii 1862; iv June 1865	Bonn: N. Simrock, 1866	X:5
Trio in E♭ for Piano, Violin, and *Waldhorn* (or Violoncello) Op. 40	May 1865	Bonn: N. Simrock, 1866	IX:5
High maturity			
String Quartet in C minor Op. 51 No. 1	Rewritten summer 1873 (begun in 1860s?)	Berlin: N. Simrock, 1873	VII:5
String Quartet in A minor Op. 51 No. 2	Rewritten Summer 1873 (begun in 1860s?)	Berlin: N. Simrock, 1873	VII: 6
Piano Quartet in C minor Op. 60	Winter 1873/74 (i and ii [in C♯ minor] 1855)	Berlin: N. Simrock, 1875	VIII: 4
String Quartet in B♭ Op. 67	Summer 1875	Berlin: N. Simrock, 1876	VII: 8
Sonata in G for Piano and Violin Op. 78	Summer 1878 and Summer 1879	Berlin: N. Simrock, 1879	X:1
Piano Trio in C Op. 87	June 1882 (i June 1880)	Berlin: N. Simrock, 1882	IX:3
String Quintet in F Op. 88	May 1882	Berlin: N. Simrock, 1882	VII:3
Late works			
Sonata in F for Piano and Violoncello Op. 99	Summer 1886 (ii in early l860s?)	Berlin: N. Simrock, 1887	X:6
Sonata in A for Piano and Violin Op.100	Summer 1886 (begun in 1883?)	Berlin: N. Simrock, 1887	X:2
Piano Trio in C minor Op. 101	Summer 1886	Berlin: N. Simrock, 1887	IX:4
Sonata in D minor Op. 108	Summer 1886	Berlin: N. Simrock, 1889	X:3
Piano Trio in B Op. 8 (revised version)	Summer 1889	Berlin: N. Simrock, 1891	IX:2
String Quintet in G Op. 111	Spring–Summer 1890	Berlin: N.Simrock, 1891	VII:4
Trio in A minor for Piano, Clarinet (or Viola), and Violoncello Op. 114	Summer 1891	Berlin: N. Simrock, 1892	IX:6
Quintet in B minor for Clarinet (or Viola) and Strings Op. 115	Summer 1891	Berlin: N. Simrock, 1892	VI:5
Sonata in F minor for Piano and Clarinet (or Viola) Op. 120 No. 1	Summer 1894	Berlin: N. Simrock, 1895	X:6
Sonata in E♭ for Piano and Clarinet (or Viola) Op. 120 No. 2	Summer 1894	Berlin: N. Simrock, 1895	X:7

[a] *Johannes Brahms Sämtliche Werke* (Complete Edition of Brahms's works, 1926–7)

Table 5.2. *Repudiated, 'occasional', and doubtful works*

Work	Date	Comments
Early period		
Sonata in A minor for Piano and Violin Anh. IIa Nr. 8	by 1853	Rejected for publication by Bartholf Senff
String Quartet in B minor Anh. IIa Nr. 5	by 1853	Considered for publication but rejected
Piano Trio in A Anh. IV Nr. 5	by 1853?	Doubtful; composed by Albert Dietrich?
Hymne zur Verherrlichung des grossen Joachim! Anh. III Nr. 1 (= Trio for two violins and contrabass or cello)	1853	Published Hamburg: H. Schuberth & Co., 1976
Scherzo in C minor to the F–A–E Sonata for Piano and Violin WoO posthum 2	1853	First movement composed by Albert Dietrich; second and fourth movements composed by Robert Schumann; entire collaborative work published Berlin, 1935. Brahms's scherzo published separately, Berlin: Deutsche Brahms-Gesellschaft, 1906.
Piano Quartet in C♯ minor	1855–6	See Table 5.1, under Op. 60.
Serenade in D for Flute, Clarinet, Horn, Bassoon, and Strings	1858	Later revised as Serenade in D for Large Orchestra Op. 11
First maturity		
String Quintet in F minor	1862	See Table 1 under Op.34.
High maturity		
Piano Trio in E♭ (first movement) Anh. IIa Nr. 7	1880	Conceived as companion to C major Trio Op. 87

time, though released after his death, most notably the Scherzo in C minor for violin and piano from the composite 'F–A–E' Sonata, written in collaboration for Joachim by Dietrich (first movement), Brahms and Schumann (Intermezzo and finale). Still other compositions, such as an early Piano Quartet in C♯ minor (1855–6) and a somewhat later String Quintet in F minor (1862), though they left Brahms unsatisfied in their original incarnations, eventually were preserved, at least in part, in compositions that did pass muster. Table 5.2 summarises the scanty documentary evidence pertaining to such works; unfortunately, we shall never learn the full extent of Brahms's activity, since, as is well known, he ruthlessly destroyed most traces of his compositional workshop.

This massive output reflects Brahms's creative development more fully than any other extended genre. For the most part, Brahms adhered to tradition in the overall disposition of these compositions. For example, every work save one begins with a complex sonata or sonata-like form in a moderately fast tempo; only the Horn Trio Op. 40, with its rondo-like opening Andante, stands apart in this respect. The majority of the finales likewise are in sonata form of one kind or another, usually in a somewhat broader tempo than that of the opening movements and in one instance (the Piano Quintet in F minor Op. 34) being preceded by a dramatic slow introduction. The most notable exceptions here are the Third String Quartet Op. 67, the Clarinet Quintet Op. 115 and the Second Clarinet Sonata, each of which concludes with a set of variations. In both the quartet and quintet, moreover, Brahms weaves into the fabric of the finale a recollection of the main theme from the first movement.

Most works contain the standard four movements. In thirteen of the four-movement cycles the slow movement precedes the faster 'dance' movement (or its substitute); in the other seven this arrangement is reversed. The slow movements of the Second String Sextet Op. 36, and Second Piano Trio Op. 87, are in variation form; elsewhere Brahms favours ABA form.[2] Although Brahms did not always use the heading 'Scherzo', a number of cycles include fiery movements of the type that is normally associated with that tradition. On the other hand, the String Quartet in A minor Op. 51 No. 2, includes a 'Quasi Menuetto'; and in two cases, the String Quartet Op. 51 No. 1 and the Third Piano Trio Op. 101, both in C minor, Brahms employs duple rather than triple metre in the livelier of the two inner movements. As for the five three-movement cycles, the First Cello Sonata Op. 38 – which, like the A minor String Quartet, includes a 'Quasi Menuetto' – contains no slow movement (although Brahms had originally written one); the First Violin Sonata Op. 78 eschews the normal 'dance' movement; the First String Quintet Op. 88 and Second Violin Sonata Op. 100 combine elements of both traditional inner-movement types in their central movement; and the Second Clarinet Sonata concludes, as noted, not with a traditional finale, but with a set of variations in moderately slow tempo.[3]

In the light of this impressive record it is little wonder that Brahms has generally been credited with upholding the chamber music tradition at a time when the interests of Wagner, Liszt and other 'progressive' composers lay in the radically different directions of music drama and symphonic poem. His achievement is all the more remarkable since he was by no means alone in his devotion to chamber music. Many leading musicians of the day, including such friends and members of Brahms's professional circle as Carl Reinecke, Bernhard Scholz, Otto Dessoff, Robert Fuchs and Heinrich von Herzogenberg, made important contributions to the repertory; among the works of Robert Volkmann, Karl Goldmark and even Hermann Grädener are several, now largely forgotten, that remained in the repertory until well into the twentieth century. Indeed, performances of new chamber works by composers such as these abounded during the second half of the nineteenth century, not only within the private homes of the educated middle classes (such as Brahms's viola-playing friend, the great surgeon Theodor Billroth), but – as a glance at any music periodical of the day will show – in increasingly numerous public concerts. In many cities such concerts were convivial social events, really, for which composers willingly supplied the kind of 'healthy' and unpretentious music that was expected on such occasions.

In contrast to many of his contemporaries, however, Brahms took up the most serious aspect of this tradition, stemming from the Viennese classics. He revivified this tradition through the sheer quality and innovation that characterised his works. One cannot overestimate the size of his achievement. This is all the more significant in that by around 1860, when he produced his first mature chamber works, and wrote the Manifesto against the New Germans, chamber music had, as Dahlhaus has put it, 'been shunted on to the sidelines of history, both in its influence and its quality'. He continues:

> In the history of musical performance, chamber music was in the main a private affair and its key works were largely esoteric. It was overshadowed by public music life: the opera, the virtuoso concert, and the 'grand concert' with mixed program, which gradually gave rise to the symphony concert. Nor did it any longer seem particularly relevant aesthetically, as a means of reflecting on the evolution of musical language and technique. The decisions that affected the history of composition were made in the music drama and the symphonic poem, genres dominated by the 'progressive party' of the 'New Germans'. Chamber music, in contrast, did not exist for Wagner, Liszt, or Berlioz. It was a nature reserve for conservatives too dazed by the new music to do anything but cling to the old.[4]

Through formal experimentation, innovations in harmony and, perhaps most strikingly, his treatment of theme and melody, Brahms proved to be a great progressive, to use Schoenberg's famous description. Echoing Schoenberg, Dahlhaus emphasises that Brahms's characteristic practice of constructing a theme on the principle of 'developing variation', to be found in his dense thematic connections and complex thematic processes, represents the critical evolutionary stage between the balanced 'architectonic' form of the later eighteenth century and the rigorous 'logical' form of Schoenberg's twelve-note music.[5] The chamber music is particularly rich in such features. Just how highly Brahms was regarded in this respect by his contemporaries is indicated by the number of works – no fewer than nineteen – dedicated to him by other chamber composers. Among the finest was the Piano Quartet in E Op. 6 by Hermann Goetz, who wrote thus to the composer on 6 June 1870:

> I have allowed myself to set your name over the enclosed quartet. That is only fair, since it was your piano quartets in A major and G minor that first set me thinking to write in this form. I simply cannot let the occasion pass without telling you how salutary and lifting the effect of your artistic works has been on me for many years.[6]

It is in the unusual context of 'conservative' outer forms containing 'progressive' content that we can begin to understand the bewildering range of reactions with which Brahms's chamber music was greeted from all sides of the critical spectrum. Eduard Hanslick's initial response to the two piano quartets Opp. 25 and 26, in his review of Brahms's first concerts before the Viennese public in November 1862, is well known: 'For one thing', wrote Hanslick with regard to Op. 26, 'the themes are insignificant. Brahms has a tendency to favour themes whose contrapuntal viability is far greater than their essential inner content. The themes of this quartet sound dry and prosaic. In the course of events they are given a wealth of imaginative derivatives, but the effectiveness of a whole is impossible without significant themes.' Even more strongly put is the following reproach from the pen of Ludwig Bischoff, the notoriously conservative founder of the *Niederrheinsiche Musikzeitung*:

> Even Robert Schumann is already outdone by the imitators of his mannerism ... The greater the talent with which this occurs – as, for example, with Johannes Brahms in his newest Piano Quartets – the more it is to be regretted ... The question of whether genius consists in stuffing each fist with notes and moreover allowing three bows to saw away without any respite or repose on a violin, viola, and cello, all in order to maintain an endless rhythmic confusion and ensnarl everything without distinct melodic motives in such a way that it is only with difficulty that one can recognize a key – this situation will be brought near to its decision by such 'achievements'; an opposing reaction cannot fail to ensue.[7]

In time, of course, Brahms won over many such 'conservative' critics, most of whom, at least in the Vienna of the 1880s and 90s, were drawn, ironically enough, from the city's liberal political and economic Establishment. These members of the educated German and German-Jewish middle and upper middle classes championed the ostensibly 'conservative' music of Brahms, valuing above all its rational and logical basis; quite naturally, the focus of musical life for this group fell on chamber music. The anti-liberal (and increasingly anti-Semitic) alliance, which eventually gained power in the year of Brahms's death, tended, by contrast, to take up the cause not only of the late Wagner but of Anton Bruckner, whose monumental symphonies, all but ignored previously, came to be valued for the powerful and direct emotional impact they could have upon the larger masses. It is a further source of irony, then, that Bruckner's single major essay in a chamber genre, the sprawling String Quintet in F, brought him one of his earliest triumphs in the Imperial City; meanwhile, in the anti-liberal newspapers Brahms's symphonies were dismissed as being mere 'chamber music,' a charge that had originated some years earlier in Wagner's essay 'On the Application of Music to Drama' (1879).[8]

Brahms's chamber music, then, presents the critic with a very rich field indeed, and the survey that follows must be selective. After the briefest mention of the early works from the mid 1850s (to which we shall return), we take up a representative sampling from the composer's 'first maturity', 'high maturity' and late style. Along the way we shall focus on such issues as formal innovation and thematic structure, inter-relations within and between Brahms's works and those of other composers, and questions of autobiographical resonance.

Scherzo in C minor ['FAE' Sonata]; String Quartets Op. 51; Piano Quintet Op. 34; String Sextet Op. 18; Piano Quartet Op. 26

As noted, Brahms's first published work, the Trio Op. 8, was to be very thoroughly revised in 1890, involving cutting and extensive recomposition. Only the scherzo survived more or less intact. Indeed, this movement had a precedent in the equally effective scherzo from the 'F–A–E' Sonata, which, with its rhythmic drive, anticipates certain of Brahms's later efforts in the key of C minor, including the scherzi of the Piano Quintet in F minor and Piano Quartet in C minor, and the opening Allegro of the First Symphony. This C minor scherzo thus stands as compelling testimony of the early age at which the composer acquired an assured sense both of his own style and of the tradition in which he aspired to take part.[9]

But if Brahms was initially satisfied with the Piano Trio it was to be different with the most intimidating of the chamber genres, the string quartet, with which he struggled long and hard – and this because he chose, as he did in the case of his first symphony, to meet Beethoven face to face, with an uncompromising example in the earlier master's 'C minor mood'. The first movement of Brahms's First Symphony was in hand by June 1862 but then laid aside. In contrast, the First String Quartet Op. 51 No. 1 (which, together with the Second in A minor Op. 51 No. 2, Brahms dated in his hand-written catalogue of compositions as having been 'written for the second time Summer 1873, Tutzing, begun earlier') seems to have been completed in some form or another by the middle of the 1860s. In December 1865, Joachim enquired, 'Is your String Quartet in C minor finished?' The following August, Clara noted in her diary that Brahms had played for her 'some magnificent movements from a German Requiem . . . then also a String Quartet in C minor'. Soon thereafter she gave word of these pieces to Joachim: 'Johannes has been here for 14 days and has made a magnificent German Requiem, which you will like. He has also completed a string quartet in C minor.' On 16 March 1869, Simrock implored the reluctant composer: 'I . . . can only repeat for the umpteenth time that I expect more soon: the [string] quartets and the symphony; come out with them finally – I'll give you no peace!'[10] Indeed, in his pocket calendar book for 1869 Brahms assigned the two quartets the opus number 51. In the event, however, the quartets were revised and did not appear until four years later; the symphony remained in limbo even longer, until 1876, by which time Brahms had composed his third (and what would prove to be his final) string quartet.[11]

Although Brahms struggled with the genres of symphony and string quartet after 1860 (the year of his public 'Manifesto' against the music of Liszt and the slanted editorial policy of the *Neue Zeitschrift für Musik* in promoting the New German School), he fared better with other, less historically freighted works. Indeed, the first half of the 1860s was an especially fertile time that saw the publication of one duo sonata (for piano and cello), one piano trio (with *Waldhorn* replacing cello), two piano quartets, a piano quintet and two string sextets. As James Webster has shown, the influence of Schubert's sonata forms was especially strong in these works. Indeed, nearly all the most distinctive features of Brahms's own sonata forms here can be traced back to the Viennese master: long lyrical themes in closed forms; transitions that either hesitate to leave the tonic until the last moment and then lurch suddenly into a remote key, or else imply one key only to establish another; and 'double second groups' and three-key expositions.[12]

Tovey pointed to the Piano Quintet in F minor as the 'climax of [this] first maturity', and to Schubert as Brahms's single greatest source of influence at this time (indeed, the striking D♭–C conclusion of the quintet's scherzo alludes plainly to the ending of Schubert's posthumous String Quintet in C, D. 956); and in a more general sense, as Tovey noted, one can easily imagine Schubert watching over Brahms's shoulder as he wrote 'the second subject of the first movement, the main theme of the slow movement, and the whole body of the finale'.[13] But Schubertian lyricism and interest in harmonic colour are joined at every turn in this work by Beethovenian dynamism and integration of motive and form. Two of Beethoven's own masterpieces in F minor, the *Appassionata* Sonata Op. 57, and the *Quartetto Serioso* Op. 95, loom especially large. The tonal plan of Brahms's first movement (i–♭vi–♭VI) resembles not so much a three-key model of Schubert's as a kind of conflation of the key plans of the *Appassionata* (i–♭III–♭iii) and the *Serioso* Quartet (i–♭VI); all three of these works, moreover, include significant Neapolitan relationships. The quintet and piano sonata both make much of the motive $\hat{5}$–♭$\hat{6}$–$\hat{5}$, and each begins its recapitulation over a $^6_4$ bass. In addition, the finales of Op. 34 and Beethoven's Op. 95 share a similar pattern of dramatic slow introduction, binary form with the development 'replaced by a considerable

Example 5.1 Brahms, Sextet Op. 18, movement 1
(a) bars 10–13
(b) bars 20–3
(c) bars 41–3
(d) 61–2

discussion between the recapitulation of the "first subject" and that of the second' and presto coda.[14] At the same time, however, the work stands out as a truly impressive example of Brahms's favourite technique of 'developing variation' (in both the motivic-thematic and metric-rhythmic dimensions), whereby a collection of only a few motives, continually reworked, is sufficient to sustain long stretches of music.[15]

The first movement of the String Sextet in B♭ Op. 18 (1860) offers a somewhat earlier example of this synthesis of lyrical and dramatic impulses and artful use of developing variation. The work begins with a large, song-like first-theme group (A A′ B C). Although parallels can be drawn with the first group of Schubert's posthumous Piano Sonata in B♭, D. 960, in Brahms's hands matters take on a dramatic urgency that is lacking in the earlier work. The opening A phrase concludes, in the manner of an antecedent, on the dominant (at bar 9). But the ensuing A′ phrase (beginning in bar 11) does not act as the expected consequent, with a full cadence in the tonic; instead, it comes round to a second close on V. Both the B and C phrases (bars 20ff. and 31ff.) expand the dominant, and closure in the tonic is thus withheld until the elided full cadence at bar 43, whereupon the transitional theme (based on A) is introduced.

Of particular interest in this open-ended process is Brahms's handling of the little stepwise motive introduced at bar 10 (Example 5.1a). The initial status of this motive is not clear. Is it the final bar of the opening A phrase? Does it stand alone? The answer is uncertain, but when the same motive returns at bar 20, there is no doubting that now it is acts as the first bar in the ensuing B phrase (Example 5.1b). By the time the end of the C phrase is reached, however, the motive has taken on the unmistakable role of concluding gesture (Example 5.1c); and yet when, in bar 61, the second group begins, in the distant key of A major, the same motive is now once again clearly an opening gesture (Example 5.1d).

In Brahms's treatment of this tiny detail we find another sign of the

Example 5.2 Brahms, Piano Trio Op. 101, movement 1
(a) bars 1–4
(b) bars 22–4
(c) bars 81–3
(d) bars 38–41

early age at which he found his distinctive compositional voice. Consider the first movement of the late Piano Trio in C minor Op. 101 (1886), a work that Heinrich von Herzogenberg rightly described as being 'ripe and wise in its incredible compactness'.[16] The piece begins with a dramatic opening gesture, rich in contrapuntal relations between the related outer voices (motives x and y); the counterstatement (bars 22ff.) and reprise (bars 81ff.), in turn, offer new permutations of the same pair of related motives (Example 5.2a–c). Especially notable in the reprise is the augmented form of motive y: with that Brahms underscores the genetic similarities existing between the dramatic opening and lyrical second groups (Example 5.2d).

This second theme begins with the same 'ambiguous' gesture that we had discovered in the earlier Sextet in B♭. In its first appearance in the trio, as also in its first appearance in the sextet, its status is equivocal (Example 5.3): although the stepwise ascent from $\hat{5}$ to $\hat{1}$ is characteristic of an anacrusis, as the theme unfolds we are more likely to hear bar 38 in retrospect as the first strong beat in a four-bar hyperbar. The theme progresses in this leisurely manner for four such hyperbars (bars 38–53), but when it elides into a varied counterstatement, we find that the new 'strong beat' is now what had been the first 'weak beat' of the hyperbar, and that the stepwise motive that had formed the old 'strong beat' has at last assumed its role as an anacrusis (cf. bars 38 and 53). And if all this is handled more subtly in the 1880s than had been the case in the string sextet from

Example 5.3 Brahms, Piano Trio Op. 101, movement 1, bars 36–58

twenty-five years earlier, the adroitness of the younger Brahms in handling such details is none the less astonishing.

For a broader examination of one of the works from Brahms's 'first maturity', let us turn to the third movement of the Piano Quartet in A, Op. 26 (1861). As Tovey noted, this 'scherzo and trio are a pair of binary movements developed far beyond the limits of mere melodic form, and constitute in their alternation a movement fully on the scale of the others', adding, with more than his usual impatience regarding such matters, that 'a hundred years earlier Bach had impudently plagiarised Brahms's main theme in the overture to his Fourth Partita in the *Clavierübung* [Part I BWV 828]; no doubt with Brahms's full pardon'.[17]

Tovey's scepticism notwithstanding, this movement invites a close examination of Brahms's characteristic practice of allusion-making. In addition to Bach – the head motif of Brahms's opening theme does indeed recall the beginning of the 9/8 section of Bach's Ouverture (bars 36ff.) – both Beethoven and a number of later composers are represented here. The opening theme draws directly from that in the first movement of Beethoven's late String Quartet in E♭ Op. 127 (bars 7ff.), with which it shares not only the same general melodic shape and flowing character in triple metre (both are marked *p dolce*), together with a comparable basic structure of 'statement–texturally varied counterstatement', but even an unusual attenuated opening harmonic progression – implied in the case of Brahms's unison melody – of (roughly) ii^6–I^6–ii–V–I^6. By the same token, Brahms's transitional theme (bars 25–33) recalls a very similar passage in staccato quavers from the scherzo of Schubert's Piano Trio in B♭ Op. 99 (bars 83ff.).

The most telling allusion, however, comes in the second group (bars 33ff.). As Clara Schumann remarked, after having read through the manuscript in the summer of 1861,

> The second subject reminds me very much of a passage in Robert's string quartet:

> not precisely melodically but in the layout and mood.[18]

Here Clara has quoted the lyrical second theme in the opening Allegro of her husband's String Quartet in A Op. 41 No. 3 (bars 46ff.), and we can easily imagine that it was Brahms's use, in a similar theme, of paired descending fifths set in a comparably expressive dotted rhythm (♩. ♪ ♩) that sparked Clara's response. When, a few months later, Joachim was sent the score, he too noted a parallel between the same two themes, and, drawing from his own practical experience as a performer of Schumann's quartet, he warned Brahms that his off-the-beat accompaniment would prove difficult to bring off.[19]

These are only the most obvious threads, however, in a remarkable allusive web. As Brahms would have noticed, in his own quartet Schumann himself seems to have borrowed from Beethoven's Op. 127, beginning, in like fashion, with a brief slow introduction that ends tenu-

ously before yielding to a main theme which sets out from the same super-
tonic harmony in first inversion – although we might find an even closer
model for Schumann's first theme, with its falling fifth on $\hat{6}$ and $\hat{2}$ supported by full ii$^6_5$ harmony, in Beethoven's Piano Sonata in E♭ Op. 31 No.
3. Brahms, in turn, incorporates into his own first theme the same falling
fifth $\hat{6}$–$\hat{2}$, together with its complement $\hat{5}$–$\hat{1}$ (which, though only implied
in Schumann's first theme, is patent in his second).[20]

But the most striking point of comparison between Beethoven's Op.
31 No. 3 and Schumann's Op. 41 No. 3, on the one hand, and Brahms's
scherzo, on the other, concerns the handling of large-scale form.
Significantly, at the presumed beginning of the development, following a
full repetition of the exposition, both Beethoven and Schumann most
unusually offer a *third* tonic statement of the first theme. Of particular
interest here is Schumann's handling of this situation: his development
really gets under way only six bars after the double bar, when the first
theme's original perfect fifth on $\hat{6}$ and $\hat{2}$ (F♯–B) gives way to the new
diminished fifth F♮–B (bars 107ff.), now forming a part of a dominant
ninth chord on G. And the development soon comes to a conclusion
when, after a regaining of the original perfect fifth at bar 144, the music
slows and comes to half cadence in the tonic, out of which, following a
general pause, the reprise of the second theme emerges (bars 154ff.).

In a memorable, if unfair, judgement, the late Hans Keller described
the appearance of Schumann's main theme for the third time in the tonic
following the double bar as 'the most blatant tautology in the history of
great music.'[21] However that may be, Brahms avoids any such tautology,
and does so in a way that suggests his awareness of – and lack of congeni-
ality with – Schumann's practice. Already as his exposition draws to its
close Brahms teases with two hints of the first theme's head motif
(E–F♯–B), with the repeated pattern D♯–E–B followed by another on
E–F♮–B. But, in the event, the original head motif is not restored, and it is
the latter pattern, with its falling tritone, that carries over into the first bar
of the development, where it is harmonised at once as part of a dominant
chord on G that is similar to the one which Schumann had held in reserve
until after the 'redundant' repetition of the main theme.

By the same token, the end of Brahms's development shows its own
characteristic differences from the model found in Op. 41 No. 3. In bar
117 the violins reintroduce the altered head motif (E–F♮–B), and then two
bars later – and this amounts to a complete contrast to the palpable seam
occurring at the analogous location in Schumann's score – the development is subtly elided to the beginning of the recapitulation. At bar 119 a
return of the original head motif leads to a complete statement of the first
theme, but over a dominant pedal in the manner of a retransition; then,

continuing the process of variation within the recapitulation proper, the ensuing passage combines elements from both the first theme and its texturally varied counterstatement as found in the exposition (cf. bars 127ff. with bars 1ff. and 9ff.).

Piano Trio Op. 87

This relaxed and expansive Piano Quartet in A major was conceived simultaneously with the rather more turbulent and intense Piano Quartet in G minor, and the two works appeared together in print in 1863. Brahms was in the habit of publishing such pairs of contrasting realisations of a genre: joining the piano quartets in this category among the chamber works are the C minor and A minor string quartets (1873), and the two clarinet sonatas (1895). As we have seen, the composer seems to have undertaken a similar pairing in 1880, when he composed the first movements of piano trios in E♭ and C. It is tempting to speculate that the example of Schubert's masterly piano trios in B♭ (Op. 99) and E♭ (Op. 100) – works that Schumann had contrasted as representations of the 'feminine' and 'masculine' respectively – might have lain in the background of this project. Alas, we shall never be able to judge the character of Brahms's own Trio in E♭; he seems never to have finished the work and evidently destroyed the score of the one completed movement. Yet the opening Allegro of the C major Trio Op. 87, which survived Brahms's self-criticism and was joined in 1882 by the remaining three movements, is clearly weighted toward the 'masculine' side; indeed, its loud and sharply etched unison beginning recalls the very similar design of the opening of Schubert's Op. 100.[22]

In the matter of form, however, Brahms did not follow the model of Schubert's trio, although it includes all the typical Schubertian features to which he had responded so productively during his 'first maturity'. Instead, the opening movement of Op. 87, which may be taken as typifying the style of Brahms's 'high maturity', offers for study an especially rich example that combines elements of two very characteristic Brahmsian formal types – sonata form in which both the development and recapitulation begin with the main theme in the tonic (as in the first movements of the Violin Sonata in G and the Clarinet Sonata in E♭), and what John Daverio has recently termed 'amplified binary form', consisting of a more or less conventional (albeit unrepeated) sonata-form exposition that is followed, first, by a restatement in the tonic of a part of the main theme (as in a sonata rondo), then by development and/or episodic treatment of material from the remainder of the first group and transi-

Table 5.3. *Brahms, Piano Trio in C major, Op. 87, first movement*

	Part 1			Part 2	
Bar	Description	Key	Bar	Description	Key
	First group			*First group/ Development*	
1	1a	C	129	1a (= bars 1–4 + new accompaniment [x] and new version of head motif [y])	C
13	1b		132	on end of 1a′	
			141	on 2c	g
			165	waltz-like transformation of 1a	D♭–c♯
21	1c	on V	189	on 1c: sequential + y (from bar 129); becomes 'retransition'	on V/a to V/C
33	1a′	C	209	1a′ + x (from bar 129)	C
			213	1b, then development based on y (from bar 129)	
37	Transition (on end of 1a′, then new idea)	to g: iv^6–V^7	223	Recomposed transition (on end of 1a′, then new idea)	to c: iv^6–V^7
	Second group			*Second group*	
57	2a	G (ends on ii^6)	235	2a	C (ends on ii^6)
80	2b	ii^6–V^7/G	258	2b	ii^6–V^7
90	2c	to V^7/G	268	2c	to V^7
	Closing group			*Closing group*	
102	3a	G, with flat-side emphasis	280	3a	C, with flat-side emphasis
115	3b	G–V/C	293	3b	C–V^9
				Coda	
			309	waltz-like transformation of 1a	c–A♭/g♯–f♯–A
			363	1a	C

tion, and finally by a recapitulation in the tonic of the secondary and closing groups and either an extended coda on the material of the opening or a more exact restatement of that material in the tonic.[23]

The exposition of the trio's opening Allegro comprises three contrasting thematic groups (see the left-hand 'Description' column in Table 5.3). The first four bars present an angular, triadic motif that becomes the work's most significant and often heard idea (Example 5.4a). This beginning (1a) is followed, in turn, by two additional ideas, both marked by canonic treatment. The first (1b), starting in bar 13, derives from the original motif but sets its triadic notes as $\hat{3}$–$\hat{5}$–$\hat{1}$ rather than $\hat{1}$–$\hat{3}$–$\hat{6}$, as before (Example 5.4b); the second (1c), beginning on the dominant in bar 21, builds great tension through its chromatic lines and leads to a remarkable counterstatement of the opening at bar 33 that superimposes three separate versions of the head motif (1a′). A new developmental continuation of

Example 5.4 Brahms, Piano Trio Op. 87, movement 1
(a) bars 1–5
(b) bars 13–14
(c) bars 164–71
(d) bars 313–33

this passage (serving as the transition) ends in a half close in G minor at bar 53.

Although the second theme (2a) emerges at bar 57 in the orthodox dominant, the evident conviction with which it begins is soon called into question: the counterstatement (2a′), starting hesitantly at bar 65 (where it makes an enharmonic play on the A♯ appoggiatura from the original statement), lingers for a moment on a G minor chord, and not until the following bar is the major key restored and the theme allowed to take its course once more. But closure in the second key is again withheld, and the counterstatement dies down instead in an inscrutable ending with an ascending fourth (E–A) suspended over a quiet ii⁶ chord (A minor). Emerging now in the piano out of this same interval and harmony, and set in counterpoint against a descending stepwise idea in the strings (2b), is a strange 'digressive' allusion to the passage from Beethoven's Op. 127 String Quartet on which Brahms had previously drawn in the scherzo of Op. 26. Yet soon enough it is all gone: at bar 90 the allusion to Beethoven is drowned out, as it were, when piano and strings join forces in a louder version of the stepwise idea alone (2c), now duly emphasising A minor, and leading, at last, to a full and secure close in the dominant at bar 102. [24]

If the *grazioso* character of the ensuing closing theme (3a) is new, the material itself abounds in references to earlier ideas: its sequential ascending sixths (bars 102ff.) recall the rising sixth of the first theme, and in its flat-side bias (now involving E♭) it brings to mind the major–minor play of the second theme. Yet another full cadence in the dominant ushers in the retransition (3b), beginning softly with material derived from the second theme and gradually building to a dramatic return of the main theme and tonic key at bar 129.

What follows at this point is a complex succession of paragraphs that incorporates elements of both development and recapitulation (see the right-hand 'Description' column in Table 5.3). Bars 129–32 epitomise this conflation of formal processes: we recognise at once both the return here of material that recalls that of the opening bars and the introduction of two important new ideas: the accompanying chords in the piano and the more animated version of the head motif in the cello (a double diminution of lb). The development soon continues with a vigorous treatment of the stepwise motive 2c, the only such treatment of any material outside the first group (bars 141–64). This leads, in turn, to a broad lyrical passage in which the once angular main theme is transformed into something like a lilting waltz, played first by the cello in D♭ major, then by the violin in C♯ minor (bars 165ff.). [25] In this way Brahms realises the implication that had been denied in the second group of a repetition in the parallel mode of a theme that is heard originally in the major. At the same time, he makes obvious what had only been suggested at a much earlier moment in the piece, namely, that the notes of la might be heard not as $\hat{1}$–$\hat{3}$–$\hat{6}$–$\hat{4}$–$\hat{2}$–$\hat{7}$–$\hat{5}$, but as $\hat{3}$–$\hat{5}$–$\hat{1}$–$\hat{6}$–$\hat{4}$–$\hat{2}$–$\hat{7}$ (Example 5.4c). And with that, the roots of the unusual emphasis on A minor in the second group are shown to lie in the very first bar of the piece.

Coinciding with the firm arrival on the dominant of A minor at bar 189 is the return of lc, which is soon joined ever more insistently by the animated version of the head motif that had been introduced sixty bars earlier; together these two figures build in tension and serve, in effect, as a powerful retransition. But to what? With its forceful presentation of the head motif, the passage at bar 209 sounds like the beginning of the recapitulation, and that impression is only strengthened, to be sure, by the subsequent return of lb at bar 213. Yet the structural parallel here is not to the original version of the main theme (1a'), but to the counter-statement (1a), to which are now added accompanying chords that are similar to those introduced at the earlier return of the main theme in bar 129 (the real counterpart to 1a). Moreover, 1b soon yields to a passage that reintroduces the animated version of the head motif, leading by way of another harmonic digression to material that is related to the earlier transition. And it is only at this point, really, that the two halves of the form come into true alignment: the second and third thematic groups from the exposition now recur without essential change in the tonic key.

With the coda (bars 309ff.) comes a renewed focus on the waltz-like transformation of the main theme that had been introduced in the development. Now, however, instead of paired statements in parallel keys (D♭ major and C♯ minor), with the head motif treated in both instances as 3̂–5̂–1̂–6̂, we find a 'regular' statement in C minor elided to another that is far more complex (Example 5.4d). Creating a final redefinition of material – a unification, really – this repetition begins in A♭ major/G♯ minor, with the first two notes of the head motif treated as 1̂ and 3̂ (as in la); as the melody continues, however, its next two notes sound as 1̂ and 6̂ in E major (as in the waltz-like transformation). After this the melody seems finally to settle into the remote key of F♯ major, only to move deceptively at the last moment towards an implied cadence in A major. Yet that key, too, is skirted by means of a deceptive cadence to F (♭VI of A), and at bar 337 the head motif reappears in a stretto involving both the familiar animated guise (violin) and still another distinctive version (cello), leading to a boisterous climax based on the ending of the head motif. A final statement of the complete opening idea, now sounding for the first time through several octaves in all three parts – as in Schubert's E♭ Trio – brings the movement to a vigorous close.

String Sextet Op. 36; Violin Sonata Op. 78; Piano Quartet Op. 60; Piano Trio Op. 8 (revised version)

Brahms's extra-compositional allusions in the Piano Quartet in A and Piano Trio in C are to some degree autobiographical: they tell us much about the composer's own keen sense of music history and his awareness of his place within it. In other works, the autobiographical dimension is of a far different kind. Here Brahms evidently intended to speak not to posterity but to a more intimate audience – consisting in some cases, perhaps, of only himself – that might be expected to recognise and make sense of his use of 'ciphers' and personally 'telling' melodic allusions.[26] It is only from Brahms's passionately charged letter to Clara of 7 February 1855, for example, that we can know that the theme of the slow movement of the String Sextet No. 2 in G (1864) had originated nearly a decade earlier as an expression in music of a longing for Frau Schumann that the younger Brahms evidently dared not to express in words.[27] With its initial ascent through two perfect fourths, this melody later served as the point of departure for the main theme of the splendid opening movement, whose paired ascending fifths set into motion one of Brahms's finest essays in the

Example 5.5 Brahms, String Sextet Op. 36, movement 1
(a) bars 162–8
(b) bars 525–7

Schubertian style of his 'first maturity'. Nor is the exuberant finale (composed later than the rest, in 1865) untouched by this 'Clara theme', whose paired ascending fourths figure into both of its primary thematic elements.

By the same token, were it not for Joachim's letter to Brahms of 27 September 1894, we would be hard pressed to discover that the first movement of the same work contains a pointed reference to Agathe von Siebold, to whom in the late 1850s Brahms was briefly engaged to be married. As Joachim informs us, the ecstatic theme that comes at the climax of the second ('feminine') group contains a musical cipher of the young woman's name (Example 5.5a).[28] This piece of evidence, in turn, provides a suggestive context for Brahms's earlier use of the same motif in the tenth of the Twelve Songs and Romances for Women's Chorus Op. 44 (c. 1860), which dates from about the time when Brahms called off the engagement and in whose text the poet sings of a young girl who has died from a broken heart. In a provocative reading, Dillon Parmer has argued that Brahms's use of the 'Agathe cipher' in the secondary group in Op. 36 might be emblematic of a sexual relationship that, for whatever reason, Brahms was unable to consummate in reality.[29] To be sure, the extraordinarily high register of the setting, the 2–3 dissonance that sounds in the upper voices, and the full texture and loud dynamic marking of the whole imparts to the passage a certain sexual *frisson*. But we must not leave unaddressed Brahms's subsequent handling of the cipher. In Schubertian fashion, he derives the material for the closing paragraph from the secondary theme. The closing tune, played by the first violin, is clearly related to the Agathe cipher and is set in counterpoint against a transposed version of the cipher itself, which is played six times, in turn, by various supporting instruments (beginning in the pickup to bar 191). Moreover, and this seems especially significant, Brahms has designed the tonal patterns of this sonata form in such a way that in the recapitulation the literal spelling of Agathe's name is withheld until this very closing group, where, now marked *dolce*, it sounds six times once more in the counterpoint (Example 5.5b).

Still another example of this kind of autobiographical expression may be seen in the finale of the Violin Sonata in G, Op. 78 (1878–9), a rondo in G minor whose main theme alludes to Brahms's settings of Klaus Groth's 'Regenlied' and 'Nachklang' Op. 59 Nos. 3 and 4 (1873). The composer put his friend Billroth on the trail when he wrote, in his wry manner, that the finale 'is not worth playing through more than once' and 'requires a nice, soft, rainy evening to give the proper mood'; and the allusion did not remain unnoticed for long.[30] Only recently, however, has a serious attempt been made to understand how the literary context that Brahms thus created for his work helps to clarify the expressive trajectory of the music – how, in that sense, the work is 'programmatic'. As Parmer has shown, the pessimistic narrative that is unfolded in the pairing of Groth's poems – of a nostalgic but futile attempt to recapture the innocence of youth – provides a suggestive metaphor by which to understand the succession of events in Brahms's sonata, from its overall tonal plan (G major to G minor) and its incorporation of a funeral march (in E♭ minor) as the B section of the Adagio to the palpable thematic relationships that exist between the main themes of the first and last movements and the two disruptive appearances in the finale of the main theme of the Adagio (bars 84ff. and bars 142ff.).[31]

The reappearance in the finale of the Adagio's main theme bears closer examination in the present context. One precedent for such a recollection, known only to the closest members of the Schumann circle, may be found in Robert Schumann's late Violin Concerto (1853), a work which Clara, Joachim and Brahms jointly decreed was to remain unpublished (and did so remain until 1937). But Schumann recalled the beautiful theme of the slow movement not only in his finale but again later, as Brahms knew, in his so-called 'last musical idea,' which was set down on 7 February 1854, following a hallucination in which Beethoven and Schubert had appeared before the unfortunate composer to 'dictate' it to him. In this later form particularly, Schumann's theme anticipates a number of features of Brahms's own Adagio theme, including key, register, texture in parallel sixths, and general mood (Example 5.6). These similarities, in turn, provide a suggestive means for interpreting a recently recovered letter of February 1879 from Brahms to Clara, written during the fatal illness of her youngest son Felix and preserved on the back of a leaf containing an early version of Brahms's melody (inscribed here *Adagio espressivo*): 'If you play what is on the reverse side quite slowly, it will tell you, perhaps more clearly than I otherwise could myself,

Example 5.6
(a) Schumann, 'Last musical idea'
(b) Brahms, Violin Sonata in G Op. 78, movement 2

how sincerely I think of you and Felix – even about his violin, which however surely is at rest.'[32]

With this sonata we return, finally, to the most significant subject of Brahms's autobiographical musings – his complex, lifelong involvement with Clara Schumann. Two examples loom especially large, and both are deserving of close attention, not least because each originally dates from the composer's early period and was then extensively revised at a later date. Striking, too, is Brahms's use of thematic allusion to establish the sense of tragic irony that lies at the core of each work's mode of expression.

We can begin with the Piano Quartet in C minor, Op. 60 (published in 1875). A number of mysteries surround the genesis of this *Sorgenkind*. In his hand-written catalogue of his works, Brahms wrote 'Movements 1.2 / Movements 3.4 / 1 and 2 earlier; 3, 4 Vienna [18]73–74'. Coupling this information with evidence gleaned from a number of letters, James Webster has made a convincing case that the quartet was originally conceived during the mid 1850s in three movements only, with outer movements in C♯ minor (a gloomy essay in a most unusual sonata form and a 'concise finale' filled with 'terse' passion) surrounding a 'wunderschönes Adagio', as Clara Schumann described it, in E major. [33] Perhaps it was in something like this form that Brahms finally thought to publish the work some fifteen years later, when, in his calendar book for 1869, he assigned the composition a tentative opus number of 54. In any case, the quartet remained far from being ready, and by the early 1870s, when the last two movements were composed, the tonality of the original outer movements had been changed to C minor, the 'beautiful Adagio' destroyed and a new slow movement in the same key composed, and the original 'concise finale' (as Webster neatly speculates) revived as the trio-less scherzo that now stands as the pithy second movement. Writing to Albert Dietrich after first hearing this final version, Clara noted: 'He had already written the first two movements earlier (I don't particularly like the first one – but what a Scherzo!), and now the last two are also entirely works of genius: an intensification right up to the end that fairly takes your breath away. It is strange how the mood remains unified, despite the quite different dates of the various movements.'[34]

Of the three original movements, the first to be conceived was the opening Allegro, which Brahms shared with his beloved Clara in the spring of 1855, as his adoring passion for her was reaching its heights. Clara's impressions during that heated time were rather different from what they were to become twenty years later. In March of that year, for example, she reported to Joachim that Brahms had sent her 'a magnificent first movement of a piano quartet'. There can be no mistaking the identity of this work: Dietrich later informed Kalbeck that he had 'a clear recollection from the y[ear] 1855 of the beginnings of a very sombre piano quartet and of a very melodic and expressive second theme, which my friend Dr H[ermann] Deiters also recognised again later in the Third Piano Quartet (C minor)'. [35] Then late in the following year, after Brahms had read through the now completed work with Joachim in Hamburg, she brought up the work once more in her correspondence with the violinist: 'I'm very much looking forward to Johannes's quartet – perhaps if he's there at the moment he'll play it, otherwise I will, with a thousand joys. But do you remember when you wanted to have nothing at all to do with the quartet? where Joh[annes] and I were completely miserable. You found an unforgiving misanthropic mood in the first movement, where I had always found a beautiful, deep seriousness. Why, what a moody man you are!'[36]

On several occasions in the 1860s and 1870s – in some of his frankest remarks about the poetic content of his own work – Brahms pointedly likened this music to the tale of Goethe's *Werther* (whose protagonist commits suicide out of his guilt for having loved the wife of an older, respected friend).[37] And when we recognise that Brahms began his quartet with an allusion to the beginning of Schumann's Symphony No. 4 in D minor, with similar sustained octaves yielding to Schumann's familiar musical transliteration of Clara's name, we may assume that he knew that Schumann had originally intended the Fourth as a kind of 'Clara Symphony' (Example 5.7).[38] But whereas Schumann's symphony ends triumphantly in the major mode, Brahms's quartet ends in a very different mood altogether.

Significantly, the long opening theme of Brahms's finale, with its lyrical melody in the violin and running quaver accompaniment in the piano, anticipates the minor-key finale of the Violin Sonata in G – which itself, as have seen, draws on Brahms's songs 'Regenlied' and Nachklang'. Basil Smallman has suggested that it was 'the apt relationship of the "rain-drops"/"tears" symbolism of the songs to the tragic character of the

Example 5.7

(a) Schumann, Symphony in D minor, movement 1, bars 1–2

(b) Brahms, Piano Quartet in C minor, movement 1, bars 1–6

quartet [that] prompted the first borrowing; and that the effectiveness of its violin and piano presentation in the quartet suggested, later, a more literal appropriation of the material for the sonata'.[39] At all events, there can be little question that the finale, with its 'intensification right up to the end', is a tragic work through and through. It is ironic, then, that Brahms should allude, at the very outset of the movement, to the first movement of Beethoven's Fifth Symphony – the piano introduces the famous Fate motif in the accompaniment (♪ ♫ ♩), while the violin presents the first two pitches of Beethoven's notable motto (G–E♭) – ironic because, unlike Beethoven's Fifth (and Schumann's Fourth, for that matter), Brahms's quartet is destined to end in the same tragic mood in which it began (Example 5.8a).

But it is in the first movement of another work in the same key, Mendelssohn's late Piano Trio in C minor Op. 66 (1846), that we find the most suggestive connections. Most striking is the clear similarity between Brahms's initial piano accompaniment and the main theme of Mendelssohn's opening Allegro (Example 5.8b). According to the singer George Henschel, Brahms himself acknowledged the similarity, which was among the most often remarked during the composer's lifetime, but added that what with the earlier composer was the principal subject was with him 'simply an accompanimental figure'.[40] Hardly so: this figure quickly assumes the greatest importance within the movement. Not only is it adumbrated in the second theme (bars 55ff.), but the development

Example 5.8

(a) Brahms, Piano Quartet in C minor Op. 60, movement 4, bars 1–4

(b) Mendelssohn, Piano Trio in C minor Op. 66, movement 1, bars 1–4

offers it up continually in inversion, augmentation and double augmentation.

Although this kind of contrapuntal tightrope walking is typical of Brahms's style, its appearance here clinches the allusion to Mendelssohn's trio, in whose coda we find displayed something of the earlier composer's own contrapuntal prowess, with the theme played by the piano in its original guise combined with an augmented version of the same idea played by the strings (bars 353ff.). Brahms goes much further in all this, however. In the development he introduces his 'accompanimental figure' in the piano against a doubly augmented version of the same idea in the strings (bars 173ff.); and shortly thereafter, when the violin introduces the main theme in a 'false recapitulation' in B minor, the piano, continuing in its steady quaver rhythm, offers a doubly diminished form of that idea (bars 189ff.).

But where Brahms most significantly parts company with Mendelssohn – though now the point of comparison is with the last movement of Mendelssohn's trio – is in the coda. As Michael Musgrave has observed, Brahms's cadential group (bars 75ff.), marked by an unusual alternation of a chorale-like theme in the strings and scalar material in the piano, recalls the second couplet in the rondo finale of Mendelssohn's Op. 66, in which five short chorale-like phrases in the piano are interspersed by fragments of the movement's opening theme in the strings.[41] Here, too, the allusion ultimately serves the purposes of irony. In Mendelssohn's piece the chorale recurs just before the coda in a majestic guise, with quasi-orchestral scoring (bars 268ff.); it is in this triumphant mood that the once turbulent work is concluded. In Brahms's hands, all this is turned upside down. To be sure, the chorale itself eventually recurs triumphantly, played *forte* with full chords in the piano; yet suddenly everything is lost: the main theme recurs, and the work concludes in complete despair.

In its own way, the Piano Trio in B Op. 8 embraces an even longer period of compositional process. Brahms published the work in 1854, soon after he had written it; and in this form the trio eventually became one of his most widely performed works.[42] When, more than thirty years later, Simrock acquired the rights to this and several other early works that had originally been published by Breitkopf & Härtel, the composer was given the opportunity to make revisions. Brahms did so in the summer of 1889, and though he reported that he 'did not provide [the now ageing trio] with a wig, but just combed and arranged its hair a little', in effect he rewrote the whole.[43] To be sure, the first themes (and thus the essential identity) of each of the four movements were retained; elsewhere, however, with the exception of the scherzo (which remained relatively untouched), Brahms made extensive cuts, replacing such 'youthful excesses' as the massive secondary group of the first movement (with its lengthy process of 'Lisztian' thematic transformation) with 'tighter', more 'disciplined' paragraphs that reflect the sensibilities of the mature composer.[44]

Like the 'Regenlied' Sonata, with which it shares the unusual progression from a major-key first movement to a minor-key finale, the trio is essentially a tragic work; and like the Op. 60 Piano Quartet, its numerous allusions stamp the music, as Eric Sams has suggested, with 'an unmistakable undertone of autobiographical fantasy'.[45] Among the most telling sources of these allusions is Schumann's opera *Genoveva*. Brahms, after all, could hardly have overlooked the parallels between the story of this opera and his own predicament in the weeks following Schumann's suicide attempt on 27 February 1854 and subsequent removal to the asylum in Endenich: Golo, whose duty it is to watch protectively over Genoveva in the battle-time absence of her husband, Siegfried, instead

Example 5.9
(a) Schumann, 'Meines Weibes nimm dich an' (*Genoveva*)
(b) Brahms, Piano Trio in B Op. 8, movement 2, bars 1–4
(c) Brahms, Piano Trio in B Op. 8, movement 2, bars 113–24

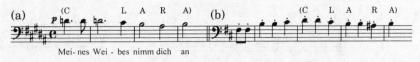

falls hopelessly in love with her. Of particular interest is Schumann's setting of Siegfried's departing charge to Golo to 'take care of my wife' ('Meines Weibes nimm dich an'). This B minor version of Schumann's 'Clara cipher' later served Brahms as the basic thematic idea in the scherzo of his piano trio (Example 5.9).[46]

Suggestive, too, are the evident allusions in the original version of the trio's third and fourth movements to, respectively, Schubert's setting of Heine's 'Am Meer' (in the B section, bars 33ff.) and the last number in Beethoven's song cycle *An die ferne Geliebte* (as the secondary theme, bars 105ff.), both of which were eliminated in the revised version of 1889. Brahms's allusion to *An die ferne Geliebte* was observed in print already in 1884, only four years after the first published notice of Schumann's own version of the same theme in the finale of his Second Symphony. With that in mind, Kenneth Hull has suggested that Brahms removed the reference to Beethoven's song in order to forestall any public speculation that the 'Geliebte' in both instances might have been Clara.[47]

There can be little doubt, to be sure, that the allusions would have been motivated by autobiographical considerations. As Sams has noted, 'Am Meer' is set in Brahms's home town of Hamburg and concerns bitter tears, tragic parting and hopeless love.[48] Moreover, as Brahms knew, Schumann himself had often quoted *An die ferne Geliebte* as a means of alluding to Clara. Yet Brahms authorised Simrock to continue selling the original version of the work, and in the revision he did not so much eliminate the allusion as artfully disguise it in a way that was better in keeping not only with the models that he had found in Schumann but with the painful circumstances of his own experience.[49]

To appreciate all this, we must first consider Schumann's earliest allusion to Beethoven's song, appearing in the first movement of the *Fantasie* Op. 17 (1836). Written at a time when the young Clara Wieck was being

Example 5.10
(a) Beethoven, 'Nimm sie hin denn, diese Lieder' (*An die ferne Geliebte* No. 6, bars 9–10)
(b) Schumann, *Fantasie* in C, movement 1, 'Adagio' (15 bars before end of movement)
(c) Brahms, Piano Trio in B Op. 8 (first version, 1854), movement 4, bars 105–10.

kept apart from Schumann by her father and was thus a 'distant beloved' in a most literal sense, this music, as the late Peter Ostwald put it, 'conveys Schumann's passion for the woman he could not possess'.[50] Although Beethoven's theme is hinted at time and again, it emerges fully only at the very end, where, coinciding with the first appearance in the work of the tonic chord in root position, it is understood to have been the goal of the entire piece (Example 5.10a–b).[51] Brahms's allusion to *An die ferne Geliebte* in the original version of his finale, by contrast, shows no comparable subtlety in either musical or metaphorical application; it is indeed among the most patent of allusions to be found in his *œuvre* – and one that can cause listeners who know only the later version to cringe in discomfort (Example 5.10c).

At first hearing, the revised version would seem to bear no trace of Beethoven's melody (Example 5.11). The new secondary theme (bars 64–87), a large binary form in the relative major with written-out repetitions, relates instead to the second theme of the Scherzo of the A major Piano Quartet and thus to the second theme in the first movement of Schumann's String Quartet in A Op. 41 No. 3: once more we meet the same combination of a long, lyrical tune with a prominent descending fifth set over an off-beat accompaniment. Of greater interest, however, is the little stepwise cadential motive that had originally introduced the new theme in bars 63–4 and then, in a rhythmically diminished form that is first heard in bars 67–8 (henceforth motive x), gradually assumes considerable importance as a kind of countermotif to the main melody.

This idea, when it returns in the piano in bar 91, following a strange stepwise passage in contrary motion, seems to herald a firm close in the tonic; yet when it is taken up by the strings a few bars later, it leads instead to a counterstatement of the preceding stepwise passage. Motive x reappears in due course at bar 101. But set now over a dissonant V^9/IV chord, it no longer carries its promise of closure, and this time it offers a

Example 5.11 Brahms, Piano Trio in B Op. 8, movement 4, bars 61–112

Example 5.11 (*cont.*)

significant new motivic shape, ending not with stepwise motion downward but by leap from the dissonant E♭ to B. And with that the stage is set
for the cello, in the tenor range, to unfold the final step in a critical motivic
process and, in so doing, to offer a fleeting reference to the *An die ferne
Geliebte* melody (bars 102–3). The allusion is brutally cut off, however, as
the cello leaps downward to a low D, over which the entire process is
repeated in a kind of augmented form before the music eventually comes
to an uneasy close on the tonic in bar 107.

In the revised version, then, we find what had been missing in the orig-

Example 5.12 Brahms, Piano Trio in B Op. 8, movement 4, bars 235–52

inal version: now, rather than simply quote Beethoven's tune as he had done thirty years earlier, Brahms unfolds a thematic process that is analogous to that which Schumann had employed in the *Fantasie*. But whereas the earlier composer's search for the distant beloved is ultimately successful – as it was to be in reality – Brahms's quest, in another example of tragic irony, comes to naught. Yet 'Clara' remains a shadowy presence in the work. Indeed, the transition back to the main theme and tonic key of B minor is brought about immediately when in bar 108 the cello reclaims the tenor register that it had lost a few bars earlier and, in a continuation from its sustained D, recalls, in a kind of misremembered form, the Clara cipher that had figured so strongly in the scherzo (cf. Example 5.9c). Matters become even bleaker at the end of the recapitulation. Just when the allusion to *An die ferne Geliebte* is expected the cello intrudes instead with its sustained D, now in the tenor register, and from that note leads directly to the coda, wherein the main theme of the movement is now made to incorporate still another misremembered form of the Clara cipher (Example 5.12).

Clarinet Trio Op. 114

As we have seen, Brahms contemplated retiring in the early 1890s with the publication of the revised version of Op. 8 and the Second String Quintet – both of which, tellingly, contain significant 'autumnal' auto-biographical references to the composer's *Sturm und Drang* period in the mid-1850s.[52] Yet still to come were those four masterly late compositions for clarinet in which Brahms's style is distilled to its essence – in which, as Walter Frisch has put it, the composer 'reduces the dimensions but increases the density of what he wants to say.'[53] The Clarinet Quintet and the two clarinet sonatas have received the lion's share of critical comment to date, and we might begin to redress that imbalance here by concluding with a few remarks regarding the first movement of the Clarinet Trio.[54]

This work, wasting not a single note, begins in the solo cello with a plaintive theme in the tenor register whose first three pitches – nothing more than a bare ascending arpeggiation of the tonic triad – encapsulate the tonal plan of the ensuing three-key exposition (A minor–C major–E minor). Not only the keys, moreover, but even the motivic substance of each of the subsequent thematic groups can be related to this unadorned opening. (It is no wonder, then, that Brahms dispenses with the exposition repeat.) The second theme, an antecedent–consequent period beginning at bar 44, is set in the mediant; yet it opens with a descending arpeggiation of the same chord of A minor, an idea that had already been introduced by the piano in bars 4–5 and which now, in the antecedent, serves also as the basis of the piano's accompaniment to the beautiful tune in the cello (e.g. bars 45–8). This thematic process is continued in the consequent (bars 52ff.). Now the piano and clarinet join forces to carry the tune (beginning E–C–A–G); meanwhile the cello, starting on its dark open C string, plays the inversion of the same idea (C–E–G–A) and with that anticipates the melody with which the exposition ends (beginning E–G–B–C). What is more, this closing tune (bars 67ff.), appearing in the key of the minor dominant and, like the second theme, set off against images of itself in the accompaniment, not only anticipates the return of the main theme itself in E minor following the double bar at bar 83 but, as we shall see, has a still larger role to play in the work's unusually compact form.[55]

Let us begin to address this matter by making a closer examination of the first group and transition, the most complex of the exposition's larger sections. Among the most striking features of the beautiful opening theme (1a) is the complete absence of the leading note in both the melody, which is shared in turns by the cello and clarinet, and the piano's accompanying harmonies. Indeed, the only chromatic note to appear is C♯, which brings the tune to a quiet, wistful close on the Picardy third in bars 10–12. The clarinet is left sounding its sustained low E alone, and when the piano enters with a triplet figure a few moments later at bar 13 (1b), it not only restores the darker hues of the minor mode, but introduces a significant new stepwise 'axial' figure centred on the tonic note A.[56]

A brief bridge-like passage in bars 18–21, hinting at both the arpeggiated motif 1a (in the clarinet) and the axial motif 1b (in the cello), carries over to a loud counterstatement in which both thematic elements are dramatically transformed (bars 22ff. and bars 33ff., respectively). The first (1a′) concludes with a forceful tonicisation of the dominant, but the scalar figures in the clarinet and cello that are elided to make this close lead, unexpectedly, to D minor harmony, supporting the second transformation (1b′), begun as a passionate utterance in the cello and soon evolving into the transition, with both halves of the axial figure now sounding against one another in note-against-note counterpoint and settling eventually into a full close in C major (bar 44). The remainder of the exposition follows on the course that was described above, and we need add here only that the entire passage dies down with a repeated plagal cadence (bars 79ff.) that leads very smoothly to the return of the main theme in E minor at bar 83.

Although the material on the one side of the double bar is comparatively straightforward in respect to form, that on the other is less so. To be sure, by introducing the development with a repetition of the main theme in the dominant minor, Brahms renews one of the oldest traditions of sonata form; and the ensuing rehearsal in F♯ minor of 1a′ (bars 91–6) and a new chorale-like transformation of 1b (bars 97–105) are in keeping with the norms of sonata form, too. Yet we look in vain later in this piece for anything like the 'double return' of main theme and tonic key that is a hallmark of sonata form. The development is marked by a relatively strong arrival on V$^6_5$ at bar 119, it is true, but this leads not to a recapitulation of 1a but to a climactic presentation of material drawn from the other important thematic element in the first group (bars 126ff.): here the passionate 1b′ (cf. bars 34ff.) takes the lead, but each of its two halves are followed by the fragment from 1b that had originally led to the bridge-like passage in bars 18–22 (cf. bars 128 and 131 with bars 15 and 17). Moreover, when, following the revised bridge that grows from this encounter, the main theme does return, it reveals a tenuous new transformation (bars 138–46). The melody itself, articulated in quiet gasps by the clarinet, is hesitant; and, far from appearing as the goal of a tonal process, the passage seems instead to be itself in search of a goal: the tonic in root position is avoided, and the melody breaks off in a deceptive cadence. After a moment the second theme steals in for its reprise in F major.

In fact, the first significant return of the tonic key – more than that, the first significant perfect cadence in A minor in the entire movement – does not occur until the beginning of the closing group at bar 169 (3a). When 3b recurs on course four bars later, we meet, in one sense, the other half of the postponed 'double return': the genetic similarity between 1a and 3b is made very clear now with the presentation of the ascending tonic triad (A–C–E) in the cello's same tenor register (cf. bars 1 and 173). And additional 'weight' is provided by the repetition of the tune as the coda emerges, first by the clarinet (bars 177ff.), and then, in the tonic major, by the piano (bars 185ff.). The movement ends with the chorale-like transformation of 1b, in A minor (Poco meno Allegro and *pp sempre*) and then 'evanesces into imitation of the passionless beauty of an Aeolian harp, with the semiquaver scales in liquid contrary motion on clarinet and cello'.[57] The leading tone is avoided throughout this passage, and the strange final cadence – G^7–A – only enhances the sense of quiet dissolution.

Postscript

A few years after the appearance of the Trio in A minor, the young Viennese composer Alexander von Zemlinsky produced a clarinet trio of his own, in D minor. In 1896 this work took third prize in a competition of the Wiener Tonkünstlerverein. The following year, on Brahms's generous recommendation to Simrock, the trio was published as Zemlinsky's Op. 3.

The younger composer later recalled 'how even among my colleagues [in those days] it was considered particularly praiseworthy to compose in as "Brahmsian" a manner as possible'.[58] Indeed, Zemlinsky's emulation of a 'Brahmsian' style is everywhere apparent in his D minor Trio. The clarinet's atmospheric tremolando passages in the slow movement and the rehearsal of the first movement's main theme at the end of the entire work both seem indebted to Brahms's Clarinet Quintet; at the same time, the last movement sounds for all the world like a paraphrase of the finale of Brahms's own Clarinet Trio. And throughout the work Zemlinsky endeavours to unfold his themes by means of Brahms's beloved technique of 'developing variation'.[59]

In Zemlinsky's trio we find signs of a condition that led Hugo Leichtentritt to pronounce, in 1922, that 'from around 1880 all chamber music in Germany is in some way indebted to Brahms'.[60] To put this sweeping appraisal in some perspective, we might note that the conservative Max Bruch (whose last works included two unpublished string quintets and a string octet) had been dead for only two years when Leichtentritt wrote, and that Arnold Schoenberg was at that time less than a year away from completing his first twelve-note compositions (the Five Piano Pieces Op. 23, the Serenade Op. 24 and the Piano Suite Op. 25). And if the characteristic styles of Bruch and Schoenberg would seem to have little to do with each other, it is all the more remarkable that neither can be comprehended without significant reference to Brahms.

With all this we return, finally, to those larger issues of context and reception that were broached at the outset of this essay. In truth, we ought to know more than we do of the music of Bruch and his ilk – music that was 'correct' in the academic sense of adhering to formal norms and established standards of harmonic propriety and melodic beauty, and, for that very reason, music that could make its way easily through the prevailing institutions of performance and publication. Only then could we really begin to measure for ourselves Brahms's achievement by the standards of his own day, sorting out those features of style that belong to his personal idiom from those that were more widely shared as conventions and so achieving a fuller understanding of why Brahms's works were canonised while those of most of his contemporaries eventually fell from favour.

Yet both Bruch and Schoenberg can step into the breach here. In a conversation with Arthur Abell from 1907, Bruch is reported to have acknowledged that

> Brahms was a far greater composer than I am for several reasons. He cared not at all about the public reaction or what the critics wrote. I had a wife and children to support and educate. I was compelled to earn money with my compositions. Therefore I had to write works that were pleasing and easily understood. I never wrote down to the public; my artistic conscience would never permit me to do that. I always composed good music but it was music that sold readily. There was never anything to quarrel about in my music as there was in that of Brahms. I never outraged the critics by those wonderful conflicting rhythms, which are so characteristic of Brahms. Nor would I have dared to leave out the sequences of steps progressing from one key to another, which often makes Brahms' modulations so bold and startling. Neither did I venture to paint in such dark colours – à la Rembrandt, as he did. All this, and much more militated against Brahms in his own day, but these very attributes will contribute to his stature fifty years from now, because they proclaim him a composer of marked originality. I consider Brahms one of the greatest personalities in the entire annals of music.[61]

Can we not imagine Schoenberg's nod of assent? Growing up in Vienna in the last quarter of the nineteenth century, he experienced the entire living repertoire of Brahms's time in a way that, despite our best efforts, we can never hope to duplicate. What he admired most in Brahms is what he could find nowhere else: the dense motivic processes, asymmetrical phrase structures, and 'expanded' tonality of 'musical prose'. And it was of course in the older composer's chamber music that all these familiar hallmarks of 'Brahms the Progressive' seem most at home.

6 Formal perspectives on the symphonies

KOFI AGAWU

Since the completion of the last of them in the summer of 1885, all four Brahms symphonies have enjoyed a more or less regular stay in the core repertory. Though they represent a small output relative to the vast output of chamber music, as well as to the symphonies of his contemporaries and successors, Brahms's symphonies have established a major position in the concert hall; a challenge to orchestras both in balance and in the quality of playing in all departments, they still represent a means by which the highest orchestral standard is judged. Yet for the listener they have an added dimension. Perhaps more than any of the symphonic works with which they might be compared in the later nineteenth century, they embody a complex set of musical statements, gestures or 'utterances' that open up different structural interpretations and relations of ideas. For some listeners, the framework for the apprehension of these features is the classical exterior and the secure grounding in an Austro-Germanic musical tradition, giving these works their unique emotional, spiritual and intellectual appeal; others will cite the creativity with which Brahms met the very challenge of symphonic composition after Beethoven, a challenge inseparable from that of symphonic composition in the time of Liszt and Wagner. The aesthetic contradictions and paradoxes inherent in his solutions are an essential part of the works' appeal.[1]

Brahms's biographers have often remarked that these large-scale works were composed within a single decade, 1875–85. To some extent, then, they spring from a single creative impulse. Although traces of it extend as far back as 1862, the First Symphony was not completed until September 1876, the bulk of the composing having taken place in 1875–6. Within the space of a single year, however, the Second Symphony followed. Then there was a lull, as Brahms turned to other projects, among them the Violin Concerto and the Second Piano Concerto, completed in 1878 and 1881 respectively. The Third Symphony was finished during the summer of 1883. And, as with the First–Second pair, the Fourth Symphony was completed only a year after the Third. The many kinds of parallel between them are in part a consequence of this compositional history. Not that there is any obvious redundancy of idea or uniformity in the works themselves. Obvious points of contact between movements –

such as the use of sonata form and ternary form, the prevailing lyricism, the similar orchestral complement, and an orchestral character that often reflects a string-based texture – these and other features are always fresh in their individual context. Much has been made of the intellectual dimension of Brahms's composing, of a supposed academic or overly learned manner. It is true that Brahms's devotion to Bach, Schubert and Beethoven, not to mention composers of what was long referred to as 'early music', made possible an ongoing dialogue with a generalised musical past, conferring on his manner a uniquely historicist compositional mode that distanced him from those purveyors of a so-called 'Music of the Future', Liszt and Wagner. But critical labels apart, the future lay as much with Brahms as with his contemporaries, and not merely because he, too, wrote some intensely chromatic music.[2]

It is somewhat paradoxical that some listeners' most enduring impression of the symphonies has less to do with the academic side of Brahms's craft than with the (apparently spontaneous) moments of great lyrical outpouring. The purpose of this chapter is to illuminate these responses by offering commentary on formal aspects of the symphonies, necessarily selective in view of their size and rich content.

Perspectives on form

'Form' is a slippery term. It may be used in a broad sense to refer to everything that makes for a meaningful shape, or dynamic trajectory, anything that promotes or undermines the coherence of the whole. In an essay identifying issues in composition, Carl Dahlhaus construes musical form as 'the sum of the associations between all the elements of a composition'.[3] He then draws a distinction between architectural form and logical form. Form as architecture, complete with plans and designs, is enshrined in the music of the Viennese masters of the late eighteenth and early nineteenth centuries. Their outer forms (like sonata form) are subject to a prescribed pre-compositional plan. Logical form, by contrast, dispenses with the outer design of architects and assumes a form prescribed by the nature, will and destination of the musical ideas themselves. The result is a fluid discourse in sound that may or may not satisfy the prescriptions of architectural form. Even superficial acquaintance with the Brahms symphonies will show that neither concept of form fully represents Brahms's practice and that we need the benefit of both perspectives. The architectural sonata form, for example, is a clear point of reference for all of the first movements, most of the last movements and several of the interior movements. Statistically, sonata form has the greatest priority in

Brahms's formal schemes. It does not follow, however, that the most productive mode of perception of these movements resides in an awareness
of the design itself. For Brahms's thematic premises are often distinct and
individual, seeming to forge their own path of elaboration, so that the discourse in sound takes on the character of an improvisation. The creative
tension between architectural and logical form, two fundamentally
opposed compositional impulses, lies at the heart of Brahms's style. On a
more concrete level of musical structure lie a number of elements that
may be said to have provided stylistic opportunities for Brahms's composing.[4] A look at the genres, forms and associated techniques of his
musical language suggests that it is formed from (at least) a triple heritage: the already mentioned Viennese classical school; a contemporary
'romantic' sensibility; and an archaising or perhaps 'archaeological'
manner.[5] By choosing the central genres of the first Viennese school
(string quartets, piano trios, symphonies and concertos), Brahms
accepted the normative challenge of writing in the high classical style.
And with this came an acceptance of the corollary challenge of composing
in their principal forms: sonata form, various ternary shapes, variation
form, minuet and scherzo. There is, however, nothing mechanical about
Brahms's appropriation of these channels of expression, for each
appropriation is marked by elements from another heritage, allowing the
composer to speak in a fundamentally mixed or syncretic language.

Harder to define technically but no less pertinent is the romantic
sensibility, whose intimate manifestations invariably invite a 'poetic'
response. Devices range from the play of periodicity and anti-periodicity
in melody, through the circulation of fragments and dislocated wholes, to
the occasionally descriptive or tone-poetic passages. Included here also
are a tendency towards the epigrammatic and a Schumannesque sentimentality. The heritage of the archaic covers Brahms's use of materials
and procedures from the distant rather than recent musical past, including devices drawn from Renaissance and Baroque choral music.[6]

The modal writing at the beginning of the slow movement of the
Fourth, for example, is both archaic in origin and 'modern' in effect.
Similarly, the choice of a passacaglia theme (based on one by J. S. Bach) as
structural premise for the finale of the same symphony betrays an
'archaic' influence, even though here the thirty-odd variations that follow
owe as much to Viennese as they do to archaic influences (Beethoven's
Diabelli Variations, for example, are assimilated in this movement). To
this archaic tone must belong the traces of a folk idiom in Brahms, in particular passages whose modal ambivalence and plagal inflection impart a
floating, less goal-oriented, perhaps even exotic quality – in contrast to
the more usual directed motion.

Example 6.1 Second Symphony, movement 1, bars 455–77

Translated into technical terms, our 'triple heritage' enables some simple generalisations. The harmony functions within closed formal designs, based on a traditional distinction between tension and resolution, and regulated by a strong bass line. Chromaticism is always contained. Periodicity is secured by cadential action, even where enormous trajectories are involved. Although parallel periods do sometimes occur, the normative duality of classical phrase structure is no longer held as a rigid premise. Melody remains fresh, frequently assuming the shape of a dynamic curve with a clear high point and a complementary resolution. A heightened exploitation of thematic invention results in a new logic of 'developing variation'.[7] Moments of self-contained and especially memorable melody contrast with periods of fragmentation. These (and other) dimensional processes combine to produce more complex profiles, profiles that are not easily described by means of single, overarching characterisations – which is why ultimate meaning must be sought in individual contexts.

Turning points

Deep into each of Brahms's sonata form movements (and sometimes others as well) is a significant turning point, a moment of reversal that announces closure. In the first movement of the Second Symphony, the moment of reversal, although adumbrated harmonically in bars 294–302, is given profile by a reduction in the rate of harmonic movement (bar 451 introduces a dominant pedal), a lowering of dynamics and, perhaps most poignantly, a new and memorable melodic event: the emergence of a resigned solo horn melody that moves unhurriedly but purposefully to its own high point (B♭ in bar 469) before subsiding in a cadence on to the tonic (Example 6.1). The shape, terminal position and poetic effect of the

Example 6.2 First Symphony, movement 1, bars 486–95

Example 6.3 First Symphony, movement 1: 'Norm' and Brahms's variant in bars 491–95.

horn melody render further thematic and harmonic activity redundant. All that is needed is cadential assurance. Not that the movement has been lacking variety in fragmentation: but the turning point invites us to forget the fragments, or rather to recall them from within the relative security of a 'traditional' coda. In a highly detailed and wide-ranging study of the Second, Reinhold Brinkmann writes similarly of this passage: 'the horn is sounding a farewell, gathering the movement together, conducting it to its fulfilment'.[8]

A comparable moment of reversal occurs in the first movement of the First Symphony, where Brahms signals the beginning of the end by means of a sweet, perhaps sentimental melodic fragment that closes with an archetypal $\hat{3}$–$\hat{2}$–$\hat{1}$ descending motion (Example 6.2). Here, too, there can be no turning back. Nor is the sense of ending here achieved only by retroactive means. On the contrary, the sequencing of bars 478–81 as 482–5 suggests further thematic and harmonic exploration. But the intervention of a subdominant harmony in bar 488 reorients the tonal narrative. And the deliberateness of the little melody quoted in Example 6.2, its unfolding over a dominant pedal (from bar 490 on) and its expansion of an underlying four-bar phrase by an extra bar (see the 'norm' and Brahms's variant in Example 6.3): all these conspire to create a sense of closure. Furthermore, at the actual cadential moment (bar 495), the timpani enter and persist, thus calling to mind the very opening of the movement, and reminding us of the reciprocal relationship between beginning and ending.

A heightening of the lyrical element may be heard in some slow movements as well. At bar 108 in the second movement of the Third Symphony, an expressively marked new melody, played an octave apart by first and

Example 6.4   Third Symphony, movement 2, bars 108–11

second violins, signals the beginning of the end, giving an epigrammatical sense to the conclusion of an altogether warm and broadly expressive movement (Example 6.4 extracts on one stave the outer voices only). Secondary factors such as the violas' triplet accompanying figure and Brahms's expressive marking 'p cresc. poco a poco' combine with the high register and subsequent melodic appoggiaturas to draw attention to this passage. Moments like this acquire a revelatory, perhaps even transcendent quality. They remind us of the composer's deep sense of classical oratory, which assures the organic shape of his first movements.

Not all turning points are quiet, lyrical or sentimental; and not all of them are marked by a new theme. The one in the first movement of the Third Symphony features nothing less than the heroic main theme of the movement (Example 6.5), prepared by the two-bar motto theme that opens the movement (see bars 181–2). The crucial difference here is the sounding of the beginning of the theme over dominant rather than tonic harmony. The resulting $^6_4$ chord (bar 183) and the immediate indication of a turn towards the subdominant (bar 184) confer the necessary element of novelty upon this moment of reversal. In the slow movement of the Fourth Symphony, the turning point is signalled by a tiny detail: a marking of the subdominant moment, delaying the inevitable arrival on the cadential dominant. This event, which occurs during the recapitulation of the extraordinarily beautiful second main theme of the movement, emerges from the following context. First, the two strains of the second theme are heard, now in the tonic of E major (bars 88–97). Then the first strain of the melody is repeated in a broad, luscious and thickly scored mode (bars 98–101). For the second strain, the scoring is reduced for strings only (bar 102), and the arrival on the subdominant chord (bar 103) is highlighted by a familiar romantic *topos* of closure, the string pizzicato. In addition, clarinets and bassoons seem to get stuck on a rhythm (bars 103–5), thus retarding the progress towards closure.

Heard as moments in the narrative unfolding of each movement, the turning points mentioned above point to one aspect of Brahms's form: the fluid processes associated with 'logical form'. We have noted however that Brahms's sonata forms embody a basic conflict between such fluid processes ('romantic form') and the architecture of classical form.

Example 6.5 Third Symphony, movement 1, bars 183–87

Architectural design, evident from the additive processes by which periods and paragraphs are arranged to constitute a whole movement, provides a framework for understanding how the discourse of each sonata form movement is articulated and sustained. Let us turn, then, to some of the ways in which Brahms plays with the elements of sonata form.

Playing in sonata form

In their outer form, Brahms's sonata form movements follow classical protocol. Each exposition features a contrast of theme(s) and key(s), the development elaborates upon the exposition's materials, and a recapitulation restates the material of the exposition with the appropriate tonal adjustment, which means either returning all 'dissonant' keys of the exposition to the tonic or arranging them symmetrically around the tonic. But there the similarities end and the differences begin, for the formative ideas or thematic premises of these symphonies are strikingly different, each group of ideas propelling its own path to closure, thus articulating sonata form discourses with greater or lesser degrees of explicitness.

Consider the first movement of the Third Symphony, which features 'local' thematic contrast as well as 'global' thematic integration, encouraging a hearing of the tripartite formal scheme as a more or less single, undivided form. The source of this 'undivision' is the so–called motto theme with which the movement opens (Example 6.6, which includes a single-stave chordal summary). Not merely a theme, the motto subtends a nexus of ideas that in turn determine the course of the tonal narrative of the movement and of the symphony as a whole. Among these is modal interchange, not just the primary interchange between F major and F minor, but the secondary mixture that allows the third-related keys of D♭, A♭, and even A to be brought into the orbit of the home key. Another is the series of neighbour-note motions (C–D–C, C–B–C, A–G♯/A♭–A, A–B–A) by which the F chord is prolonged. Brahms employs this Schubertian technique to effect several subsequent modulations. Derivative progressions

Example 6.6 Third Symphony, movement 1, bars 1–3 (motto theme)

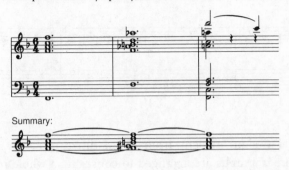

Summary:

appear as part of a cadential group (see, for example, bars 15–35) or as a link between sections (see bars 49–50 or the equivalent passage in the recapitulation, 158–9). In addition to generating local progressions, the motto theme participates in a longer-term process. Each subsequent appearance is a reinterpretation of a previous appearance, so that the entire succession acquires an organic, goal-oriented sense. To mention but one instance of this reinterpretation: observe the four-bar expansion of the motto theme in bars 120–3.

Consider also the first subject (bars 3–15), which forms a closed, detachable thirteen-bar period, complete with a twofold elided repetition of its final cadence. When this passage returns in the recapitulation (bars 124–36), Brahms makes only a minor change, but when the same material comes towards the end of the movement, the twofold statement of the cadence is now multiplied to a fivefold statement (bars 202–10). To juxtapose these three passages is, again, to gain some sense of Brahms's long-range planning, although this particular cumulative process is perhaps less obvious than the one involving the motto theme. Enhancing but at the same time contradicting this cumulative process is another involving the treatment of the first subject material in the development. Here Brahms offers not the expected 'working out' but a restatement in a distant key (see bars 112ff.).

At more local levels of structure, the temporal profile of the movement is more complex, less single-minded. And this results in part from the extensive use of repetition. Consider, for example, the bridge passage between first and second key areas (bars 15–31). Beginning as if confirming the cadence that concluded the first subject, the bridge features two transpositionally equivalent passages, the first in F (bars 15–23), the second in D♭ (bars 23–31); the music settles eventually on A (bars 31–6) as both preparation for and anticipation of the second subject. The major third relation between F and D♭ takes up one of the harmonic ideas implicit in the motto theme, even as it breaks up the linear intensity that might derive from fifth- or semitonally related motion. The second subject, too, features a statement and repetition of the same idea (bars 36–40 and 40–4) before yielding to another (bars 44–50). And the passage that follows (bars 51–72) makes use of both sequential and non-sequential repetition, before bringing the exposition to a close in the mediant minor, A minor. Overall, then, the exposition proceeds in terms of repeated utterances, gaining part of its character from the juxtaposition of phrases, without losing the sense of a cumulative tonal process.

The shape of the development, especially the manner in which discrete tasks of elaboration are carried out, follows the precedent set by the exposition but not its ordering of ideas. The development is given over mainly to the elaboration of the second subject material. After the lead-in to the development (based on the arpeggio figure that ends the exposition, bars 70–7), the first phase of development elaborates (by transposition and modal reinterpretation) the second subject (see bars 77–90). Specifically, the theme is heard in C♯ minor (bars 77–81) followed by a suffix (bars 81–2); then the exact process is repeated in bars 83–7 and 87–9. Further elaboration follows in bars 90–100, involving fragmentation and the inclusion of a syncopated subsidiary idea first heard in bars 44–50. As the syncopated figures are liquidated in bars 97–9, the motto theme and first subject return in a strikingly different affective guise, supported by Brahms's favourite syncopated accompaniment (the beautiful 1874 song 'Sapphische Ode' Op. 94 No. 4, comes to mind). Minor adjustments notwithstanding (the recapitulation of the second subject in bars 149–59 includes a statement of its main idea but not a restatement as we had heard in bars 40–4), the recapitulation behaves normally. The negotiation of the movement's global close, however, is marked for attention not only because it involves the normative excess of Brahms's closing moments but because (from our point of view) it gives rise to intertextual resonances with two Mahler movements, the fourth movement of the Seventh and the first of the Tenth. We have seen that the climax in bars 183–7 of the Brahms engenders a heightened rhetoric that begins to subside around bar 202 and achieves definite closure on the downbeat of bar 209, the period between bars 202 and 209 given over to cadential reiteration. The last of these cadences involves a familiar $\hat{3}$–$\hat{2}$–$\hat{1}$ descent. Unlike the passage from the first movement of the First that we cited earlier as a sign of closure (see Example 6.2), however, the $\hat{1}$ in this passage is isolated and sounded with no support (see bar 209 of Example 6.7a). Far from weakening the sense of closure, this particular dramatisation strengthens it by making the close that much more precious. It is not unlikely that Mahler remembered this closing strategy while concluding

Example 6.7a Third Symphony, movement 1, bars 203–16

Example 6.7b Mahler, Seventh Symphony, movement 4 ('Nachtmusik 2'), bars 369–76

Example 6.7c Mahler, Tenth Symphony, movement 1, bars 238–43

the second 'Nachtmusik' movement of his Seventh, for there, too, the
$\hat{3}$–$\hat{2}$–$\hat{1}$ descent (also in F major) leaves the terminal element unsupported
(see Example 6.7b). Again, in the first movement of the Tenth, the close on
the tonic, F♯, is executed in exactly the same way (Example 6.7c). In all
three passages, a sense of fatigue follows the attainment of $\hat{1}$, allowing
only imperfect reminiscences of fragments of melody. Brahms underlines
the sense of an ending by playing back quietly (as if in a whisper) the
opening of the main theme of the movement. He will do the same at the
end of the finale.

To turn from the cogent, closely argued, and lightly textured first
movement of the Third to the first of the Second, another sonata form
movement, is to turn to Brahms in a more lyrical, less heroic, but also
quite self-aware mode. Here the seams of sonata form are quite plain, and
nowhere more so than in the development section (bars 180–302).
Proceeding mainly in two- and four-bar increments, Brahms first elaborates upon the first theme of the first subject (see bars 180–204, whose
antecedents are in bars 1–44). This process then spills over into a passage
of stiff, formal counterpoint, an instance of the so-called 'learned style' in
the form of a fugato (bars 204–25). The subject of the fugato is derived
from the first subject of the movement (see Example 6.8). Brahms's
manner here recalls Beethoven, specifically the first movement development of the *Eroica* Symphony. Then, as if consulting a thematic index,
Brahms proceeds methodically to develop the themes of his exposition,
leaving intact the somewhat predictable periodic structure.

The exposition, by contrast, is considerably more fluid, the phrase
structure more supple and the tonal orientation enriched by ambiguity.
Whereas the tonal issue in particular remained in the background in the
first movement of the Third, it is projected as a feature of the foreground
in this movement. The opening period of the first subject (bars 1–44) provides some illustration of this. Orientated towards the dominant (it is 'on'
rather than 'in' the dominant), the period seems to withhold closure in
order to unfold a number of thematic fragments. This process weakens
the sense of an inaugural tonic while transferring the first structural

Example 6.8 Second Symphony, movement 1, bars 6–8 as origin of bars 204–6

accent on to the lyrical theme that enters in bar 44. It is interesting that
when this opening material returns at the start of the recapitulation,
Brahms takes the plunge and presents all of the first part over a dominant
pedal, thus building on a tendency implicit in the earlier presentation
while extending the sense of development into the recapitulation. The
second subject (bars 82–118), too, is tonally ambivalent, beginning not in
the dominant but in the mediant minor, F♯ minor, and turning towards
the tonic, D major, by its eighth bar. In another eight bars, a plagal cadence
coloured by the minor submediant is reached (bars 97–8). This obviously
'wrong' harmonic goal is immediately and literally cancelled by a four-bar
transitional passage (bars 98–101), leading to a restatement in F♯ minor of
the second subject. From a tonal-harmonic point of view, very little in the
first 118 bars of this movement is unequivocally clear; little seems permanent and secure.[9]

Although it feels a shade premature, the arrival of the first of the exposition's two cadence themes in bars 118–27 brings a stability unprecedented in the movement. Its two phrases, five and six bars long
respectively, cadence decisively in the dominant key. If the second subject
left us with a sense of ambivalence about its tonal orientation, this
cadence theme rebukes the doubting listener. A second cadence theme
(bars 127–31) at first reinforces the sense of the new key, A major, before
serving as a jumping-off point for an enormous phrase expansion based
on an off-beat rhythmic pattern. What should have been a classical
cadence in which the 'dominant of the dominant' leads to the dominant
and eventually to the tonic (here, bars 152–5, A major) is undercut in bar
155 by a resolution to a first inversion rather than a root-position A major
chord. Then, as if to make another bid for closure, the second subject is
restated (bars 156ff.). This time tonal ambivalence is redirected to lead to
a proper cadence in A major.

The articulation of sonata form in the first movement of the Fourth
Symphony is of a different order from the first movements of the Second
and Third. The initial chain of descending thirds on the foreground sug-

Example 6.9 Fourth Symphony, movement 1, bars 1–4 as origin of bars 80–3

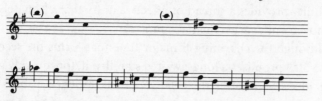

gests a discourse dominated by tight motivic work. But Brahms's plan is more complex. In what turns out to be a surprisingly wide-ranging movement, passages of careful motivic work are interspersed with topical allusions and fantasia-like disruptions of periodicity. The net result is a mixed discourse, a discourse grounded in a verse-like structure but enriched by a prose-like process.

Consider the way in which ideas are introduced from the onset of the movement. The single period that begins the exposition (bars 1–19), although harmonically expanded by the events in bars 4–8, nevertheless maintains a dynamic trajectory that is brought to a decisive close in bar 19. Immediately following is what appears to be a parallel period (bars 19–45). But Brahms does more than restate the first period; he redirects it (beginning in bar 28), adding more thematic material in the process. Between bars 45 and 73, three distinct thematic ideas are introduced. First is a sweeping melodic gesture, heard in two parallel phrases (bars 45–9 and 49–53), the second of which begins as a transposition up a fourth of the earlier one. Second is a fanfare-like figure (bars 53–7), and third is an appoggiatura-laden melody initiated by a rising seventh and reminiscent of Tchaikovsky's sentimental melodic manner (bars 57–73). There is no obvious causality here in the unfolding of ideas, no sense of an urgent or anxious first movement discourse. On the contrary, Brahms is at his most additive, juxtaposing contrasting passages, and allowing the musical form to emerge from the nature of the material.

The rest of the transition to the second subject (bar 95) is similarly broken up thematically. Bars 73–80 feature the wind fanfare. Then comes a passage of broken rhetoric (bars 80–6), reminiscent of the introduction to the finale of the First. This apparently new 'Klangfarbenmelodie' is melodically derived from the opening of the movement (see Example 6.9). Then a passage based on an F♯ pedal stays matters for five bars, before being interrupted by a passionate outburst (bars 91–4), a summarising gesture that sets up the second subject. The heterogeneity of ideas in this exposition is striking, second perhaps only to the heterogeneity of the scherzo movement (to which we will return). Yet it would be wrong to infer a loss of cogency in the movement's form. An underlying sense of instability provides a thread of affective unity that ultimately subsumes the movement's varied thematic process.

Although the charming B major tune that forms the second subject (bars 95ff.) promises a long-awaited stability, it, too, quickly gives way to other ideas. Soon after the relatively weak cadence in bars 106–7, the fantasy-like passage interrupts, suspending a sense of harmonic direction and periodicity. Then the fanfare passage is heard (110–13), interrupted by the fantasy (114–19) and followed by an intensified form of fanfare (119–37), leading finally to the structural cadence that closes the exposition (bars 136–7). If the idea of sonata form as a flexible, fantasy-driven scheme was merely implicit in the first movements of the Second and Third Symphonies, it is explicit here. The mechanical repetitions that we encountered in the development section of the first movement of the Second now lie in a distant horizon. Here, in the last of Brahms's symphonies, a seamless manner emerges strongly.

This first of the Fourth is the only one among Brahms's symphonic first movements whose exposition is not formally repeated. The absence of a repeat sign, however, masks a written-in repeat (beginning in bar 145) that enables Brahms to play on the listener's expectations. Before long we are in the throes of a rhythmic canon (starting in bar 153 but reaching a point of culmination in bar 169), whose learnedness we associate with formal development. Perhaps the most striking feature of the development is the 'false reprise' that begins in bar 219, a reprise that is thematically correct (it brings back the descending third melody from the beginning of the movement although in an altered orchestration) and harmonically 'wrong' (it is in G♯ minor not the expected E minor). This Haydnesque trick (bars 219–26) is not made much of, however, for the return to the main key is accomplished by a leisurely and deliberate retransition (bars 226–46) based on bar 9 of the first subject, in which the descending thirds of the first subject are also adumbrated (bars 242–6).

The augmentation of the first subject at the start of the recapitulation (interspersed after each group of four notes with the fantasy material) may remind us of the pervasiveness of such techniques in Brahms. Such manipulation of thematic ideas is built into the very fabric of his language. The four brief instances assembled in Example 6.10, chosen more or less at random, speak to this point. Although a proper assessment of the role of augmentation and diminution techniques in Brahms requires a contextual explanation (such a study would include extensive data about the finale of the Fourth), it is worth emphasising the normality, indeed the ordinariness, of such learned 'speaking' in Brahms. Brahms's usage of

Example 6.10 Four brief instances of thematic augmentation or diminution
(a) Fourth Symphony, movement 1, bars 1–4 and 247–58
(b) Second Symphony, movement 1, bars 1–2 and 63–6
(c) Second Symphony, movement 1, bars 18–19 and 19–23
(d) Third Symphony, movement 2, bars 1 and 80

such techniques is made to appear inevitable, an essential part of his everyday language.

Sonata form remains a point of reference for some of Brahms's slow movements. On first hearing, that of the Fourth Symphony may suggest a bipartite form. And the most memorable thing about that hearing may well involve the profoundly beautiful melody which gives profile to the second key, B major, and which is later recapitulated in the tonic, E major. Memory of this theme, especially of its contrasting tonal levels, anchors the formal process for the first-time listener. We note an exposition comprising two successive key areas (bars 1–30 and 41–64) linked by a bridge (bars 30–41) and a recapitulation offering the same material with the appropriate tonal adjustment. The events following the attainment of $\hat{1}$ in bar 113 further suggest a coda.

The trouble with such schemes, however, is that they do not always accurately represent the 'facts' of the movement. For one thing, there is no development section – which might suggest that Brahms's model here is a so-called sonata form without development. Moreover, to speak of a dramatisation of key areas is to misplace the rhetorical emphasis, for the second movement of the Fourth is less 'about' a polarised key conflict than about an intricate motivic and variational discourse. In utilising a sonata form scheme, then, Brahms draws upon the properties of a standard tonal space; it would have been a quite different challenge to make palpable the invariant rhetoric of this particular tonal opposition.

How, then, does the more palpable motivic discourse unfold? The movement begins with an introduction in bare octaves for horns and winds only. The metrical emphasis on E and the intervallic expansion up and down a third from that central E produce a collection referable to the Phrygian mode, sending a signal that the modal interplay may well play a role here. Indeed the way in which the notes B and G♯ are added to the note E in bar 4 confirms the significance of this juxtaposition of modes. The nature of the introduction, however, remains normative: to prepare the principal theme of the movement by reiterating its head motif. The shape and subsequent treatment of the first theme are, by contrast, not normative. The first theme is presented in bars 5–13 as an open rather than closed theme, its overall shape mimicking a metaphorical crescendo. (The expression is intensified as the music moves to the mediant minor for a repeated cadential gesture.) As if beginning again, the music in bar 13 leads via a sequential passage featuring a fanfare motif to a second beginning in bar 22. It is this second beginning (actually third, if one counts the beginning of the movement) that is to succeed, achieving closure in bars 29–30 by extending the falling fifth clarinet gesture from bars 11–13 in order to reach the tonic. As so often happens in Brahms the cumulative rhetoric created by the threefold gesture (see the clarinet melody in bars 28–9) underlines the music's organic shape, overriding the symmetries that derive from phrase and sub-phrase organization.

The functional ambivalence of this opening period sets the tone for the rest of the movement. Immediately following the cadence in bars 29–30, we are presented with a broad tune with a confirmatory stance, an assurance that the initial period has been brought to a decisive close. The confirmation function proves short-lived, however, as the music assumes a transitional function, leading us towards the next key area. And after the big statement of the second theme in bars 41–50, complete with a full cadence, a passage of confirmation immediately follows, but it, too, takes an elaborate turn, meditating for a while on the cadential material before circling back to the dominant of E both to prepare the recapitulation (bars 50–64) and to deny the possibility of development.

A tiny chromatic detail at the beginning of the reprise (bars 64–7) reminds us of Brahms's long-range tonal thinking: the C♮ and D♮ of the equivalent passage in the exposition (bars 5–6) are replaced by C♯s and D♯ in the first two bars of the reprise (bars 64–5). C♯ persists in the third and fourth bars (66–7) but D♯ is replaced by D♮. As a pointer to the sub-dominant, itself a signal for closure, D♮ contributes to marking a major turning point in the movement.

Set alongside that of the Fourth, the slow movement of the First, also in E major, reveals some striking parallels in sound and content as well as equally striking divergences in overall strategy. This movement is in ternary form (1–39, 39–66, and 66–128) with a greatly expanded reprise. Of special significance is the way in which the movement is brought to a close. The end begins in bar 90, where the earlier and memorable oboe melody (bars 17ff.) is rescored for horn and solo violin. Lying two octaves apart and punctuated by a pizzicato cello figure, the melody acquires an epigrammatic sense. The expected cadence arrives in bars 99–100, followed by a four-bar tonic pedal that seems long and weighty enough to absorb earlier tensions. But there is a further twenty-four bars of music to follow, music that might be described in terms of a gestural excess, a surplus of closing signs. The surplus here does not consist of a relentless reiteration of a cadence figure, however. Initially (bars 105–14), the sense of a surplus derives from a breaking up of familiar material, a textural disintegration enlivened by dialogue, leading eventually to a cadence (bars 113–14). Then there is a striking moment of recall, a moment of melodic tenderness that sends the listener to two pasts: first (bars 116–20), the immediate past of the first movement, part of whose chromatic opening (bars 1–3) is reproduced in the harmonic progression of bars 117–18, complete with simultaneous textural ascent and descent; secondly, a more distant past, the Quintet from Act 1 of *Così fan tutte*. Example 6.11 compares both passages. Finally, the plagal cadence in bars 123–4 confirms that the movement's structural cadence has already taken place, and that this plagal inflection is part of a large-scale extension of the tonic in the closing twenty-four bars of the movement. Themes of death, dying and closure assumed increasing importance in Brahms's later work. Here we are offered a glimpse of that dark side of the composer.

Example 6.11
(a) Excerpt from the Quintet, Act 1 of *Così fan tutte*
(b) Brahms, First Symphony, movement 2, bars 117–20

Towards a modernist aesthetic

More than any of his other symphonic movements, the scherzo of Brahms's Fourth Symphony seems radical and modern. This is not to underplay the originality of other movements. The finale, for example, is often discussed in terms of a self-conscious archaism that is shot through with romantic feeling. The slow movement is vintage romanticism, an exploration of predominantly dark sentiments by means of an inwardly turned, lugubrious counterpoint. And the first movement harks back to the thematic consistency and integration of some of Beethoven's first movements, even as it makes several gestures towards the theatre rather than the concert-hall. The scherzo, however, is a different kettle of fish. Its C major 'home' is exploited here with only an occasional sense of tonal desire. (The exception – and a dramatic one at that – is the long dominant pedal that begins the coda (bars 282–308).) In this robust and adventurous movement, musical ideas are juxtaposed freely, creating the aura of a mosaic rather than a linearly charged atmosphere.

One source of the movement's unique character is its unabashed intertextuality, its imbrication in other texts. Each listener will construct his or her own intertextual horizon, but mine includes, on the future side, Mahler, especially the Mahler of the second movement of the Ninth. There, beginning and ending in a pristine C major, fragments of diatonic melody are presented through varying harmonic spectra (the keys of E,

E♭, F, D and B♭ are visited), some superimposed one upon another. Brahms, likewise, eschews the long line of his slow movements (or even of the 'Intermezzo' third movement of the Third) for a more earthy arrangement of musical ideas. The loud bang in bar 5 and elsewhere, for example, this rude disruption of an otherwise orderly procession, this juxtaposition of textural blocks: this is what Stravinsky was to exploit to the full in the *Rite of Spring* and in other works. Bars 159–80 of Brahms's scherzo, for example, offer a succession of keys and ideas, deriving their coherence less from a unity of idea than from an underlying energy that drives the scherzo as a whole. Bartók, too, seems not too far away in passages such as bars 137–59 where triads and scalar patterns are traded by different instrumental groups and frequently repeated. His *Music for Strings, Percussion and Celesta* (1936) and the Concerto for Orchestra (1943) leap to mind immediately. To suggest affinities with Stravinsky and Bartók is to attempt to rescue Brahms from the overburdened and overdetermined Beethovenian tradition, to claim him for a tradition into which he fits neither comfortably nor obviously: that of fin-de-siècle non-German modernism. The point here is not, of course, to suggest that Brahms's role in furthering the Austro-Germanic symphonic tradition could ever be underestimated (one need only recall his influence on Schoenberg to see the futility of such a historical revision). The point, rather, is to hint at what lies in the margins: affinities with other musical traditions in which metrical, textural and phrase-structural play serve to inaugurate a modernist trend.

The scherzo of the Fourth, however, owes as much to a past influence. Beethoven and Schumann are implicated here. Beethoven is recalled in the energetic character of the scherzo, and in specific 'Stravinskian' juxtapositions. The passage in bars 93–105, for example, may be usefully compared to a passage from the first movement of the first of the 'Rasumovsky' quartet Op. 59 No. 1 (Example 6.12). Embedded in Beethoven's polyphonic texture (b) are different voice-leading strands, each of which finds proper resolution eventually. Brahms's texture (a), by contrast, depends less on maintaining the integrity of individual 'voices' than on 'freezing' blocks of sound. Also implicated here is late Beethoven, the Beethoven who juxtaposed ideas with distinct tonal allegiances. For example, in the 'Alla danza tedesca' of Op. 130, contiguous passages in G major and C major do not necessarily invite an organic grouping between 'tonic' and 'subdominant' but point, instead, to small, closed harmonic fields (compare bars 25–40 with 41–56). Something of this transpositional procedure occurs in bars 35–44 of the Brahms movement. C major and G major (including a passing tonicisation of A minor) are juxtaposed

Example 6.12
(a) Brahms, Fourth Symphony, movement 3, bars 80–113; compare bars 93–105 with (b)

(133) 47

without a marked sense of a functional I–IV progression. There is logic in Brahms's move, however, for as Example 6.13 makes clear, the reharmonisation of a $\hat{6}$–$\hat{5}$–$\hat{3}$–$\hat{2}$ melodic fragment (level a) in bars 8–10 (level b) is precisely the harmonization that Brahms uses in the G major version in bars 40–2 (level c) (Example 6.13). The last two harmonies of level (b) are identical to the first two at level (c). Finally, Schumann enters into this intertextual world both generally, in the grandness of tone and design,

Example 6.12 (*cont.*)

(b) Beethoven, String Quartet in F major Op. 59 No. 1 movement 1, bars 85–92

154 *Kofi Agawu*

Example 6.13 Reharmonisation and transposition of melodic fragment
in Brahms, Fourth Symphony, movement 3
(a) bars 6–8
(b) bars 8–10
(c) bars 40–2

Example 6.14 Brahms, Fourth Symphony, movement 3:
melodic fragment and its variant

and specifically, in a $\hat{6}$–$\hat{5}$–$\hat{3}$–$\hat{2}$ melodic fragment (see Example 6.14). Beginning as if from a distance, resisting closure in spite of its inner tendencies, this melodic fragment, like several in Schumann, is retrospectively marked, sending us back, so to speak, as if we were only half-remembering.

As an illustration of Brahms's phrase discourse and the manner in which ideas are organised, let us examine the first twenty-three bars of the movement. Example 6. 15 displays the melodic content of these bars in four columns (I, II, III, IV) in order to emphasise difference in the succession of ideas and sameness in their treatment. Each idea is immediately repeated in varied form, the only exception being the F/A dyad that intrudes in bars 5–6. The fact that it is unintegrated with any of the other paradigms reinforces its independent and disruptive quality. Note especially the wider range of variation among the segments in column IV.[10]

Talk of variation procedures in this scherzo may recall ideas of 'developing variation'. The process enshrined in Example 6.15 represents not the variation of a single, parent idea but a succession of different ideas

Example 6.15 Brahms, Fourth Symphony, movement 3: paradigmatic analysis of bars 1–23

each of which is immediately varied. The impression then is not of an ongoing, organically based thematic process; it is rather of a juxtaposition of seemingly heterogeneous ideas. Talk of heterogeneity may seem somewhat exaggerated, however, since the fundamental security of Brahms's outer forms is, in the end, never threatened, not even in a wide-ranging scherzo like that of the Fourth. The challenge is to appreciate the containment of heterogeneity, to see how Brahms controls a thematic process that could easily have by-passed the 'revolutionary' procedures associated with modernism for a playful 'post-modern' juxtaposition of ostensibly incompatible ideas. This last was left to Mahler, and to other composers of the early twentieth century. What is inspiring about Brahms's symphonic output is not only how much of the past is consolidated therein, or how much of the present is domesticated by him, but how – and this is only possible with the benefit of hindsight – significant subsequent practices may be traced to him.

7 'Veiled symphonies'? The concertos

MALCOLM MACDONALD

Ever since Schumann, in 'Neue Bahnen', told the world that a twenty-year-old unknown from Hamburg had played him 'sonatas, or rather veiled symphonies'[1] ('Sonaten, mehr verschleierte Symphonien'), Brahms's works have been open to charges of inconcinnity, or at least ambiguity, of genre. Wagner, in 'On the Application of Music to Drama' ('Über die Anwendung der Musik auf das Drama', 1879), suggested a contrary formal mismatch: for him the Brahms symphonies were essentially 'transplanted' chamber music, 'quintets and the like served up as symphonies'. This leitmotif was long recycled by Brahms's detractors, and some of his more discriminating friends. All polemics aside, certainly in Brahms the streams of orchestral, chamber and instrumental music flow in unusually close proximity. Seemingly these genres did not require any sharp differentiation in his expressive aims, or the means of their realisation: all partook equally of his highly personal synthesis of romantic, classical and pre-classical techniques, and his ongoing development of post-Beethovenian sonata discourse.

Brahms's orchestral scores, moreover, reflect his development of a genuine and original orchestral style which deployed colour neither for its own sake, nor for merely pictorial or anecdotal effect. His orchestration relates colour to structure, to embody and articulate a dramatic but intricately developing musical argument with the directness and clarity, the identity of idea and expressive medium, of the smaller, 'purer' ensembles of his chamber and instrumental works.

Ultimately, however, the close kinship of genres in Brahms's *œuvre* is a function of his musical language, in which – for whatever reason, emotional, spiritual or psychological – intimacy (both confessional and secret) and grandeur (heroic, tragic or elegiac) are in continual counterpoise.

This central paradox of Brahmsian expression is fully reflected in the four concertos. Here, in the full tradition of the genre, instrumental soloists, as individuals, engage in contest or dialogue with the massed forces of the orchestra. Yet here too the other categories (even choral works and *Lieder*) are suggested in different ways. The concertos emerge from an imaginative continuum embracing symphonic, vocal and instrumental impulses.

Three of the concertos date from Brahms's full maturity, composed in fairly quick succession during the years 1878–87. However, the First Piano Concerto (1854–9) stands apart. It belongs to a much earlier phase of the composer's career; its *Sturm und Drang* character, and its long and particularly difficult parturition, made it a work of apprenticeship and self-discovery, a hard-achieved masterpiece of youth.

Brahms wrote his piano concertos in the first instance for the soloist he knew best: himself – and both, it can be suggested, contain autobiographical elements. The Violin Concerto and Double Concerto were both written for, and with a measure of collaboration from, Joseph Joachim, though the professional and personal relations of composer and violinist changed drastically over the intervening years. But Joachim was also intimately involved, much earlier, in the First Piano Concerto's genesis, as mentor – and provider, in his own works, of compositional parallels. So one aspect of these three concertos is the way they chart the course of Brahms's friendship with the great violinist-composer. Moreover, the Second Piano Concerto (1881), through its scherzo movement, bears a now unquantifiable relationship to the original plan of the Violin Concerto, the most 'Joachim-directed' work of the four.

Brahms's intense and difficult affections, both personal and musical, are surely sources of his music's intimacy of utterance, even in such large forms as these concertos. And the piano concertos, as most specifically 'his' works, are (in their slow movements) also the most overtly 'Clara-directed'. In their very fabric, the concertos commemorate friendship, and more.

Piano Concerto in D minor Op. 15

The First Piano Concerto grew directly out of Brahms's youthful series of piano sonatas – the first genre in which he had achieved mastery and characteristic expression on a large scale. Of the three sonatas we possess (last in a sequence of at least five[2]), the F♯ minor Op. 2 (1852), a species of fantasy-sonata deriving all its movements from a germinal motif, relates more directly to contemporary musical romanticism than to the classical traditions evoked in the C major Op. 1 (1852–3), whose first movement refers unmistakably to the opening of Beethoven's *Hammerklavier*. The huge F minor Sonata Op. 5 (1853) unites classical and romantic impulses in a powerful synthesis. Its five-movement form manifests structural and expressive innovation: the second of its two Andantes (the 'Rückblick'), with its remarkably 'orchestral' pianism, is a funereal and elegiac negative image of the warmly lyrical first Andante. If none of these sonatas entirely avoids surplus rhetoric, all impress by their capacity for sustained and serious thought on a broad canvas, their challenging bravura technique and Brahms's unusual contrapuntal skill, canonic imitations and other devices 'uniting . . . the old contrapuntal art with the most modern technique', as Adolf Schubring noted in an important early critique.[3] Nevertheless, despite their external complication the emotional life projected by these works is comparatively simple – even in the F minor, with its strong sense of an implied narrative of youthful aspiration, love, misfortune, despair and final victory.

Completed in October 1853 (but not refined for publication until December), that work may well have convinced Brahms he had driven the genre of solo sonata to its current limits. The work vividly exemplifies Schumann's phrase about 'veiled symphonies'; one formal model, indeed, could have been the five-movement narrative of Berlioz's *Symphonie fantastique*. The sheer magniloquence of Brahms's first movement and finale, and the orchestral shadings of his 'Rückblick', already implied a bigger medium. The next keyboard sonata, three movements of which were sketched by April of 1854, was designed for two pianos, not one. This is the work which became the First Piano Concerto. The metamorphoses which produced that result are known in broad outline, but there is much we do not understand. By June, Brahms found that his 'D minor Sonata' for two pianos (begun in the immediate aftermath of Schumann's madness and attempted suicide – a shattering blow for his young protégé) required yet larger forces for the proper expression of its ideas. It demanded to be nothing less than an orchestral symphony, justifying and fulfilling Schumann's prophecy and ardent hope that Brahms should assume the mastership of that form straight away. This symphony was intended, too, as a kind of memorial to Schumann's tragic fate. Brahms envisaged a four-movement design: the dramatic opening movement; an unusual 'slow scherzo' in sarabande tempo; a slow movement *per se* and a finale. Lacking experience in orchestration, however, he continued, through the summer of 1854, to evolve the work in two-piano score, for subsequent instrumentation. The finale was in fact never completed.[4] One problem seems to have been that genuine piano writing, rather than symphonic composition sketch, kept intruding into Brahms's chosen four-hand medium. With J. O. Grimm's assistance, he essayed only an orchestration of the first movement, completed in late July, which provoked Joachim's derision. There matters rested until, in February 1855, Brahms wrote to Clara Schumann how he had dreamt he was playing a piano concerto based upon his 'hapless symphony', consisting of 'the first movement and scherzo with a finale, terribly difficult and grand'.[5] Encouraged by Grimm and Joachim, he slowly effected this transformation. A new version of the first movement was completed in April 1856. However, the scherzo was discarded along with the other symphony movements. (Elements of it eventually found their way into the second movement of *Ein deutsches Requiem*.) It used to be thought that the symphony's slow movement was retained as the concerto's Adagio, but this is a new movement, completed in January 1857, probably after Brahms had achieved his rondo finale, 'difficult and grand' indeed. However, Brahms continued to revise and recast the concerto until 1858: a preliminary version of the whole work was tried over in Hannover, under Joachim's baton, in March of that year, and underwent further revision before the public premiere in 1859.

Had Brahms set out from the first to compose a piano concerto, would he have produced one on a scale so much larger than Mendelssohn's, Liszt's and even Schumann's concertos? The monumentality and symphonic breadth, unheard since Beethoven's E♭ Concerto, proved problematic for audiences and critics of early performances. These aspects were determined, obviously, by the concerto's origins in a symphony that must have been, in Michael Musgrave's phrase, 'the most powerful orchestral utterance in German music since Beethoven's Ninth Symphony in the same key'.[6] But the symphony's first movement was evidently shorter than the concerto movement we know – perhaps even quite terse, though slower in tempo,[7] after the manner of the first movement of Beethoven's Ninth. Refashioning for piano and orchestra presumably justified the more pianistic passages of the symphony sketch, but also brought considerable expansion: not just through the intercalation of entries for the soloist. Joachim's letter of 3 January 1858 to Clara Schumann indicates far-reaching compositional modifications: 'He has added many beautifully quiet connecting passages, which I am sure would please you. The second theme, in particular, is broader and more satisfying. The whole thing seems to me almost too rich. But that is a good fault!'[8]

This suggests Brahms had to expand the movement to accommodate passages of dynamic contrast, balancing the monumental with more lyrical elements. Perhaps also to extend the range of modulation: one thinks immediately of the B♭ minor section, with its effect of remoteness, beginning at bar 45 and anticipating part of the second subject.[9] Though Joachim's phrasing is ambiguous, either the second subject itself was thoroughly revised – making it 'broader and more satisfying' than its original form – or the subject we know replaced, at this late stage, a previous one deficient in those qualities.

The latter interpretation may seem drastic, but Brahms's 1889 revision of the first movement of his B major Trio – composed, like the D minor Sonata/Symphony, in 1854 – jettisoned the original second subject entirely in favour of a new one, causing the whole movement to be recomposed after that point. We tend to assume that Brahms required the thirty-five-year lapse to perform such ruthless surgery. But his painstaking self-criticism was ingrained very early. If the concerto's second subject is indeed new, this might explain why its shape is echoed in the rondo subject of the finale: the echo would then be the original, the resemblance back-composed into the first movement's material.

Joachim's involvement in bringing the D minor Piano Concerto to birth can hardly be overstated. The great violinist, though only two years older than Brahms, had far more extensive orchestral experience, both as composer and as conductor. Brahms, just before he began his two-piano Sonata, attempted an orchestral overture, and it seems likely that both projects were partly engendered by the two-piano transcription of Joachim's *Overture to Shakespeare's 'Hamlet'* he made in the winter of 1853–4. The full scores of the concerto's movements went repeatedly to Joachim for advice and approval. But though Tovey once remarked that 'it is no exaggeration to say that [Brahms] learnt orchestration from Joachim',[10] the relationship was not simply that of pupil to master. In 1855–6, Joachim too was engaged in orchestrating a symphonic work from a two-piano original: Schubert's C major Sonata, the 'Grand Duo' D. 812, which Schumann had thought an arrangement of a lost symphony. And it is Tovey again who records that Joachim bowed to Brahms's advice in perfecting this score.[11]

Most significant of all: throughout 1856–8, Joachim was writing a concerto of his own – in the same key, D minor, as Brahms's and likewise of a size, difficulty and seriousness of purpose hardly approached in the previous thirty years. This was his Second Violin Concerto Op. 11, better known (where it is known at all) as the Concerto in the Hungarian Manner,[12] and still one of the most formidable works in its repertoire. The 'Hungarian Manner' refers, of course, to the full range of melodic and rhythmic imprints, cadential and decorative formulae and exotically inflected scales which made up the 'gypsy' style familiar to Central European café society and already enthusiastically exploited for purposes of local colour by Joachim's fellow countryman Liszt. Brahms too had begun his lifelong romance with this exotic resource in his early *Hungarian Song* Variations. Joachim, however, was at this period in full withdrawal from Liszt's circle, where previously he had been a protégé. What was unusual in Joachim's case was his determination to ennoble this nationalist style – take it, as it were, out of Liszt's hands – by absorbing its characteristics into the fabric of a work which is otherwise a very fully developed post-classical concerto. The historical process which till recently consigned Joachim's *Hungarian Concerto* to near-oblivion consequently exaggerated the solitude of Brahms's achievement. Probably we should see the First Piano Concerto as emerging out of a shared concern to restore Beethovenian dignity and architectural logic to the concerto form: a concern maybe more pressing for Joachim (who had already perpetrated a one-movement concerto in the approved Lisztian manner) than Brahms, to whom Joachim's concerto is dedicated and who once wrote that his ideal concert programme would consist of his First Piano Concerto followed by his friend's *Hungarian Concerto*.

Despite their wide divergences of musical character, these two D minor concertos descend directly from Beethoven's Piano Concerto in C minor: especially in the scale of their opening tuttis and the determined integration of the solo instrument into an unfolding symphonic argument (in which virtuosity serves the more vividly to delineate musical ideas). Above all, the respective finales are clearly modelled on that of Beethoven's concerto, both in their large modified rondo plan and in such details as the phrase-structure of their principal subjects, the placing of cadenza-like links and the occurrence of a fugato-variation of the rondo theme.[13] Brahms's D major Adagio, however, stands equally remote from Joachim's ternary 'Romanze' movement in G and Beethoven's poised sonata-form Largo (which, were Beethoven's concerto in D minor, would be in F♯ major). This is the most personal area of the First Piano Concerto, and one which – like all Brahms's concerto slow movements – seems to draw almost explicitly on vocal archetypes. In his autograph full score, Brahms underlaid the words 'Benedictus qui venit in nomine Domini' beneath the serene violin–viola theme in the opening bars, syllabically broken in the manner of a singing text – and, as George Bozarth has shown,[14] he considered having the words thus printed in the score as eventually published in 1871, but finally decided against. This text caused some early commentators to suspect the theme to be a quotation from the lost a cappella Mass he was working on at the same period. When movements of this so-called 'Missa Canonica' resurfaced in recent years, it proved to have a quite different Benedictus. Yet it can hardly be denied that the orchestral writing of the concerto's Adagio owes much to Brahms's study of Renaissance religious polyphony, especially Palestrina.

The Benedictus quotation points rather to a possible literary origin for such polyphonic textures. Siegfried Kross has noted acutely that, in E. T. A. Hoffmann's novel *Kater Murr*, this is the inscription over the door of the Benedictine Abbey of Kanzheim, where Kapellmeister Johannes Kreisler finally gains a measure of peace.[15] *Kater Murr*, of course, was one of the young Brahms's favourite books, the principal source for his adopting his Hoffmannesque *alter ego* of 'Johannes Kreisler junior'. This does not necessarily negate the more traditional view that the Benedictus text refers to Schumann, whom Brahms and Joachim both called 'Mynheer Domini'. Indeed it seems more reasonable to assume that the Adagio as a whole enshrines several levels of reference. The idea of an instrumental Requiem – latent, as it were, in the original plan of the D minor symphony – may hover over the movement, not only here at the opening but in the chorale-like writing for the woodwind choir after bar 70, and in the generally withdrawn and contemplative style of the solo part. This latter aspect, however, reminds us that Brahms also described the movement to Clara Schumann as 'a gentle portrait of you'.[16] The quality of intimate dialogue between piano and orchestra underlines the effect that here, after the very public heroics of the first movement, we are permitted to glimpse a far more private side of the composer. The piano writing is more improvisatory and decorative in effect than elsewhere in the concerto, and the delicately understated cadenza may reflect aspects of Clara's pianism as well as Brahms's.[17]

Violin Concerto in D major Op. 77

Almost twenty years elapsed after the completion of this concerto before Brahms returned to the genre with a violin concerto of his own for Joachim: a task he might have been expected to fulfil much earlier, given his closeness to Joachim and the latter's international eminence as a soloist. Perhaps, among many possible deterrents, he scrupled to spoil the *Hungarian Concerto*'s chances to establish itself in the repertoire. By 1878 he probably felt he had waited long enough – and in the meantime had attained a complete command of the orchestra, demonstrated most recently in the two symphonies completed in 1876–7. The Violin Concerto evolved through the second half of 1878 in close consultation with Joachim, their collaboration continuing well into the following year, after the premiere, with extensive refinement of the solo part. Though Joachim's role in this was vital, it was not always decisive for the final form of particular passages.[18]

In this concerto too, though evolved over a much shorter period than the First Piano Concerto, Brahms made drastic modifications to his original design. Once again he had planned a work in four movements. Almost unprecedented in a violin concerto, this scheme would presumably have produced a work even larger than Joachim's; but at a late stage Brahms decided to jettison his two middle movements – one of them a scherzo – in favour of the single slow movement we know (which he termed 'a feeble Adagio'). As the four-movement Second Piano Concerto bears out, it is unlikely that even his original intention was to create a symphony-concerto hybrid.[19] Rather, that he felt the need (to which he surrendered in that work) for a large canvas with the optimum number of areas of contrast, provided by four rather than three well-defined musical characters. For over twenty-five years he had been accustomed to such formal resources in his concerted chamber music. Perhaps the prospect of undue length eventually deterred him, considering the slow progress which both his Piano Concerto and Joachim's *Hungarian Concerto* had so far made in the world. None the less, the Violin Concerto certainly manifests affinities with Brahms's Second Symphony of the previous year: they share the same key, and their first movements – in each case a large, unhurried Allegro non troppo in 3/4 time, romantic in instrumental colouring – evoke a similar sense of opulent and sometimes shadowed pastoral.

Here, however, the 'symphonic' elements are held in an ideal balance with (which means they give the impression of having been subordinated to) the demands of an eloquent violin part. It is, in fact, the weightiest and meatiest violin solo since – Joachim's *Hungarian Concerto*. Yet the impression it creates is mercurial, voluble, rhapsodic: a sustained evocation of the effect of spontaneous improvisation, even though every phrase plays its role in a consummately planned symphonic scheme. Truly we may say of this concerto, as Brahms wrote to Clara Schumann: 'It is a magnificent piece, of remarkable freedom in its invention; it sounds as if [the composer] were fantasising, and everything is masterfully conceived and executed.'[20]

These words, however, described the Concerto No. 22 in A minor by Viotti, published in 1803, which Brahms also called 'my very special passion'. It was a passion he shared with Joachim, who wrote a cadenza to it, and whose playing belonged to the classical French school of which Viotti was considered the founder. The A minor Concerto had a direct bearing, as we shall see, on Brahms's own Double Concerto in that key. But this letter (of June 1878) demonstrates that it was very much in his thoughts while composing his Violin Concerto as well. Brahms, indeed, ranks it with the Mozart concertos: no idle comparison, for it is a work of substance as well as brilliance, with a strain of turbulent proto-romantic feeling underlying its smoothly deployed classical forms.

Despite all the differences of period language and formal decorum, we can sense a community of expression between Viotti and Brahms. Yet if Viotti's concerto represented the expressive ideal which Brahms felt himself striving towards, there are few archaising tendencies in his own work. The Adagio's striking opening on paired woodwind and horns, recalling the plangent wind-band sound of the 'Corale St. Antoni' which Brahms took from an eighteenth-century Feld-Partita for his *Variations on a Theme of Haydn*, is a notable exception, but in sonority only. Here as throughout he brings to bear the full resources of romantic harmony and instrumentation to produce the most substantial violin concerto since Beethoven: indeed, a work clearly composed against the background of Beethoven's concerto. In this slow movement, however, the character is of a song without words subjected to intense variation, the solo oboe and then the violin taking the place of a female voice.[21]

Modern instrumental virtuosity, in the traditions of Paganini, Ernst and Joachim himself, likewise receives its full due. Aside from the actual technical challenges of the solo part, this aspect is most prominent in those elements of the 'Hungarian Manner' with which the work is so richly endowed, entirely appropriate in a work intended for, and in part as a homage to, Joachim. The manner is firmly established in the soloist's very first utterance, dramatically entering on the lowest G and passion- ately and volubly spanning its entire gamut in bravura recreation of what had been the bucolic, triadic simplicity of the work's opening theme; and it is confirmed many times over before we reach the finale, which some commentators have gone so far as to term a 'gypsy rondo'. Yet Brahms, who loved the 'Hungarian Manner' as deeply as any composer of his century, and deployed it copiously in intervening chamber and instru- mental works, tends not, in this concerto, to use the 'gypsy' melodic for- mulae which were such a piquant stylistic component of Joachim's *Hungarian Concerto*. Hungarian traits are achieved by more generalised suggestion: the rondo theme in thirds, the cimbalom-like rush of the accompaniment, the rhythmic structure and syncopation.

But Brahms's most striking homage to the virtuoso tradition (though it might be counted another 'archaising' element) is his decision to leave the first-movement cadenza to be supplied by the performer: a gap which Joachim filled in so exemplary a fashion that his remains the standard model, entirely of a piece with the rest of a concerto conceived to reflect, and with the benefit of, his playing style. The existence of so many later cadenzas of merit, however, shows that Brahms had set a problem of enduring fascination.[22]

Second Piano Concerto

1878 was also the year Brahms began his Second Piano Concerto, in B♭, only to lay it aside to concentrate on the Violin Concerto. Completion was delayed until 1881. This time Brahms had planned a work in three move- ments, which he subsequently expanded to four, introducing as the second movement a scherzo derived in some degree from the scherzo drafted for the Violin Concerto.[23] The result was his longest concerto, still one of the largest in the repertoire, and one in which the potential of the concerto form as a symphony manqué seems most patent.

Yet among Brahms's concertos the B♭ has the fewest classical affinities. Its expressive stance is, from its opening bars (piano musingly duetting with the woodland mysteries of the horn), frankly romantic and personal, in places maybe even confessional. If the work mimics another genre it is not the symphony, but the concerted chamber ensemble, especially those large works for piano and strings of which Brahms was by now such a settled master: such as the three piano quartets, and in the first movement, with the soloistic horn, the Horn Trio as well. Despite the heroic outbursts and large paragraphing the predominant effect is one of intimacy, an intimacy most openly displayed in the last two movements but palpable from the horn–piano dialogue of the very opening. The pianist is often a listener and responder to other instrumental voices: true dialogue, a sharing of the melos, chamber-musical give and take of ideas and mutual exploration of their consequences, seem to be part of this concerto's essential meaning.

Whereas the First Concerto was a work of youthful aspiration – and in that sense also a clear continuation of the early piano sonatas – the Second is very much a product of mature reflection, apparently informed by a lifetime's experience, and by long memories. The piano part, which most players agree is even more taxing that that of the First, bristles with the kind of virtuoso technical challenges which had excited Brahms's lively interest for decades. It represents (above all in the first movement) a continuation of the modern (indeed, 'post-Lisztian') bravura approach demonstrated in the Op. 35 *Variations on a Theme of Paganini*. Yet as the concerto proceeds the soloist recedes from his heroic prominence, until in the third (and most 'chamber-musical') movement he has become an accompanist to sweeter voices.

Is it fanciful to see in this shift the changing role of pianism in Brahms's own life? Though he remained an active player in concertos, chamber music and song, his early ambitions as a solo virtuoso, so manifest in the piano sonatas, had been laid aside by the 1860s in favour of the act of composition. In the early 1850s the young Brahms's vigorous and original pianistic talents were the very basis of his musical personality – the basis, too, of his compositional work – but after the First Piano Concerto this was no longer the case. The piano, always vital, came gradually to occupy a different role in his life, less for public display, more for private study and intimate meditation.

Thus in one aspect the B♭ Concerto suggests itself as a kind of pianistic autobiography. The first movement, whose quality of carefully structured improvisation is even more marked than in the Violin Concerto, plausibly presents a portrait of the young virtuoso, responding to the voice of Nature (the horn theme) with a hugely confident display of pianistic technique. A lion of the keyboard discovers a most ample stage on which to flex his powers. But the scherzo intervenes, in D minor. For Brahms this is a key of catastrophic associations – of Schumann's suicide attempt and his own personal crisis, to judge by the First Piano Concerto's 1854 origins, and by the D minor Ballade, also of that year, whose dramatisation of the Scots Border Ballad 'Edward' appears to symbolise the tangle of Brahms's feelings for both Schumanns. This agitated movement is a *tragic* scherzo, directly opposing the boundless confidence of the first movement. The almost neo-Baroque, Handelian style of its robust and enlivening central trio perhaps represents the saving grace of study, the power of the music of the past to strengthen and stabilise the composer – as Brahms's Baroque studies had strengthened him, issuing at length in the Op. 24 Handel Variations.

The Andante slow movement then indicates a period of withdrawal, of self-communing at the keyboard, almost of self-effacement. In Brahms's own solo output this mood is most clearly felt in the long series of late pieces which had begun during the 1870s with the Op. 76 *Klavierstücke*. The wonderful main theme, however, is entrusted to the solo cello: the piano muses round it, decorates it, dialogues with the cello as a subordinate partner, and is essentially an accompanist to the clarinets in their contrasting F♯ episode. The extent to which this movement resembles a cello–piano duo suggests (quite apart from the tenderness of the main idea) some imaginative connection with Clara Schumann. The Romanze slow movement of her own Piano Concerto, even more of a cello–piano duo, could be cited as a forerunner here.

The finale, with its Hungarian rhythms, its relaxed evocation of dance and song, evokes another side of Brahms's pianism: his sizeable output of *Unterhaltungsmusik*, music for enjoyment and relaxation, most notably in the Hungarian Dances and *Liebeslieder-Walzer*. This finale remains of the highest artistic quality (and is no relaxation for the pianist); but the popular elements blent in it are essential to any rounded portrait of its composer.

Any such interpretation of the B♭ Concerto must perforce remain speculative, and attempts to force Brahms's music into a strictly programmatic scheme are likely to be misguided. Yet the wealth of acknowledged personal reference in his music generally encourages a 'reading' of this concerto; and speculation hovers most legitimately around the Andante, whose intimate tones have intrigued commentators for over a century. Here again, as in the Adagio of the Violin Concerto, the music evokes a vocal rather than instrumental conception. It is an ancient commonplace of Brahms scholarship that the cello theme resembles, or rather presages, his *Lied* Op. 105 No. 2, 'Immer leiser wird mein Schlummer' ('Ever fainter grows my slumber') – a song of the approach of death, composed in 1886. More recently, Constantin Floros has drawn attention to the fact that in the F♯ major episode the first clarinet quotes the lines 'Vater in der Höhe, / aus der Fremde fleht dein Kind' ('Father in Heaven, from afar thy child implores') from Brahms's Schenkendorf setting 'Todessehnen' ('Yearning for death') Op. 86 No. 6.[24]

This is an impressive identification, for the allusion is not simply melodic. Allowing for re-shaping to the Andante's 6/4 metre and to the concertante nature of the piano part, the allusion is literal as regards key and pitch, and nearly so for harmonic background. The song dates from 1878, therefore contemporary with Brahms's initial work on the concerto, and is rich in indications (among them the use of the shared Schumann–Brahms 'Clara motif') that it addresses Clara Schumann.

Schenkendorf's opening stanza asks 'who will rid my soul of the secret, heavy burden that, the more I hide it, clings the more strongly to me?' The F♯ minor line to which Brahms sets this question clearly evokes the Dies Irae,[25] suggesting that the burden will only be released by death. Later the text states that the poet and the 'sisterly being' may only be wed ('vermählt') in death. The appeal to the Heavenly Father quoted by the clarinet is for entrance to that realm where 'the language of spirits calls life by the name of love'.

Perhaps this most intimate and dreamlike of Brahms's concerto movements should therefore be considered in the light of 'Todessehnen' as a whole? Though the cello theme is in no direct sense a quotation of the song's opening, the rhythmic and intervallic profiles are such it seems legitimate to hazard that the song theme may be the background out of which it emerged (see Example 7.1).[26] One could speculate further that the cello–piano duo enshrines a symbolic dialogue with Clara Schumann; and that the secrets of that dialogue touch upon the approach of death and the mysteries of the hereafter, if there is one. On this reading the subsequent reinterpretation of the cello theme in 'Immer leiser wird mein Schlummer' probably arises from a continuing association of the ideas of death and slumber with this basic musical shape.

Concerto for Violin and Cello [Double Concerto] Op. 102

The solo cello's prominence in this Andante already presages Brahms's final and most remarkable contribution to the concerto genre, the Double

Example 7.1
(a) Brahms, 'Todessehnen' Op. 86 No. 6, bars 1–4
(b) Brahms, Piano Concerto in B♭ Op. 83, movement 3, bars 1–3
(c) Brahms, 'Immer leiser wird mein Schlummer' Op. 105 No. 2, bars 1–3

(a) Langsam

Ach, wer nimmt von mei - ner See - le die ge - hei - me, schwe - re Last,

(b) Andante

(c)

Im - mer lei - ser wird mein Schlum - mer

Concerto for violin and cello. Joachim's quartet partner since 1879, the cellist Robert Hausmann, had attempted over several years to persuade Brahms to compose a cello concerto, but what Brahms eventually produced in 1887 was a virtually unprecedented form: a duo-concerto where the cello, though often the instigator of musical events, shares the glory in equipoise with the violin. Specifically, in the first instance, Joachim's violin. The year following their collaboration on the Violin Concerto had brought a serious breach in their friendship, when Brahms chivalrously took Amalie Joachim's side when her husband instigated divorce proceedings against her. Joachim did not return to speaking terms with Brahms until 1883, and the relationship never regained its previous cordiality, which the Double Concerto was obviously in part an attempt to restore.

Though Brahms was not wholly successful, Joachim deeply appreciated the gesture. His professional esteem and admiration for his friend's music had never flagged, and once again he contributed to a significant extent in the shaping and refinement of the new concerto's solo string parts.[27] In October 1887 he partnered Hausmann in the Cologne premiere, under Brahms's baton. Among the features which indicate to whom the work is especially addressed are the violin's first entry after the tutti exposition, shaping the first theme's salient three-note figure to Joachim's personal 'F–A–E' motto; and the second subject, long recognised as referring to a favourite work, namely Viotti's A minor Concerto, already involved in Brahms's other concerto for Joachim. The model for

Example 7.2
(a) Viotti, Violin Concerto No. 22 in A minor,
movement 1, bars 1–2
(b) Brahms, Double Concerto in A minor Op. 102,
movement 1, bars 1–2

(a)

(b)

Brahms's theme is Viotti's opening subject; here, however, there is no question of simple quotation but rather the kind of creative allusion best shared between close friends (Example 7.2). Brahms's adoption of a concertino-like solo duo might indicate a throwback to the principles of the Baroque concerto grosso, unsurprising in a composer who had drawn so many fruitful lessons from the music of that period; but the behaviour and phraseology of the Double Concerto hardly bear this out. No doubt his available models included Bach's two-violin Concerto, but Mozart's violin–viola Sinfonia Concertante and Beethoven's Triple Concerto were surely more significant influences,[28] and the result is in fact the most frankly romantic of Brahms's concertante works, in his most advanced style.

Even more than the B♭ Piano Concerto, the Double Concerto is 'chamber music for soloists and orchestra', and takes its place in the grand sweep of Brahms's late chamber music, passionate and exploratory in its handling of instrumental resources, that stretches from the F major Cello Sonata to the G major String Quintet. The conception, perhaps, is closest to that of an expanded piano trio, the orchestra assuming the place of the pianoforte; and there are strong expressive links between the Double Concerto and Brahms's C minor Piano Trio Op. 101, completed the previous summer. The trio's four concise movements have yielded in the concerto, however, to a three-movement plan dominated by a large opening movement not merely symphonic in outline but enlarged by a brilliant cadenza-like introduction presenting cello and violin, separately and together, in bravura solos significantly marked in *modo d'un recitativo*.

Chamber music or not, the Double Concerto extends to its whole design the analogies with vocal music adumbrated in Brahms's previous concerto slow movements. The very idea of two soloists in dialogue and duet suggests operatic parallels. It is maybe significant that some of Brahms's friends, in the year of the work's composition, had gained the idea he might be writing an opera; and that when the Landgrave of Hesse asked him about this, he replied that he was 'composing the entr'actes'. The idea of treating a concerto soloist like an opera character goes back at least as far as Spohr's *Gesangszene* for violin and orchestra, but by employing two instruments of contrasted range and tone Brahms vastly enlarged the dramatic potential. He invests the utterances of cello and violin with something of the sexual polarity of baritone/tenor hero and soprano heroine. Perhaps there is a further implication that the soloists, in this work conceived in the cause of friendship, represent Brahms and Joachim themselves: if so it is mildly ironic that Joachim, who could only be represented in his own instrument, and who Brahms believed had wronged his wife, should therefore have to take the feminine part of the discourse. No less ironic than that Brahms, so often self-conscious about his high tenor voice, should award himself the deep masculine cello register.

But of course the music itself, in the fantasy and imagination with which its materials are developed, transcends any such narrow interpretation. The warmth and strength of romantic feeling, palpable throughout the first movement and reaching its apogee in the slow movement with its ardent evocations of song and choral serenade, make the protagonists representatives of love in all its aspects. But virtuosity for mere display is avoided: the soloists are entirely integrated into the ongoing development of the work's material. Though violin and cello are strongly characterised as individuals, Brahms just as often combines them texturally as a single entity, in the manner of string–piano chamber music. Thus their ideal union occurs in the service of the musical ideas, typified by the ecstatic string roulades of the coda after the wit and geniality of the finale – once again a 'Hungarian' rondo in honour of Joachim, resolving all remaining conflicts in the spirit of the dance.

8 The scope and significance of the choral music

DANIEL BELLER-MCKENNA

If he will only point his magic wand to where the powers amassed in the orchestra and chorus lend him its might, yet more wonderful glimpses into the mysteries of the spirit world await us.
(ROBERT SCHUMANN, 'NEUE BAHNEN', 1853)[1]

Commentators from Brahms's century and our own have largely interpreted Schumann's prophetic remark about the 'powers amassed in the orchestra and chorus', on which Brahms should draw, as a reference to the Beethovenian symphonic tradition at mid-century and, specifically, the challenges posed by the choral finale of Beethoven's Ninth. Robert Schumann had certainly led his readers in that direction when, earlier in 'Neue Bahnen' ('New Paths'), he refers to sonatas that were 'veiled symphonies' among those pieces the twenty-year-old Brahms played for Clara and himself in October of 1853. Nevertheless, it is likely that Brahms and his contemporaries understood Schumann's comment to refer at least as much to orchestrally accompanied choral music as to choral symphonies or symphonic music more generally. Schumann, after all, produced many of his large choral works during the last decade of his life, by which time his own style had veered decisively towards Mendelssohn's more traditional legacy. And when Brahms did finally establish himself as a major force on the German music scene in 1868 he did so with a major choral work of his own, *Ein deutsches Requiem* Op. 45, the largest piece he was ever to compose.

Given the tremendous success of that work and the various shorter works for chorus and orchestra that followed around 1870 (*Alto Rhapsody* Op. 53, *Schicksalslied* Op. 54, *Triumphlied* Op. 55), it is easy to lose sight of the fact that by 1868 Brahms had already produced a large number of choral works of more modest proportions and that he continued to compose choral music of all types for the next two decades. And whereas Brahms's status as a composer of choral music is much acknowledged in the choral world, his signficance in this area among musicians at large has been overshadowed by his reputation as a symphonist and chamber music composer. To wit, a survey of scholarly literature on Brahms from the last quarter century reveals a wealth of material on his instrumental music and songs, but little on the choral music. Since Siegfried Kross's comprehensive dissertation *Die Chorwerke von Johannes Brahms* was published in 1958 only subsequent publications of Hans Michael Beuerle and Virginia Hancock's 1983 dissertations have substantially dealt with the choral repertoire.[2]

Modern scholars' focus on Brahms's symphonies as the realisation of Schumann's prophecy probably stems from the trend, already begun during Brahms's career, to elevate the aesthetic status of instrumental music as a professional art over vocal music, especially above choral music, whose performance fell more and more to amateur groups from the middle of the nineteenth century on.[3] Indeed, the tension between the relative status of choral music as compared with such genres as chamber music and the symphony (and, for that matter, the *Lied*) played a direct role in Brahms's own career. For whereas he presented himself to the Schumann circle in 1853 as a piano virtuoso with a ready made catalogue of solo and chamber works for his instrument, it was only through a study of contrapuntal techniques during the later 1850s that Brahms honed his compositional skills. [4] The product of those endeavours was a wealth of small-scale choral pieces that served as examples of the archaic techniques he was mastering and also as material for the choirs he concurrently directed at Detmold (1857–9) and Hamburg (1859–60). Thus choral music formed an important vehicle through which Brahms developed the style of his 'first maturity'.

Playing the role of a professional directing amateurs may also have satisfied a social need for Brahms. It is telling that he was never able to commit himself for very long to a major position with an orchestra: i.e. as a leader of other *professional* musicians. Rather, most of his directing positions were with non-professional choral organisations. Hans Michael Beuerle has even suggested that his early choral positions at Detmold and Hamburg might have provided Brahms, son of a working-class musician, with a sense of bourgeois respectability.[5] Brahms initially continued this pattern during his early years in Vienna when he directed the amateur Vienna Singakademie in 1863–4. His only post as an 'orchestral conductor' *per se* came with his duties as conductor and artistic director for the Musikverein of the Gesellschaft der Musikfreunde in Vienna from 1872 to 1875, which included the society's orchestra as well as its Singverein.

Each of his conducting positions brought Brahms into contact with one or more of the choral music traditions of his century. As mentioned above, his experience with choirs during the late 1850s provided Brahms with an opportunity to try out his own 'exercises' in the study of early music. More importantly, perhaps, it allowed him to enter a nineteenth-century tradition of performing music of earlier eras, ranging from a cappella works by Renaissance masters like Isaac, Palestrina and Byrd to examples from the German Baroque including Bach cantatas and Handel choruses.[6] Similarly, Brahms's own folk-song settings shared the stage at Detmold, Hamburg and Vienna with like-sounding works by his nineteenth-century predecessors in that genre, as did his more artful choral settings of romantic poetry.[7]

By the time he assumed his last steady post in 1872 as conductor of the Musikverein, however, Brahms had already composed many of his own larger choral works: *Rinaldo* Op. 50, *Ein deutsches Requiem* Op. 45, the *Alto Rhapsody* Op. 53, the *Schicksalslied* Op. 54, and the *Triumphlied* Op. 55. And whereas he was certainly familiar with the large-scale oratorios, cantatas and odes by many leading choral composers of the eighteenth and nineteenth centuries, his performance of that repertoire in the early 1870s did not influence his own compositions in those genres so much as it reflected his status as a major composer of choral music in Germany by that time and his subsequent desire to explore the existing choral/orchestral repertoire as a conductor.

The early choral works

Although there is some indication that Brahms composed choral music during his teens, his first true efforts in choral composition stem from a series of contrapuntal exercises that he exchanged between 1856 and 1860 with his close friend the violinist and composer Joseph Joachim.[8] Brahms embarked on the counterpoint project as a means towards mastering all types of contrapuntal writing.[9] Given the nature of the repertoire on which he sought to model his exercises (keyboard fugues of the eighteenth century and a cappella vocal music of the sixteenth to eighteenth centuries), Brahms's output predictably fell into two categories: (1) preludes and fugues for organ and (2) choral works. Among the early choral works that can be securely connected to the composition exchange are the motet 'Schaffe in mir, Gott, ein rein Herz' Op. 29 No. 2, the *Geistliches Lied* Op. 30, Nos. 1 and 2 of the *Drei geistliche Chöre* for women's chorus Op. 37, and the 'Missa Canonica', WoO 18 (portions of which were later reused in the motet 'Warum ist das Licht gegeben' Op. 74 No. 1).

Most of these works bear traces of the technical exercises from which they emerged, as demonstrated by the earliest entry in the exchange, a four-voice (SSAT) Benedictus that Brahms sent to Joachim on 24 March 1856 (Example 8.1).[10] Although some portions of the 'Missa' pointed up Brahms's inexperience as a choral composer, the Benedictus already displays his budding potential as a contrapuntist.[11] Brahms artfully constructed a tonally symmetrical canon by bringing in the four voices as a

Example 8.1 Benedictus in F major from 'Missa Canonica' in C major WoO 18

pair of entries at the (lower) fourth: F–C (soprano 1 – soprano 2), B♭–F
(alto–tenor).[12] Together with its gently proportioned arc-like phrases,
the balance of this symmetrical tonal structure creates a romanticised
caricature of Palestrina style. And if the Benedictus is perhaps too perfect
to pass for sixteenth-century counterpoint, it is nevertheless finely
crafted and full of evidence for the careful attention to phrasing and
structure that would soon become a hallmark of Brahms's style. Other
remnants of the composition exchange with Joachim are more daring in
their use of contrapuntal devices. Accompanying the Benedictus in the
letter to Joachim of 24 March was the opening portion of a five-voice
(SATBB) setting of Luther's translation of Psalm 51, v. 12, which Brahms

Example 8.2 Schaffe in mir, Gott, ein rein Herz' Op. 29 No. 2, bars 1–25

later used as the opening section of the motet Op. 29 No. 2 (Example 8.2). Here Brahms ably conceals the augmentation canon between soprano and bass 2 amidst a German Baroque stylistic veneer. More impressive still is the well-crafted double canon at the ninth that undergirds the modern-sounding *Geistliches Lied* Op. 30 for SATB and organ, one of the few accompanied choral items from the composition exchange.

The presence of the Benedictus and the first two *Geistliche Chöre* from Op. 37 in the part books of the Hamburg Women's Chorus shows that Brahms pressed his studies into service when repertoire was needed for his fledgling choir.[13] Moreover, he also composed several works directly for this chorus, including the sacred accompanied works *Ave Maria* Op. 12 and *Psalm 13* Op. 27. Brahms also composed one accompanied choral work for Detmold, the *Begräbnisgesang* Op. 13 (1858). Any hint of archaic style in these non-canonic works merely colours their overwhelmingly modern affect. Siegfried Kross rightly points to the 'astounding dependence on Mendelssohn' as a defining style feature in these works, especially when compared with the a cappella sacred choruses and more folk-like choral works of this period, Op. 22 and Op. 44 (discussed below), in which he 'completely found his own voice'.[14]

Although these latter *opera* point towards the separate role that folk-song played in defining Brahms's musical style, as do the numerous folk-song arrangements that he made for his Hamburg and Vienna choirs, we should not overlook the historicist connection between the two concepts (archaic counterpoint and *das Volk*) and their respective importance for Brahms's approach to choral music.[15] Each of these concepts represented a connection to the cultural past, and each had been idealised in its own way by German Romantics from the turn of the century to the generation that preceded Brahms. Choral music was able to capture both of these romantic ideals in distinct ways: sonically, the a cappella choir represented the musical purity of the sixteenth century and, by extension, the religious purity of the Catholic era to which the music of Palestrina and his predecessors was attached;[16] socially, the choral movement had taken on democratic and *völkisch* connotations during the post-Napoleonic era.[17] And although all of the choirs with which Brahms worked were decidedly bourgeois institutions (even aristocratic in the case of Detmold), the folk-aura had become thoroughly dispersed through the various social strata that choral groups occupied by 1850, as witnessed by the numerous sophisticated choral settings of folk or folk-like poetry in the repertoire of that era. The best example of this within Brahms's own *œuvre* from c. 1860 are the Twelve Songs and Romances Op. 44 for women's voices (SSAA) with optional piano *ad libitum*. Brahms's ambivalent use in this set of the piano, which often provides more than mere doubling of the vocal parts, reflects the highbrow distillation of folk art so typical for the choral-*Lied* genre.

Perhaps the most interesting admixture of folk-song and religion within Brahms's choral output are the seven *Marienlieder* Op. 22, most of which also belonged to the repertoire of the Hamburg Frauenchor.[18] Brahms's predilection for texts on the Marian legend are attested by his multiple performances of Eccard's 'Übers Gebirg Maria geht' and the many texts on the subject that he copied out of various folk-song collections.[19] Although he retained the older melodies that accompanied some of the texts to Op. 22 when he set them in other contexts (i.e. solo songs

Example 8.3a 'Der englische Gruß' Op. 22 No. 1, bars 1–6

and alternate choral settings), for the *Marienlieder* Brahms fashioned his own melodies and surrounded them with suave yet simple choral accompaniments.[20]

When Brahms described the set as 'somewhat in the style of old German church- and folk-songs' he may well have been referring to the subtle contrapuntal infusions to the otherwise homorhythmic choral setting, as is evident in the opening bars of 'Der englische Gruß', the first number in the set (Example 8.3a). Brahms merely suggests imitative counterpoint through the separate entrances of the soprano and bass against the alto–tenor pair. For as the identical text and rhythm in each voice reveals, the consecutive entrances in bars 1 and 2 produce little more than a thickening of the texture from two, to three and then to four voices. And whereas a canonic effect is implied by the soprano's initial arpeggio E♭–B♭–G (an inversion of the tenor's preceding G–B♭–E♭), such triadic repetition has less to do with imitation *per se* than with the unfolding nature of Brahms's melody, which seizes on the dyad B♭–G to emphasise the words 'Gegrußet' and 'Maria', before expanding into a complete descending scale fragment (B♭–A♭–G–F–E♭) to round off the opening phrase on the words 'Mutter der Gnaden'. Even when Brahms abandons the strophic form of the song in the sixth and final verse to introduce an initial period that is indeed imitative, the counterpoint is pictorial: the gradual increase in texture and volume depicts the chorus of angels ('sie sangen alle') in its song of praise to Mary (Example 8.3b).

In this song, and in the *Marienlieder* generally, Brahms employs counterpoint for an atmospheric or colouristic effect, i.e. to invoke the idea of 'old German church-song'. Likewise, the Catholic-tinged subject of the texts should be understood as a romantic effect and not as a religious statement by Brahms. Similarly, the frequent use of strophic settings, diatonic harmonies and simple melodic phrasing add a modernised folk-like aura to these Marian texts that have been stripped of their authentically *völkisch* melodies – a thoroughly nineteenth-century

Example 8.3b 'Der englische Gruß' Op. 22 No. 1, bars 38–52

approach to the melding of high art, low art and (through the displaced religiosity of the texts) stylised spirituality.

A different sort of affectation is evoked by the Five Songs for men's chorus Op. 41, which were composed between 1861 and 1865. These TTBB *Lieder* are the only a cappella works for *Männerchor* that Brahms composed, a surprisingly meagre output in a genre which thrived during the nineteenth century and for which Brahms's predecessors and contemporaries produced comparatively large numbers. Some of these choruses (especially Nos. 2 and 5) speak to a chauvinistic and blatantly militant side of Brahms's well-documented German patriotism, a quality that helps account for the low esteem in which Op. 41 is generally held nowadays.

The middle-period choral works

If *Ein deutsches Requiem* Op. 45 looms large in Brahms's overall career, it positively dominates the choral music of his middle period. Although Brahms continued to compose a cappella and piano-accompanied choral works during these years, they are few in number and primarily continue the line of such works from the early 1860s. By contrast, the *Requiem*, completed in 1868, marked a monumental step forward on every level in Brahms's development as a composer. Whether one accepts Op. 45 or the First Symphony of 1876 as the rightful fulfilment of Schumann's expectations in 'Neue Bahnen,' *Ein deutsches Requiem* proved Brahms capable of handling larger forms and extended performing forces. A handful of earlier works had already pointed the way towards some of Brahms's achievements in Op. 45, particularly the *Begräbnisgesang* Op. 13, a multi-sectional work for SATBB chorus and wind band (2 oboes; 2 B♭ clarinets; 2 bassoons; 2 E♭ horns; 3 trombones; tuba; timpani in C and G) composed for Detmold in 1858–9. Whereas the text alone, a sixteenth-century funeral ode from the *Gesangbuch der böhmischen Brüdern* (1531), points towards the general character of the *Requiem*, certain details of its musical composition foreshadow specific movements of the later work: the dark timbre of the wind writing resembles the low string scoring (minus violins) in the opening movement of Op. 45; and the tightly fashioned arc-shape of the opening melody in Op.13 resembles (in various ways) that of the choral entrance in the second movement of the *Requiem* (Example 8.4a–b).[21]

Another significant 'study work' for *Ein deutsches Requiem* is the cantata *Rinaldo* Op. 50, on Goethe's adaptation of a scene from Tasso's *Gerusalemme Liberata*. Although it was not premiered until 1869, most of this semi-dramatic work for tenor solo, male chorus and orchestra was composed at Hamburg in 1863 (the separate final chorus 'Auf dem Meere' was added for the first performance at Vienna in 1869). *Rinaldo* shows a far more sophisticated use of the male chorus than Op. 41, and as the closest thing Brahms wrote to a musico-dramatic work, it provides a glimmer of what opera might have sounded like in his hands. Most importantly though, *Rinaldo* is his only work for chorus and full orchestra to predate the *Requiem*, and it displays a fairly secure use of 'the powers amassed' there by the thirty-year-old composer.

Although scholars have long speculated that Brahms may have begun composing the early movements of *Ein deutsches Requiem* in 1859 as part of a less extensive sacred cantata, documentable evidence for most of the piece points to 1865–6 as its primary years of composition. Only portions of the second movement can be dated earlier with any confidence: Albert Dietrich, Brahms's close friend from the Schumann circle, identified the 'funeral march' (presumably the opening orchestral statement, bars 1–22) as part of the aborted D minor sonata/symphony of 1854 from which Brahms eventually fashioned his Op.15 Piano Concerto (1859).[22] The earlier D minor piece was begun in response to Robert Schumann's attempted suicide in 1854 and, together with many of Brahms's later remarks, the connection of that work to movement 2 of Op. 45 suggests that Brahms intended the *Requiem* (in part) as an homage to his mentor. A more immediate impetus, however, was the death of Brahms's mother in 1865. Following his return to Hamburg for her funeral, Brahms devoted most of the winter and spring of 1866 to composing Op. 45 while travelling through Germany and Switzerland.

Example 8.4a *Begräbnisgesang* Op. 13, bars 1–10.

Example 8.4b *Ein deutsches Requiem*, movement 2, bars 22–33

Example 8.5 *Ein deutsches Requiem*, 'germinal' motive

Many commentators have attempted to demonstrate that the *Requiem*'s seven movements are united by a germinal motive, which is articulated in the chorus's first entry: a melodic third followed by a step in the same direction (Example 8.5).[23] In addition, Brahms's own reported comment that a well-known chorale 'lay at the root of the entire work' has led to much speculation about motivic unity in the piece. Scholars generally agree that the chorale in question is 'Wer nur den lieben Gott läßt walten', although some have questioned its identity, most notably Christopher Reynolds, who offers the chorale 'Freu' dich sehr, O meine Seele' as a convincing alternative.[24]

But while certain melodic ideas certainly do reappear, the *Requiem*'s cohesion probably owes more to a general symmetry in its overall

Example 8.6a *Ein deutsches Requiem*, movement 6, bars 82–93

musical form than to some hidden or pervasive motivic unity. One hears this balance most immediately between the first and last movements, which are marked by the textual connection 'selig sind'. Both movements begin in F major with the same distinctive dissonance between the low strings' initial F and the middle strings' ensuing E♭. Then, after a middle section in a contrasting key, each movement returns to the key of F major

Example 8.6b *Schicksalslied* Op. 54, bars 104–24

and ends with the same descending melodic phrase passed among the
voices of the choir, while the harp plays a series of rising figures. Similarly
the second and third movements seem to form a pair that balances with
the sixth: all three move from a minor to a major key and end with a long
contrapuntal choral section. These musical connections aside, however,
symmetry and unity in the *Requiem* ultimately stem from its text.
Brahms carefully combined seventeen separate passages from the Old
and New Testaments and the Apocrypha to create a poetic web of biblical
imagery. The text of movement 1 includes a series of oppositions:
sorrow–comfort, tears–joy, sowing–reaping. Some of this imagery is then
picked up by the text of the second movement, where the farmer waits for
the fruit of the earth before receiving rain, and where joy and gladness

shall replace pain and suffering. In a larger sense, the whole text of the second movement projects the minute oppositions of the previous one, as the transience of human flesh at the movement's outset is pitted against the eternal endurance of the Lord's word at its conclusion. Similar connections across the work's seven movements help to carry the piece through its various views of life and death. In the end, Brahms finds comfort in the knowledge that the dead can rest from their labours because 'ihre Werken folgen ihnen nach' ('their works follow after them').

After a performance of the *Requiem*'s first three movements in Vienna in December 1867 garnered a lukewarm response there, the premiere of the complete work (still lacking movement 6, however) in Bremen on Good Friday, 10 April 1868 earned widespread acclaim and quickly established Brahms as one of Germany's leading young composers. In one great stride, Brahms had combined his years of contrapuntal study with the large-scale gestures of *Rinaldo*. The *Requiem*'s German biblical text provided a historical grounding and philosophical depth to couch Brahms's mixture of modern harmonic language and archaic contrapuntal techniques. And together, the music and text of the *Requiem* captured a personal, philosophical brand of spirituality at mid-century that was uniquely German: a truly *deutsches* Requiem.

In the aftermath of the *Requiem*'s tremendous success, Brahms produced three shorter works for chorus and orchestra: the *Alto Rhapsody* Op. 53 (1869), the *Schicksalslied* Op. 54 (1871) and the *Triumphlied* Op. 55 (1871). Leaving aside momentarily the last work, which is in three movements and based on a biblical text, Op. 53 and Op. 54 may be grouped with the somewhat later *Nänie* Op. 81 (1881) and *Gesang der Parzen* Op. 89 (1882), forming a core repertoire of single-movement works for chorus and orchestra that are based on the highest-quality German authors of Brahms's immediate past: Schiller (Op. 81), Goethe (Op. 53 and Op. 89) and Hölderlin (Op. 54). Each of the works owes something of its musical language and choral style to the *Requiem*, even surpassing it in some instances. For example, the violently rushing C minor string figures that set Paul's prophecy, 'For the trumpet shall sound' ('Denn es wird die Posaune schallen'), from Op. 45 movement 6 are sharpened and more threatening when they reappear in the same key in the Allegro sections of the *Schicksalslied* (Examples 8.6a, 8.6b). At the opposite expressive extreme, the imitative entries of the chorus that are woven into a dance-like rhythmic fabric in the *Requiem*'s fourth movement find a broader, more satisfying realisation in a similarly transitional passage from *Nänie* (Examples 8.7a, 8.7b).

Subject matter also binds three of the four single-movement works, Opp. 54, 81 and 89: these deal in some manner with questions of human

Example 8.7a *Ein deutsches Requiem* Op. 45, movement 4, bars 23–36

Example 8.7b *Nänie* Op. 82, bars 46–55

Example 8.7b (*cont.*)

transience and powerlessness in the face of the gods, who are consistently cast in Grecian (not Judeo-Christian) terms. There is, then, a connection between the philosophical mind-set that lies behind these works and the secularised Lutheran values that inform *Ein deutsches Requiem*. By the middle of Brahms's career, choral music had come to serve as a vessel for the composer's weightiest thoughts and as a means of connecting with German literary traditions.[25]

As the only one of these works to feature a soloist, the *Alto Rhapsody* stands apart from the rest. Moreover, it strikes a decidedly dramatic tone in comparison to the elegiac character of the others. Like the equally dramatic *Rinaldo*, which was also completed and premiered in 1869, the *Alto Rhapsody* is based on a text by Goethe and is set for soloist, male chorus and orchestra. But whereas *Rinaldo* presents its drama in a stylised, artistically removed fashion, the *Alto Rhapsody* has long been understood to be a more genuine expression of the composer's own psyche. Brahms composed the piece during the summer of 1869, as he lamented the betrothal of Clara Schumann's second daughter, Julie, for whom he had recently expressed a thinly veiled marital interest of his own – he sarcastically referred to the work as his 'bridal song for the Schumann princess'.[26]

The excerpted text from Goethe's 'Harzreise im Winter' (verses 5–7) places poignant emphasis on the pain of the misanthrope before dissolving such suffering in a plea to refresh his heart and open his eyes:

Example 8.8a *Alto Rhapsody* Op. 53, bars 17–34

Ach, wer heilet die Schmerzen	Ah, who can heal the pains
Des, dem Balsam zu Gift ward?	Of a man for whom balm has become poison?
Der sich Menschenhaß	Who imbibed hatred of mankind
Aus der Fülle der Liebe trank?	From the Abundance of Love?

Example 8.8b *Alto Rhapsody*, bars 116–19

Brahms sets the bleak text of verses 5–6 to some of his most anguished music, signalled not only by the singularly dissonant bass appoggiatura (B–C beneath a tonic harmony) with which the C minor piece opens, but by the tortuous contour of the vocal line which adorns the return of that figure at bar 18 (Example 8.8a) and which 'loses its way in the thickets'. Similar dissonances mark the tripartite Poco Andante middle segment of the work (bars 48–115), most notably at the thrice repeated word 'Menschenhaß'.

Brahms resolves the tension of the first two sections through a turn to the parallel major and a rocking harp-like pizzicato at the closing Adagio prayer to the 'Vater der Liebe' ('Father of Love'). Also worth noting here is a conspicuous emphasis on plagal cadences, most noticeably at the F–C cadence that concludes the work. Still more telling, perhaps, are the inflected plagal cadences in bars 117 (and 147) (Example 8.8b). The passing B–D dyad on beat 2 in the tenors implies a superimposed dominant harmony against the F–A in the outer parts, an effect more commonly found at the end of works in nineteenth-century sacred choral music: Brahms would later use it to good effect in Op. 74 No. 1 and Op. 109 No. 1. It serves here as a rhetorical marker of the sacred amidst an otherwise secularised prayer. And when heard as an overtly secular statement that contains a prominent influx of spiritual sentiment, the *Alto Rhapsody* may be understood as a counterfoil to *Ein deutsches Requiem* completed just one year earlier.

Of all the choral-orchestral works that Brahms composed around 1870, the *Triumphlied* Op. 55 seems the most unusual to modern audiences. A three-movement work on selected verses from Revelation 19, Brahms began the *Triumphlied* as a 'deutsches Te Deum' during the Franco-Prussian war of 1870 and completed it after the defeat of France and the establishment of the German *Kaiserreich* under Wilhelm I and Chancellor Bismarck in 1871. In Brahms's century the *Triumphlied* was considered the sister work and equal to his *Requiem,* and it remained one of the composer's personal favourites until the end of his life. However, two world wars have rendered this boisterous German praise for a God who 'hat das Reich eingenommen' ('ushered in the Kingdom') nearly intolerable – for German as well as non-German audiences – and the work is now rarely performed.

The later choral works

Brahms composed nearly all of his works for large performing forces between 1868 and 1885; the choral works just discussed derive from the same impulse as all four of Brahms's symphonies, two of his concertos (for Violin Op. 77 and No. 2 for Piano Op. 83) and both of his overtures. In the summer of 1886, just one year after he completed his last symphony, Brahms showed a marked shift towards smaller performing forces by composing a series of three chamber sonatas, one for cello (Op. 99) and two for violin (Opp. 100 and 108), and a piano trio (Op. 101). Similar tendencies were evident in his choral output around this time. Following the *Gesang der Parzen* of 1882, nearly all of Brahms's remaining choral works were a cappella: two groups of secular settings, the Six Songs and Romances Op. 93a (1883) and the Five Songs Op. 104 (1888); and two sets of sacred works, the *Fest- und Gedenksprüche* Op. 109 (1889) and the Three Motets Op. 110 (1890).[27] In addition to these newly composed works, Brahms published in 1891 the Thirteen Canons Op. 113 for women's chorus, a collection made up largely of previously composed canons, including several he wrote for the Hamburg Women's Chorus more than thirty years earlier. The latter set betokens a nostalgic impulse that dominates Brahms's last decade, witnessed as well by the retrospective forty-nine *Deutsche Volkslieder* published in 1893 (WoO 33) and the widely observed introspective mood of so many late instrumental works, most notably the sets of piano pieces Opp. 116–19.

A similar inclination to reminisce may have already motivated the two

Example 8.9 'O Heiland, reiß die Himmel auf' Op. 74 No. 2, bars 56–73

motets of Op. 74, since each contains music that substantially predates their 1878 publication date. The first motet, 'Warum ist das Licht gegeben', re-uses several portions of the youthful 'Missa Canonica', which Brahms apparently abandoned around 1862.[28] Brahms extended his highly chromatic Agnus Dei fugue from that early work into the lengthy first section of the later motet, retexted with Job's agonised complaint and existential 'Why?', which Brahms reiterates as a chordal refrain. An expanded version of the Missa's F major Benedictus (with two bass voices added for the cadential extension of bars 96–103) and a reworking of its

'Dona nobis pacem' are followed by a newly composed cantionale setting of Luther's graveside chorale 'Mit Fried und Freud ich fahr dahin'. Like the *Requiem*, to which it is often compared, the 'Warum' motet displays Brahms's familiarity with the Bible and his ability to fashion from scripture a modern philosophical statement on the meaning of death.

Although the second motet in Op. 74, 'O Heiland, reiß die Himmel auf' also predates 1878, its exact origins are unclear.[29] Whereas the 'Warum' motet presents a variety of historical styles from Palestrina to Bach, Op. 74 No. 2 is a more straightforward imitation of Baroque chorale-variation technique, much along the lines of Bach's cantata *Christ lag in Todesbanden* BWV 4, which Brahms conducted several times, or the a cappella motet *Jesu meine Freude* BWV 227, with which he was familiar. Brahms sets each of the five stanzas from 'O Heiland, reiß die Himmel auf' with a different Baroque imitative technique, and Virginia Hancock has rightly labelled the piece 'a compendium of almost all the early music techniques Brahms had used in his choral writing up to [1864]'.[30]

Brahms's setting of the chorale's fourth stanza, 'Hie leiden wir die größte Not' ('Here we suffer in greatest distress'; see example 8.9) displays a rich mixture of Baroque rhetorical figures with modern chromatic writing and shows the closest resemblance in Op. 74 No. 2 to the musical language of the companion 'Warum' motet. While the bass intones the chorale tune as a slower-moving cantus firmus, the loosely imitative upper voices are saturated with a typically Baroque 'sighing' motive that aptly reflects the darker text of this stanza. Many of these sighs are emphasised with chromatic passing tones, which become especially poignant at the wedge figures that appear in bars 62ff. (see for example the soprano and tenor against the bass in bar 62, the alto and tenor against the soprano in bar 63, or the tenor against the soprano in bar 64). Particularly when these wedge figures are capped by an échappée, as in the tenor's leap to a neighbour-note F on the downbeat of bar 65, the material in this passage is strongly reminiscent of the dense contrapuntal writing in the first section of Op. 74 No. 1: compare, for example, the same figures in bars 43ff. of that motet, which do not derive from the earlier Missa, and whose date of composition is therefore presumably closer to that of 'O Heiland reiß die Himmel auf'.

If the Op. 74 motets look backwards to earlier material in Brahms's output, his next choral opus, the Songs and Romances Op. 93a, evokes a different sort of nostalgia, one that is both generic and material. Generically, Brahms returned to a designation, 'Songs and Romances', that he had previously used for his settings for women's voices in Op. 44 (pub. 1866). Like the earlier set, Op. 93a is based primarily on folk-like poetry. And although it is not entirely clear what distinguishes these groups (or others so named in Brahms's solo song repertoire) from many that he simply labelled 'Lieder', the term 'Romanze' apparently connotes an aura of *völkisch* simplicity for Brahms, according with a slightly earlier understanding of the Romanze as a song whose melody consists of 'artless, naive, and peaceful song'.[31] Compared to his youthful Op. 44, however, Brahms's Op. 93a is ripe with the expressive techniques he had developed over twenty prime years of his career; any 'artless naiveté' that might be implied by strophic settings or homorhythmic choral texture in these later Songs and Romances is overwhelmed by lush harmonies and a general air of sophistication, which is partly accounted for by a highly refined use of motivic development.[32]

The fourth song sets Rückert's bittersweet 'Fahr wohl', and evokes nostalgia strongly enough to have been selected by the Vienna Singverein (the choir Brahms directed from 1872 to 1875) to perform when Brahms's cortège paused outside the Gesellschaft der Musikfreunde building during the funeral processsion.[33] Ruckert's poem dwells on metaphors for separation (wandering bird – falling leaf – parting love), and Brahms's setting obliges with a constantly shifting and richly coloured harmonic background. In bars 2–4, Brahms affects a linear descent in all four voices, enriched by subtle chromatic inflections, thereby symbolising the drifting away of which the voices sing. A depth of harmonic background here marks this song (and all of Op. 93a) as the work of a mature artist working in a world in which romantic fascination with the simple and the naive has been superseded by melancholy and a heavily laden sense of 'lateness'.[34] In 1885 a complete edition of Heinrich Schütz's music began to appear, edited by Brahms's close friend Philipp Spitta. It is usually assumed that the wealth of new Baroque a cappella (and particularly polychoral) music that Brahms encountered in these volumes inspired his last two choral *opera*, the *Fest- und Gedenksprüche* Op.109 and the Three Motets Op. 110.[35] Given the post-dating of most of the material in the motets of Op. 74, it is quite likely that these choral works from the late 1880s were Brahms's first new sacred music in nearly two decades. The former set, Op.109, comprised three ceremonial settings of biblical texts; the latter set, Op.110, included one on biblical texts (No.1, 'Ich aber bin elend'), and two on hymn texts (No. 2, 'Ach, arme Welt' and No. 3, 'Wenn wir in höchsten Nöten sein'). A clear link between these two *opera* is the normative use of a cappella eight-voice polychoral writing, a new format for Brahms. (Only Op.110 No. 2 is set for a single, four-voice choir.) In Opp.109 and 110, polychoral writing is one compositional means by which Brahms reflects the plural voice or references to a community that occur in most of the texts, through phrases like 'Unsere Väter', 'unser Gott', and 'Wenn *wir* in höchsten Nöten sein'.

Example 8.10 *Fest- und Gedenksprüche* Op. 109 No.1, bars 1–16

To begin the *Fest- und Gedenksprüche*, for example (Example 8.10), Brahms employs polychoral textures that depict separate groups in the most vivid musical terms possible. Choir 2 opens the piece with a unison arpeggiated F major triad that is immediately embellished by choir 1 through highly figured four-voice counterpoint. Out of this initial gesture, a pattern emerges in which starkly simple statements by choir 2 are followed and elaborated by a more sophisticated and learned tone in choir 1. Of the Op.110 motets, only No. 3, 'Wenn wir in höchsten Nöten sein', matches the *Fest- und Gedenksprüche* for its handling of the polychoral format. After the two choirs delineate themselves through 'echo' phrases to set the first verse of this sixteenth-century German translation of a contemporaneous Latin hymn, all eight voices join together at the second verse 'So ist das unser Trost allein, daß wir zusammen ins gemein dich rufen an, o treuer Gott, um Rettung aus der Angst und Not' ('Thus is our only comfort that we call to you, O faithful God, all together as one, for deliverance from fear and distress').

These last two sets of choral pieces were nearly the last works Brahms composed before his brief retirement in 1890. Thereafter, Brahms relegated his compositional activities to more private and introspective works. Nostalgia for the romanticised German culture in which Brahms

194 *Daniel Beller-McKenna*

Example 8.10 (*cont.*)

grew up, as represented by the Songs and Romances of Op. 93a, or for the patriotic fervour of 1870, as alluded to in the *Fest- und Gedenksprüche* Op. 109, was no longer appropriate to Brahms's quieter musical utterances of the 1890s. Although the choir would seem to be a fitting vehicle for this late-life exploration of spirituality, his last two works, the *Vier ernste Gesänge* Op. 121 (1896) and the Eleven Chorale Preludes Op. 122 posthum. (pub. 1902), suggest that he preferred the more intimate confines of the solo *Lied* and the keyboard near the end.

9 Words for music: the songs for solo voice and piano

MICHAEL MUSGRAVE

Brahms's view of song

Brahms wrote songs throughout his life.[1] They provide a constant back-cloth to his larger instrumental works, to which they often relate quite tangibly. A solid core has remained in the repertory since Brahms's time, and they are well represented in the current recording catalogue, as prominent as those of his predecessors Schubert and Schumann, whom he so admired. Yet there has always been a discernible tendency among critics to exclude Brahms from an ultimate canon of great German *Lieder* composers comprising Schubert, Schumann and Wolf; indeed Brahms is even sometimes included in a list with much lesser figures of the genre such as Mendelssohn, Franz and Cornelius. There are obvious reasons for this. First of all, the fact that Brahms did not set the greatest poems, rather preferring the work of minor figures, whose verse he might more easily transform: from this it is assumed that he lacked the knowledge of or the discernment of the composers who did. Since by this reckoning, great songs are seen as critiques of great poetry, responding to the challenge presented by a poem which is independently known, Brahms's songs are excluded since they offer no such comparisons. To this conclusion is harnessed the fact that Brahms is sometimes seen as displaying awkwardness in the musical rendering of verbal accentuation, a consequence of his emphasis on rounded melody. One might further add in such an assessment that Brahms avoids the lengthy groups or cycles that show a capacity for reflecting psychological development. In short, that he is an instrumentally rather than verbally driven composer.

These are negative comparisons, ones which ignore that Brahms's songs were based on a wide and discerning knowledge of German literature; that as a corpus they display a remarkable range of expression in both vocal and instrumental domains; and that they have great qualities of their own which are based on a clearly held aesthetic. Certainly Brahms did avoid setting the famous lyrics and cycles which are so central to the literature of nineteenth-century German song: for example, the lyrics from Goethe's *Wilhelm Meister* or his *Faust*, or the cycles by romantic poets such as Heine and Eichendorff. There are hardly any comparable settings by Brahms. Although he later admitted to having set 'the whole of

Eichendorff and Heine' when young, [2] few survive, namely of Eichendorff in Op. 3 Nos. 5 and 6, Op. 7 Nos. 2 and 3 and the single 'Mondnacht' (WoO 21);[3] his own surviving Heine settings were apparently written much later. But this is in itself no evidence of insensitivity to poetry. On the contrary, Brahms's choices were based on a passion for literature apparent from childhood. He believed that a great poem gained nothing from musical setting: consider his familiar comment on Goethe settings by Schubert, whose songs he greatly admired: 'in my opinion, Schubert's "Suleika" songs are the only of his settings where the music enhanced the words. In all other cases the poems are so perfect that they need nothing added.'[4] Instead, he explored more widely, using foreign poems in translation and including verse with special personal association – with friends and with his home region. It was only in large-scale choral music that he allowed himself more freedom: all four major works with orchestra to secular texts use important poetry.[5] On the other hand, he did not align himself with those who sought to interpret poetry by shifting the balance decisively towards music. As he commented to Henschel: 'there are composers who sit at the piano [and compose the poem] from A to Z until it is done; they see something finished, something important in every bar'.[6] His aims differed both from those of Schubert and Schumann and from those of the 'composers who sit at the piano', but they were clearly defined; and his settings always show the composer responding to distinctive technical challenges within his defined terms of reference. Brahms's aesthetic emerges clearly through his contact with Henschel, and through his teaching of Gustav Jenner, his only pupil, in the 1870s and 1880s. It was based on the principle of strophic composition. Jenner comments: 'I always thought he valued strophic songs more than any others [though] he never expressly said so.'[7] He insisted on the close relation of the rhythm and form of the poem to that of the music: it was well known that Brahms's aesthetic canon demanded that the metre of a song should reflect, in one way, or another, the number of metrical feet in the poem.[8] Elsewhere Brahms asserted that he set the words and not the emotions or imagery of the words, as when he commented of the *Magelonelieder*, 'my music has . . . nothing whatever to do with [Ludwig Tieck's *Phantasus* and the love story of Peter]. I have really only set the words and nobody need be concerned about the landscape',[9] by which he seems to mean that he set the qualitative and quantitative properties of the words and their larger patterning within the structure of the poem, rather than as topics for individual depiction or 'expression' through traditional 'word painting'. His remark is, of course, a trifle disingenuous. His melodies and their accompaniments do create atmosphere, and mark a new stage of expressive development;

but rounded, self-sufficient melody and clear harmonic support allied to natural verbal rhythms remained central to his style.

The ideal he had in mind emerges clearly in a comment made to Clara Schumann in 1860: 'song composition is today sailing on so false a course that one cannot too often remind oneself of the ideal, which for me is folk-song'.[10] As much could have been deduced from his previous output, in which he had already made extensive use of folk-song texts in original settings as well as arrangements, including fourteen settings for Clara's children; and his interest was to last to the end of his life when he released his arrangements of *49 Deutsche Volkslieder* for solo voice and piano, claiming that no work had given him as much pleasure. Other unpublished solo arrangements also survive, as well as settings for many choral groupings.

His favourite folk-songs were all extremely simple in structure, with balancing phrases and a syllabic style, implying a simple harmonic support, and with no repetition of text. They represented a romantic ideal, songs whose very simplicity and stylisation embodied a quality of perfection. That Brahms made his comment in 1860, the year of the 'Manifesto' against the New Germans, when he was so aware of dividing paths and the discarding of old values, suggests a polemical ring, an extreme statement of principle. In reality he was expressing faith in a set of values: of a particular melodic character, of formal clarity, of the direct relation between melodic and poetic structure. But his relationship with them needed flexibility to be of use to a creative composer. Brahms's later original settings of some of the folk-song texts would show him breaking down the stylised form. In 'Spannung' Op. 84 No. 5, using the text 'Guten Abend, Guten Abend, mein tausiger Schatz' (No. 4 of the *Deutsche Volkslieder*), the six verses are set with a contrast melody for verse 3, a variant of the original in the major mode in verse 6, as well as developing keyboard figuration, where the setting of the original melody only varies the accompaniment in verses 4–6. In 'Dort in den Weiden steht ein Haus' Op. 94 No. 7 (No. 31 of the *Deutsche Volkslieder*), he extends the first cadence from a 2/4 to a 3/4 bar to shift the whole emphasis of the words to the end of the line (he also omits the structural repetition in the original, to give an entirely different mood), as well as varying the accompaniment for verse 3. Sometimes his melody is a response to a pre-existent melody: the famous 'Wiegenlied' Op. 49 No. 4 incorporates another lullaby known to and sung by its dedicatee, Bertha Faber (formerly Bertha Porubszky); thus his melody extends an original by contrapuntal or complementary means.

The folk idiom remained central to a vast part of Brahms's melodic language. In the songs there is an especially large stock of folk-like melodies, or melodies of a rounded character which clearly relate to them. An example of the first, 'Der Schmied' ('The Smith') Op. 19 No. 4, is subtly distinguished from the melodies in the *Deutsche Volkslieder* by its leaping chordal shape and extended cadence. 'Vergebliches Ständchen' Op. 84 No. 4 includes internal repetition in voice and piano; 'Sonntag' Op. 47 No. 3 plays on repetition to give a much more extended structure than is implied by the simple opening figure. More distantly, a folk-like quality remains in many Brahms songs which are of a more expansive kind, with more developmental melodies and with freer, more active and elaborate accompaniments. One might take such examples as 'Sommerabend' Op. 85 No. 1, 'Dein blaues Auge' Op. 59 No. 8, 'Auf dem See' Op. 106 No. 2 and 'Von waldbekränzter Höhe' Op. 57 No. 1, where basic scalic and chordal patterns still lie at the root. Brahms also wrote in a very strict 'alt-deutsch' chorale style, entirely syllabic and scalic with stark, root-position accompaniments, in settings for solo voice and piano which also appear for four-part chorus: 'Vergangen ist mir Glück und Heil' Op. 48 No. 6; 'Ich schell mein Horn ins Jammerthal' Op. 43 No. 3.

Yet the world of folk-song, however subtly extended, was clearly very limiting to a composer with Brahms's pronounced lyrical gifts, wide stylistic range and love of structural variation. For all his use of folk-song, Brahms had long shown a capacity for a wider range, and some of his earliest songs are highly dramatic, almost expressionistic: his earliest known song, 'Heimkehr' Op. 7 No. 6 (1850), and the second setting of 'Liebe und Frühling', Op. 3 No. 3, are both almost like operatic *scenas*, with dramatic piano introductions and throbbing accompaniments to the vocal line. Brahms's first published song, 'Liebestreu' Op. 3 No. 1, controls its powerful expression by a strong canonic movement between the voice and the bass part of the piano. Such songs had existed side by side with the most intimate types from the first ('Heimkehr' is preceded in Op. 7 by the song 'Volkslied' and the folk-song setting 'Trennung'). The stylistic range of the Op. 32 songs to texts by Platen and Daumer, and the *Magelonelieder* Op. 33, all written between 1859 and 1862, show no desire to restrict the dramatic aspect; on the contrary. But it is now given a new character, with a more rounded melody and a more supportive than illustrative accompaniment, and the structure is becoming more extended.

Given Brahms's ideals and stylistic preferences, what were the issues governing his mature settings? Essentially, he sought to expand the strophic type into varied strophic forms and to adapt those to a wider stylistic range. This did not happen chronologically (from one type to another in one period): rather, a constant synthesis was at work between different types throughout, with the elements always drawn into an integrated whole. The vehicle was both musical and poetic: on the one hand, the adaptation of the musical form to provide greater expressive capacity; on the other, the choice of interesting poetic forms which would determine a comparable musical response. This essay presents selected examples to illustrate the broader trends in the output as a whole.

Modified strophic form

The strength of the modified strophic form lay in its focus – one sentiment embodied in a self-sufficient principal melody, yet with opportunities for musical variation mirroring subtle changes in either the poetic content or its metrical structure. It offered many musical possibilities, ranging from the slight variation of a repeated verse through more extensive recomposition to alternation with a contrasted verse (A A B A), or combinations of these patterns. Only slight irregularity in the disposition of a poetic stanza itself was necessary to give opportunities for striking musical variation and development. And musical variation of an anticipated formal norm might also serve to reveal a meaning more fully: to reveal humour, pathos, irony, for example. The following examples trace some typical stages of variation of the strophic folk-like type as demonstrated in Brahms's *49 Deutsche Volkslieder* and in his original settings of folk poems.

A first stage can be seen in the setting of Gottfried Keller's 'Therese' Op. 86 No. 1.[11] Here Brahms chooses a folk-like melodic idiom for the stylised folk-like poem, in which an experienced older woman gently rebukes the advances of an amorous youth and teaches him a lesson. The style is conversational, its stepwise questioning mode similar to the earlier folk-song setting 'Trennung' Op. 7 No. 4 with its similarly prescribed vocal range and varied third verse. It is in three equal strophes; in strophes 1 and 2 she demands what he wants of her, though in a coquettish, knowing way; in verse 3 she sends him away to look in an old sea shell and find its answer.

Du milchjunger Knabe,	You young, young boy,
Wie schaust du mich an?	Why do you look at me so?
Was haben deine Augen	What are you asking,
Für eine Frage getan!	What would you know!
Alle Ratsherrn in der Stadt	All the councillors of the town
Und alle Weisen der Welt	And the wisest men on earth

Bleiben stumm auf die Frage	Will remain dumb at the question
Deine Augen gestellt!	I see in your eyes

Eine Meermuschel liegt	A seashell lies
Auf dem Schrank meiner Bas,	In my cousin's cupboard;
Da halte dein Ohr dran	Put your ear to it,
Dann hörst du etwas!	Perhaps it will tell!

The syllabic pattern of each stanza is similar and the poem could therefore be set in a repetitive form. But Brahms adapts both the vocal idiom and the strophic form to bring out the meaning better. The melody lies between the third and sixth degrees of the scale and never resolves to the tonic; stanzas 1 (Example 9.1a) and 2 both end on the third, which Brahms harmonises as III♯ (F♯ in D major), followed by a composed pause – an augmented rhythm for the cadence: all these features create suspense. But stanza 3 (Example 9.1b) is totally transformed musically. It is marked slower, 'etwas gehalten', with much softer dynamics to emphasise the radical harmonic shift, whereby the F♯ chord now serves as the dominant of B major (D major's submediant major), and the melodic shift, whereby the newly fashioned melody with wider intervals, beginning with rising fourth and falling octave, makes the response. In repeating this melody on the tonic after expressive chromatic movement in the bass and middle parts, the melody does not finally end on the tonic; only the piano, shadowing the material of the introduction, really concludes the song. Expansion in the piano part before this final phrase further secures the expressive goal. This final phrase and piano conclusion show an unusual balance between vocal and pianistic claims within the norms of Brahms's style, especially in such a folk-like vein.

The idiom of the setting of Heine's 'Es liebt sich so lieblich im Lenze' Op. 71 No. 1[12] is, by comparison, of a more open-air, triadic type, in accordance with its narrative topic. It uses a more elaborate folk idiom in its expanded range (spanning a tenth in the mirror-like opening arpeggiac phrase) and in its onward development of an essentially alternating musical design; it greatly extends its basic materials in projecting a small drama around the stylised rustic scene. The poem tells of a hopeful girl making garlands by the river in springtime. To whom will she give them? A fine rider comes by, sporting a plume, but he passes on, leaving her bereft. The refrain, repeated again in the last line, 'Love is so lovely in Springtime' gives the poem an ironical, bittersweet quality.

Die Wellen blinken und fließen dahin –	The waves gleam and flow by –
Es liebt sich so lieblich im Lenze!	Love is so lovely in Springtime!
Am Flusse sitzet die Schäferin	The shepherdess sits by the riverside
Und windet die zärtlichsten Kränze.	And weaves the loveliest garlands.

Example 9.1 'Therese' Op. 86 No. 1

(a) verse 1, bars 1–14

(b) verse 3, bars 25–39

Das knospet und quillt und duftet und blüht –	The buds, the water, the fragrance, the bloom –
Es liebt sich so lieblich im Lenze!	Love is so lovely in Springtime!
Die Schäferin seufzt aus tiefer Brust:	The shepherdess gives the deepest sigh:
'Wem geb' ich meine Kränze?'	'To whom shall I give my garlands?'
Ein Reiter reitet den Fluß entlang;	A rider rides by the riverside;
Er grüßet so blühenden Mutes!	He greets her so boldly in passing!
Die Schäferin schaut ihm nach so bang,	The shepherdess watches, her heart so sore,
Fern flättert die Feder des Hutes.	The plume of his hat disappearing.
Sie weint und wirft in den gleitenden Fluß	She weeps, and in the flowing stream,
Die schönen Blumenkränze.	Throws her beautiful garland.
Die Nachtigall singt von Lieb und Kuß –	The nightingale sings of love and embrace –
Es liebt sich so lieblich im Lenze!	Love is so lovely in Springtime!

Brahms modifies the strophic setting in three ways: by extending the strophe itself through repetition; by providing a contrast verse setting, and by extensive melodic and harmonic recomposition of the last verse: thus the pattern is A A B1 A1. Though the poem has balancing four-line stanzas, Brahms concludes his verse with a repetition of the text to extend the phrase length to 2+2+2+3 bars and thus to emphasise the end of each stanza. Following the sense of the poem, the same music is used for stanzas 1 and 2. In stanza 3, the image of the galloping horse is reflected in a more strident melody, with a triplet piano figure and a shift to the mediant (F♯ in D major), though continuing to develop earlier material. Stanza 4 (Example 9.2b) further develops the opening theme through harmonic variation, though it moves firmly to the subdominant G major for the third line at the image of the nightingale, before coming to a robust new conclusion of the theme, the piano postlude dying away (perhaps with the vanishing rider). The change of mood in verse 4 is obviously intended to express irony: Brahms had apparently sought to capture this in the redirection of the harmony, the modulation through G and the almost overcheerful, too culminative conclusion. Whether he has done so is perhaps doubtful. At least he seems more intent on bold humour than irony through these means. Viewed differently, however, the whole setting could be taken as ironical, given the obvious relation of the opening theme to the inverted and repeated figure in the introduction (Example 9.2a) which seems wilfully apparent in octaves, and to impart a false sense of innocence to the confident vocal idiom.

Example 9.2 'Es liebt sich so lieblich im Lenze' Op. 71 No. 1
(a) verse 1, bars 1–6
(b) retransition to verse 4, modulation to G major and conclusion, bars 34–52

Example 9.2 (*cont.*)

In the setting of Klaus Groth's 'Wie Melodien zieht es mir' Op.105 No. 1,[12] another strophic structure is provided with a very different kind of melody: not an elaborated folk type, but a chordal opening (Example 9.3a) treated in an essentially instrumental way (the same basic contour reappears as the second subject of the A major Violin Sonata Op.100) and standing apart from the essentially repetitive or alternating material of the previous examples. Brahms adopted this musical character because of the subject of the poem, which evokes the power of music to arouse feeling which mere words cannot express:

Wie Melodien zieht es	It runs, like melodies
Mir leise durch den Sinn,	Quietly through my senses,
Wie Frühlingsblumen blüht es	It blossoms like Spring flowers
Und schwebt wie Duft dahin.	And clings there like perfume.
Doch kommt das Wort und faßt es	Then a word comes to hold it
Und führt es vor das Aug',	And brings it in front of my eyes
Wie Nebelgrau erblaßt es	And it dispels like fog
Und schwindet wie ein Hauch.	And vanishes like a sigh.
Und dennoch ruht im Reime	And, for all that, in this rhyme
Verborgen wohl ein Duft,	There lies hidden at least a scent of it,
Den mild aus stillem Keime	Which, from a silent bud, is gently
Ein feuchtes Auge ruft.	Coaxed by a tearful eye.

The three stanzas of 7 6 7 6 syllables could again be set to a repetitive structure, a b a b for each stanza. However, this would be to diminish the poem's meaning, which grows in interest, purpose and focus as it unfolds towards the conclusion. Likewise, the simple rhythmic scheme of the verse gives insufficient opportunity to symbolise the expressive content in the music. Brahms follows the natural rhythms for most of the verse, lines 2–4; but notably transforms the opening line of 7 syllables to an equivalent of 10 syllables in length by doubling the length of the syllables 'di-en zieht'. Not only this, but he places the opening three syllables as an anacrusis to these extended syllables. The reason is obviously to attract attention to the key word by exposing it, and likewise the parallel words in verses 2 and 3, 'Wort' and 'Reime'. Additionally, Brahms repeats the last line so that, with the piano postlude, a total of twelve bars results where eight would have been predicted, to make a more conclusive ending. The settings of the second and third verses vary this model to reflect the comparison presented by the poet. In the second verse, the music is led from the second line into the relative minor (F♯ minor) via the subdominant (D). The lowering of the melodic G from G♯ at 'schwindet wie ein Hauch' ('vanishes like a sigh') immediately reflects the textual contrast. In verse 3, the recomposition is delayed a little later to take the music into F major, the lowered VI degree, though its direct resolution onto the dominant and closure is beautifully delayed by its acting as dominant to B♭, from which the music returns chromatically into the tonic: then the tonic returns with added freshness, including an emphasis on the word 'feuchtes' ('tearful') by a melisma as part of a now expanded response which takes in lines 3 and not just 4 to make sixteen bars from twelve (Example 9.3b). Thus the composer achieves a remarkable diversity of harmonic resolution in such a short space.

To a second category belong settings which modify the strophic form through metrical factors within the poetry itself, rather than by musical means alone. Several stages of complexity can again be observed.

In Hölty's 'Die Mainacht' Op. 43 No. 2,[14] the vocal style is again close to a folk type, the opening built on the decoration of a triad with answering phrases a b a b, though one destined to develop more dramatically at its close. Brahms gave this song as an example of how an idea, once discovered, could develop unconsciously over time to reveal its full potential in the completed song. The poem evokes the poet's loneliness, sharpened against the idyllic moods of nature – the silvery moon, the trembling leaves, the warbling nightingales, and symbolised in a pair of cooing doves. Where will the poet find balm for his tears?

Wann der silberne Mond	When the silvery moon
Durch die Gesträuche blinkt,	Shines through the trembling leaves,
Und sein schlummerndes Licht	And its slumbering light
Über den Rasen streut,	Spreads softly o'er the grass,

Example 9.3. 'Wie Melodien zieht es mir' Op. 105 No. 1
(a) verse 1, bars 1–5
(b) verse 3, complete, bars 28–46

(a)

(b)

Example 9.3. (*cont.*)

Au - ge ruft.

Und die Nachtigall flötet,	And the nightingale warbles
Wandl' ich traurig von Busch zu Busch.	I wander sadly from glade to glade.
Uberhüllet vom Laub	Roofed in with foliage
Girret ein Taubenpaar	A pair of doves coo
Sein Entzücken mir vor;	Their rapture at me,
Aber ich wende mich,	But I turn away,
Suche dunklere Schatten,	Seek deeper shadows
Und die einsame Träne rinnt.	To be with my tears alone.
Wann, O lächelndes Bild,	When, O smiling image
Welches wie Morgenrot	That comes like the sunrise
Durch die Seele mir strahlt,	Flowing through my soul,
Find' ich auf Erden dich?	Will I find you on earth?
Und die einsame Träne	And the lonely tear
Bebt mir heißer die Wang' herab.	Flows hotter down my cheek.

Here four equal lines are followed by successively extended fifth and sixth lines in the syllabic scheme 6 6 6 6 7 8, thus again placing a focus at the end of the verse. Though there is no actual rhyme scheme between them, they fall into complementary pairs in verses 1 and 3 and Brahms reflects this pattern in his melody, with an cadential augmentation to conclude the verse. In verse 2 (Example 9.4a), however, the stanzaic structure demands musical variation. Here the six lines are structured as two pairs of three lines as, in a changed image, the doves distract the poet with their intimacy and he turns away from them. The music mirrors this, moving into B major, enharmonically reached from the minor chord on E♭, but the 'turning to deeper shadows' brings a declamatory re-transition to the tonic and a massively elaborated cadence to accommodate the melisma on 'Träne'. This wonderful new phrase is then repeated twice in verse 3, which unites the music of verse 1, first part, and verse 2, second part. When 'Träne' recurs, reaching its goal through a lowered II degree in the progression II–v–i, the melisma is now given to the word 'Wang' ('cheek'), so that the textual intensification is exactly mirrored in the music (Example 9.4b).

Example 9.4 'Die Mainacht' Op. 43 No. 2
(a) verse 2, bars 15–32

Example 9.4 (*cont.*)
(b) verse 3, bars 39–51

Like 'Die Mainacht', Brahms's setting of Daumer's 'Wir wandelten . . .'
('We walked . . .') Op. 96 No. 2[15] also uses a chordal pattern; however, the
melody is not as independent, relying on the piano for its completion, and
the irregularity of the stanzaic structure prompts further the individuality of the setting. The text describes the recollection of unspoken
thoughts by a lover, who has questioned, but remained in a state of bliss.

Wir wandelten, wir zwei zusammen,   We walked, we two together.
Ich war so still und du so stille;   I was so still and you so still;

Ich gäbe viel, um zu erfahren,	I would give much to know,
Was du gedacht in jenem Fall.	What you were thinking at that time

Was ich gedacht – unausgesprochen	What I was thinking – unuttered
Verbleibe das! Nur Eines sag' ich:	Let it remain! Only one thing I say:
So schön war Alles, was ich dachte,	It was all so lovely, that I thought,
So himmlisch heiter war es all.	So celestially serene it all was.

In meinem Haupte die Gedanken,	The thoughts in my head,
Sie läuteten wie gold'ne Glöckchen;	They chimed like golden bells;
So wundersüß, so wunderlieblich	So passing sweet, so passing lovely
Ist in der Welt kein and'rer Hall.	In all the world there was no other sound

The irregularity of the phrasing arises from the metre and stress, with lines of 9 9 9 8 syllables, the first line requiring musical extension because of the natural stress on 'zus*a*mmen'. The stress becomes the focus of the setting of line 1, which takes 2½ bars. Since it does predict a responding vocal phrase, Brahms uses the piano's developmental accompaniment to link to the second line, of basically the same length: '-sammen' balanced by 'stille'. As in 'Die Mainacht', the meaning of strophe 2 determines an internal variation in its structure; lines 1 and 2 are continuous, with a separate thought, 'Nur Eines sag ich', ending line 2 and preparing for its consequent: 'So schön war Alles . . .' Brahms reflects this in his setting by presenting an entirely new melody for the latter in a new key and preparing it by the repetition of the former in augmentation for emphasis (one bar in 3/2). This thought continues until the end of verse 3 in the poem. Brahms satisfies the requirements of his strophic form by returning to the opening melody at line 3 of verse 3 'So wundersüß . . .', but reflects the continuity by accommodating the quaver figure which he has subsequently introduced into the vocal part (perhaps to evoke the bells of the text). Thus, one melody embodies the basic thought, but the changing details are also accommodated.

In his setting of Hermann Allmers's 'Feldeinsamkeit' as Op. 86 No. 2,[16] Brahms treats the chordal idiom in a different way. Rather than essentially articulating a chordal progression through balancing answering phrases, he here focuses all attention on the constituent intervals within the opening octaves themselves, as the starting point of a melody of extraordinary focus, manipulating them to telling effect (Example 9.5). The melody is now completely removed from any suggestion of folk-like origin. Equally its character permits a remarkably simple harmonic progression for the verse, with a move to the dominant and quick return to a long tonic in the second half of the stanza. Thus, mirroring its text, it stands apart from other melodic types. The musical texture is grounded

Example 9.5 'Feldeinsamkeit' Op. 86 No. 2, verse 1, bars 1–9

in the quiet throbbing of the piano bass pedal points. Static chords float above, continually fluctuating like the changing cloud shapes the poet watches so raptly. This organic character develops further in verse 2 with subtle internal modulations to intensify the words. The poem describes the vast peace experienced by one lying and gazing at the boundless sky, when time and identity are suspended.

Ich ruhe still im hohen grünen Gras	I lie still in the high green grass
Und sende lange meinen Blick nach oben,	And gaze raptly upwards,
Von Grillen rings umschwirrt ohn' Unterlaß,	Crickets chirp around unceasingly,
Von Himmelsbläue wundersam umwoben.	The blue of the sky weaves wondrously around.
Die schönen weißen Wolken zieh'n dahin	The beautiful white clouds pass by
Durch's tiefe Blau, wie schöne stille Träume;	Through the deep blue, like beautiful quiet dreams
Mir ist, als ob ich längst gestorben bin	It is as though I had long been dead
Und ziehe selig mit durch ew'ge Räume	And was passing with them through eternal space.

The rhythm of the four-line stanza alternates pairs of ten and eleven syllables (10 11; 10 11). The pattern also contains end-rhyme between lines 1 and 3 and 2 and 4 – 'Gras/-laß; 'oben'/'-woben', in each verse.

Brahms might therefore have set it in a musical pattern a b a b for each stanza. However, this would have been less effective than the structure he eventually built, which provides a good illustration of music's need of greater space to capture mood than the spoken poem, where meaning can be imparted by the merest inflection of the voice. A rhythmic balance of the first line would have tied the poem unduly. Brahms's wonderful melisma at 'meinen Blick nach oben' requires a balancing response as the music comes to the dominant. Thus extended (2+2 = 4) the second half of the verse places emphasis on the fourth line with a new figure, thus requiring balance by extension (2+2+4) to make a balance of 6+8, a total of fourteen bars (with an interpolated piano bar) where the opening two-bar phrase might have predicted only eight. In verse 2 the most beautiful harmonic recomposition of the material and extension of the vocal line prolongs the length to sixteen bars.

Finally, the case of Brahms's setting of Daumer's 'Wie bist du, meine Königin' Op. 32 No. 9[17] shows the strophic form with stepwise, rounded melody at its farthest remove from a folk-like source. The melody stands as apart from most examples as the previous song in its 'artful' character: ongoing and continuous (though not in the instrumental, developmental sense) and obviously conceived in equally close association with the piano part, and here avoiding the strong chordal progressions that underpin more straightforward melodies in favour of inversion-based progressions and stepwise part-movement (Example 9.6). These arise in response to the poem, which offers no strong accentual model and cultivates a rapt and focused mood. It is an ecstatic declaration of love and devotion to an idealised woman, who is compared to springtime and the freshest flowers, and who represents coolness and balm which even nullifies the bitterness of death:

Wie bist du, meine Königin,	How wondrous art thou, my queen
Durch sanfte Güte wonnevoll!	Through your soft goodness!
Du lächle nur – Lenzdüfte weh'n	You need only smile – and spring fragrances
Durch mein Gemüte wonnevoll!	Waft through my spirit – wondrously!
Frisch aufgeblühter Rosen Glanz,	The brightness of fresh-blooming roses
Vergleich' ich ihn dem deinigen?	Shall I compare it to your brightness?
Ach, über alles was da blüht,	Ah, above all that blooms
Ist deine Blüte wonnevoll!	Is your bloom wondrous!
Durch tote Wüsten wandle hin,	Wander through dead wastes
Und grüne Schatten breiten sich,	And green shadows will spread themselves,
Ob fürchterliche Schwüle dort	Even if fearful sultriness reigns endlessly,
Ohn' Ende brüte, wonnevoll	Wondrously.

Example 9.6 'Wie bist du meine Königin' Op. 32 No. 9, verse 1, bars 1–24

Laß mich vergeh'n in deinem Arm!	Let me die in your arms!
Es ist in ihm ja selbst der Tod,	Even death itself,
Ob auch die herbste Todesqual	Though the sharpest pangs pierce the heart,
Die Brust durchwüte, wonnevoll!	Comes wondrously!

The poetic stanza is of four lines of eight syllables (8 8 8 8) falling into two parts: lines 1–2 and 3–4 (though in verse 1, less regularly: 1–2, ½, 1½). There is no consistent internal rhyme: rather, the distinctive rhyming feature is the final word 'wonnevoll' – 'joyously', a resonant word which recurs in each strophe as its goal. This word becomes the focus of Brahms's setting. He intensifies the continuity of lines 3–4 of each stanza by shortening the note values of the third line to enable its expansive statement and repetition in line 4, in which the piano plays an essential part in balancing the phrase by anticipating to or responding to the word. The natural stress on 'wonnevoll' requires that the whole melody possess a downbeat character, though it fits verses 2 and 4 better than 1 and 3 (the more natural accentuation is 'Wie *bist* du'; 'Du *lächle* nur'). Lines 3 and 4 come out as an eight-bar section if the insertion of 'wonnevoll' in the piano is omitted. This insertion is also a feature of lines 1–2, enabling the voice to echo the piano, thus making a six-bar setting of lines 1–2, where five bars could have served, as is the case in the piano introduction based on the same material (repeated as a postlude at the end of verse 1). Verse 3 is set separately as a variant to capture the darker colouring of the text. Here the rhythm is stretched further by syncopated augmentation at 'Ohn' Ende' to make five bars of the original four, whilst the recomposition of the material involves an additional repetition of 'wonnevoll'. The setting has been criticised for its 'faulty' scansion. Yet a setting in the alternative metre of 4/4, which reflects the verbal stresses more closely, would tie the rhythm down too much for the sense of suspension and wonder which is the poem's essence. Brahms's ravishing melody in 3/4 embodies an aesthetic choice, in focusing on mood and distributing the accents sufficiently evenly without undue stress to give the singer every opportunity to inflect them and communicate the sense. All the same, the different stress which has thereby to be given to the same key word ('wonnevoll' having to take an end stress where it occurs at the end of line 2 in strophe 1) shows the sacrifice Brahms occasionally had to make in the service of his larger aesthetic.

Instrumental and dramatic songs

A composer of Brahms's stylistic and formal range could hardly have restricted himself in over 200 original songs to essentially rounded and syllabic melody. Despite the preponderance of such types, there exist many which explore much wider stylistic territory. Two types stand out: songs of an instrumental melodic character, and songs of a dramatic character.

Of the instrumental types, the most striking example comes in the intimate relationship between the third movement of the Violin Sonata in G Op. 78 and the settings of Klaus Groth's poems 'Regenlied' and 'Nachklang' Op. 59 Nos. 3 and 4. The sonata movement is a rondo, its first

Example 9.7

(a) 'Regenlied Op. 59 No. 3, bars 1–12

theme a continually evolving sixteen-bar structure with a continuous semiquaver accompaniment (Example 9.7c). Both songs share their opening four-bar phrase with the sonata theme. The first, 'Regenlied' (Example 9.7a), uses its rhythm and opening pitch repetition (three C♯s) as the motive of a four-bar introduction. Thereafter it is structured as a sixteen-bar continuous melody to an eight-verse strophic text, though it stays closer to the opening phrase than does the sonata theme, which develops a new figure based again on the memorable opening rhythm. The text describes the memories of childhood evoked by the patter of rain on the window pane (which is seemingly reflected in the animated accompaniment). The second verse takes a different route, its latter part developing widely and concluding with an augmented cadence to make twenty bars from the earlier sixteen. The growing intensity of the memories extends the treatment for stanzas 3 and 4 with a new and more truly instrumental melody, ending with further repetition and cadential augmentation to make twenty-four bars. Stanzas 5 and 6 offer a new melody in a contrasting key and metre, until a return of the music of lines 1 and 2. Thus, the six stanzas embody the continuous principle of the instrumental rondo movement with quite independently generated material

Example 9.7 (*cont.*)

(b) 'Nachklang' Op. 59 No. 4, bars 1–8

(c) Violin Sonata in G major Op. 78, movement 3, bars 1–9

within a large A B A scheme reflecting the poem. The following, second setting of a similar subject – 'Nachklang' ('Echo') Op. 59 No. 4 (Example 9.7b) – reworks the material yet again for a shorter poem. But the brevity includes greater formal subtlety, the irregular two stanzas permitting a freer phraseology in which the piano shares as an integral partner, the second stanza extended from sixteen to twenty-five bars, including piano interpolation. It begins, like the sonata movement, with no introduction.

As has been noted, the song 'Wie Melodien zieht es mir' Op. 105 No. 1 relates closely to the second subject of the Second Violin Sonata in A Op. 100. The relation is not as literal as in the Op. 78 movement, but is rather an identity of melodic shape between the opening phrases of song and sonata subject, unmistakable despite rhythmic dissimilarities. The sonata theme is again of sixteen bars' length; the song stanza is of twelve bars, though again of continuously evolving character.

In the Two Songs for Alto with Viola Op. 91, the relation of instrumental and vocal idioms is made tangible in two songs with voice and instrument on equal terms, the alto voice simulating and complementing the viola idiom. The second song offers a further synthesis of influences: it opens with a purely instrumental stanza to represent the text, the viola playing the well-known folk-song lullaby 'Lieber Josef, Josef mein', depicting the sleeping Jesus (Brahms placed the text under the melody in the score). The remaining seven stanzas of the eight-stanza poem explore the imagery of swaying palms to symbolise his passion to come. The voice enters in stanza 2 with a theme drawn from the opening of the folk-song by augmentation and inversion, the viola sharing with the piano more animated movement. In stanza 3 the voice begins to share this movement, conversing with the piano and viola in animated trio style and modulating through A major before restoring the tonic for the second part of its first-stanza theme ('stille die Wipfel'). Stanza 4 brings a more intense tone – a new metre, melody and texture at the prospect of the burden to come – but soon returns to the musical succession of stanzas 2 and 3, and the instrumental cradle song provides the coda, mirroring the introduction. Op. 91 No. 1 is a hymn at twilight to peace by Friedrich Rückert, four stanzas in which the poet reflects on the futility of human assertion in the presence of the stillness of nature. The instruments again take the first section, though with no associated text, and the first vocal stanza is again a counterpoint or complement to the repeating instrumental part. In stanza 3, the voice takes the viola part of the opening and the viola counterpoints with a much more florid semiquaver pattern. As in the following song, stanza 4 presents stark contrast, here of tonality and mood; however, the opening material is quickly restored in the major, though not the key signature, which reappears only with the music of stanza 2 over a dominant pedal, followed by that of stanza 3 for the completion of the setting. Thus both settings involve the sharing of material, yet also the generation of new material specific to the medium of voice, viola and piano.

In other later songs without such instrumental participation, Brahms employs an instrumental idiom in the voice or piano or both. The example most closely related to those just discussed is a setting of Candidus's 'Alte Liebe' Op. 72 No. 1. Here the continuously evolving melody in 6/4 time recalls the rhythmic pattern of the first movement of the Op. 78 sonata in its opening dotted minim chords and distinctive anacrusis, though the range is for the viola, not the violin. The melody is constrained in its growth by the poetic strophe of four lines (7 6 7 6), but its potential is developed in the following four stanzas of the 5-stanza poem: the return of spring reawakens bitter feelings of a lost earlier love; the poet feels contact, hears sounds, smells scents from his memory, but cannot escape his thoughts. In the musical form, each stanza grows from the last, shared rhythms gaining new shapes and original shapes being worked into new contexts with wider modulation to evoke the growing memories, before the return of the opening and the source of bitterness – the beloved – to make an overall pattern for the five stanzas of A – A1 – A2 – development – A. The song could certainly be played as an effective viola solo.

In other songs, the instrumental role is given to the piano, the voice adding a commentary as a variant, and thus sharpening the distinction. One of the most striking is the setting of Heine's 'Meerfahrt' ('Sea Journey') Op. 96 No. 4, where the piano right hand has a bold venturesome melody of instrumental character – it could be a passage for cellos or solo horn if orchestrated – which evokes, with its strident left hand accompaniment and uneven, seamless phrasing, a boundless infinitude of sea, on which an unheeding couple are adrift: the 14-bar introduction divides memorably into phrases of 6+2+4+2 . Three stanzas evoke the sea, a phantom island, and the sea again, the voice entering with an independent melody to the opening accompaniment, though growing in animation, modulating widely and sharing the instrumental line and its striking dissonances against the harmony. The form is continuous, introduction A B development (including references to the introduction), with the postlude recalling the opening. In 'Verzagen' ('Despair') Op. 72 No. 4, the piano again begins with a strikingly instrumental main theme and florid accompaniment in 3/4 which could almost serve as a solo composition, over which the voice enters independently, with a simpler, contrasted line; it takes on an instrumental idiom in verse 3, shadowing and elaborating the piano to depict the text in which the poet compares his fears and woes to the waves dashing on the beach, unconsoled by the fact that they disappear in spray and that the clouds come and blow away. In contrast to the other settings the music of stanza 1 is marked for repeat in stanza 2. In other songs, the piano theme and texture dominate, or play an equal role with the voice: in 'Abenddämmerung' Op. 49 No. 5, the piano creates a shimmering atmosphere of twilight; in 'Es schauen die Blumen' Op. 96 No. 3, the piano evokes the metaphor of blooming flowers and rushing streams; in 'Botschaft' Op. 47 No. 1, the dancing piano introduction realises the breezes carrying messages of love.

There are no comparable models for songs of dramatic character. Brahms wrote no opera, and there are few examples of the kind of dramatic recitative that seems to lie in the background of his many declamatory and dramatic songs. Only in the opening solo passage of the dramatic cantata *Rinaldo* is there any obvious precedent, and this is of an old-fashioned type from opera or oratorio as used in early Wagner and Mendelssohn. Brahms's declamatory idiom soon took on a more lyrical form in the Op. 32 and Op. 33 songs, partly under the influence of the singing of Julius Stockhausen: a new lyrical-declamatory *arioso* style which adapted to the need to merge formal sections. Within this idiom he was to couch numerous expressive types. The idiom comes to an early flowering in the *Requiem* with its two baritone movements requiring the intonation of biblical prose rather than poetry, though he equalises the syllabic inequality through melodic means, involving repetition ('Herr, lehre doch mich' in movement 3; 'Siehe, ich sage euch ein Geheimnis...' in movement 6). If there is a 'goal' to his dramatic style in the *Lied*, it is in the other biblical settings for solo voice, the *Vier ernste Gesänge* ('Four Serious Songs') Op. 121. In Op. 121 No. 3, 'O Tod, wie bitter' (Example 9.8), there is an obvious quality of recitative, where the stark words are given focus through repetition and shifted accentual position; but there is also a clear contrast to the more lyrical response 'wenn an dich gedenket ein Mensch' in a much more *arioso* style. After the opening has recurred, the consequent is transformed into an even more intense lyricism in the major key: 'O Tod, wie wohl tust du', and finally, ecstatically (in 3/2 metre), 'wie wohl, wie wohl bist du'.

The subtle but distinct recitative–*arioso* relation in Op. 121 No. 3 finds a clear forebear in the late song 'Auf dem Kirchhofe' ('In the Churchyard') Op. 105 No. 4, in which the poet describes the wind-lashed cemetery, the graves almost covered over, the names marked 'departed' ('gewesen') – but then the revelation of the word 'healed' ('genesen') on these tombs with the clearing skies. Here the declamatory opening over pedal-based arpeggios in the piano yields to a clear quasi-recitative style with short uneven phases building to a repetition of the opening (Example 9.9a). With the transformation of the text, the music is also transformed, into the clear major mode and the timeless shape of a chorale phrase

Example 9.8 'O Tod, wie bitter bist du' Op. 121 No. 3
(a) bars 1–7

(b) bars 18–25, transformation of theme into major

Example 9.9 'Auf dem Kirchhofe' Op. 105 No.4
(a) bars 1–17

(acknowledged by Brahms to have been prompted by the chorale 'O Haupt von Blut und Wunden'), worked into a new melody to conclude the song (Example 9.9b).[18]

A possible model, or at least a forerunner, for this pattern, is the *Alto Rhapsody*, where Goethe's imagery of wild thickets on all sides as a metaphor for the lack of direction of the misanthropic subject of the poem is followed by a lyric *arioso* passage for the one 'for whom balm has become poison'), and eventually a chorale-type passage for chorus to the words 'Is there in your Psalter, father of love, one word to refresh him?' The form is essentially recitative, *arioso* and chorus, and its opening two sections

Example 9.9 (*cont.*)
(b) bars 27–37, closing 'chorale'

could certainly be part of a staged dramatic work. The distinctive character of the opening, with its active bass figure seeming to determine the movement of the rapidly shifting harmony, finds another successor in Brahms's later song 'Steig auf, geliebter Schatten' Op. 94 No. 2 to a text by Friedrich Halm. Here the imagery is again comparable: 'Arise, Beloved Shadow, in dead of night appear', though here the declamatory opening is part of a more continuous totality before it returns to complete the song.

That the recitative–*arioso* distinction was conscious in Brahms's songs can be inferred from the presence of the term 'recit.' in the early song 'An eine Aeolsharfe' Op. 19 No. 5, written before Op. 32. This is the only song in which this indication appears, and it indicates the character of the passage as well as how it should be sung. The text uses the imagery of the Aeolian harp, or wall harp (whose strings vibrate freely with the wind), as the image of the recipient of messages from nature, here from the dead lover who has just been buried on the hillside with flowers. Cast in three stanzas, the text recalls the mystery of the ancient harp and its ballad of mourning: the winds bring the scent of springtime, and suddenly the wind quickens and the flowers are strewn at the lover's feet. The contrast between description and invocation in verse 1 is reflected in the distinction between the 'recit' bars to describe the harp, and the lyrical response over repeated 'harp chords' in the piano to convey the desire for the message. The pattern is repeated for stanza 3 of the three-stanza structure.

One might well see Op. 19 No. 5 as prefiguring such a quiet, reflective idiom as that of 'Herbstgefühl' Op. 48 No. 7, in which the closing autumn is taken as a metaphor for resignation; 'why play like the wind at leaf and stem . . . only be at peace'. Verse 1 is tentative, with the piano interpolating bars to give a story-telling quality, bleak and unresolved, built on the dominant of the key: it acts as a preparation for the outburst of verse 2 to a new idea, 'thus a cold, night-dark day sends shivers through my life', a dramatic contrast before the return of the opening material, which only at the end is resolved.

The idiom of the Heine setting 'Der Tod, das ist die kühle Nacht' Op. 96 No. 1 is strikingly Wagnerian. Its opening phrase (Example 9.10a) is almost identical to that of 'O sink' hernieder, Nacht der Liebe' in Act II of *Tristan* (Example 9.10b) and uses the same accompanimental rhythm of syncopated repeated chords and chromatic dissonance in the voice, which almost floats above it in a slowly lyrical declamation of the utmost concentration. Here again there is a skeletal recitative–*arioso* distinction between opening and continuation in both cases. But Brahms's single strophic poem imposes a structure, the first half continuing in a frag-mented *arioso*, the second transforming the opening into a more expan-sive and periodic melody with a regular accompaniment figure and a touching final vocal cadence. The similarity arises from the analogous text, with its quintessential Wagnerian themes of night, death and love; it must be a homage on Brahms's part to a composer he greatly admired, whose idiom has been adapted here to the needs of periodic song. Brahms's text (by Heine) contrasts the coolness and clarity of night with the sultry day, which saps energy, in the opening recitative-like passage. The poet hovers between contemplating the peace of sleep and death and suffering the exhaustion of life. The nightingale sings of love as the 'aria' unfolds, but its ecstatic vision is soon quelled in the setting: the poet hears it only as if 'in a far-off dream', touchingly suggested by the refrain of this phrase before the hushed conclusion.

The setting of Brentano's 'O kühler Wald' Op. 72 No. 3 also inhabits this idiom, with slow repeated chords and arpeggio bass against the same rising tone in the melody (Example 9.11). But here the harmony adjusts to the dissonance, and Brahms adapts the idiom to produce a rounded melody in two complementary parts, the second with an extended cadence, the whole varied for the second stanza; however, he modifies this form even further by commencing the second verse with a new phrase in a slower rhythm – to reflect the words 'Im Herzen tief' – before continuing with the original material, more suited to the animated text 'da rauscht der Wald', which here requires a repetition of the second line to accom-modate the repeating melody; the verse concludes with an even more

Example 9.10

(a) 'Der Tod, das ist die kühle Nacht' Op. 96 No. 1, bars 1–6

(b) Wagner; 'O sink' hernieder, Nacht der Liebe', *Tristan und Isolde*, Act 2 duet, opening

Example 9.11 'O kühler Wald' Op. 72 No. 3, bars 1–13

extended cadence. The text portrays the murmuring of the cool forest which sends the lover's messages; he asks if its echo understands his song; the murmuring mirrors his feelings and when the echo falls asleep in sorrow the song floats away. The setting creates a striking effect at its final cadence: not only are the last words 'sind verweht' repeated to a chromatically rising melodic line that mirrors the text, but the metre is changed from the prevailing triple to duple and the accompaniment to offbeat chords – further to suspend the sense of time – before the opening pattern of the accompaniment, again displaced rhythmically, rounds off the whole.

In conclusion, a particularly striking example of the synthesis of some

Example 9.12 'Mein Herz ist schwer' Op. 94 No. 3, bars 1–15

of these basic types can be identified in the setting of Geibel's 'Mein Herz ist schwer' ('My heart is heavy') Op. 94 No. 3 (Example 9.12). The idiom is not unlike that of 'Alte Liebe': it is set in the same original key, G minor, in the same alto range and with the same compound metre and pervasive rhythm (though it alternates its basic 9/8 metre with 6/8): its opening motive suggests that both are variants of the same idea. But the melody never develops as freely as that in 'Alte Liebe' because of the power of its accompaniment, a stark contrary-motion pattern in octaves which holds the melody in a declamatory brace dramatising the text 'my heart is heavy, my eyes awake, the wind rides sighing through the night'. This quality continues into the second stanza, first with a simple repeated speech rhythm underpinned with syncopated piano chords; then the lyrical potential comes to the fore as the melody modulates widely: but it never loses the declamatory, constrained regular phrasing that prevents it from becoming a purely lyric or instrumental song akin to 'Alte Liebe'. Even in a genre where synthesis is so often to be observed, this example stands out and again illuminates how the principles of variation and adaptation of style and structure to new contexts permeates Brahms's music at every level: and how deep this traditional sense of craft, of the re-use of material, lies even within music as highly charged in expressive content as many of Brahms's more elaborate and dramatic solo songs.

PART III

Brahms today: some personal responses

10 Conducting Brahms

ROGER NORRINGTON WITH MICHAEL MUSGRAVE

An approach to the music

The completion of my series of Brahms recordings with the London Classical Players provides an opportune moment to reflect on my approach to them.[1] I have come to Brahms as the latest stage in a long exploration of musical performance from a historically-informed viewpoint which began with the Baroque era, continued into the classical era with Haydn and Mozart, and has stretched through the works of Beethoven and Schubert to the Romantics Mendelssohn, Berlioz and Schumann, and eventually to Brahms, Wagner and Bruckner. The aim has been to seek to restore as much as possible the relationship between the scores, which have not changed, and the instruments, forces and performing styles, which most certainly have. I wanted to find out how things actually *were* in the performing situation, to get the relationship right in order to enable the music to sound fresh and natural. The use of earlier instruments and playing styles does not force us to be old-fashioned: on the contrary, it ought to help us to re-create these masterpieces afresh. Like Schumann, Brahms has long had a reputation as a poor orchestrator, his textures being seen as overloaded and unclear. Though Brahms's scoring has had many detractors, I have never agreed with their objections. But there is equally no doubt in my mind that using the resources of his own time can tell us much about his orchestration, and about the music itself.

The performance of standard repertory from an 'early music' point of view has always engendered a good deal of resistance – the suspicion that a speculative view of how things *might have been* is being forced onto a hallowed repertory of great works. Such a view has never been my starting point. I studied orchestral conducting at the Royal College of Music with Boult in the standard repertory and I still conduct 'conventional' orchestras in this music, and much else. My interest in 'early music', especially the choral music of the Baroque, was an extension of this. But whatever the medium, the aims are always the same: to bring the music to life; not as 'early music' but as good music played properly. With the London Classical Players in the Brahms works, I have used all the available resources to seek to get as close as possible to the music as conceived and first experienced. In this respect, of course, existing orchestral tradition has been of little help – I had to start much further back. I want to know what originally lay behind tradition, to distinguish a true tradition from a false one (one hallowed simply by time and association with great artists). The Italians have an expression 'Tradizione e una maschera' – 'tradition is a mask', and if you take the mask away there is a skull. A playing style may have had its roots in something valuable, but these roots may now be little worth preserving. I have to admit that it is sometimes very difficult to decide. Take the way they play the waltz rhythm in Vienna. I'm sure there is something there that goes back a very long way – but you just can't tell, and I am not prepared to let anything in without a thorough examination. Mahler said that tradition is laziness – 'Schlamperei' (slovenliness, or bad habits, if you prefer). One must certainly always be alive to new possibilities. But I object to letting things be before we have even established what the composer originally wanted; one must first try to find out what he meant. We have found out a great deal already, and whatever choices one finally makes (performance is full of choices) one cannot afford to ignore the historical evidence where it exists.

Looking through nineteenth-century performance history decade by decade, I kept expecting to find the evidence to justify the styles of Brahms performance we have become familiar with in the twentieth century, but never did so. This is because the changes happened at the end of his life. The orchestra was transformed under the influence of Mahler and Strauss in the wake of Wagner's theatrical innovations: larger forces, with more penetrating strings, to balance more powerful brass and wind, originated in response to the new demands of the scores, larger halls and bigger audiences. Brahms has a special place within this change because, unlike Wagner, he was an avowed classicist. The transformation of playing forces and styles probably had a more distorting effect on the performance of his music than it did on Wagner's, with its heavier scoring and expressive slowness so determined by theatrical pacing. Brahms is significantly different, essentially classical in his intricate contrapuntal structure, rhythmic precision and interplay of figures, which is so often likened to chamber music. All classical music has a certain 'innocence' associated with it, and I want to capture that sonic quality in Brahms. But as well as doing justice to the sound, it is also important to get it right for expressive reasons, in view of the very false image that still persists of 'the bearded Brahms'. He was a man in vital early middle age when he wrote his *Requiem* and his symphonies. Indeed, he was even thought in many quarters to be a radical. There is an amusing example of the reception of his Second Symphony in Boston. One critic suggested that there should be a emergency sign in the concert hall – 'exit in case of Brahms' – portraying him as a firebrand, a Stockhausen of the time. The historical image of Brahms has certainly suffered from his promotion by the anti-programmatic criticism stemming from the 1930s, which viewed his music as abstract because of his mastery of large forms and his interest in articulating complex structures. But I am suspicious of Stravinsky's notion that music must not be allowed to be 'about' something. Brahms's soul is writ on every page of his music.

Though Brahms's symphonies are instrumental, I have never been able to understand the view of them as 'abstract'. For me his works are always full of meaning and of drama. I find them almost Byronic; they become 'overwhelmed by grief and joy' just as much as Beethoven's. We are all familiar with the view of Mahler and Sibelius of the symphony as a 'world', a view stemming ultimately from Beethoven's Ninth, with its attendant notions of the composer's lofty role and of the deep significance of the symphony in reflecting the highest aspirations and most powerful experiences: William Walton said that 'you cannot write a symphony unless something terrible has happened to you'. I suspect that Brahms would have concurred. Of his symphonies, Beethoven claimed, 'I always see pictures.' Brahms too had his secret mental images: we know that many of his melodies were inspired by texts now forgotten and that he used secret pitch-ciphers. The fact that he so carefully suppressed the sources of his stimuli does not alter the effect of the result. This is highly charged emotional music.

So I try to come to Brahms without some of the prejudice which gathers round his name. For me his music mirrors his life. He was not simply intellectual, though he had extraordinary mastery of 'learned' devices. His mode of expression is certainly different from that of other composers, especially his great symphonic contemporaries Tchaikovsky and Bruckner, yet he was driven to composition by the same forces of desperation, inner conflict, joy and resolution. Indeed, his classicism may even have been a way of controlling the sprawling emotion. Of course, his drama is not like Tchaikovsky's 'primal scream'. His inner conflict is more contained, his whole musical personality more inward. It is much more 'lump in the throat' music – the contained emotion one feels at the end of Edith Wharton's *The Age of Innocence*. And he is likewise different from Bruckner, with those massive effects of contrast, those Wagnerian aspirations. Brahms's sense of change and transmutation is more organic. Neither is there the bluntness of expression of Beethoven. Brahms is always modulated, and essentially lyrical. He comes out of a long German tradition of virtuosity in 'serious' composition that extends back through Bach to Schütz and even before.

234 Roger Norrington with Michael Musgrave

I am by nature a dramatic conductor, at home in the opera house as much as in the concert hall. I respond to what I take to be the personal character of a work, or at least the emotion that it expresses. For me, to deny the emotional or evocative aspect of Brahms is as absurd as to suggest that Dickens, Hardy or Wharton could write a novel 'in the abstract'. I find something very personal going on in Brahms's symphonies, a quality that is just as strong as in the works of other romantic composers. I see the symphonies as psychic dramas; each one is biographical, making a sort of life cycle – perhaps one might think of it as Brahms's *Ring*. I know it is controversial to say these things in an artistic climate which (unlike that of the Romantics) still favours a 'structural' or 'objective' view of meaning. Yet I can't avoid such thoughts when I experience the music and consider the powerful events in his personal life.

Of course, Brahms left few clues to these inner dramas; it is for each listener to fill out the picture with his own imagination. But the cast of 'characters' includes Robert Schumann, Clara Schumann and their children, together with the violinist and composer Joseph Joachim. And the subject matter is Brahms's innermost feelings: his joy, his loneliness, love and deprivation, deep depression and artistic triumph. It is an absorbing and compelling tale, a non-verbal landscape of the heart.

Instruments and performing styles

Many kinds of evidence can be drawn on in providing a context for historically informed performance, both in the physical and the interpretative dimensions. First the physical, starting with the instruments themselves. The radical changes in instrument design in the nineteenth century affected the stringed instruments least of all. The basic features which distinguish the modern violin from the Baroque prototype – the angled neck, the extension of the fingerboard, added sound posts, the higher bridge and modern bow, the cello spike and the violin and viola chinrest – were all achieved early in the nineteenth century. Only in the use of gut strings rather than metal does the sound differ – more mellow, less bright. The rediscovery of earlier performing traditions is made possible by surviving teaching materials. At every stage in my historical quest with the London Classical Players it has been possible to find treatises which clarify much about string technique and performance values: J. J. Quantz about Handel and Bach, Leopold Mozart about Amadeus Mozart and Haydn, Louis Spohr about Beethoven, Pierre Baillot about Berlioz. Brahms is no exception to this. His greatest adviser in matters orchestral was Joseph Joachim, the leading German classical violinist of the nine-teenth century. Joachim's *Violinschule* of 1902–5 gives many points of guidance towards the performance of Brahms's works.[2] In the light of twentieth-century traditions of Brahms performance with large orches-tras, modern instruments and modern playing styles, it is a surprise to find how much of Joachim's treatise represents a direct continuation of earlier traditions, respected by him until his death in 1907. Three tech-niques are of special interest in orchestral string playing: vibrato, *porta-mento* and *portato*.

In discussing vibrato Joachim quotes directly from Spohr,[3] emphasis-ing the vocal origins of the device: 'the singer in the performance of pas-sionate movements, or when forcing his voice to its highest pitch, produces a certain tremulous sound resembling the vibrations of a pow-erfully struck bell. This, with many other peculiarities of the human voice, the violinist can closely imitate. It consists in the wavering of a stopped note ... this motion, however, should only be slight in order that the deviation from purity of tone may scarcely be observed by the ear ... the player, however, must guard against using it too often and in improper places.'[4] He gives four species of vibrato for particular expressive effect in solo playing – slow and quick vibrato and variants of these. But in his comments Joachim repeats the caution that 'the pupil cannot be sufficiently warned against the habitual use of the tremolo, especially in the wrong place. A violinist whose taste is refined and healthy will always recognise the steady tone as the ruling one and will use the vibrato only where the expression seems to demand it.'[5] Since the purely symphonic repertoire calls for so few of these effects, if any, it follows that his caution is even more binding for this music, not least for Brahms.

Joachim's emphasis on the vocal model shows the importance of phrasing in instrumental music: as well as a pure singing quality, it must have an intimacy like speech to be fully expressive. The style he describes is thus very different from the style of 'obligatory vibrato' that came about in the early twentieth century. Heifetz and other players used it on every note, and the resultant brightness and projection has been an intimate part of the 'concert machine' tradition, gathering momentum from the 1930s, by which modern orchestras have been judged. But it is certainly not what Joachim wanted of string players, or what Brahms would have expected. Vibrato solves problems of tone and sometimes of intonation, but it does not address the question of musical sense. The nobility that both sought in music comes from not having instant gratification – salt and sugar all the time: rather, the gratification comes from waiting for the ear to lead to where the music is going, to a chord change or to the top of a phrase, for example. Lack of vibrato gives a 'pure classical tone'; if you use it too much, you endanger the 'classical' style (for instance, you wouldn't dream of using vibrato on the clarinet – it would instantly suggest jazz). Brahms would have *known* vibrato playing from the gypsy violin music he loved so much, but this was a totally different style from that of his orchestral music. Nor does vibrato always increase volume. One can often obtain a louder sound from non-vibrato playing.

Another device Joachim discusses is *portamento:* 'the audible change of position ... if two notes occurring in a melodic progression, and situated in different positions, are to be made to cling together. [It is likewise] borrowed from the human voice (Italian: portar la voce = carrying the voice, French = port de voix). . . The *portamento* used on the violin between two notes played with one bow-stroke corresponds, therefore, to what takes place in singing when the slur is placed over two notes which are meant to be sung on one syllable.' But Joachim again counsels against the 'constant use of wrongly executed *portamenti* [whereby]. . . the performance of a piece can become so disfigured as to result in mere caricature [and one should use] taste and judgement'.[6] The device is still to be heard in early twentieth-century performances, for example of the Elgar symphonies in the 1930s. But is interesting that, while vibrato has become commonplace, the twentieth century has shown increasing reserve towards *portamento*, which is often seen as tasteless and has largely disappeared from the performance of classical music. We follow Joachim in using some for special effects of expression, but always with lightened bow and the two notes unstressed, never weighted and stressed (which gives the vulgar 'whine' Joachim criticises). In my opinion, the next twenty years could see a similar decline in unplanned continuous vibrato. This fashion could change as that for *portamento* has.

The device we do make much use of is *portato* – a semi-slurring of the bow. Joachim says little directly on this in his treatise, through the subject emerges repeatedly in correspondence with Brahms in connection with markings for the Violin Concerto. It is described by Spohr and Baillot in the same expressive context as vibrato. However, its meaning has certainly changed. Baillot applies it to a single open string or stopped note. '*Portato*, the undulation produced by the bow alone [indicated by dots over the note covered by a slur], is of a calm and pure expression, because, on the one hand, it is generally used in slow or moderate tempi and on an open string, and on the other hand, when it is played with one finger on the string, which does not move, the intonation of the note remains fixed.'[7] The classification in *Grove* places it under 'slurred staccato', the 'distinct separation between two or more notes with the same bow-stroke indicated by dots or strokes over individual notes all under a slur, an on-string stroke at moderate speed, [the] separation depending on the character of the music': that is half way between legato and staccato, played on the string.[8] A frequent illustration is the second theme of the Mendelssohn Violin Concerto. Brahms took a keen interest in the device, but disputed with Joachim how it should be notated. Brahms disliked the use of strokes covered by a slur, preferring dots covered by a slur for all such cases, commenting to the effect that 'you are still using this sign for staccato, but I still mean portato', and citing Beethoven's comparable usage to justify his choice.[9] Florence May observes that he 'made very much of the well-known effect of two notes slurred together: 'I know from his insistence to me on this point the mark has a special significance in his music.'[10] The variety and combination of these devices gave music before the twentieth century much greater animation and intimacy, some of which has been lost in modern orchestral performance. When Brahms indicates 'espressivo' he really wants more phrasing, not more volume. Phrasing and attention to the different bow-markings enhance expression and also really clean up the texture.

In contrast to the strings, which can tune the scale by ear, the need to obtain an equivalence of interval and resultant good intonation led to radical changes in brass and woodwind design during the nineteenth century: the introduction of valves and more keys respectively. Flute players would have had access either to the late eighteenth-century or early nineteenth-century simple-system instruments of German or Austrian design or to the modern Boehm system, perfected around 1850, with larger tone holes for greater sound and with improved intonation. The oboe known to Brahms would have been the Viennese Sellner instrument, a thirteen-key oboe which remains the basic Viennese instrument of today, though the Boehm design was available from the mid-century. The older instruments still retained features of the Baroque instrument, which was designed to have 'pockets of sound' like the harpsichord's 'dark' notes, different registers giving different effects: thus the scale was not smooth like that of the modern instrument, but had more variation and character. The bassoon and contrabassoon displayed similar qualities. In the case of the clarinet we have a better idea of the instruments Brahms knew and preferred thanks to his contact with Richard Mühlfeld, principal clarinettist of the Meiningen court orchestra. His instruments were of the Baermann design of the early nineteenth century, derived from Müller's so-called simple system, not from Boehm. Müller's tutor of 1825 illustrates an instrument with thirteen keys, two of which have extra levers for the right thumb. The Boehm design was slow to overtake the

Müller in Germany, though the fingering was easier. Mühlfeld's surviving instruments have a lighter and sweeter tone, and the instruments are more strongly melodic in character, performing some intervals much more easily.

Valves were available on horns and trumpets from the mid nineteenth century and they gained steady acceptance, soon replacing the natural instruments with crooks whose highly developed technique had first been codified in the mid eighteenth century. Brahms continued to write for instruments with crooks in all his orchestral music. His technique of writing for the horn is of particular interest. He had known the natural instrument since childhood, since it would have been played by his father. Brahms followed the classical composers in using relatively few stopped notes in his orchestral music, though, like them, he is much more adventurous in chamber music – notably in his Horn Trio Op. 40, where the stopped notes at the end of the slow movement show a remarkable grasp of the technique and the effects available. Like the classical composers, he covered the tonal range by specifying changes of crooks between and within movements and by scoring for pairs of instruments to cope with modulations. On the rare occasions he wanted the contrast of a stopped note for its particular effect, he indicated it and expected it to be played as such. Nevertheless there is evidence that many players would have performed his works on the horn in F, the standard valve instrument in Germany in his time, and this is the instrument we use in our recordings. It still differed greatly from the modern instrument in its more delicate sound.

Brahms's intimate knowledge enables him to score very effectively for the horn and find the best parts of the range. He treats it like an extension of the woodwind instruments, using it to blend with them in contrapuntal writing and to provide a bridge between purely solo and 'harmonic' tutti writing. The heavy brass chorus in Bruckner or Wagner (or even Schumann in the fourth movement of the *Rhenish* Symphony) is rare in Brahms. He wanted a particular sonority and used a full range of registers in his writing. The early valve horn, like the natural horn, can produce a forced sound with less distortion than the otherwise more mellifluous modern instrument: it has a characteristic rasping 'brassy' effect when blown hard.

Brahms generally treats the trumpet as a chorus instrument in the orchestra. In contrast to his use of the horn, his writing for trumpet solo is simple and chordal, as when it takes the opening motive in the closing bars of the first movement of the Second Symphony. Though he writes for the capabilities of the natural instrument, the instrument of his time in Germany was the 6-foot trumpet in F (or, rarely, in G) which could be crooked down to C and sometimes B♭. The F trumpet, being longer than the B♭, had a less bright tone and blended better with the horns and trombones. In Brahms's writing for the trombone, he still observed a distinction between the B♭ instrument for the highest part and the B♭/F instrument for the second and bass parts; after his time all parts were played on the B♭/F instrument. The bass instrument would have had a wider bore than the second, giving a more distinctive bass to the section than in the modern ensemble, though still of a lighter and more vocal character than the modern instrument. The tuba was the only brass instrument to possess valves from its invention (in 1835): Brahms's bass tuba in F would also have been lighter than the usual modern instrument (the contrabass tuba). The timpani in Brahms's time would have been covered in skin, not plastic, tuned manually rather than by chromatic pedal, and played with leather-headed, not felt, sticks. The resultant sound is much more distinct and less muffled. Therefore the timpani parts assume a much clearer role in the texture: not a reinforcement or background to the orchestra, but a distinct voice, another form of counterpoint (except when they are used for an atmospheric function).

To turn from the instruments themselves to their combination and balance in the orchestra, the size of orchestra may well come as a shock to concertgoers accustomed to modern performances. German orchestras of the 1870s were generally no bigger than those of the 1830s, when Mendelssohn was in charge of the Leipzig Gewandhaus Orchestra: that is, eight to ten first violins was still the tradition. This naturally affects the balance of strings, woodwind and brass. The Gewandhaus layout was of nine firsts, eight seconds, five violas, five cellos and four basses. When Joachim gave the first British performance of Brahms's Symphony No. 1 at Cambridge, he had nine firsts, nine seconds, six violas, four cellos, and three basses. Brahms was obviously happy with this number: for the premiere of No. 4 at Meiningen he was offered more but turned them down. Although it is true that there were sometimes large string forces for festivals and charity concerts (just as in Haydn's and Beethoven's time), it was then customary to double the woodwind in proportion. The Vienna Philharmonic, with its unusually large string body (twelve firsts instead of nine), regularly performed with doubled wind. The modern complement of seventy string players creating a 'wall-to-wall' string sound against single woodwind considerably alters the balance Brahms would have assumed.

Though orchestra size solves many problems of clarity, some problems of balance remain. One is required to decide on the quality of one particular 'forte' against another. Brahms was very sparing in differentiating dynamics within a chord (unlike Mahler, who within tuttis can give as many as seven different dynamic markings at a time). One has to assume that there was a tradition of orchestral balance, and adjust as seems necessary. The orchestral layout of the time complements the musical texture: between 1750 and 1950, violins I and II were seated on opposite sides and, usually, horns and trumpets too. Our double basses are at the rear, and often divided in the manner described by Henschel to Brahms in his early experiments with the Boston Symphony Orchestra.[11] This plan reflects the musical structure of the scores, where the first and second violins, for instance, frequently respond to each other. The overall sonic design (three 'choirs' of strings, wind and brass) reminds me of the contrasting choirs in the motets of Giovanni Gabrieli and Schütz.

In considering issues of balance, one cannot of course ignore the most important factor in the production of sound from the orchestra – the room and its acoustic properties. Halls can work for or against the character of the music. We must realise how intimate the whole business was in such halls as the old Leipzig Gewandhaus, the Zurich Tonhalle and the Basel Casino. At Bad Kissingen, Bavaria, the surrounding galleries are so close around you that you could almost shake hands with the audience. In such halls one can use 'chamber music' gestures, as for example with the delicate return of the main theme of Symphony No. 2's first movement on the horns, an effect very different from the more public and generalised sound we often hear. Our recordings give an opportunity to hear the chamber music proportions of nearly all orchestras of the time. There is a striking difference, and, for me, the context fits the classicism of Brahms's writing.

The use of the resources of Brahms's time gives a significantly different sound from that with which most listeners will be familiar: first in the orchestra as a whole, and secondly in the main instrumental groups and solo instruments, and their relation to each other. This different balance is clearest in passages designed by the composer to share the same material among different instruments. In Variation 4 of the *St Antoni Variations*, for example, the inversion of the parts in the repetition involves oboe and horn against violas and lower strings (bars 1–5), full strings against flute and clarinet (bars 11–15), all in perfect balance with each other, not least the horn. In the canon by inversion in Variation 8, the lower string parts remain much clearer than in some modern performances – not least when the composer inverts the theme in canon in the second half, where the effect is often very muddy with full vibrato. In general, the orchestral parts are much clearer, the timbres of each section better heard, including the timpani. As in contrapuntal vocal music, each voice is heard as an individual in a crowd, never submerged. This is especially important for Brahms, whose complex rhythms and intricate motivic texture are *meant* to be heard: his scoring is never impressionistic in intent, but always thematic and related to the whole. Our results, I believe, disprove the traditional view of Brahms as a 'muddy' orchestrator – rich and intricate certainly, but beautifully calculated and balanced. I am reminded of one critic of our Schumann recordings, who commented, 'so Schumann was an orchestrator of genius'. The same applies to Brahms. The balance reveals the strings as participatory instruments in a complete texture, rather than the dominant group. It also shows more fully just what an active texture Brahms achieves, with all players sharing in the thematic material.

As regards the individual departments of the orchestra, one immediately notices our strings: the various techniques outlined earlier create a very different effect in some familiar passages. The lack of vibrato often gives the great string themes a different character – or seems to place them in a different perspective. In the fourth movement of Symphony No. 1, the great finale theme for violins, which Brahms indicated to be played on the G string, seems to point forward more. In the first movement of No. 2, the minor-key second theme on cellos sounds much more pensive and reflective; the main theme of the second movement has a more distant quality. As was mentioned above, we follow Joachim in using *portamento* rarely; but there is a place for it, as in the expressive elaboration of the first phrase of the second movement of No. 1, where it adds a subtle colouring in bar 13 (first violins). Of much greater importance to us, however, is the role of articulation and phrasing, especially the bow-determined device of *portato*, which stands out the more in the absence of constant vibrato. In the main theme of the first movement of No. 3, the clear marking of a two-note *portato* both contrasts with and complements the broad phrasing of the opening phrase, so that when the figure eventually comes on separate staccato bows at the climax and highest register of the theme, it really has an effect (bar 4). In the following transition theme a similar effect is implied, though not marked, with three notes marked with one slur and thus to be taken in one bow. In the second episode of the third movement of No. 2 the lack of vibrato really brings out the effect of the *portato*, especially when, placed in the lower parts, it contrasts with the legato of the upper parts (bar 114). In contrast, Brahms also indicates heavy staccato with wedges and separate bows for the strings, as in the passage at bars 97–100 in the first movement of No. 1. He gives numerous opportunities for varieties of bow-stroke and for contrast between them. His frequent indication 'pizzicato' is just one aspect of a constantly changing surface of articulation which I work very hard at in rehearsal to bring to the fullest expression.

In the brass and woodwind ensemble writing, one immediately notes the blend of the different instruments. They do not merge into a homogeneous sound – a synthetic sound where all lose some of their individual character – but retain their individual timbre and identity to a much greater extent than in some modern performances. The problem of the omnipresent horn in modern Brahms performances, tending to muddy the texture with its doublings and contrapuntal role, disappears with the lighter and more agile instrument of the period. In the coda to the slow movement of No. 1, the horn is usually held back in its melodic role in order not to overpower the violin; here the smaller-scaled horn and the light-vibrato violin balance more easily than the modern instruments. Earlier in this movement, the transition theme, which soars out on full violins, sounds pure and liquid, as though responding to the delicate tone of the oboe in the opening theme preceding it – a true balance.

Of the woodwind instruments themselves, it is the quality of the oboe which is perhaps most immediately notable in imparting character to a theme. The 'Quasi Andantino' of the third movement of No. 2 is a rustic dance melody over a folk-like pizzicato bass, the true character of which is perfectly revealed in the 'unevenness' of the period instrument, each phrase giving a slightly different effect according to its register, unlike the mellifluous modern instrument with no 'breaks'. The exposed high oboe writing in the introduction to the first movement of No. 1, creates a similarly distinct effect, especially when the line is continued down into the non-vibrato cellos. Variation 4 of the *St Antoni Variations* exploits its middle register. The clarinet has a similar melodic effect in the first movement of Symphony No. 3, another quasi-Baroque moment with an unfolding melody over a drone bass, which the timbre of the earlier instrument brings more fully to the surface. The fluid arpeggio melodic writing Brahms uses in the last movement of No. 2 and the first of No. 3 appears much more fresh and lively with the lighter period instrument. The clarity of the flute, though it has less melodic work, is everywhere apparent, from the opening of the first movement of No. 2, where it responds to the brass chorus, to the famous echo of the 'Alphorn theme' in the finale of No. 1.

' Music is not about sound'

Proper resources are necessary prerequisites for performance of this music as the composer would have imagined it. But music is not about 'sound' as such: it is about its sense, its direction, its shape, what it is saying. Music must 'speak' as well as sing. One might characterise sound as 'the noise an orchestra makes'. Its problem is that it can be so seductive that one sometimes forgets the larger issues. Central to these is gesture. Gesture and phrasing are always as important as sound and intonation. In seeking shape and line, as with tempo and dynamics, one inevitably comes up against the issue of 'interpretation'. Interpretation has long been one of the keywords of modern music making – that quality which enables a performance to stand out amidst numerous others and which reinforces the cult of the virtuoso conductor who is associated with it, giving it a certain 'authority'. Yet the concept stems only from the early twentieth century and the age of the professional virtuoso conductor. Prior to this, for example in the time of Brahms's contemporary George Henschel, there was no such thing as 'interpretation'. One just played the music as well as one could.[12] The approaches of other conductors were not important, because one heard them too infrequently to perceive a 'tradition'. Brahms offered few aids to the performer and was wont to avoid questions on performance, seeming to accept performances coming from different traditions. There is thus no one way to play it. Brahms heard Nikisch, who was very free, and the young Weingartner, who was very classical, and he was apparently happy with both. Some composers are never happy with changes – Britten was very insistent on his markings, whereas Tippett did not mind as much. Brahms may likewise have been easy-going; he was certainly open to change for practical reasons when necessary.

There is nevertheless plenty of evidence to orientate us towards the range of possibilities which he accepted as his framework, especially as regards speed and to a degree dynamics. To some extent this tradition has been lost in modern performance. When critics speak of 'the great tradition' of performance, they are referring to the style and individuality of recent great orchestras and conductors, not to the tradition in which the music was actually written. For example, I find Furtwängler amazing and very dramatic. But he tends to use the score as a support for a structural improvisation. I want the drama without the excess. Toscanini is much stricter in tempo. Weingartner's recordings are also very convincing (although they were made long after he had earned Brahms's approval).

Brahms often used tempo directions which are difficult to interpret: with their qualifying 'più' and 'poco', they give the impression of a tempo which he had yet to finalise or perhaps one slightly different from the basic tempi suggested by single-word indications. The opening of Symphony No. 1 is the most tantalising example: just 'un poco sostenuto' out of nothing, which then has to be defined in relation to the 'Allegro' which follows for the main part of the movement. And in any case, how do we

244 Roger Norrington with Michael Musgrave

determine a suitable tempo even for the basic tempo names, 'allegro', 'andante' and 'adagio', which are so often modified in his scores? Here a clue can be obtained by reference to the metronome marks which he provided for several works including the German Requiem. Though he did not want them regarded as absolutes – he had them all removed from the Requiem in the fullness of time, saying that everyone eventually changed their tempo – the fact that they were associated with the first complete performance gives them interest; they do at least give an indication of the relation between tempo name and speed of the beat, and (as important) of the relative speeds of the tempo names.

They are as follows:

1	Ziemlich langsam und mit Ausdruck	80
2	Langsam, marschmäßig	60
	etwas bewegter	80
	poco sostenuto	56
	allegro non troppo	108
3	Andante moderato	52
4	Mäßig bewegt	92
5	Langsam	104
6	Andante	92
	Vivace	112
	Allegro	100
7	Feierlich	80

I use these at least as a guide in my performance of the Requiem, keeping Brahms's faster Andante (movements 1, 2 [opening sections] and 4 were originally marked 'Andante') and a balance between the tempi of the movements 1 and 7 to facilitate the return of the first movement material.[13] The tempo-name /speed relation emerging from these marks demarcates the following ranges: Adagio 40–60; Andante 60–90; Allegro 90–120. They are especially notable for the wide range of the 'Andante' band, much wider than today. The relevance of the markings can be further confirmed by reference to the other works with metronome marks. The Andante movement of the Second Piano Concerto, for example, is crotchet = 83. Now this whole tradition of tempo has been lost and performance in the Andante and Adagio range has become much slower, radically affecting the performance of Brahms's works.

In choosing a speed to match a tempo name, I have assessed each symphony movement individually: every one of the sixteen is different with regard to character, and almost every one with regard to metre. My results are often different from customary tempi for these movements. The tempi of some of the main themes of each movement are as follows according to time unit (crotchet, dotted crotchet, minim, dotted minim):

Symphony/movement/metronome mark

	Symphony No. 1	Symphony No. 2	Symphony No. 3	Symphony No. 4
Allegro range	1 Allegro 108	1 Allegro non troppo 106	1 Allegro con brio 66	1 Allegro non troppo 63
	4 Allegro non troppo, ma con brio 116	4 Allegro con spirito 108	4 Allegro 80–84	3 Allegro giocoso 4 Allegro energico e passionato 108
Andante range	2 Andante sostenuto 50		2 Andante 70	2 Andante moderato 76
Adagio range	4 (1) Adagio 46	2 Adagio non troppo 48		

That these correlations are in line with the conventions Brahms would have known emerges from detailed comments by Fritz Steinbach (Hans von Bülow's successor at Meiningen and a favourite conductor of the composer) on his own performances of the symphonies, which were recorded by his pupil Walter Blume.[14] It is also interesting to note the obvious continuity from earlier generations of composers: Schumann gives 66 for the dotted minim beat of the opening Allegro of the *Rhenish* Symphony, which is almost identical to Beethoven's dotted minim = 60 for the first movement of the *Eroica* Symphony, a movement of a very similar type. Schumann gives crotchet = 52 for the Ziemlich langsam opening of Symphony No. 4 and crotchet = 66 for the Andante un poco maestoso of No. 1. The Beethoven–Schumann continuity gives an obvious model for the first movement of Brahms's No. 3, the third member of the *Eroica–Rhenish* succession, with its close rhythmic and thematic link to the *Rhenish*. Our tempo for this Allegro con brio is identical, at dotted minim = 66, though the metre is broader, 6/4 rather than 3/4. Steinbach does not give metronome marks, but he does give many details which help to characterise basic tempi as well as to decide on details of tempo modification. To return to some of the problematic tempo names, he comments of the 'un poco sostenuto' at the opening of the first movement of No. 1, for example, that 'the emphasis should be on "poco", therefore not too slow', so that one can beat the half bar, though 'initially in six'. The time signature 6/8 is after all very different from 6/4, where the subdivided beat, the crotchet, has a larger role in the inner rhythm. This treatment of the opening creates a very different effect from the majestic six-beat pattern adopted in so many performances. Of the main theme of the finale, 'allegro non troppo, ma con brio', Steinbach emphasises the importance of long breaths for its great line, and points out that its structure is of two-bar phrases, the end of each indicated by a descending dynamic wedge.

If the sense of a proper basic tempo for the character of the ideas and their relation to one another is essential, so, of course, is a sense of modification. Brahms was against rigid, metronomic tempi, though also against an excess of modification, as emerges from his comment to Henschel that tempo modification was nothing new and should be taken *con discrezione*.[15] This was probably a dig at Wagner, who claimed the credit for its invention through his many freedoms with tempi as a performer. My general conclusion is that tempi should be spacious but forthright, tempo variation sensitive but simple. The music must have inner rhythm, but if you 'pull the rhythm around' too much you may lose it, since so much is built in, as, for example, with the hemiola pattern. My belief is that Brahms wanted few major changes and was happy with essentially straightforward tempi. I try to be sensitive to the structure and to the ebb and flow of the music. Brahms used very few tempo markings, only the essential ones to give the basic structure. Apart from sectional changes within movements, such as the contrast sections in ABA or scherzo–trio forms, they are almost all at the end of a movement or section to indicate slowing, usually marked 'più lento', 'poco rall.' etc. Separate coda sections with their own marking only occur in two of the symphonic movements – briefly in the first movement of No. 1 ('meno allegro' from 'allegro') and much more expansively in the first movement of No. 2. None the less, even here Brahms marks the 'tranquillo' and 'sempre tranquillo' sections 'in tempo'. Speeding up in a movement is very rare. He marks the return of the main theme of the fourth movement of No. 1, 'animato' (bar 220), later restoring the tempo with the marking 'largamente'; however, the lower-case printing suggests that this is to be only a slight change. Indeed, he intended these markings only for the full score and not for the parts.

My aim is never to contradict large-scale structural markings, or to anticipate them, thus undermining their effect. I assume that he intended his tempi to be basically 'straight' or, when marked for change, to be clearly changed, so that the change is an event, not just another tempo variation. We therefore avoid some of the freedoms which can be heard in traditional performances, such as in the 'Un poco sostenuto' opening of No. 1, which I keep quite clear and strict. Likewise, I take the concluding 'meno allegro' not too slow, but different from the opening, not a 'sostenuto' effect. In the coda of the first movement of No. 2, I try to match Brahms's difficult markings of 'tranquillo' and 'sempre tranquillo' in tempo, with no real slowing at the end of the coda, so that the closing chords come quickly. The 12/8 central section of the second movement is kept in strict tempo since Brahms gives no tempo change. In the last movement the second theme 'largamente' represents a significant slowing, and so must the 'tranquillo' and 'sempre tranquillo' sections of the middle section.

In main development sections of outer movements, we even receive encouragement from Steinbach to press forward in helping to sharpen the contrasts of tempo when they come. Of the development of the last movement of Symphony No. 3, for example, he says, 'at H [bar 134] the strings play on the bridge until the forte entry [at bar 141]. The driving tempo is valid above all [from] here . . . and following. In spite of having already arrived at fortissimo before K, we crescendo further one bar before K [bar 172] in all instruments up to the climax . . . at the triplet episode [from bar 252] one calms the tempo down. The semiquaver figures in the strings at O [bar 261] are played so that one dwells some-what on the first semiquaver, quasi tenuto.'[16] We follow this description of movement 1 so that the 'agitato' (from bar 77) presses on until the 'poco rit.' which leads to the 'un poco sostenuto' retransition to the main theme, marked 'Tempo 1'. Another example of a strict and driving Allegro tempo is that of the *Tragic Overture*, which contains much internal contrast. I keep this strict, and also the proportional relation of the central section, marked at exactly half speed. These 'strict' tempi make the modifications, where they come, all the more telling and enable them to be subtle too. In the first movement of Symphony No. 1, the slight holding back for the reflective second theme, which seems so natural, benefits from not having been exploited in the parallel passage of the introduction. Keeping the 'poco sostenuto' until the exact point marked at the end of the third movement of No. 2, rather than earlier reinforces the touching contrast of the strings in the scoring. Likewise an exact observance of the 'poco rit. . . . un poco sostenuto' in the first movement of No. 3, helps to keep the basic shape of the movement. One is always tempted to do more shaping with tempo change. But once a performance goes out of shape it is ruined. One senses that shape in performance, as in structure, was always paramount for Brahms.

Tempo relationships are also vital to the structure of a whole work, the temporal dimension complementing the musical substance. The subject is especially interesting where the composer has achieved a reprise of opening materials at the close, thus implying a return to the same or a related tempo. This feature characterises two major works, the Requiem and the Third Symphony. As mentioned, Brahms recalls the closing section of the first movement of the Requiem at the close of the work via a transition from the main part of movement 7. Though the movements bear different markings – 'Ziemlich langsam und mit Ausdruck' and 'Feierlich' – it is clear from the MM crotchet = 80 that he wants something of the same tempo; indeed, he gives no tempo change for the dramatic return of the very contrasted opening material. Taken literally, his mark-ings impart no sense of shape to the last movement, since the main part is of a different character and clearly needs more animation than the reflective close. Yet he gives no suggestion that the end should be significantly slower. I therefore take the main section slightly quicker in order that the close can be around the marking of the first movement, and seem like a relaxation from the earlier part of the movement, allowing for a slightly slower tempo at the very end to signal the close of the entire work.

The tempo relationship in the Third Symphony is somewhat different. The recall of the opening theme in the closing bars of the work comes at the end of a coda marked 'Un poco sostenuto' following an Allegro movement, and gradually transforms its rhythmic and dynamic character – a calm dissolution of its original tensions. However, despite the transformation of mood, the fact that the first movement is marked Allegro con brio, suggesting a faster tempo than Allegro, must indicate that the eventual 'un poco sostenuto' marking for the theme cannot actually signify a much slower speed than that of its first appearance. The 'poco sostenuto' recalls prominent ideas from the second and third movements as well as the opening motto; if slowed a little as Brahms asks, the recollection of the slow movement can occur at exactly its original speed. In many performances the end gets too slow too soon. One must keep it moving so that it is a glowing sunset, but doesn't go on all night: it must be a climax, not an endless good-bye; its classical character must be acknowledged. This quiet ending is always a shock to the uninitiated listener, but it is one of the golden moments in the Brahms canon.

Brahms's dynamic markings are much more straightforward than his tempo marks. They generally cover only the range *pp–ff*. The extremities of *fff* and *ppp* are unusual and reserved for special moments – for example the atmospheric string tremolos under clarinets in thirds followed by oboe at the end of the second movement of Symphony No. 4, or for a contrasted repetition (third movement of No. 1, bars 39–40). But one notes immediately the constant use of dynamic 'hairpins' for expression, which occur throughout the texture. Their importance is confirmed in the fact that they even exist on individual notes as well as in phrases, as, for example, in the continuation of the first theme of the first movement of No. 4. They are further evidence of the importance of nuance and phrasing to the life of this music, and we may expect that many similar features of dynamic shaping were assumed by Brahms even when not marked in the score: Steinbach's markings, for example, add much that must be taken as part of the Brahms style. Perhaps most indicative is his comment on the opening of the first movement of No. 3. He points out that the two opening chords marked *forte* should be given a slight dynamic shaping by a diminuendo on each rather than a crescendo. These chords can sometimes seem a little feeble in effect, lacking any sense of relation to what follows. Nor is the scoring very bright, with the second trumpet obscured at the bottom in unison with the bassoon. Steinbach's suggestion for the dynamics, taken with a tempo quicker than in many performances, makes the whole effect more convincing. There are many places where such an approach enlivens the music. The many long pedals in Brahms, where the lack of harmonic movement can lead to monotony on the basis of the given marks, also benefit from dynamic shaping. In the introduction to No 1's first movement, I phrase the timpani part in one-bar phrases, with a crescendo at the end of each, creating a larger dynamic curve to reflect the music above. In the pedal fugue of the Requiem (movement 3) I reflect the dynamics of the choir and the structure of the fugue in the dynamics of the pedal, none being marked by Brahms. In contrast, I make use of preliminary diminuendos to intensify the ensuing crescendos and help to build the climax. Such details were simply the norm in eighteenth- and nineteenth-century music-making.

In conclusion, the use of historical resources does not solve performance problems. The subtlety of great music requires a comparable sensitivity on the part of the performer, and many different approaches to tempi and expression can be taken. But the immediacy of the result can bring back to Brahms performance something which, to judge from decades of negative and rather bland Brahms criticism, it has lost (compare, for example, reviews of his day with our own). I find that these approaches interest performers of many kinds, not just of original instruments; that string players in 'conventional' orchestras begin to ask about the role of vibrato, for example; that attitudes towards tempi in 'conventional' performances are changing perceptibly. Not least among young audiences, there is a tangible enthusiasm for historically informed approaches which will surely be significant for the future of classical concert music, and Brahms in particular.

11 The editor's Brahms

ROBERT PASCALL

How Brahms gave his music to the world

There are two compelling descriptions of Brahms composing: one by Brahms himself talking to his young friend the singer (and later conductor) Georg Henschel on 26 February 1876 during a train journey between Koblenz and Wiesbaden, the other by his biographer Max Kalbeck, who happened to meet him on one of his composing walks.[1] Both in their different ways testify to intense mental activity away from manuscript paper: Brahms composed in the main, not at the piano or at his desk, but in his head. It is no surprise therefore to find his musical handwriting, when he came to write a piece down, characterised by a certain urgency. Of course he sketched and drafted (mostly destroying such material after it had served its purpose); but his writing out of the full form of a composition was usually as a working copy, which had running corrections as he changed his mind on details. The script is characteristically fluent, and all sorts of short-cuts are employed – including notational abbreviations, or ways of forming characters which are really economical (he used to combine leger-lines and note-stems into one stroke of the pen, and he developed a way of writing natural signs with one stroke too). His correction methods needed to be similarly efficient, and the two most common are surely also the two fastest – smearing the ink when still wet, then writing in the revised notation over the smear, or crossing something out in ink and replacing it alongside; on occasions he also used a knife to scrape out mistakes. The meaning of dynamic and articulation signs is usually clear as he wrote them, though the placement of crescendo and decrescendo hairpins can be approximate, increasingly so perhaps towards the bottom of pages.

When he had completed the full writing down, he would then wish to try over the work and consult friends and colleagues. Often he would have the work copied, and performance materials would have to be generated for larger-scale works – these materials were mostly copied by hand, though later in life, Brahms had string parts for orchestral music engraved for the trial performances. One hundred and two different copyists have been distinguished by their writing, but the two professional copyists he most regularly used were Franz Hlavaczek and William

Kupfer, both working in Vienna. With Kupfer, a fellow Hamburger, he struck up a friendship, keeping the Hamburg newspapers for him, and showing other kindnesses.[2] A copyist's job of course was to imitate, reproducing precisely what he had in front of him. Copyists worked as speedily as they could, however, and human error crept unavoidably in: omissions, misplacements, misreadings (Brahms's quaver rest could on occasion be interpreted as a note, for instance!). But Brahms corrected and used these copies; and a copied orchestral score would now replace his autograph for most practical purposes – conducting performances, retouching the work. He would then prepare this copyist's score as the engraver's model – polishing, clarifying and giving instructions to the publisher's reader and/or engraver in the margins. In the run-up to submission, he would also discuss the layout and format of the coming edition with the publisher. Since music with parts would characteristically be engraved score-from-score, parts-from-parts, it was most important that the manuscript parts should agree with the manuscript score (though on some rare occasions Brahms intended the parts to have fuller markings, for instance at the opening of the Second String Quintet Op. 111 – thus causing a real problem for today's editors). Brahms's chief publisher was the firm of Simrock (Bonn, and later Berlin), and for Brahms's major works Simrock employed as reader (analogous to today's sub-editor) Robert Keller: thoroughly good at this job, he had an eagle eye, and came to take enormous pride in his involvement with Brahms's music.

For Brahms's music, the best available engravers were employed. Their job was to reproduce the music too, but also to regulate and amplify signs according to the then current notational practice (hairpins for instance would be, then as now, from notehead to notehead), and to produce an object of pleasing graphic appearance. The engraving was done on a single metal plate for each page, and if one has had the luck to see an engraver at work, one never forgets the impression of enormous skill and judgement involved. It has first to be decided how much music should be fitted on each page, after which there are the three principal activities: mapping out where the bars and notes should go – done with light scratch marks; graving (or engraving proper) – the gouging out, or graving, of staves initially, and, towards the end, adding the necessary slurs and hairpins in this way; and punching – using punch and hammer to put in the clefs, key and time signatures, notes, dynamics and some articulation signs. The plate is in mirror-image, but engravers rapidly became used to working (by our standards) backwards. Hairpins (except for very long ones) and slurs were done freehand, and hairpins were begun at the point (a right-handed engraver therefore would turn the plate upside-down to engrave a descrescendo hairpin). Thus the page of note-text would be made up piecemeal on the plate, and according to all available evidence, a plate would take around five hours for a complex piece. Mistakes could be corrected either by hammering out the plate from the back, or by pouring on liquid metal. In some later printings from the old plates, evidence of corrections can resurface – naturally of great interest to today's editors.

With all this skill and care, engravers nevertheless sometimes mis-interpreted what they had in front of them, or regulated the notation in inappropriate ways. But proofs were read carefully: at the publishers (by Robert Keller for the larger-scale works), by Brahms himself and by any friends he called in on specific occasions. Brahms would characteristically use this opportunity to give the work a final compositional polish. Such polishing had been going on since the writing down and through the trial performances, and it tended in general to become less extreme the further Brahms was along the road to publication: so the autographs can show quite major changes – bars, sections inserted, new transpositions and orchestrations – whereas the copyists' scores generally have less of sub-stance, with significant attention paid instead to dynamic and articulative profiling; the same is true of the proofs. Where the proofs do not survive, we may deduce the corrections they must have contained by comparing the engraver's model with the first edition. Seventeen proof copies marked by Brahms do survive, but one needs to know their provenance in order to determine whether they were functional proofs or copies for record which had not been returned to the publishers. From the heavily marked proof of the piano four–hand arrangement of the Second Symphony, and from other corroborative evidence, we can readily see that the exact placement and extent of hairpins, slurs and articulation signs did matter to Brahms.

The first editions are, however, of very considerable significance. Brahms wrote in 1873 in connection with his *Variations on a Theme of Haydn* Op. 56a: 'It is not the manuscript that is definitive but rather the engraved score, which I myself have corrected.'[3] But he also recognised that mistakes could get through into the print uncorrected, and in the case of the Second Symphony he suggested to Fritz Simrock in 1878: 'For the Symphony you will probably think of printing the minimum possible – so that we can carry on finding mistakes?'[4] Thus the first editions could contain both improvements and errors, and today's editor has to dis-entangle these by careful work on the entire range of sources available, and by thorough understanding of the habits of copyists, engravers and (most importantly) the composer himself.

After the work had appeared, Brahms would take a copy of the print into his library and use it for most subsequent purposes – performances, post-publication correction and polishing. These 'Handexemplare' contain all sorts of marks: conducting indications, corrections to mistakes, a few polishings, experiments for possible revisions, alterations for specific performances. Furthermore, after Brahms's death these volumes were then taken into the Archive of the Gesellschaft der Musikfreunde in Vienna, where they could be used and marked by performers, editors and other interested musicians (happily this is now no longer the case). Every mark on them has to be assessed for its significance before it can be decided whether Brahms intended an alteration to his public text. When he found something he very definitely wanted to be changed, he wrote off to the publisher requesting that the plates be altered; and since his correspondence does not survive intact, today's editor has to use an appropriate printing from first edition plates issued after his death as a control text.

Perceiving the need

Thus in general terms we have a picture of a composer actively and intimately concerned with the whole process of publication of his music, and working with a dedicated team of publishers and engravers. It is therefore easy to understand that until roughly the 1970s everything looked relatively straightforward for a would-be Brahms editor. Indeed there did not seem any real need for an editor in the scholarly sense at all: Brahms himself had supervised publication of almost all his compositions, and his post-publication alterations had been taken into the old Complete Edition of 1926–7 (*Johannes Brahms Sämtliche Werke*) along with the few remaining pieces not published during his life.

During recent times, however, two principal factors have come together to change this view: intensive research on sources has made clear how many of these have survived, and how few had been used in the preparation of the old Complete Edition; and detailed scrutiny of the texts has demonstrated that mistakes had remained uncorrected in the first editions, as also in the old Complete Edition. Accordingly, discussions and preparations during the late 1970s led to the involvement of the publisher G. Henle of Munich, then to the formal foundation of the Society for the (new) Johannes Brahms Complete Edition (*Johannes Brahms Gesamtausgabe*) and to the establishment of a staffed Research Office at the University of Kiel, Germany. In 1991 the Konferenz der Deutschen Akademien der Wissenschaften in Mainz granted the long-term financial support necessary to ensure the proper completion of the project. The first volume of the new edition – the First Symphony – appeared in 1996. (Most of the detailed exemplification below is drawn from the research behind this volume). There will be some sixty to sixty-five volumes in the new Complete Edition, issued at the planned average rate of two per year.

An important difference between the old and the new Complete Editions is the inclusion in the latter of all Brahms's arrangements of his own music for piano, principally for duet. These four-hand arrangements are wonderfully written for the instrument, as one might expect, and they shed a different light on the compositions concerned; they were of course of great significance in the spread of Brahms's music in the nineteenth century. But the most important issue is this: in the new Complete Edition, the end-product of the editor's activity is the provision of a musical text free from transmission errors, which comes as close as possible to the notational intentions of the composer and which offers the scholar and performer alike a reliable basis for interpreting the work.

Today's editor sets to work

So, what does a Brahms editor now have to do to accomplish this primary objective, how does he/she go to work, and what differences does it make? The tasks for the contemporary Brahms editor can be viewed as falling into three related categories of activity: historical, source-critical and editorial. Historical enquiry traces the genesis of the work at issue and its emergence into the public domain; it is thus concerned with compositional process, early performances, early reception and publication. Since much historical material on Brahms is already available in the literature, the main work here is that of refinement – dating undated or wrongly dated letters, checking other factual details. Most of the historical material appears in the introduction to a new Complete Edition volume.

The source-critical work seeks to give a full bibliographical description of each source, to relate the sources and to assess their significance and use. Here the main work is that of technical description, chronology and evaluation, and the outcome of this work is the first part of the Critical Report. The editorial activity deciphers readings, and identifies, lists and explains the history of all variants, particularly concentrating on whether these have arisen through error or compositional improvement. This is the basis for deciding which reading Brahms actually intended, and the outcomes here are the second part of the Critical Report (the Editorial Report) and the note-text itself. In practice, these three categories of task are closely intertwined, and they are best done in conjunction: the role each source played in the history of the emergence of the work conditions our assessment of the status and significance of the source, which in turn has great bearing on the editorial decision-making.

How, then, does the editor accomplish all this? There are a number of ways to answer this question. Every complete edition has its formal guidelines, which describe technically what is required (those for the new Complete Edition can be obtained from the Research Office in Kiel). A few selected points from our early planning stage may well be of interest in showing strategic alternatives. We had to decide whether to publish the critical reports separately, as do some current complete editions, or to include these under the same covers as the main music texts, as do some others. There are advantages both ways. A separate volume means that critical report and note-text can be compared simultaneously by users. On the other hand, separate critical reports can become mislaid in libraries and elsewhere, and for some volumes in other complete editions, critical reports have not yet been published. Furthermore – and this could be considered the overwhelming argument for inclusion – unless an editor has thought through the histories of the variant readings as deeply as possible, the editorial decisions can so easily be intuitive and/or wrong. Or again, we did not know whether to publish the piano four-hand arrangements in score (the format of the autographs) or secondo on the left and primo on the right of each opening (in the format of the first editions). Here too there are advantages both ways: scholars find working with scores easier, performers the opposite. Our computer age provided the ideal solution: the library edition will be in score, the practical edition in performers' format. Or again, concerning the control of sources and argumentation, we decided to work with three categories of source: the main source (*Hauptquelle*: that source in which the necessary corrections are the slightest), reference sources (*Referenzquellen*: those sources closely related to the main source) and marginal sources (*Randquellen*: for instance sketches and drafts, which, while they have great historical interest and importance, do not provide strong input into the editorial decision-making).

Two additional answers to our question are important, however. In order to understand what happened in the particular case of one piece, one needs to know the normal methods of work of composer, copyist, reader and engraver. And in general one needs to have a strong detective instinct, wanting to find out what ostensibly indecipherable marks on manuscripts actually indicate, wanting to reconcile apparently conflicting information in historical source-material, wanting to investigate untackled problems and issues. As to the differences all this makes, we will, in general, be considerably better informed on the history of the musical work, and I expect the new texts will show a significant number of changes of detail – a few different notes, many altered dynamic and articulation indications. These will affect the way a work is played and heard, and it is to be hoped that performers, analysts and critics will want to consider the new readings and their implications. When there are relatively few or even no changes to a particular text, it is still important to have had that text confirmed by the research.

Historical problems

Detailed historical work on Brahms is in one sense no different from all such work: documents have to be found and assessed. But for this great composer, who has already received so much scholarly attention, there is the additional matter of identifying and correcting previous errors. Let us consider briefly selected examples concerning the genesis and early performances of the First Symphony.

As is well known, Brahms took many years to complete this work. Having shown a version of the first movement to his friends Clara Schumann and Albert Dietrich in 1862 (when it was without its slow introduction), he did not finish composing the whole work until shortly before the first performance, on 4 November 1876 – and even then he had not really finished, since between first performance and publication he radically revised the slow movement and retouched other movements. Between 1862 and 1876 there is only one surviving document of musical substance, the greeting Brahms sent on 12 September 1868 to Clara Schumann for her birthday the next day, which contains an early version of the Alphorn theme in the last movement of the symphony. Two interesting questions surround this greeting:[5] is it really a quotation of a melody Brahms heard in the Alps, or might it rather be an original melody? And, is it possible to say whether the Alphorn melody was already planned to be part of the symphony's finale at this time? The reasons these questions arise are: (i) that the autograph object itself raises some questions: for instance, both the archaic form of the heading ('blŭs' instead of blies) and the presence of words rather suggest Brahms was indulging (as it were) in a poetic conceit; and (ii) that some claims in the Brahms literature seem overdetermined on the evidence ostensibly available. Slight melodic resonances with a yodel from Lower Austria had been discovered in the 1920s by Felix Pöschl, but if Brahms had known that melody at the relevant time, one should rather speak of a starting point which Brahms evolved into something quite new. A search through nineteenth-century alphorn anthologies and enquiries at the Volksliedarchiv in Freiburg im Breisgau failed to produce any specific source for Brahms's theme. For the text, similar topoi may be found in folk-song (for instance in Erk/Böhme, *Deutscher Liederhort*: 'Hoch aufm Berg und teuf im Thal / Soll ich denn um dich truren wohl überall?') and in Eichendorff's 'Aus dem Leben eines Taugenichts' ('Wohin ich geh' und schaue, / In Feld und Wald und Tal, / Vom Berg ins Himmelsblaue, / Vielschöne, gnäd'ge Fraue, / Grüß ich dich tausendmal').[6] But again no actual exact source for Brahms's text has come to light. On the evidence available at the moment then, it seems likely that Brahms followed appropriate style and topoi but composed melody and text himself, 'pretending' otherwise to Clara.

The first stage in answering our second question above (whether the Alphorn melody was already planned to be part of the finale) is to understand whether the finale of the symphony had already been conceived, or perhaps even partially composed, by 1868, but this is regrettably not knowable on the presently available evidence. In fact, apart from the greeting to Clara Schumann, nothing at all is known to us of this finale until 1876. What can be stated with certainty is that in the finale this theme has undergone some very interesting revisions: the preliminary 'intonation' bar has been cancelled, the rhythm modified and a second horn brought in to establish a seamless legato. The general result of this inquiry, then, is that we have set the boundaries of current knowledge, and, until additional evidence becomes available, future commentators on the symphony should exercise appropriate caution.

One of the important historical problems in Brahms research is an issue surrounding his correspondence. The published editions of his letters contain many clear errors of dating and transcription, and these need to be put right in order to follow the genesis of a musical work properly. During the course of work on the First Symphony for the new Complete Edition, dating was revised for thirteen letters, transcription of contents was made more accurate for a further one letter, and three unpublished letters proved of significant use in establishing aspects of the history of and/or preferred textual readings for the music. To demonstrate how today's editor goes about the revision of dating and transcription of letters, let us take the example of a letter Brahms wrote to his publisher Fritz Simrock after arriving in Pörtschach in June 1877. This letter affects the dating of work on the piano arrangement of the symphony in a relatively small way, but provides a neat example of what has to be done. In the published correspondence Brahms's letter is dated 14 June and transcribed as: 'Ich wohne also: Pörtschach am See, Kärnten. / Seit Vorgestern und Gestern habe ich schon 4 Seiten cmoll zu 4 Händen geschrieben!'[7] What Brahms actually wrote was: 'Ich wohne also: *Pörtschach* am See, *Kärnten*. Seit Vorgestern, u. Gestern habe ich schon 4 Seiten *cmoll à 4 ms.* geschrieben!' . . . The omitted comma proves crucial, and its restoration alters the sense entirely. The published version implies: 'Since the day before yesterday and yesterday I have written four pages of the C minor for four hands', but that comma makes Brahms's meaning plain as: 'I am staying at *Pörtschach* am See, *Carinthia*, since the day before yesterday, – and yesterday I wrote out four pages of the C minor for four hands!' This in turn makes the dating of the letter itself relatively straightforward, since Brahms put in his diary that he was to arrive or had arrived in Pörtschach on 9 June. If Brahms had arrived there quite late, he could have counted the beginning of his stay in his letter to Simrock either from the date of his arrival or from the next day, his first full day there. Thus either 9 or 10 June would be the 'day before yesterday', and he wrote this letter on either 11 or 12 June 1877.

On the programme leaflets for early performances of the First Symphony, it can be observed that the tempo indications for individual movements varied. For instance, at the time of the first performance, the second movement was marked Poco Adagio, which Brahms changed to the final reading Andante sostenuto between the first and third performances; and the main part of the finale was marked Allegro con brio, which Brahms changed on or shortly before 19 November 1876 to the still interim Allegro moderato ma con brio. Dating the change to the second movement's marking is made possible by a press report of the third performance which gives the new marking; and dating the change in the finale is by simple deduction from the copyist's score of the movement; Brahms sent his autograph off to be copied on 19 November, and the copy gives the new marking with no evidence of alteration. Here the documents can be assessed adequately only when considered together. (During publication, Brahms altered the marking of the finale again, and it now reads *Allegro non troppo, ma con brio*.)

A final brief example is of particular interest to us in Britain. Hans von Bülow conducted the First Symphony in Scotland in December 1877: according to Brahms's biographer Max Kalbeck 'not in Glasgow, but on 10 December in Edinburgh'.[8] This may seem a relatively tangential issue, but no editor should leave resolvable contradictions however small. Since there was conflicting information on this date elsewhere, the matter needed clarification, and the Public Library Records in Scotland show clearly that he conducted the work twice, in Edinburgh on 17 December and in Glasgow on the following day.

Source-critical problems

During the work, and as a matter of good fortune rather than a result of enquiries, thirty-two engraver's models for Brahms's music were redis-covered in Switzerland, among which were the engraver's models for movements 1 and 4 of the First Symphony.[9] These enabled a much clearer picture to emerge of the development of variant readings. Brahms himself had both copies made (at different times and places, and by different copyists), used them for performances and prepared them as the engraver's models for the publication process. The stemma relating the sources for the symphony is complex, showing varied patterns of provi-sion, use and survival for each movement. The first movement autograph does not survive, indeed was probably destroyed quite early on by Brahms, who had had the movement copied in Vienna before the final main compositional thrust on the symphony as a whole in the summer of 1876. The second movement was finished and performed in a version superseded in May 1877, shortly before publication; uniquely among the movements of the work, the printed orchestral parts for the slow move-ment were engraved from the score as model. The third movement auto-graph served as engraver's model, as did the fourth movement copy. Brahms was characteristically involved in the publication process, pre-paring material for the engraver, discussing and deciding on format and appearance, reading proofs, and keeping in regular contact with pub-lisher and reader. After the first edition, Brahms continued correcting and retouching, and he requested two corrections and one retouching by letter to the publisher, which he also entered into his personal copy of the printed score. As noted above, we need to use posthumous prints from the first edition plates as control texts – though one has to be careful about losses of image due to plate deterioration. In the case of the First Symphony, there are no further corrections or retouchings in evidence in these posthumous printings of the score (the parts however were revised).

Editorial problems

Let us consider bars 27–31 of the finale – the dramatic change from the chromatic minor slow introduction to the emergence of the Alphorn melody. In order to understand the full range of the editor's work, we must include consideration of the autograph, the copyist's score, used as engraver's model, and the first edition for these bars (see Plates 11.1–3).

Plate 11.1 Autograph: from the finale of the First Symphony (bars 27–31)

The first thing we have to do is to account for all of Brahms's compositional emendations in the sources:

bar 28^{1-2}: autograph, Violin I: The legato slurs were originally over only the demisemiquavers, and Brahms has lengthened them backwards in ink to include the preceding quaver in each case.

bar 28^{2}: autograph, Violin II: Brahms has altered the original double-stop $e_\flat{}^1/g_\flat{}^1$ in ink to $g_\flat{}^1/e_\flat{}^2$.

bar 28^3–29: autograph, Horn 1/2: Brahms has changed the original semiquavers $c^3/e_\flat{}^2$ (sounding $c^2/e_\flat{}^1$) followed by quaver, crotchet and full-bar rests in ink into the printed version.

bar 28^3–29: autograph, Timpani: Brahms has altered in bar 28^3 the original crotchet c in ink into the printed version. In bar 29^{3-4} he originally notated the tremolo on each beat as a dotted crotchet with semiquaver abbreviation-signs and the number 6 above, indicating the semiquaver triplet motion (compare bar 30^{1-2}). Later he has altered the tremolo in bar 29^{3-4} into demisemiquaver abbreviation-signs, corrected the 6 in bar 29^3 accordingly into a 12, and deleted altogether the 6 in bar 29^4.

Plate 11.2 (a and b): Copyist's manuscript: from the finale of the First Symphony (bars 26–37)

Plate 11.3 First edition (Handexemplar): from the finale of the First Symphony (bars 28–34)

The copyist Josef Füller took over this version for his copy of the finale, and added a 12 in bar 29^4 for completeness' sake. This is also the version found in the first edition of score and parts.

Subsequently (probably at the time of working on the piano four-hand arrangement) Brahms further altered the reading in the autograph score. In bar 29^4 he cancelled the dot after the crotchet, so that duple demisemiquaver motion and hence a more graduated written-out ritardando came into being (this is also the reading in the autograph and the first edition of the piano four–hand arrangement). That this difference between the score and the piano arrangement was intentional is confirmed by Brahms's letter to Robert Keller of 28 September 1877: 'In sending back the proofs of the Symphony, I cannot but

Example 11.1 First Symphony, movement 4, bars 30–1

thank you in the warmest possible way for the great trouble you have taken with the work. Especially, I am most grateful for the blue-crayon marks (and not just the one on p. 48). On that very page, I will leave the triplet motion for the Timpani, because this is the main point of the succeeding passage, and the player will be able to capture it more securely in performance.'[10]

bars 30–1: autograph, Trombone 1–3: Brahms has altered the original version (see Example 11.1) in ink into the printed version. The original bass-note *G* in Trombone 3 is a residue of the intonational opening to Brahms's Alphorn theme, as first written down in 1868.

bar 31[1]: autograph, Horn 1/?2: At the beginning of the bar Brahms has deleted the original semibreve g^1 (sounding *g*) in ink; this could have been for either Horn 1 or Horn 2. If for Horn 1, then we see Brahms composing in his seamless legato for this theme by giving the sustained note to Horn 2.

bar 31[1]: autograph, Viola: Brahms has made an illegible alteration in ink, which may just be clarifying an obscurity in the original notation.

The copyist Josef Füller copied the score of the finale for Brahms between 20 November and 10 December 1876. One of the things Brahms asked was that the original clarinet parts for C clarinet should be transposed for B♭ clarinet. As we have noted above, Brahms used this copy to conduct from, then prepared it as the engraver's model, so it contains some further emendations to the text of significance for the final state of his intentions:

bar 28[1–3]: Tutti: Brahms has altered the original staccato dots in pencil into vertical dashes (Strichpunkte), and made a marginal note.
bar 31: Horn 2: Brahms has added *f* in pencil.

Then we have to look at the changes in readings between the sources and explain those, intervening editorially in the cases of error:

bar 27[1–2]: Flute 1, Oboe 1, Bassoon 1, Contrabassoon: In Füller's copy, and hence also in the first edition, the *cresc.* has been carelessly copied into beat 2. It needs to be restored to where Brahms intended, as shown in the autograph.
bar 28[3–4]: Timpani: The *dim.* has been carelessly copied before beat 4, and the printer has taken it back even further. Here too we need to restore the sign to where Brahms intended, on beat 4 itself.

bar 30^1: Horn 1: Füller omitted the *Solo* indication here, as did the engraver, and it should be restored according to the autograph.
bars 30–1: Trombone 1: Füller omitted the legato slur for Trombone 1 (bars 30^3–31^4) as did the engraver, and this must be restored, following the autograph.

With minor alterations of detail to suit the current context, this documentation is as it appears in the new edition of the First Symphony, and it will be noted that one of the innovations with this list is that it is in complete sentences (making it user-friendly). However, there is an important regard in which the list is different here. Because we are presently concerned with demonstrating a method, the list is in three sections; in the new edition, there is a single unified list, which has the perceived advantage of presenting all the material on a particular crux together.

The editor and performer

Considered simply, editorial activity seems to precede musical performance: editors deliver texts to performers. But notation always denotes sound, and editorial activity must be carried out with this in mind. As we have now seen, in Brahms's music there are often differences of reading between the engraver's model and the resulting print; in the absence of the mostly lost corrected proofs, the editor does not initially know whether a compositional improvement has taken place or whether a mistake has crept in. The first question then is: which reading makes more musical sense? – bringing us firmly into the realm of sound and its perception. For instance, argumentation from phrase-structure, where perhaps an engraver has erroneously carried over articulation signs from the end of one phrase to the beginning of the next, or with parallel motion between instruments marked with divergent crescendo or decrescendo hairpins. But more practical matters can also enter in: in the third movement of the First Symphony the autograph engraver's model shows a double-stop for viola in bar 103 first quaver, which in the print has become a triple-stop. This triple-stop is not performable at the required tempo, and orchestral players of today agree a *divisi* amongst themselves. Thus we can assume here that the engraver made a mistake, and the editorial decision is therefore for the original double-stop (in this case however with a footnote, since the cause of the variant reading remains an assumption on our part).

Musical notation is always developing, and every musical work is written in the notation of its time and place. Even after we as editors have made any cautious modernisations that seem desirable, the transparency of meaning can still be deceptive. For instance, *espress.* for strings proba-bly implied in Brahms's times 'with vibrato' – this is quite well known by string players today, but what is much less well known is that normal tone-production was in those times without vibrato. Or: Brahms took great pains over his tempo markings, but only relatively infrequently gave metronome indications (we have these for just nine works). In *Ein deutsches Requiem* the metronome marks indicate clearly that choral fugues were characteristically taken distinctly slower then than is custom-ary now, and therefore we ought to interpret his tempo indications without metronome marks in other choral works in the light of this. Or: Brahms's use of the indication *dolce*, often in combination with *p*, shows considerable care in the manuscripts, often being deleted or inserted (sometimes both). But what did it mean to him? We are not yet fully able to answer this question, especially as the mark occurs for accompanying parts and held notes as well as melodies. But in principle we can now maintain: notation without knowledge of performance practice remains only seemingly transparent, and the question of the meaning of the nota-tion always leads into the field of performance practice research.

Information concerning historical performance practice properly belongs in a complete edition, even if it does not have a central role there. The new Brahms Complete Edition volumes are planned to include material on early performance history and reception in their introduc-tions; and information, for instance, on orchestral size, instruments and their sound, durations and speeds, technical and expressive issues in per-formance, will naturally find its way in. As a telling example, the critic of the *Karlsruher Zeitung*, commenting on a performance Brahms gave of his First Piano Concerto on 3 November 1865, found fault with the 'unremitting spreading of chords in the slower tempi'.[11] Since it is well established that this aspect of interpretation was widely practised in the nineteenth century, and there are other accounts of Brahms's use of it, we should take this remark to mean: Brahms spread chords more than the critic could take or was used to. Our Critical Reports give complete information on all alterations to the sources of compositional significance, including retouchings of tempo. For two of his most impor-tant works, the Second Piano Concerto and the Fourth Symphony, Brahms wrote tempo modifications into the autographs, as an aid to the first performers of the music, which he later erased for publication pur-poses. Since these erased marks are still decipherable, we have before us direct evidence of how Brahms himself considered this music should be performed. He referred to the tempo modifications in the Fourth Symphony in an important letter to his erstwhile friend Joseph Joachim:

I have pencilled in a few modifications of tempo into the score. They seem desirable, useful, even perhaps necessary, when dealing with a first performance. Unfortunately they then creep into print (with me and with others), where in the main they do not belong. Such exaggerations are only really necessary as long as a work is unfamiliar to an orchestra (or virtuoso). In this case I can often not do enough with the pushing on and holding back, so that the expression of passion or calm comes out as I want it. But when a work has got under the skin, my view is that there should be no more talk of such things, and the more one departs from this, the more artificial I find the performance. My experience with my earlier works often shows how all this happens naturally and how superfluous many such markings of this type are! But how readily performers today seek to impress with this so-called free artistic interpretation – and how easy it all is, even with the worst possible orchestra and one rehearsal! A Meiningen Orchestra will have to make it a matter of pride, to show the opposite way. Do forgive the rambling gossip. . .[12]

All this belongs in the relevant volume of our Complete Edition, and a detailed analysis of this complex letter will have to wait till then, or some other future occasion. (As a contrary example, however, we could consider Joachim's extensive commentary in his *Violinschule* on how one should/could play Brahms's Violin Concerto, together with a complete reproduction of the solo part edited with his performance markings. Of course this is important, but it is only indicative and to include all of it in a Complete Edition volume would not be feasible on space grounds.)

In the first volume of our new Complete Edition, I carried through Brahms's third proof-correction for him, in a manner of speaking, and made 281 interventions in the text of the first edition (corrected *Handexemplar*) of the First Symphony. There are only ten corrections to pitch/rhythm, and the chief matters corrected are directly performance-relevant: extent and placement of hairpins, erroneous and wrongly placed dynamic and articulation signs. As we have noted above, for Brahms's music, the best available engravers were employed, but nevertheless they often dealt with such signs in a relatively approximate fashion. For instance at the beginning of the fourth movement of the First Symphony Brahms wrote the crescendo hairpin in bar 2 beginning on beat 3; the copyist copied somewhat approximately, extending it back to beat 2 for most of the instruments, and the printer regulated incorrectly, starting it quite soon after the *fp* on beat 1, again for most instruments.

These kinds of approximations Brahms accepted on occasion, but not always entirely without protest, as some of his interventions in copies and proofs clearly demonstrate. If hairpins have been engraved too long (often the case), the dramatic effect in performance is to some extent compromised, or at the very least changed.

In Britain at least, Brahms has now been captured for 'Early Music'! This is surely a very positive development, and performers are increasingly concerning themselves with the accuracy and historical meaning of his note-texts. Today's Brahms editor, therefore, has now a role to play extending distinctly beyond the purely musicological.

12 A photograph of Brahms

HUGH WOOD

There exists an early photograph – a shadowy person, a stretch of wall – which dates from 1824: three years before Beethoven's death. It sets the mind racing with the thought that just such a primitive apparatus might well have been turned on Beethoven himself. Just as the early gramophone captured the last castrato, so a spectral image could well have existed of this extraordinary little man who even in his lifetime had become one of the great mythic figures of the civilisation of the West. Only a few years were to pass, and the next generation – Schumann, Berlioz, Chopin (beautifully, in that nakedly revealing tragic late photograph by Bisson) – are all recorded. Musicians, and many others: the heroic age of photography produced, in the hands of Nadar, startlingly immediate images of Baudelaire, which make him peculiarly our contemporary. Such images lend to the historical existence of those depicted something which all the documentation in the world cannot: this immediacy, this contemporaneity, this sense of Now. The invention of the camera created a great dividing line in our experience of the past.

Such thoughts arise when one gazes at the many existing photographs of Brahms. They put him in a different category to Beethoven, whom the passing of time has cut off from us, has reduced to a history-book figure. Brahms, by the aid of the camera, can be imagined as tenuously alive, as a real person to be seen walking about the streets of Vienna. The arguments for the greater truth of character portrayal achieved by the art of the portrait painter are still occasionally rehearsed and (more rarely) justified. It is also true that the typical nineteenth-century photograph is a posed one; whereas we esteem in a photograph a touch of the arbitrary, the fortuitous: the 'snapshot'. There are certainly enough posed photographs of Brahms and his colleagues. Typically, one hand is placed on a doily-covered table or on the back of an ornamental chair; neither prop has any significance or real existence outside the photographer's studio: the subject is dressed up in his best clothes; there is a set expression on his face.

Nevertheless, even posing reveals. The earliest images of Brahms show a boy both exceptionally vulnerable and utterly determined: a youth already sure of his genius. There is no weakness in the chin; but both the fashion of the time and, perhaps, the sort of person he turned into dictated

Plate 12.1 Brahms and Alice Barbi on the Ringstrasse

that by his mid-forties he should have grown a beard. To turn abruptly to the end of his life: the latest photographs have nothing of the studio about them, and were mostly taken in informal circumstances. Brahms at Ischl – looking strangely clerical, a Victorian parson in his floppy off-duty summer suit – beside his close friend Johann Strauss II, moustached, dapper in his check trousers. In other snapshots, Brahms is made much of by, and responds with heavy flirtatiousness to, a series of dashing young ladies of the 1890s – grand-daughters of the generation of young ladies that their cosseted old bear fell so fruitlessly in love with when, many centuries ago, he was young. They all know that – in spite of his sharp tongue and his yokel-like lip-smacking salaciousness – he is quite harmless really. But the most compelling of these late photos, obviously taken by happy chance and on the spur of the moment, is of a tubby, elderly Brahms in his best clothes, a little black derby perched on his head, a happy-looking Alice Barbi at his side, walking in the Ringstrasse (Plate 12.1). In so far as one can detect an expression on his shadowed face, it is that of a gentleman surprised during a walk, conscious of an intrusion. In that year of 1891 when the photo was taken, Brahms had written the Clarinet Quintet and the Clarinet Trio: and no photograph can come to terms with the significance of that astounding fact.

In between youth and age there are endless photographic portraits of varying degrees and formality. One characteristic they all have in common: he never looks happy. The vulnerability of his youth has settled into a naked helplessness in the face of a hostile, alien world. Who was it who said that the eyes were windows of the soul? Look at the eyes: the camera reveals them as bottomless pools of sadness and despair. The rarely recorded – and then always superficial – manic counterbalance to this deep and perennial depression is hardly caught on camera. Truly, Brahms was the most profoundly unhappy of all the great composers.

This fact is quite central: and everything else flows from it. Schubert said: 'Do you know any jolly music? *I* don't'; and Brahms would have agreed with him. And

> Since someone will forever be surprising
> A hunger in himself to be more serious . . .

this quality of seriousness – springing, in Brahms's case, from acute personal misery – is something which appeals, and will always appeal, to large numbers of people who feel that they can respond to it; and who esteem it accordingly.

Brahms's eyes can tell us a lot: more so, his choice of texts. Goethe's *Harzreise im Winter* might have been written for him to set: the young man, bereft, wanders through a landscape as cold and barren as his own inner state. It is also the metaphor of *Winterreise*, which it anticipates by some forty years. Brahms seized on the text when his personal affairs were at their usual particularly low ebb. A touch of ludicrous insult added to injury came when Clara Schumann's good-looking daughter Julie took it into her head to marry an Italian nobleman named Vittorio Radicati di Marmorito. The unlikely consequence – Brahms offered it as his 'bridal song' – was the sombre masterpiece the *Alto Rhapsody*. We are more justified in suggesting a causal connection here than between, say, Mozart's G minor Quintet and the untimely death of his friend Count von Hatzfeld: for, after all, this was the nineteenth century, and Art and Life had now got themselves much more thoroughly entangled.[1]

Brahms begins with the words

Aber abseits, wer ists?	But who is this that has turned aside?
Ins Gebüsch verliert sich sein Pfad,	His path wanders into the undergrowth
Hinter ihm schlagen	and is lost,
Die Sträuche zusammen,	The bushes close

Das Gras steht wieder auf,	And the grass rises again behind him,
Die Öde verschlingt ihn.	The wilderness swallows him up.

The gesture of turning aside has already appeared in the Hölty text *Die Mainacht*, which Brahms set in 1866. This time the protagonist is wandering through a nocturnal landscape far from barren, full of blossoms and the sounds of nightingales and doves. But, as the music gathers itself to an almost Tristanesque moment,

Aber ich wende mich,	But I turn away,
Suche dunklere Schatten ...	Seek deeper shadows

He was always, in fact, to be turning away, seeking the deeper darkness: it soon became the pattern of his personal life.

Of course, all this is driven by the engines of a vast self-pity, and this automatically repels some. So was the poetry of Housman, and the results are magnificent. There are some other resemblances: both embattled, vulnerable, 'difficult', they none the less possessed everyday aspects of their existences which remained virtually untouched by the inevitable erosion of spirits. Of the two, Brahms emerges the more richly endowed character. Housman, the precise, demanding scholar, his chosen field cramped and specialised to the point of pedantry, confined himself to adding footnotes to minor ancient authors like some obscure kinglet taking possession of marginal, infertile territory. Brahms's scholarship and his public performing life were wide-ranging and fruitful; at least in this aspect he was fulfilled.

There is another comparison to be drawn. Housman's self-pity and pessimism were not just those of the Shropshire Lad disguised as a university professor. It has a cosmic dimension: 'I, a stranger and afraid / In a world I never made'; and the world was to be met with a stoicism learnt directly from the ancient world. Brahms had similarly imbibed this sort of wisdom through German literature.

The overwhelming lesson was that good things were only to be surveyed from afar, a huge extension of the text:

Dort, wo du nicht bist,
dort ist das Glück.

At the time of the premiere of the German Requiem in 1868 he came across (a happy chance in those days) the poetry of Hölderlin, in particular 'Hyperions Schicksalslied'. It depicts the heavenly ones in tranquil blessedness above; mortals, destined to find no resting place, below – to be hurled from rock to rock into the unknown abyss. The music moves from one level to another with abruptness. That the opening stanza, with its own ethereal music, is then repeated at the end cannot be read as an amelioration of Hölderlin's bleak conclusion, or dismissed as a capitulation to the imperatives of formal balance. It is there for a Brahmsian reason: to rub home the point about the separation of those above from those below; and the impossibility of bridging the gap.

Webern loved these works, and used to love to conduct them. The *Schicksalslied* haunted his imagination as an ideal model for *Das Augenlicht*.[2] But he also cherished and brought to performance two other choral pieces which are amongst Brahms's finest music but which are otherwise sadly neglected and unknown to the wider musical public today.[3] The *Gesang der Parzen*, also a Goethe text, presents another vision of the gods in their infinite distance, their indifference to the 'suffering Titans' who serve them, their neglect of humankind. Then there was *Nänie* – always the remote Uranus of the Brahmsian planetary system. A memorial piece, literally 'Dirge' – for the painter Feuerbach – it uses a text by Schiller in order to lament the transience of all things beautiful: 'see, even the gods and goddesses weep that beauty must fade, that perfection must die'. The evocation of the world of classical mythology is complete. And since music is the transient art *par excellence*, it is the perfect vehicle for the transmission of such sentiments. Yet the piece is far from being an example of what it represents: it is fashioned austerely to fulfil all the requirements of timelessness, of durability, that are the true hallmarks of classic art. It is also one of Brahms's most inspired and greatest works, as calm as a statue, with the same enigmatic eyes.

All these four texts were set by Brahms in between 1869 and 1882, between his thirty-sixth and forty-ninth years. It is as if, in these years of artistic maturity, he was staking out his psychological territory, proclaiming it with the clarity of a manifesto. But his concentration upon romantic and ancient classical themes did not preclude the setting of religious words. The theme of transience – to be returned to in *Nänie* – provides the link with his selection of texts for *Ein deutsches Requiem*, meditated upon since the death of his mother in 1865: 'all flesh is as grass'.

It has often been remarked, particularly by his contemporaries, that Brahms's work carefully skirts round any mention even of the name of Christ or any recognition of his Incarnation; and that Brahms successfully parried attempts by conventional believers to modify such exclusions. Nor – in spite of the sixth movement's substantial overlap with Handel's *Messiah* texts ('the trumpet shall sound . . .', 1 Corinthians 15) – is there much affirmative joy shown in the possibility of Resurrection. Yet the whole discriminating choice from a wide range of scripture – the Psalms, Isaiah, the Apocrypha; but the Gospels not so prominent as the Epistles and the Book of Revelation – show an intimate and long-standing acquaintanceship with the Lutheran Bible, suggesting not only regular reading of it, but that that reading was suffused with deep piety.

Those without religious sense may minimise this, pointing out that knowledge of the Lutheran scriptures was just as much and as conventional a part of the cultivated German's *Bildung* as a grounding in the classics of German literature: Brahms was one of many working within a Greco-Judaic tradition. The music itself gives the lie to any such superficial dismissal. It is difficult for late twentieth-century man to appreciate the religious sense; we are doing well even if we conjure up some sense of the numinous; of awe; of the impossibility of understanding the natural world and the realisation that there is something beyond it. We are far more familiar with the cocksure, noisy, media-hungry atheists of our own day, the heroes of the television chat show, who know that no courage is required for their bold stand, backed as it is by the implicit acquiescence of a materialistic audience.

In comparison, how profoundly religious these nineteenth-century unbelievers were, how acute their sense of mortality and transience, how serious and troubled, indeed anguished, they were in their awareness of something missing, something they could not find but much wished to. That quality is encountered at its most sympathetic in Brahms. It was inevitable that he should turn naturally to the Book of Job, as he did in the finest of his motets, Op. 74 No. 1. He might have written the text himself:

> Wherefore is light given to him that is in misery,
> and life to the bitter in soul;
>
> Which long for death, but it cometh not; and dig for it
> more than for hidden treasures;
>
> Which rejoice exceedingly, and are glad, when they can
> find the grave?
>
> Why is light given to the man whose way is hid, and whom
> God hath hedged in?

Typical too that Brahms should have composed these words during the same summer holiday that produced the Second Symphony. But then I have always found reports of that work's jolliness and lightheartedness to be greatly exaggerated.

Brahms's dark vision – of goodness impossibly far off, of the mortality and the transience of beauty, of the inevitability and omnipresence of personal misery – is best expressed by a twentieth-century voice:

> They give birth astride of a grave, the light gleams
> an instant, then it's night once more.

The resonances of Brahms's music are not unfamiliar to those who dwell in the age of Beckett.

The image which recurs is, of course, that of Philoctetes and his bow (now, there's a subject for a truly Brahmsian opera!). Philoctetes – left behind on an island in his cave, nursing the Amfortas-like wound which pains him every waking moment, but always aware that the wound is of a smelly repulsiveness which must exclude him from the sympathy or even the company of others, who would identify him only as the object of wary, horrified pity. However: he has the bow, and only he can wield it. The artist as a wounded creature, both subversive and *lebensunfähig*, outside civil society yet living off it as a parasite – this is very much like a nineteenth-century notion. But the true Philoctetes is not the happy-go-lucky, tragic, irresponsible, scrounging inhabitant of *La Bohème*, not the Dubedat of Shaw's *Doctor's Dilemma* (in the value of whose pictures we can never, in any case, quite believe), but the lonely sublimated obsessive with the petit-bourgeois life-style, seeking neither wealth nor fame and disregarding them if they come, giving his money away in many a secret benevolence while living the life of a clerk. The stoicism of the bachelor apartment: that is truly Philoctetes in his cave, and that was Brahms's style.

But photographs do not always bring us closer to their subjects: in many ways they distance us from them. If you look at Victorian photographs of industrial subjects, you are aware that the railway tracks and signals are recognisably familiar (like the buildings on the Ringstrasse in the background of the Barbi/Brahms photograph): but the human beings, differently dressed, are obviously of a bygone age, have now perished and are no more. Photographs can also remind us that Brahms, too, is far away and long ago. Between him and us there is a great gulf fixed: in the hundred intervening years so much has happened; and Brahms in many ways, large and small, is on the other side of this huge divide.

For instance: Brahms never learnt to ride a bicycle, and it is difficult to see him on one. But H. G. Wells was bicycling away well before Brahms died. Freud had published *Traumdeutung* just before Brahms's death, but it's difficult to imagine Brahms consulting or even meeting him. Mahler, however, was to consult Freud in 1910. German scientists were doubtless already making the experiments which led to the invention of poison gas before 1897: but Brahms did not live on into the world in which poison gas rolled across the fields of northern France. Brahms had friends amongst painters, and in particular seems to have reciprocated the admiration of Max Klinger (whose paintings I find exceptionally awful). But Brahms wouldn't have been able to make much of the later Klimt,[4] or anything of Kokoschka or Cubism.[5] A new and terrible world was lining up outside, ready to take over, at the moment of his death. The Habsburgs fell and Lenin rose; there was the Jazz Age and the Weimar Republic and the Bauhaus and the Wall Street Crash. Then came dictatorships all over Europe, another world war, the death camps and the holocaust: Sartre, abstract expressionism, the hydrogen bomb, the cold war: international terrorism: at last the fall of the Berlin Wall: the computer revolution. And here we are, standing on the further side of all this. In the far distance there is a beard, faintly waving.

But if Brahms would have found the political twentieth-century world nightmarishly strange, what would he have made of its even more alien musical aspect? Even to ask the question, we indulge in the parlour game of hypothesis. It's perhaps more honest to assume of most composers that the limits of their understanding coincide pretty closely with the ending of their natural lives. It's sentimental to opine that J. S. Bach 'might well have liked' Gershwin (really because you like Gershwin yourself). He wouldn't. He'd have found even Haydn and Mozart hard going; both offensively trivial and sometimes even incomprehensible. And Beethoven? – 'not music at all'.

The first half of our century was distinguished by what appears to us now to have been a gallant rearguard action to preserve creatively the values of the past and to continue, but along radical lines, a great tradition. At present it seems like a lost cause: the fact that the work of Schoenberg, Berg and Webern has now reached the nadir of its fortunes is more than adequately indicated by the number of university undergraduate courses on the subject – the real kiss of death – as well as their absence from the concert hall. The key figure from the immediate past upon whom Schoenberg relied – much more so than upon Wagner – was Brahms. But plonk Brahms down at a performance of *Pierrot Lunaire* and do you honestly imagine the compliment would have been returned? He could have recognised neither the homage nor the continuity, nor the similarity of the ideas in spite of the different sounds: again it would be a case of 'not music at all'.

Stravinsky he would heartily have disliked not merely because he was smart, fashionable, *mondain* (though because of that too), but more basically because he was Russian. He would thoroughly have distrusted the braggadocio of Stravinsky's attitude to the past, with its irresponsible eclecticism – that of the cultural pirate, offending the scholar in Brahms.

As for the rest of the century . . . what would he have said? That welter, that helter-skelter succession of revivals and renewals and betrayals; of re-assessments and re-creations and returns and completely new starts; that sequence of immediately trumped extremes and immediately discredited theories to support those extremes; all that ill-judged co-option of ill-digested mathematics and politics and drama and philosophy and sociology and technology; that retreat into a myriad of private worlds, at first that of the coterie and the true believer, but later, more ominously, into the infantile solipsism of the nursery; finally irresponsible, irrational pre-natal regression to the womb itself, with no past – therefore no future. Latterly we have experienced all the commercial horrors of cross-over, the voluntary espousal of all that is most ephemeral and idiotically mechanical in modern life; and. (reaction against a reaction) the resort to a cut-price religiosity which will heal all wounds, a pocket mysticism breathing some divine muzak adjusted to the attention-span of the middle-brow purchaser of a compact disc: essential easy listening, feel-good religion without dogma, without tradition, without sense. Maybe we are passing through a bad patch: but every society gets the sort of music it deserves.

Why then do I today revere Brahms as much as any other composer? The negative part of the answer lies above.

A great gulf fixed, then, between us and Brahms? This must not imply that he was cosily ensconced in his Victorian garden. He was a stranger there too: if not afraid, then certainly in a world he never had made – and had (as we have seen) great difficulties in coming to terms with. If he is remote from us, then he was equally remote from his contemporaries.

And then, is that gulf so great? The atrocities that I have detailed above would be thought marginal by many practising musicians, for whom the fabric of continuing musical society remains whole, if a bit tattered. It is only in fact my more right-on Brothers in Apollo who feel far away from this master musician (and needless to say from the idea of mastery). For some of us he has never gone away.

A story (which, like most stories, reveals my age) will illustrate both these points. I have always been enchanted by a remark of the distinguished art historian Sir Ernst Gombrich when he was introducing his choice of records on the BBC some years ago. It must be explained that his mother was a remarkable piano teacher who settled in Oxford, and gave her last piano lesson a week before she died at the age of ninety-five.

Sir Ernst chose like a cultivated Viennese – all the way through the classics to the 'Champagne Aria' from *Fledermaus*. 'And modern music?' He then said, 'With modern music I am in agreement with my mother. She used to say "I don't mind modern music *at all*. Why, I've even got *quite to like Brahms*." And that is my position also.'

The point of this story is not so much to highlight the continued existence of Brahmsian Old Incorrigibles, exhibiting a hyper-conservatism which is itself very Viennese. It is to remind ourselves that Brahms was himself modern, difficult and not accepted, found rebarbative and new-fangled and impossible, long before he became stuffy, backward-looking, old fashioned. In the last decade of his life he may well have been revered not only in Vienna and the rest of northern Europe but widely in North America as the world's greatest living composer. But this did not necessarily reflect itself in any great readiness to perform his music, which continued to be regarded as problematical, austere and forbidding (and, for those with ears to hear, remains so to this present day), or, once it was performed, in any great response to it on the part of critics or public alike. The 1894 *Grove*, which lists his works up to 1878, tempers its reverential praise with reservations along these lines.

The distinguished cultural historian Peter Gay has written an article entitled 'Aimez-Vous Brahms?', which is the most brilliant account of Brahms reception history that I have ever read.[6] His main theme is the malaise at the heart of modernism, of which he gives a very acute analysis. He gives a compelling portrait of Brahms's musical personality, and shows its curiously oblique relation to the polarities inherent in modernist thinking. He then goes on to demonstrate the surprising paucity of Brahms performances, even during the last twenty years of his life, the virtual absence of his main works from programmes in Germany and elsewhere, and the chilly reserve of the critical reaction to those which were performed. More surprisingly, even the informed inner circle – the young Richard Strauss or Max Bruch or Hans von Bülow – expressed their bewilderment. The refrain was always the same: repeated hearings were needed – a typical reaction of those well-disposed towards modern music but honestly puzzled by it to the present day. The key critical phrase was 'strangely neglected' (a cliché used to the point of parody in the pages of *Lucky Jim*).

> Brahms was not just neglected, he was strangely neglected . . . It is apparent then, that difficulty did not preclude esteem. But with Brahms it was esteem chilled by a sense of duty. Most of his contemporaries ingested Brahms like some nutritious but unpalatable diet; he was good for one.

Brahms himself realised that respect, rather than love, was the best that he could expect. Gay's section titles 'The Cerebral Sentimentalist' and 'The Alienated Conformist' summarise well the drift of his argument. He charts the change from the misleading nineteenth-century view of Brahms to the equally misleading twentieth-century view of him in a single telling sentence:

> and Brahms the frigid intellectual has become Brahms the sultry sentimentalist . . .

Sultry sentimentalist, or simply old bore: there certainly was a reaction. And it was natural enough: the oldest of generation games, that of the revolt against authority. In this country Parry and (with less individuality) Stanford had set themselves to produce surplus Brahms as a sign of allegiance. It would have been surprising if their pupils – nationalism and folk-song apart – had not stirred themselves to revolt: albeit in a very gentlemanly *English* way. The First World War gave all this reaction a political dimension; the Franco-Russian orientation was dominant here, and Brahms just another of the Old Gang, to be dismissed by those who enjoyed the scornful venom of 'Eminent Victorians'.

Those who have heard the gramophone record of Nadia Boulanger playing Brahms waltzes in duet with Dinu Lipatti will be hesitant to accuse her of a total lack of sympathy for Brahms: human beings, as every Proustian knows, are more complicated than that. At the same time, downgrading of Brahms did become a sort of unofficial academic orthodoxy amongst her pupils: I remember one of them, a lady composer of my own generation, for whom such doctrine was an article of faith.

Then there was the thirty-six-year-old Benjamin Britten (old enough to know better), who was proud in 1949 to declare that every other year or so he took down the works of Brahms to see if they were as bad as he remembered them to be – and discovered them to be worse. Even so, he had to confess a certain *tendresse* (like having a single female friend) for the Clarinet Quintet.

But the Boulanger Influence (to use a shorthand for all this spinsterly lack of response) lingers on. Only a couple of years ago, in an interview on one of these endless old-music programmes on the radio that we now enjoy as a substitute for culture, a middle-aged Scottish composeress was heard (she was enlarging upon a youthful infatuation with Stravinsky) to say: 'I wanted to get away from all that nineteenth-century *Schmalz*.' The remark comes straight out of the 1920s. In this comprehensive anathema – pronounced on the century which gave us Beethoven's late quartets, Schubert's last piano sonatas, Chopin's Ballades, Verdi's richly Shakespearean world, *Götterdämmerung*, *Parsifal* . . . all of them *Schmalz* – Brahms would certainly have been included. Such judgements, delivered without thought and without shame, illustrate in a small way our predicament *vis-à-vis* the past: a large subject, to which we must return. In this minor case the attitude is one of simple dislike fuelled by ignorance, and the uneasiness which springs from ignorance.

It is time for another photograph; and a poem to go with it. Brahms, bearded, magisterial, is reading alone in what seems to us an oppressively

Plate 12.2 Brahms reading in the library of Viktor Miller zu Aichholz

stuffy, over-furnished mid-Victorian room: a substantial volume is held up to his eyes. Brahms certainly studied Wagner; the poet Roy Fuller assumed (on what authority?) that this was a score of *Siegfried* and wrote a poem titled after the work. Fuller's approach is oblique, beginning with an adroit and witty physical description of the room and its occupant. In the last three stanzas we reach the nub:

The peering old man holds the little score so close
His white beard sweeps the page: but gives no sign
    That he perceives – or smells –
    Anything untoward.

He could not be expected to be thinking
That the legend of courage, kiss and sword arose
    From those atrocious Huns
    Who ruined an empire's comfort.

But how can he not be falling back aghast
At the chromatic spectrum of decay,
    Starting to destroy already
    His classical universe?

It is a good question, as politicians like to say. We might answer it (another politicians' trait) evasively – that is, in more general terms. Brahms's actual attitude to both Wagner in general and *The Ring* in particular has been very perceptively analysed elsewhere by Michael Musgrave.[7] As for the wider issues – such as the end of civilisation as we know it, as foreseen in the destruction of his classical universe – I think I've gone already about as far as one can into the thickets of hypothesis to explore Brahms's possible views about the future of music.

But in any case, Brahms could on occasion himself wield a chromatic sword worthy of any atrocious Hun. How on earth, for instance, did he get into E♭ minor (if that is what it is) in the development of the first movement of the A minor Double Concerto? Elsewhere there are even more sensational attempts to embrace, in a small compass, the whole chromatic field: the virtual pan-tonality of the Trio belonging to the Scherzo of the C major Trio Op. 87: or, more modestly, the same tendency in the entirely *terzverwandtschaftlich* last page of the C minor Trio Op 101. But most sophisticated of all (and predating all these examples by nearly twenty years) is the desolate – and because of this, disorientated – opening of the *Alto Rhapsody*. The initial bewildering augmented triad is soon followed by another a tone lower – taking us into remote, uncharted regions long before the tonic is at all decisively asserted. It all happens again when the voice comes in, but this time a substantial Neapolitan shelf is interposed ('das Gras steht wieder auf') before C minor is fully achieved. It matches anything in Wagner in its harmonic/tonal subtlety.[8] Brahms was here not so much falling back aghast at the chromatic spectrum of decay as enthusiastically contributing to it.

We cannot actually read the title on the spine of the book that Brahms is reading; it is equally likely that he might have had a volume of old music up to his nose. Once again, there is no need here to recapitulate the researches of Virginia Hancock,[9] which underline in a wealth of detail the now universally accepted truth that, for a man of the nineteenth century – itself a heroic age for the scholarly exploration of the past – Brahms was uniquely knowledgeable; and put his knowledge, as we now increasingly realise, to wonderful creative use. So Mozart's van Swieten-led rediscovery of Bach and Handel, Beethoven's trumpetings in his letters about old Sebastian Bach's 'Crucifixus' (and knowledge of the *Goldberg Variations* displayed in the *Diabelli Variations*), even J. S. Bach's incessant copying of Frescobaldi amongst many others – all these now fall palely into the background. It was Brahms who re-lived the past more than any previous musician in history; who developed, quite on his own, a deeper understanding of it; who was a pioneer in the acquisition of a 'historical sense'.

'After such knowledge, what forgiveness?' For Brahms was not only the first composer fully to mine the past's riches, he was also the last to be able to bear on his shoulders – Atlas-like (and *unglückseliger*, as always) – the enormous burden of what had been vouchsafed to him. That he felt this pressure is confirmed by endless utterances, always expressing his unworthiness, even in relation to the generation immediately before him. Strip off the layers of crawly self-deprecation to which he was prone – the new overtures which were unnecessary as long as those of Weber, Cherubini and Mendelssohn remained in print – and you still have to realise that Brahms's relation to his predecessors – to Beethoven in partic-ular – was not a happy one. The best-known and most frequently quoted of all Brahms quotations is worth citing in the original German:[10]

> Du hast keinen Begriff davon, wie es unsereinem zu Mute ist, wenn er immer so einen Riesen hinter sich marschieren hört.

> You haven't the faintest idea what it's like, for us lot, always to hear such a giant marching along behind one.

The threatening violence of the imagery conjures up a fairy tale by the brothers Grimm. His apprehension was shared, whether they were fully aware of it or not, by many another nineteenth-century composer. Nevertheless, he spoke from the heart there. But he might well have said the same thing about J. S. Bach.

Brahms felt the cold winds of history blowing – and had also leaning heavily on him a mass of personal inhibition and uncertainty. He went on creating none the less, and out of his predicament he built a style. Both its unique character and Brahms's acute self-awareness of his historical posi-tion are perfectly expressed in perhaps the two most eloquent and pene-trating sentences ever written about this aspect of his music:

> The sense of an irrecoverable past . . . is omnipresent in the music of Brahms, resignedly eclectic, ambiguous without irony. The depth of his feeling of loss gave an intensity to Brahms's work that no other imitator of the classical tradition ever reached; he may be said to have made music out of his openly expressed regret that he was born too late.[11]

Brahms was oppressed by and in love with (the two conditions are similar) the past, but not defeated by it. After his death, the position deteriorated, and the burden of the past became too much for twentieth-century man. We cannot come to terms with the past; for a start, it offers too much of a challenge, and we have become thoroughly screwed up in our attitude towards it. The simplest reaction is that of hostility *à l'outrance*: the cavalier attitude of the Futurists ('flood the museums') or, equally silly, of Boulez ('blow up the opera houses'). Far more widespread is plain uneasiness, which shows itself up in ambivalence. The acute self-consciousness which has ruled since Freud, and which – together with ghastly ecumenical tolerance towards everything, however nugatory, and everybody, however horrible (the most characteristic of the late twentieth century's Deadly Virtues) – is focused on how we behave towards those who came before us: what we call Tradition.

How often one has read in stupid books and articles: 'the shackles of tradition' – when one knows perfectly well that the writer has never even seen a shackle, far less recognised a tradition. Ninety years ago tradition began to be taken for granted, as if it were one of the public services; then despised, as another word for routine: *Tradition ist Schlamperei*. Now, because of this descent, we have only the *Schlamperei* left. So it has become perfectly possible simply to shut our eyes and ears, like the child in the nursery blocking out the unwelcome sight. Or – to look, to take it all in, to be appalled, to remain silent. These phenomena constitute the dilemma which is the root cause of all the strange twists and turns of twentieth-century artistic thought that I listed – it may be thought a shade too excitedly – earlier. The figure of Brahms stands before all that. He was the last person to see the whole predicament, and to be able to cope with it. That is his importance to the darkened world of today.

My favourite story – the account of an episode that has all the clarity of a snapshot – is of Brahms's meeting with the young Zemlinsky. I am haunted by it. Zemlinsky had written a string quintet; Brahms actually asked him whether he would come and see him: 'of course, only if you're interested in talking to me about it'. Zemlinsky hesitated a long time before ringing the bell of Brahms's flat.

... to talk to Brahms was no easy matter. Question and answer were short, sharp, seemingly cool and often very ironic. He took my quintet through with me at the piano. At first correcting gently, considering one part or another most carefully, never really praising or even encouraging me, and finally getting steadily more emphatic. And when timidly I tried to defend part of the development section which seemed to me to be rather successful in the Brahmsian manner, he opened the score of the Mozart quintets, explained to me the perfection of this 'unsurpassed formal design' and it sounded quite to the point and inevitable when he added 'That's how it's done from Bach to me!'[12]

'That's how it's done from Bach to me!' What a superb remark – and what an entirely justified one. At last Philoctetes flourishes his bow and extols its qualities and its heritage. Brahms – all that crawly, joky self-deprecation left far behind – shows his awareness of his own true worth: standing at his full height, he lets slip to a twenty-three-year-old student his full self-knowledge, and his realisation (as natural for him as to be taken for granted) of his place in history. Only a truly great man possesses inside himself such an accurate estimate of his worth: and that, most of the time, has to stay locked up inside him. It remains incomprehensible, indeed intangible, to the mean-minded mob of the world; and therefore the subject of their mockery.

One reflects that there is no one in the musical world today who could possibly make such a claim, or sustain it. Worse: there is no one who would wish to; who would have any interest in belonging to such a tradition, or feel it an honour to continue it. The only possible candidate – or indeed, applicant – died some forty-eight years ago in Los Angeles. Since then, we have lived without such a figure of authority.

Indeed, the existence of such a person is frowned upon, because, together with tradition, authority itself has become suspect. In an age of tyrants and monsters, we have learnt to despise anyone who stands out from the rest, whose word is law. Because we have blunted our minds to the extent that we can no longer tell the difference between good authority and bad authority, we are ready to cry 'fascist!' without even knowing what a fascist is. Because the Parisian literary critics have encouraged us not to draw any distinction between high and low art, between the lasting and the worthlessly ephemeral, we can only sigh: *Derrida-down-derry*. My Brothers in Apollo have not lagged behind the servants of the other muses in their dislike of the idea of one person being any better than another; but then it has long been obvious that the concept of anybody happening to write better music than the next practitioner of his art would have to be the next citadel to fall. Those of us who can recognise, and then respect and esteem the exceptional achievement of exceptional people are told that we are suffering from some curious psychological condition to do with our fathers. The most boring ideal of the French Revolution has come home to roost: *Liberté, Egalité, Stupidité.*

The first way – and, when all is said and done, the only important way – in which Brahms exercises authority is over the notes themselves; and that to an extent and depth only inadequately revealed by any analysis – though it helps. There is in Brahms's music a curious intensification of that air of authenticity that all great music possesses – that which impels one to realise that the notes themselves wield an authority, in the sense that they could in no way be different from what they are. Brahms's man- uscript-burning sessions – those at the end of his life, particularly, but also the earlier destruction of (it is said) some twenty string quartets before three were allowed to remain – are often idly speculated upon. It is remarked with a sort of despairing condescension that maybe better quartets perished than the ones that survived. What impertinence! The unearthings of unauthorised juvenilia by composers as various as Webern and Britten have been complete disasters. A truer corollary to be drawn is that Brahms knew exactly what he was doing; that everything he allowed to stand he intended to stand by, to be judged by. Random fits of sub- standard composing, such as every young composer nowadays considers to be the limits of his responsibility, or the cult of the fragment in 'work in progress' and all its attendant aleatory-improvisatory-participatory- jiggery-pokery-fakery, such as their elders used to go in for, would have been to Brahms repulsively alien. The concept of a corpus of work – the product of a lifetime's meditation and activity – was axiomatic for him: with us it has virtually vanished.

The interview with Zemlinsky displays another aspect of authority, the authority of example: that which is exerted by the transmission of that tradition which Brahms loved with such a bitter love – that is, by teaching, by actively demonstrating 'that's how it's done from Bach to me!' It is inconceivable to imagine Brahms as a member of any teaching institu- tion: his multifarious musical activities luckily always brought him enough money never to have to sink as low as that. Nor did these activities ever embrace regular systematic instruction either of a class or of individ- uals: that onerous and somewhat self-abnegatory activity which never- theless fed the creative careers of both Schoenberg and Messiaen. His one known pupil, Gustav Jenner, must surely have survived a good deal of putting-off noises when he first arrived, and even more subsequently.

Those who came to him for consultation were treated roughly: in the vast majority of cases, rightly so. Brahms couldn't be bothered with the second-rate, and, one may suspect, was concerned to preserve standards inside the profession: whom could we call on to perform this function today? The two most frequently cited cases are those of Hugo Wolf and Hans Rott. It's interesting to compare Wagner's reception of the adolescent Wolf with that of Brahms. Wolf's fawning ways worked, of course, with that vain old monster Wagner: they didn't with Brahms. He told him to go away and study counterpoint: a good idea. He must have found Wolf already as insufferable as many others did later on. Wolf turned out to be the sort of composer who wrote regularly for the newspapers (like Cesar Cui and Berlioz and, alas, Debussy – but then Debussy's journalism is embarrassingly bad). To Brahms it would have been inconceivable to write for the newspapers. Composers should not do so: you don't hunt with the fox and the hounds. As for Hans Rott – if you can't stand the heat, keep out of the kitchen. At least his delusion that Brahms had filled a railway train with dynamite allows a sparkle of black comedy to break through all this nineteenth-century worthiness.

If we return to the present day, we find the whole practice of composition teaching to have entirely collapsed. Even the mere interchange of information between teacher and taught is clogged up by the circumstance that the pupil is not interested in receiving it – it isn't 'relevant' to his/her needs. In most cases the student is not at all interested in music itself – not as much as the average music lover – but only in 'expressing' him/herself (whatever that means). As for the transmission of experience – well, forget it. And as for any serious criticism of a student's piece, any suggestion that it could be done differently, or (well) *better*; or that it could, possibly, be junked altogether and something else started – the degree of lack of talent possessed determines the speed with which he/she will walk out of the room, never to come back.

And of course the student's outrage is only a justifiable reflection of what the greater, grown-up world has already told him. For it is now quite bereft of anything resembling artistic standards. There are commercial considerations, and the dictates of market-driven fashion. Nothing thrives in this concrete wilderness but a thousand bad composers, who flourish through the cracks like weeds. I am not sure that Brahms could recognise much in our present-day world that really demanded to be taken seriously; but I am convinced that most of it would earn his bark of disapproval.

There is one last photograph to be presented, but this one was never taken (and never can be taken of any composer). It portrays the scene always missing from Ken Russell films about composers – or, indeed, from any romantic novel about them. It is that of Brahms working, of the silent (or noisy) hours of solitude, stretching from the first strong coffee very early in the morning, until about lunch-time: the hours of a composer's most active consciousness into which a commentator, even more so a psychologist, intrudes at his peril. Already we have surveyed the periphery of our subject: Brahms as a historical figure; his relations to his times and ours; his attitude to the past and (hypothetically) the future; his place as the last universally acceptable, and accepted, figure of authority. But what exactly resulted from these solitary hours on the Baltic coast, on the Wörthersee, in Switzerland, or at home near the Karlskirche? What about his music?

What makes Brahms not only a very great but also a very good composer? His preoccupation with the *materia musicae* absolute and total; his supreme skill in handling it; his assumption, like Bach, that counterpoint is the child of passion not calculation – that there is no conflict between technique and expressiveness, but rather that one feeds the other, and that both are mutually dependent. Every composer's virtues, but writ very large. To demonstrate in detail would be the task of a much more technical work, which would mean little to the many to whom Brahms's music appeals, who are unaware of any of these factors: once again, 'Seid umschlungen, Millionen.'

A few months ago I found myself listening by chance to the closing pages of the slow movement of the First Piano Concerto. What music could better give a sense of the melancholy with which we wander through the world, dazed and questing, scarcely able to believe in the beautiful and terrible things that we encounter, that sometimes happen to us and that sometimes we make happen. Listening onwards into the finale, I experienced, as if it were for the first time, that leap for joy which starts with the B♭ arpeggio on the strings (directly after the first double bar (bar 181)): a moment which, by definition, can only happen once.

I remember listening to the Violin Concerto in a barrack-room some forty-five years ago. The tantalising omission of the second subject proper from the orchestral exposition (you can hear the music turning aside from the spiralling upbeat figure) makes its eventual appearance in the hands of the soloist all the more ravishing. But this delayed satisfaction is outdone by the second subject's treatment in the recapitulation. It is presented in B major – which then pales into B minor, and is then overlaid by the high-register entry of violins in the home key.

The wonders of this movement are not over. After the cadenza the soloist restates the main theme in its highest register. But as the bass line falls from D to C♮, the soloist floats away higher and higher – a child's balloon ascending far, far away into the deep azure of a very Italian sky –

until it reaches a high C♯. At that moment – whether the landscape be Alpine or Mediterranean – one is truly 'Ausgesetzt auf den Bergen des Herzens'.

But at the moment my head is full of the Double Concerto – its drama and driving passion, those throbbing dissonant syncopated chords giving way to the orchestral strings which come storming in from on high: the heart-breaking, urgent tenderness of the second subject (one day I must look up the Viotti original)[13] with the breathlessness imparted by dislocation of harmony and beat. It is for me, in its vitality and virility, in the way that it holds nothing back, a deeply Schoenbergian work; Brahms's toughness, his stoic masculinity comes over superbly in this piece. The whole man is there.

It is not a bad idea to end with the heroic – beyond optimism or pessimism. 'Erst verachtet, nun ein Verächter' – this line from *Harzreise im Winter* seems a good motto for Philoctetes, his wound forgotten, his bow now performing miracles – though they are not recognised. I think about Brahms having behaved badly at some party, throwing over his departing shoulder the Parthian shot of 'if there is anybody in this room that I have not insulted – I apologise'. Another good motto from the Beard in the Middle Distance – and an admirable guide to behaviour. As I sit in reflection in the late twentieth century, I think about Brahms.

Notes

1 Brahms the Hamburg musician 1833–1862

1 Max Kalbeck, *Johannes Brahms*, 4 vols. (Berlin, 1904–14; rpt of final edn of each vol. (1921, 1921, 1912–13, 1915), Tutzing, 1976), vol. I, p. 1.

2 Richard Heuberger, *Erinnerungen an Johannes Brahms*, ed. K Hofmann, 2nd edn (Tutzing, 1976), p. 63.

3 Private collection.

4 Brahms-Archiv, Hamburg Staats- und Universitätsbibliothek, Carl von Ossietzky. The 'genealogical coat of arms' is not sufficiently exact to prove, as Kalbeck had assumed, that one of Brahms's forebears was the Albert Brahms who wrote a theory book on the 'origins of dyke and waterwork construction' in Aurich, Ostfriesland in 1745; his family connection to that of Johannes Brahms has never been established to this day; nor has that of an extensively dispersed Brahms family that can be traced in Ostfriesland and Jeverland (Kalbeck, *Johannes Brahms*, vol. I, p. 2).

5 Kurt Hofmann, *Johannes Brahms und Hamburg*, 2nd edn (Hamburg, 1986), pp. 18ff.

6 Kalbeck, *Johannes Brahms*, vol. I, p. 1.

7 Alfred von Ehrmann, *Johannes Brahms* (Leipzig, 1933), p. 7.

8 Josef Viktor Widmann, *Johannes Brahms in Erinnerungen* (Berlin, 1898), p. 95.

9 See the 'Einwohnermeldelisten', relating to the Hamburger Burgermilitär (Staatsarchiv Hamburg); see also Friedrich Ebrand, 'Vom Hamburger jungen Brahms', *Schweizerische Musikzeitung* 11 (1 November 1946), p. 3 (*Separatdruck*), with some variants of detail in the content. In 1864 Brahms's parents parted and took separate dwellings: Johann Jacob in the Grosse Bleichen 80, the mother with the daughter in a house in St. Georg, Lange Reihe 42, where the mother died on 2 February 1865. The 'Urzelle' of the Brahms family is the Ulricusstrasse, in Hamburg Valentinskamp, where the Unilever-Hochhaus currently stands. The Ulricusstrasse was first, from 1870 to 1919 under the name Winkelstrasse, a centre of prostitution, and a street of bordellos from 1934 until its destruction, a fact not broadcast in the Brahms literature.

10 Letter from Elise Denninghoff née Giesemann to Brahms of 31 October 1880 (Brahms-Archiv, Vienna, Gesellschaft der Musikfreunde)

11 *Johannes Brahms Briefwechsel XII: Johannes Brahms: Briefe an Fritz Simrock*, vol. II, ed. Max Kalbeck (Berlin, 1919), p. 112.

12 Private collection.

13 Heuberger, *Erinnerungen an Johannes Brahms*, p. 108.

14 *Joseph Joachims Briefe an Gisela von Arnim 1852–59*, ed. Johannes Joachim (privately printed, Göttingen, 2 April 1911), p. 65.

15 All printed editions referred to are in the Brahms-Institut, Lübeck, Sammlung Hofmann.

16 See *Neue Zeitschrift für Musik* 64/17 (28 April 1897), p. 195.

17 Private collection.

18 Kalbeck, *Johannes Brahms*, vol. I, p. 32.

19 See Julius Spengel, *Johannes Brahms, Charakterstudie* (Hamburg, 1898), pp. 11ff.

20 Heinrich Reimann, *Johannes Brahms* (Berlin, 1897), p. 4.

21 See Brahms's mother's letters of 15 June 1854 and 20 March 1855 in Kurt Stephenson, *Johannes Brahms in seiner Familie: Der Briefwechsel* (Hamburg, 1973), pp. 56 and 60ff.

22 Berthold Litzmann, *Clara Schumann: Ein Künstlerleben*, 3 vols. (Leipzig, 1906–9), vol. II, p. 372.

23 Brahms-Institut, Lübeck, Sammlung Hofmann.

24 Kalbeck, *Johannes Brahms*, vol. I, pp. 19ff.

25 Robert Haven Schauffler, *The Unknown Brahms* (New York, 1940), pp. 224ff.

26 Widmann, *Johannes Brahms in Erinnerungen*, p. 95; Siegfried Ochs, *Geschehenes, Gesehenes* (Leipzig and Zurich, 1922), p. 298.

27 Kalbeck, *Johannes Brahms*, vol. I, p. 47.

28 Ibid., p. 36.

29 See *Deutsches Wörterbuch von Jacob und Wilhelm Grimm* (Leipzig, 1873), s.v. 'Kneipe'.

30 Adolf Steiner, 'Johannes Brahms, 1. Teil', *86. Neujahrsblatt der Allgemeinen Musikgesellschaft Zürich* (Zurich, 1898), p. 6.

31 'Brahmsiana von A. Br.', *Neue Zeitschrift für Musik* 64/16 and 17 (21 and 28 April 1897).

32 Antje Kraus, *Die Unterschichten Hamburgs in der ersten Hälfte des 19. Jahrhunderts* (Stuttgart 1965), p. 91.

33 Florence May, *Johannes Brahms*, trans. Ludmilla Kirschbaum, 2 vols. in 1 (Leipzig, 1911), p. 66.

34 Ibid.

35 Stephenson, *Johannes Brahms in seiner Familie*, p. 55.

36 Henny Wiepking, 'Wo ging Johannes Brahms zur Schule?', *St. Georger Blätter* [Hamburg] (Spring 1966).

37 Original in Brahms-Institut, Lübeck, Sammlung Hofmann.

38 May, *Johannes Brahms*, pp. 68ff.

39 Ibid., p. 75.

40 See *Allgemeine deutsche Musikzeitung* 32/33 (10 and 17 August 1900). Elise had subsequently married the Wilhelmshaven hotelier Denninghoff.

41 Kalbeck, *Johannes Brahms*, vol. I, p. 20.

42 'Hedwig von Salomons Tagebuchblatt, Leipzig, 5. 12. 1853', in *Katalog 100: Johannes Brahms, Musikantiquariat Hans Schneider* (Tutzing, 1964), p. 7.

43 *Clara Schumann – Johannes Brahms: Briefe aus den Jahren 1853–1896*, ed. Berthold Litzmann, 2 vols. (Leipzig, 1927; rpt Hildesheim and Wiesbaden, 1989), vol. I, p. 18.

44 Brahms-Institut, Lübeck, Sammlung Hofmann.

45 Preface to reprinted edition of *Souvenirs de la Russie: Transcriptions en forme de Fantasies* (piano four hands; Hamburg [A. Cranz] before 1852), by K. Hofmann (Hamburg [Karl Dieter Wagner], 1971). See also entry 123 in Kurt Hofmann, *Die Erstdrucke der Werke von Johannes Brahms* (Tutzing, 1975).

46 Brahms-Institut, Lübeck, Sammlung Hofmann

47 *Programmzettel* in private collection.

48 Brahms-Institut, Lübeck, Sammlung Hofmann

49 Walter Hübbe, *Brahms in Hamburg* (Hamburg, 1905), pp. 5ff.

50 Hübbe, *Brahms in Hamburg*, pp. 4ff.

51 Minna Stone [née Völckers], 'Johannes Brahms als Lehrer', in *Hamburger Nachrichten* (3 April 1822), Abend-Ausgabe, Beilage. Minna Völckers was a sister of Betty and Marie Völckers, who belonged to the solo quartet of the Hamburg Frauenchor, which sang under Brahms.

52 Stephenson, *Johannes Brahms in seiner Familie*, p. 60.

53 See the exact terminology in Hofmann, *Johannes Brahms und Hamburg*, pp. 18ff.

54 Carl von Meysenbug, 'Aus Johannes Brahms's Jugendtagen', *Neues Wiener Tagblatt* 91–92 (3 and 4 April 1902).

55 Brahms-Institut, Sammlung Hofmann.

56 Private collection.

57 *Clara Schumann – Johannes Brahms: Briefe*, vol. I, p. 281.

58 *Hamburger Correspondent* 15 (17 January 1861).

59 *Hamburger Nachrichten* 28 (25 November 1861).

60 Private collection.

61 *Hamburger Nachrichten* 37 (13 February 1860).

62 Private collection.

63 Kalbeck, *Johannes Brahms*, vol. I, p. 419.

64 Brahms-Institut, Lübeck, Inventar-Nummer 1995.31.

65 Hübbe, *Brahms in Hamburg*, p. 14.

66 *Clara Schumann – Johannes Brahms: Briefe*, vol. I, p. 362.

67 The proceedings of the Philharmonic Society, Hamburg are located in the Staatsarchiv der Freien und Hansestadt Hamburg.

68 *Clara Schumann – Johannes Brahms: Briefe*, vol. I, pp. 412ff. Clara's answer is at pp.414ff.

69 Letter of Julius Stockhausen to Clara Schumann from Hamburg, 7 March 1863 (Berlin, Staatsbibliothek Preussischer Kulturbesitz, Musikabteilung mit Mendelssohn Archiv, Mus. Nachl. K. Schumann 2), p. 62. The name is spelled 'Gebweiler' in German; the town is located in Alsace (France), close to Strasbourg.

70 *Johannes Brahms Briefwechsel XVIII (n.s.): Johannes Brahms im Briefwechsel mit Julius Stockhausen*, ed. Renate Hofmann (Tutzing, 1993), p. 18.

71 Max Kalbeck's manuscript 'Notizbuch' on Brahms's Hamburg period, p. 46 (Staats- und Universitätsbibliothek Hamburg, Carl von Ossietzky, Brahms Archiv).

72 Unpublished letter of Avé to Stockhausen (Staats- und Universitätsbibliothek, Hamburg, Carl von Ossietzky, Brahms Archiv).

73 Kalbeck, *Johannes Brahms*, vol. I, p. 424.

2 Years of transition: Brahms and Vienna 1862–1875

1 Carl Georg Peter Grädener (1812–83), active as a conductor and cellist in Hamburg from 1851, was appointed to teach theory and singing at the Vienna Conservatory 1862–5, subsequently returning to Hamburg three years later. Bertha Porubszky, later Bertha Faber, was with her husband Arthur Faber one of Brahms's closest later acquaintances in Vienna.

2 Letter of September 1862 from Hamburg, Albert Dietrich, *Erinnerungen an Johannes Brahms* (Leipzig, 1898), p. 45. The letter is misdated by Dietrich as (January)1863; Brahms did not return to Hamburg until May 1863.

3 Florence May, *The Life of Brahms*, 2nd edn, 2 vols. (London, 1948), vol. I, p. 300. Further indication of his attitude to Vienna is found in his letter of acceptance of the conductorship of

the Vienna Singakademie in June 1863: 'anything coming from Vienna is doubly pleasant to a musician, and whatever may call him thither is doubly attractive', quoted in ibid., pp. 344–5. Specht points out that Joachim had already encouraged Brahms to accompany him there in 1861. Richard Specht, *Johannes Brahms*, trans. E. Blom (London, 1928), p. 122.

4 Letter of 18 November 1862, *Clara Schumann – Johannes Brahms: Briefe aus den Jahren 1853–1896*, ed. Berthold Litzmann, 2 vols. (Leipzig, 1927; rpt Hildesheim and Wiesbaden, 1989), vol., I, p. 413.

5 Letter to his parents of 30 November 1862, quoted and translated by May, *The Life of Brahms*, vol. II, p. 333; facsimile reproduced in Heinrich Reimann, *Johannes Brahms*, Berühmte Musiker: Lebens- und Charakterbild nebst Einführung in die Werke der Meister, 5th edn (Berlin, n.d. [c. 1919]), facing p. 32. He still expressed these sentiments in March 1863, giving them as a reason for returning home. Letter to Schubring, 26 March 1863, *Johannes Brahms Briefwechsel VIII*, p. 196.

6 Letter of 6 December 1862 from Christiane Brahms to Johannes Brahms, published in Karl Geiringer, *Brahms: His Life and Work*, 2nd edn trans. H. B. Weiner and Bernard Miall (London, 1948), p. 74.

7 Letter to his parents of 30 November 1862, quoted and translated by May, *The Life of Brahms*, vol. II, p. 334; facsimile reproduced in Reimann, *Johannes Brahms*, facing p. 32.

8 Letter to his father of 'Beginning October' 1864, quoted in Kurt Stephenson, *Brahms's Heimatbekenntnis* (Hamburg, 1933), pp. 62–3.

9 Geiringer, *Brahms*, p. 88. Geiringer cites an unpublished letter from Johann Jacob Brahms of 13 January 1865 (ibid., p. 91).

10 After the father's death, Brahms's stepmother continued to house his books until she later moved.

11 Letter of 30 November 1862, quoted and translated by May, *The Life of Brahms*, vol. I, p. 344, from the facsimile reproduced in Reimann, *Johannes Brahms*, facing p. 32.

12 In the short term he was of course angry. 'Now along comes this enemy of a friend and, for better or worse, pushes me aside. How rare it is for one of my kind to find a permanent position. How happy I would have been to find one in my native city.' See letter to Clara of 18 November 1862, *Clara Schumann – Johannes Brahms: Briefe*, vol. I, p. 413.

13 Letter from Joachim to Avé Lallemant, 31 January 1862, *Briefe von und an Joseph Joachim*, ed. Andreas Moser and Johannes Joachim, 3 vols. (Berlin, 1911–13), vol. II, pp. 274–5.

14 An account of the history of the Philharmonic is included in Josef Sittard,

Geschichte des Musik- und Concertwesens in Hamburg (Altona, 1890; rpt Hildesheim, 1971).

15 Letter of 27 April 1894, quoted in Max Kalbeck, *Johannes Brahms*, 4 vols. (Berlin, 1904–14; rpt of final edn of each vol. (1921, 1921, 1912–13, 1915), Tutzing, 1976), vol. IV, p. 345.

16 Letter to Joachim of 30 December 1864, *Johannes Brahms Briefwechsel VI: Johannes Brahms im Briefwechsel mit Joseph Joachim*, vol. II, ed. A. Moser (Berlin, 1908), p. 35.

17 Letter of 30 April 1869, Stephenson, *Brahms's Heimatbekenntnis*, p. 108.

18 Letter of 16 December 1869 from Chrysander to Brahms, and of 4 December 1876 from Marxsen to Brahms, quoted in Geiringer, *Brahms*, pp. 74–5: Eduard Marxsen (1806–87); Friedrich Chrysander (1826–1901).

19 Account summarised in May, *The Life of Brahms*, vol. II, pp. 343–4.

20 Remark to Klaus Groth, quoted in Geiringer, *Brahms*, p. 76.

21 Lodgings listed in Otto Biba, *Johannes Brahms in Wien* (Vienna, 1983), p. 27. May notes additionally that he also resided in the Wollzeile, as well as staying with the Fabers.

22 From a personal communication from Epstein to Florence May; May, *The Life of Brahms*, vol. II, pp. 330–1.

23 Quoted in ibid., p. 333.

24 Quoted in ibid., p. 338. Concert of 6 January, 1863.

25 Quoted in ibid., p. 387.

26 Ibid., p. 340. The circle included the following: the cellist of the Hellmesberger quartet, Heinrich Röver, the violinists Gabriel Lemböck, Anton Fischer and Josef König, the hornist Richard Lewy, the bassoonist Förchtgott, the soprano Passy-Cornet, whom he had known in Hamburg, the composer Johann Rufinatscha and the publisher J. P. Gotthard. And to them should be added the names of two leading pianists at the Conservatoire, Anton Door and, later, Ignaz Brüll, in addition to the friends around the Singakademie which included members of the von Asten family.

27 Carl Goldmark (1830–1915); (Carl August) Peter Cornelius (1824–74); Carl Tausig (1841–71).

28 Letter of [26] March 1863 to Adolf Schubring, *Johannes Brahms Briefwechsel VIII*, p. 196.

29 The Sechter canon is reproduced in Biba, *Johannes Brahms in Wien*, p. 13.

30 Letter of 12 February 1870. *Johannes Brahms Briefwechsel XIV: Johannes Brahms im Briefwechsel mit Breitkopf & Härtel, Bartholf Senff, Johann Melchior Rieter Biedermann u.A.* (Berlin, 1920), p. 183.

31 Quoted in May, *The Life of Brahms*, vol. II, pp. 330, 341.

32 Geiringer, *Brahms*, pp. 66, 71. He had already been taken with Bertha Porubszky and her singing of Austrian folk-songs in Hamburg. Geiringer, *Brahms*, p. 63.

33 Letter of 13 November 1867, *Clara Schumann – Johannes Brahms: Briefe*, vol. I, p. 568.

34 See letter of 7 February 1855 to Clara Schumann, ibid., p. 75.

35 The background is illustrated by Max Friedländer, *Brahms Lieder*, trans. C. L. Leese (Oxford, 1928), pp. 79–80.

36 Eduard Hanslick, *Aus dem Konzertsaal: Kritiken und Schilderungen aus 20 Jahren des Wiener Musiklebens 1848–1868*, 2nd edn (Vienna, 1897), p. 287.

37 Quoted in Norbert Meurs, *Neue Bahnen? Aspekte der Brahms Rezeption 1853–1868, Musik und Anschauung im 19. Jahrhundert*, vol. III (Cologne, 1996), p. 168.

38 Quoted in ibid., pp. 170–4.

39 Quoted in May, *The Life of Brahms*, vol. II, p. 336.

40 Quoted in ibid., p. 337.

41 Eduard Hanslick, *Aus dem Konzertsaal: Kritik und Schilderungen 1848–68* (Vienna, 1897), p. 320.

42 *Die neue freie Presse*, Vienna, 3 December 1867.

43 Quoted in May, *The Life of Brahms*, vol. II, p. 369.

44 Quoted in ibid., p. 513. Bernsdorff, obviously under pressure, commented on the additional presence of outside Brahms supporters.

45 Quoted in May, *The Life of Brahms*, vol. I, p. 295.

46 Kalbeck, *Johannes Brahms*, vol. II, p. 200.

47 Adolf Schubring, 'Schumanniana Nr. 8: die Schumann'sche Schule IV: Johannes Brahms', *Neue Zeitschrift für Musik* 56/12–16 (21 March – 18 April 1862).

48 See Otto Biba, *Mit den Gedanken in Wien*, trans. E. Hartzell (Vienna, 1984), pp. 26–7.

49 Undated letter to Dessoff [November 1876]. *Johannes Brahms Briefwechsel XVI*, p. 144

3 Brahms and his audience: the later Viennese years 1875–1897

1 For the most recent cases in point see David Brodbeck, *Brahms: Symphony No. 1* (Cambridge, 1997), pp. 1–19; Walter Frisch, *Brahms: The Four Symphonies* (New York, 1996); and Renate Ulm, ed., *Johannes Brahms: Das symphonische Werk* (Kassel, 1996).

2 Louis Ehlert (1825–84) studied with Schumann and Mendelssohn. He worked in both Berlin and Wiesbaden. He is perhaps best remembered for his 1878 laudatory article introducing Dvořák to the wider German reading public. See Louis Ehlert, *Aus der Tonwelt: Neue Folge* (Berlin, 1898), p. 247.

3 See John H. Mueller, *The American Symphony Orchestra: A Social History of Musical Taste* (Bloomington, Ind., 1951), pp. 187–90.

4 Siegfried Kross, *Johannes Brahms: Versuch einer kritischen Dokumentar-Biographie*, 2 vols. (Bonn, 1997), vol. II, pp. 545ff.

5 See the major analytical and biographical literature of recent vintage including Michael Musgrave, *The Music of Brahms*, rev. edn (Oxford, 1994); Malcolm MacDonald, *Brahms* (New York, 1990); Christian Martin Schmidt, *Johannes Brahms* (Stuttgart, 1994) and *Johannes Brahms und seine Zeit* (Regensburg, 1983) as well as Hans Gál, *Johannes Brahms: Werk und Persönlichkeit* (Frankfurt, 1961).

6 The argument that follows concentrates essentially entirely on Vienna from 1875 to 1897. However, it is assumed that apart from strictly local matters, the relevant circumstances described transcend Vienna and apply to German-speaking Europe. Brahms kept up his contacts with Germany, including Berlin and Leipzig. He travelled widely. Athough only two of the symphonies, Nos. 2 and 3, were premiered in Vienna, that city was the primary prism through which Brahms experienced and interpreted political and cultural currents. Subsequent first performances of the orchestral music in Vienna were therefore analogous to premieres. The reactions of the Viennese audience and press were crucial to him, particularly during the last years of his life.

7 Viktor Miller zu Aichholz, *Ein Brahms Bilderbuch* (Vienna, 1905), p. 67.

8 For a laudatory view of Herbeck, see Ludwig Herbeck, *Johann Herbeck* (Vienna, 1885); for a critical assessment see Leon Botstein, 'Music and Its Public', 5 vols. (Ph.D dissertation, Harvard University, 1985), vols. II and III.

9 See Renate Wagner-Rieger and Mara Reissberger, *Theophil von Hansen* (Wiesbaden, 1980); and Botstein, 'Music and Its Public'.

10 On the Wolf–Brahms relationship – a subject of much controversy – see Max Kalbeck, *Johannes Brahms*, 4 vols. (Berlin, 1904–8; rpt of final edn of each vol. (1921, 1921, 1912–13, 1915), Tutzing, 1976), vol. III, pp. 410–11; Frank Walker, *Hugo Wolf* (New York, 1968), pp. 84–7; and Sandra McColl, 'Karl Kraus and Music Criticism', forthcoming in *The Musical Quarterly* 82 (1998).

11 On Rott, Brahms's supposed 'cruelty' to Rott, Bruckner's advocacy and this episode, which took place in 1880, see Henry-Louis de la

Grange, *Gustav Mahler: Vers la Gloire 1860–1900* (Paris, 1979), p.128.

12 Kalbeck, *Johannes Brahms*, vol. IV, p. 508.

13 On Nietzsche's view of Brahms see the 'Zweite Nachschrift' in 'Der Fall Wagner' from 1888 in *Werke*, ed. K. Schlechta (Munich, 1966), vol. II, p. 934.

14 Friedrich Nietzsche, 'Vom Nutzen und Nachteil der Historie' in *Unzeitgemäße Betrachtungen*, trans. R. J. Hollingdale as *Untimely Meditations* (Cambridge, 1983), pp. 61–6, 78–83.

15 See Reinhold Brinkmann, *Late Idyll: The Second Symphony of Johannes Brahms*, trans. Peter Palmer (Cambridge, Mass., 1995).

16 See Richard Wagner, 'Beethoven' from 1870 in *Prose Works*, vol. V, trans. by W. A. Ellis (London 1896/New York, 1966), pp. 57–126; and Franz Liszt's writings on Beethoven in *Gesammelte Schriften*, vol. III (Leipzig, 1881/Hildesheim and Wiesbaden, 1978), particularly the essay on *Egmont* from 1854, pp. 29–36.

17 See Leon Botstein, 'Time and Memory: Concert Life, Science and Music in Brahms's Vienna' in Walter Frisch, ed., *Brahms and His World* (Princeton, 1990), pp. 3–22, and 'Brahms and Nineteenth Century Painting', *19th-Century Music* 14 (1990), pp. 154–68.

18 On Brahms the historian see the two essays – fifty years apart— by Karl Geiringer: 'Brahms as Reader and Collector' and 'Brahms as a Musicologist', *The Musical Quarterly* 19 (1933), pp. 158–68 and 69 (1983), pp. 463–70.

19 Brahms had developed this reputation a decade earlier, in the 1860s, when he conducted the Singakademie, where his repertoire included, among others, a work by Schütz.

20 See Brahms's Gesellschaft programmes in Richard von Perger and Robert Hirschfeld, *Geschichte der Gesellschaft der Musikfreunde* (Vienna, 1914).

21 For a good example see the discussion on Wagner in Hans Merian, *Geschichte der Musik im neunzehnten Jahrhundert* (Leipzig, 1902), pp. 601–20.

22 For a pro-Wagner account see Max Morold, *Wagners Kampf und Sieg: Dargestellt in seinen Beziehungen zu Wien*, 2 vols. (Zurich and Vienna, 1930), particularly vol. II, pp. 54–211. See Volker Kalisch, *Entwurf einer Wissenschaft von der Musik: Guido Adler* (Baden-Baden, 1988), pp. 11–12.

23 On Max Bruch and *Odysseus*, see Matthias Schwarzer, *Die Oratorien von Max Bruch* (Kassel, 1988) pp. 1–85; and the forthcoming 1998 recording on Koch-Schwann with the NDR.

24 Josef Suk, 'Aus meiner Jugend' (1911),

reprinted in Renate and Kurt Hofmann, eds., *Über Brahms* (Stuttgart, 1997), pp. 176–80.

25 Kross, *Johannes Brahms*, pp. 747–51.

26 See Frisch, *Brahms Symphonies*, pp. 5–27; and Hermann Kretzschmar, *Führer durch den Konzertsaal*, vol. I: *Sinfonie und Suite* (Leipzig, 1919) for a sampling of contemporary symphonic output.

27 See Angelika Horstmann, *Untersuchungen zur Brahms-Rezeption der Jahre 1860–1880* (Hamburg, 1986), pp. 199–207.

28 See the Heuberger selections cited in Hofmann and Hofmann, eds., *Über Brahms*, pp. 83 and 224–6.

29 Brahms's reaction to the B minor Sonata on his visit to Weimar is often repeated. See MacDonald, *Brahms*, p. 13.

30 See Robert A. Kann, ed., *Theodor Gomperz – Ein Gelehrtenleben im Bürgertum der Franz-Josefs-Zeit* (Vienna, 1874); and Ernst Kobau, '*Rastlos zieht die Flucht der Jahre . . .' Josephine und Franziska von Wertheimstein – Ferdinand von Saar* (Vienna, 1997).

31 Theodor Billroth, *Wer ist Musikalisch?: Nachgelassene Schrift*, ed. Eduard Hanslick, 2nd edn (Berlin, 1896).

32 See Leon Botstein 'Between Nostalgia and Modernity: Vienna 1848–1898' in Linda Weintraub and Leon Botstein, *Pre Modern Art of Vienna 1848–1898* (Detroit, 1987), pp. 10–17.

33 Cited in August Böhm von Boehmersheim, *Geschichte des Singvereines der Gesellschaft der Musikfreunde in Wien* (Vienna, 1908), pp. 44–6.

34 Ernst Kobau, *Die Wiener Symphoniker: Eine sozialgeschichtliche Studie* (Vienna, 1991), pp. 13–23.

35 See Botstein, 'Music and Its Public', vol. II.

36 For the context of this period see John W. Boyer, *Cultural and Political Crisis in Vienna: Christian Socialism in Power 1897–1918* (Chicago, 1995).

37 Cyril Ehrlich, *The Piano: A History*, rev. edn (Oxford, 1990), pp. 47–67.

38 On Steinway and Sons see Richard K. Lieberman, *Steinway and Sons* (New Haven, Conn., 1995); and D. W. Fostle, *The Steinway Saga* (New York,1995).

39 Ehlert, *Aus der Tonwelt*, p. 247.

40 Quoted in Josef Rufer, *Das Werk Arnold Schoenbergs* (Kassel, 1959), p. 139.

41 Miller zu Aichholz, *Brahms Bilderbuch*, pp. 21–3.

42 Brahms conducted the *Triumphlied* on 21 October. See Rene Karlen, 'Geschichte des Konzertlebens in der Tonhalle' in Rene Karlen, Andreas Honegger and Marianne Zelger-Vogt '*Ein Saal, in dem es herrlich klingt': Hundert Jahre Tonhalle Zürich* (Zurich, 1995), p. 51. On Brahms in Zurich, see Werner G. Zimmermann,

Brahms in der Schweiz: Eine Dokumentation (Zurich,1983).

43 On Brahms's circle of friends, particularly in his last years, see Imogen Fellinger, ed., *Klänge um Brahms: Erinnerungen von Richard Fellinger* (Mürzzuschlag, 1997).

44 On the evolution of the Viennese aristocracy in the first half of the nineteenth century see Hannes Stekl, *Österreichs Aristokratie im Vormärz* (Munich, 1973).

45 James H. Johnson, *Listening in Paris: A Cultural History* (Berkeley, 1995); and Michael Musgrave, *The Musical Life of the Crystal Palace* (Cambridge, 1995).

46 On Vienna's demographic development see A. Hickmann, *Wien im 19. Jahrhundert* (Vienna, 1903).

47 See Friedrich C. Heller and Peter Revers, *Das Wiener Konzerthaus: Geschichte und Bedeutung 1913–1983* (Vienna, 1983).

48 On Conservatoire enrolment and the efforts in the 1890s to expand the city's concert life, see Botstein, 'Music and Its Public', vols. IV and V.

49 Marsha Rozenblit, *The Jews of Vienna 1867–1914* (Albany, NY, 1983), p. 17.

50 See Carl Schorske, 'The Ringstrasse, Its Critics and the Birth of Urban Modernism' in Carl Schorske, ed., *Fin de Siècle Vienna: Politics and Culture*, 1st edn (New York, 1980), pp. 24–115.

51 See Jutta Pemsel, *Die Wiener Ausstellung von 1873* (Vienna, 1989), pp. 75–92.

52 See Margaret Notley 'Brahms as Liberal: Genre, Style, and Politics in Late Nineteenth Century Vienna', *19th-Century Music* 17 (1993), pp. 107–23.

53 In this regard it must be noted that the linkage between liberalism and the Jews of Vienna has too often been exaggerated. Billroth, for example, a close friend of Brahms's, was liberal but himself decidedly anti-Semitic. Many of the liberal literary and cultural Viennese salons with which Brahms and Hanslick were associated were overtly apolitical – politics were never discussed and therefore more heterogeneous groupings assembled, even a mixture of high aristocracy and the second society. See Kobau, '*Rastlos*', pp. 311–39; and Ernst Bruckmüller, 'Herkunft und Selbstverständnis bürgerlicher Gruppierung in der Habsburgmonarchie: Eine Einführung' in Bruckmüller, Ulrike Doecker, Hannes Stekl and Peter Urbanisch, eds., *Bürgertum in der Habsburgermonarchie* (Vienna, 1990), pp. 13–20. The Wagner episode can be found in Cosima Wagner, *Diaries 1878–1883*, ed. M. Gregor-Dellin and D. Mack with G. Skelton (New York, 1980), pp. 769–73; on the incident and the trial, see Alexander Zeiss, *Der Process*

über die Ringtheater-Katastrophe (Vienna, 1882). See also Daniel Spitzer, *Letzte Wiener Spaziergänge* (Vienna, 1894), pp. 266–7. It should be noted that Kalbeck, in addition to his devotion to Brahms, was the editor of the last volume of Spitzer's essays and a reigning expert on Spitzer (1835–93).

54 On Brahms and Schubert, see Leon Botstein, 'Realism Transformed: Franz Schubert and Vienna' in Christopher H. Gibbs, ed., *The Cambridge Companion to Schubert* (Cambridge, 1997), pp. 13–21. Kalbeck was, like Brahms, Protestant but was married to a woman of Jewish origin. Hanslick was of Jewish origin.

55 On Herzl and *Tannhäuser*, see Amos Elon, *Herzl* (New York, 1975), pp. 3 and 142. *Tannhäuser* was used to open the second Zionist Congress in Basel in 1898. See Ernst Pawel, *The Labyrinth of Exile: A Life of Theodor Herzl* (New York, 1989), p. 360.

56 See Carl Dahlhaus, 'Brahms und die Idee der Kammermusik', *Neue Zeitschrift für Musik* 134 (1973), pp. 559–63; and Notley, 'Brahms as Liberal'. See also Notley's discussion of Bruckner in 'Bruckner and Viennese Wagnerism' in Timothy L. Jackson and Paul Hawkshaw, eds., *Bruckner Studies* (Cambridge, 1997), pp. 54–71.

57 Fellinger, ed., *Klänge*, passim; see also Richard Heuberger, *Erinnerungen an Johannes Brahms*, ed. K. Hofmann, 2nd edn (Tutzing, 1976), p. 82.

58 For Schenker's views on Brahms see the short pieces of criticism written in the 1890s, especially Nos. 1, 3, 8, 13, 14, 42 and 43 in Hellmut Federhofer, ed., *Heinrich Schenker als Essayist und Kritiker* (Hildesheim, 1990).

4 Opposition and integration in the piano music

1 See for instance Denis Matthews, *Brahms Piano Music* (London, 1978); Michael Musgrave, *The Music of Brahms* (London, 1985; revised edn, Oxford, 1994); Walter Frisch, 'Brahms: From Classical to Modern' in R. Larry Todd, ed., *Nineteenth-Century Piano Music* (New York, 1990), pp. 316–54; and Malcolm MacDonald, *Brahms* (London, 1990).

2 Matthews, *Brahms Piano Music*, p. 5.

3 Ibid., pp. 12–13.

4 Musgrave, *The Music of Brahms*, p. 7.

5 One noteworthy study is Jonathan Dunsby's *Structural Ambiguity in Brahms: Analytical Approaches to Four Works* (Ann Arbor, Mich., 1981). Despite Dunsby's comment (p. 6) that 'there is no literal opposition in music, for events which are perceived independently have at least that quality in common: in one respect

at least they are similar rather than opposed', this essay regards opposition as a musical force actively exploited as a compositional premise by Brahms and readily discernible by listeners.

6 Edward T. Cone, 'Three Ways of Reading a Detective Story – or a Brahms Intermezzo' in Robert P. Morgan, ed., *Music: A View from Delft,* (Chicago and London, 1989), pp. 77–93.

7 Ibid., pp. 79–81 passim.

8 Ibid., p. 86.

9 MacDonald, *Brahms,* p. 266.

10 Robert Schumann, *On Music and Musicians,* ed. Konrad Wolff, trans. Paul Rosenfeld (Berkeley and Los Angeles, 1946), p. 253.

11 Musgrave, *The Music of Brahms,* p. 23.

12 Adolf Schubring, 'Five Early Works by Brahms', trans. Walter Frisch in Walter Frisch, ed., *Brahms and His World* (Princeton, 1990), pp. 113, 116.

13 Walter Frisch, *Brahms and the Principle of Developing Variation* (Berkeley and Los Angeles, 1984), pp. 37, 42, 56.

14 Details of the Sonata's compositional history are provided in George Bozarth, 'Brahms's *Lieder ohne Worte*: The "Poetic" Andantes of the Piano Sonatas' in George Bozarth, ed., *Brahms Studies: Analytical and Historical Perspectives* (Oxford, 1990), pp. 348ff.

15 Letter to Bartholf Senff, 26 December 1853, quoted in ibid., p. 360.

16 Bozarth, 'Brahms's *Lieder ohne Worte*', p. 360.

17 Ibid., p. 361.

18 Detlef Kraus's term; 'Das Andante aus der Sonate Op. 5 von Brahms' in Helmut Wirth, ed., *Brahms Studien III* (Hamburg, 1979), p. 51.

19 Section A: a, bars 1–10 (repeated)
    b, bars 11–24
    a', bars 25–36
  Section B: c, bars 37–44 (repeated, with variants, in 45–52)
    d, bars 53–67
    c', bars 68–76 (d and c' are repeated, with variants, in 77–100/5)

20 Both Kraus and Bozarth read the movement as a literal setting of 'Junge Liebe'.

21 Bozarth comments that the unusual tonal scheme needs to be viewed 'across the full span of the two [slow] movements', which together articulate an interrupted progression from A♭ major through D♭ major to B♭ minor. 'Brahms's *Lieder ohne Worte*', p. 364.

22 Elaine Sisman, 'Brahms's Slow Movements: Reinventing the "Closed" Forms' in Bozarth, ed., *Brahms Studies,* pp. 80, 85.

23 MacDonald, *Brahms,* p. 69.

24 Hans Gál, *Johannes Brahms: His Work and Personality,* trans. Joseph Stein (London, 1963), p. 124.

25 Karl Geiringer, *Brahms: His Life and Work,* 2nd edn, trans. H. B. Weiner and Bernard Miall (London, 1948), p. 213.

26 Musgrave, *The Music of Brahms,* p. 54.

27 Geiringer, *Brahms,* p. 214.

28 MacDonald, *Brahms,* p. 178.

29 Donald Francis Tovey, *Essays in Musical Analysis: Chamber Music* (London, 1944), p. 167.

30 Musgrave, *The Music of Brahms,* pp. 52, 53.

31 Heinrich Schenker, 'Brahms: Variationen und Fuge über ein Thema von Händel, op. 24', *Der Tonwille* 4/2–3 (1924), pp. 3–48.

32 'Der Plan in Brahms' Händel-Variationen', *Neue Musikzeitung* 49/11, 14, 16 (1928), pp. 340–6, 437–45, 503–12.

33 Dunsby, *Structural Ambiguity,* pp. 1, 16, 17.

34 Ibid., p. 4.

35 A comment made with reference to the fugue (see below) but no less relevant to the set as a whole. MacDonald, *Brahms,* p. 180.

36 In *Music Analysis* 6/3 (1987), pp. 237–55.

37 Although crude in conception (reflecting only a few compositional parameters rather than all musical elements), this diagram is analogous to an 'intensity curve', the theoretical basis of which is investigated in John Rink, 'Translating Musical Meaning: The Nineteenth-century Performer as Narrator' in Nicholas Cook and Mark Everist, eds., *Rethinking Music* (Oxford, 1998), pp. 217–38. An intensity curve is sketched in that essay in the case of a work by Liszt. Note, incidentally, that the lower-case roman numerals in Table 4.1 and elsewhere represent minor harmonies, while upper-case roman numerals denote major keys.

38 MacDonald, *Brahms,* p. 180. It goes without saying that a graph similar to that in Example 4.3 could be devised for the fugue, reflecting both its prolonged buildup of momentum and its climactic finish.

39 Musgrave, *The Music of Brahms,* pp. 57, 58.

40 His comment is made with specific reference to Op. 24. Matthews, *Brahms Piano Music,* p. 31.

41 Musgrave, *The Music of Brahms,* p. 159.

42 David Epstein, 'Brahms and the Mechanisms of Motion: The Composition of Performance' in Bozarth, ed., *Brahms Studies,* pp. 192, 198, 199. For further discussion of this topic, see Patrick Shove and Bruno Repp, 'Musical Motion and Performance: Theoretical and Empirical Perspectives' in John Rink, ed., *The Practice of Performance: Studies in Musical Interpretation* (Cambridge, 1995), pp. 55–83.

43 John Rink, 'Playing in Time: Rhythm, Metre and Tempo in Brahms's *Fantasien* Op. 116' in Rink, ed., *The Practice of Performance,* pp. 254–82.

44 MacDonald, *Brahms,* p. 266.

45 Musgrave, *The Music of Brahms*, pp. 160–1. Compare the description in Frisch, 'Brahms: From Classical to Modern', pp. 341 and 343.

46 Compare Geiringer's comment (*Brahms*, p. 219) that by Op. 76 'Brahms had relinquished his orchestral method of writing, and had approached more nearly to the style of Schumann and Chopin, which is particularly suited to the nature of the instrument'.

47 Elsewhere I have warned that 'simply rebarring Brahms's music to show implicit alternative metrical schemes, as some analysts do, inadequately defines a performance strategy', and Examples 4.6a and 4.6b should be regarded in this light, as intentional simplifications of complex phenomena. In the case of Op. 116 No. 2, by way of contrast, I have encouraged pianists 'to refer simultaneously to as many different organisational schemes in operation at a given point as possible, perhaps practising each separately and then combining them in a rhythmic counterpoint transcending allegiance to any one grouping, with elements of each surfacing here and there to tantalise the listener with hints of stability in that particular direction, only to have the music turn immediately towards another' (Rink, 'Playing in Time', pp. 277, 273). A similar 'kaleidoscopic' flexibility is also warranted in Example 4.6b.

48 It is worth noting that the dimensions of this so-called 'miniature' (a term often pejoratively applied to Brahms's later piano pieces) are exactly right to exploit to the full this fundamental metrical opposition: in a longer work, the energy level would almost certainly sag, the tensions so expertly created by Brahms either diluted or dissipated altogether.

49 MacDonald, *Brahms*, p. 355.

50 See Arnold Schoenberg, 'Brahms the Progressive' in Arnold Schoenberg, *Style and Idea*, ed. Leonard Stein, trans. Leo Black (London, 1975), pp. 398–441; see also Frisch, *Brahms and the Principle of Developing Variation*, and Michael Musgrave, 'Schoenberg's Brahms' in Bozarth, ed., *Brahms Studies*, pp. 123–37.

51 Respectively, J. A. Fuller-Maitland, *Brahms*, 2nd edn (London, 1911), p. 99; Musgrave, *The Music of Brahms*, p. 261; Matthews, *Brahms Piano Music*, p. 49; Edwin Evans, *Handbook to the Pianoforte Works of Johannes Brahms* (London, [1936]), p. 247 (italics in original).

52 See for instance Fuller-Maitland, *Brahms*, p. 99 and Matthews, *Brahms Piano Music*, p. 69. Matthews continues: 'the remainder of the orchestra, spectators so far, will join in progressively from the entry of the new theme in G♭ – until the great climax suddenly collapses, dispersing and silencing most of them again'.

53 MacDonald, *Brahms*, pp. 359–60.

54 Respectively, David Hicks, 'Chronicles. Opus 118 No. 6 of Brahms' (Ph.D. dissertation, Princeton University, 1991); Lynus Patrick Miller, 'From Analysis to Performance: The Musical Landscape of Johannes Brahms's Opus 118, No. 6' (Ph.D. dissertation, University of Michigan, 1979).

55 The 'lento' at bar 85 is perhaps best interpreted with reference to the hemiola in the previous two bars. In performance I treat the crotchets in bars 83–4 as anticipations of the lento beat, that is, new ♪ [i.e. 3 × triplet ♪] = former ♩ as suggested in Example 4.7. For further discussion of this kind of linkage (especially in Op. 116 No. 7), see Rink, 'Playing in Time'.

56 This comparison serves as a salutary reminder to analysts that 'motivic unity' in and of itself is no guarantor of interest or quality, and that what counts most is how related motives create the music's process and effect.

5 Medium and meaning: new aspects of the chamber music

1 *Johannes Brahms Briefwechsel XII: Johannes Brahms: Briefe an Fritz Simrock*, vol. II, ed. Max Kalbeck (Berlin, 1919), p. 35.

2 See Elaine Sisman, 'Brahms's Slow Movements: Reinventing the "Closed" Forms' in George S. Bozarth, ed., *Brahms Studies: Analytical and Historical Studies* (Oxford, 1990), pp. 79–103; and Elaine Sisman, 'Brahms and the Variation Canon', *19th-Century Music* 14 (1990/91), pp. 132–53.

3 Brahms seems later to have made use of the discarded slow movement of Op. 38 in the Second Cello Sonata Op. 99; see Margaret Notley, 'Brahms's Cello Sonata in F major and Its Genesis: A Study in Half-Step Relations' in David Brodbeck, ed., *Brahms Studies*, vol. I, (Lincoln, Nebr., 1994), pp. 139–60. By the same token, the middle movement of the First String Quintet derives from the early Sarabande in A Minor, WoO 5 No. 1, and Gavotte II in A Major, WoO 3 No. 2: see Robert Pascall, 'Unknown Gavottes by Brahms', *Music and Letters* 57 (1976), pp. 404–11; and Michael Musgrave, *The Music of Brahms*, rev. edn (Oxford, 1994), pp. 201–2.

4 Carl Dahlhaus, *Nineteenth-Century Music*, trans. J. Bradford Robinson (Berkeley and Los Angeles, 1989), p. 253.

5 Dahlhaus, *Nineteenth-Century Music*, pp. 252–61. See also Arnold Schoenberg, 'Brahms the Progressive' in Arnold Schoenberg, *Style and Idea*, ed. Leonard Stein, trans. Leo Black (London, 1975), pp. 398–441.

6 Quoted in Werner G. Zimmermann, *Brahms in der Schweiz* (Zurich, 1983), p. 43. The

complete inventory of chamber works that were
dedicated to Brahms is as follows: Carl G. P.
Grädener, Piano Trio in E♭ Op. 35; Ferdinand
Thierot, Trio in F minor Op. 14; Hermann
Goetz, Piano Quartet in E Op. 6 (1870);
Bernhard Scholz, String Quintet Op. 47 (1878);
Otto Dessoff, String Quartet in F Op. 7 (1878);
Robert Fuchs, Piano Trio in C Op. 22 (1879);
Antonin Dvořák, String Quartet in D minor
Op. 34 (1877); Karl Nawratil, Piano Trio in E♭
Op.9 (1881); Heinrich von Herzogenberg,
Three String Quartets Op. 42 (1884); Richard
von Perger, String Quartet in G minor Op. 8
(1886); Fritz Kaufmann, String Quartet in F
Op. 14; Giulio E. A. Alary, String Sextet Op. 35;
Anton Rückauf, Piano Quintet in F Op. 13;
Eugen d'Albert, String Quartet in E♭ Op. 11
(1893); Josef Suk, Piano Quintet in G minor,
Op. 8 (1893); Walter Rabl, Piano Quartet (with
clarinet) Op. 1; Eugen Philips, Piano Trio in D
Op. 28; Heinrich von Herzogenberg, Piano
Quartet in B♭ Op. 95 (1897); Carl Reinecke,
Sonata in G for Cello and Piano Op. 238 ('To
the memory of Johannes Brahms') (1898).
Walter Frisch, 'Dedicated to Johannes Brahms'
in Walter Frisch, ed., *Brahms and His World*
(Princeton, 1990), pp. 211–16.
7 Eduard Hanslick, *Music Criticisms 1846–99*,
trans. and ed. Henry Pleasants (Baltimore,
1950), p. 84 (in which translation the work is
referred to, erroneously, as the Piano Quartet in
G major). Robert Lee Curtis, *Ludwig Bischoff: A
Mid-Nineteenth Century Music Critic* (Cologne,
1979), p. 269.
8 For an excellent introduction to these issues,
see Margaret Notley, 'Brahms as Liberal: Genre,
Style, and Politics in Late-19th-Century
Vienna', *Nineteenth-Century Music* 17
(1993/94), pp. 107–23. On Wagner and Brahms
in this context, see David Brodbeck, *Brahms:
Symphony No. 1* (Cambridge, 1997), pp. 87–90.
9 The 'F–A–E' Sonata was written jointly for
Joachim by Brahms, Schumann and Joachim
and based on his motto *Frei aber Einsam* ('Free
but Lonely'). Brahms's contribution stands
curiously apart from the rest, however, both in
its failure to allude directly to the three notes of
the motto and in its choice of C minor (the
outer movements being in D minor, the
Intermezzo in A minor). Indeed, the clearest
allusion is rather to the opening of Beethoven's
Fifth Symphony, which Brahms plainly echoes
at the outset. On the genetic relation between
the First Symphony and the Piano Quintet in F
minor, see my *Brahms: Symphony No. 1*,
pp. 9–11.
10 *Johannes Brahms Briefwechsel VI: Johannes
Brahms im Briefwechsel mit Joseph Joachim*,
vol. II, ed. Andreas Moser, 2nd edn (Berlin,

1912), p. 40; Renate Hofmann, 'Johannes
Brahms im Spiegel der Korrespondenz Clara
Schumanns' in Constantin Floros, Hans
Joachim Marx and Peter Petersen, eds., *Brahms
und seine Zeit: Symposion Hamburg 1983*
(Laaber, 1984), p. 56; *Johannes Brahms und Fritz
Simrock: Weg einer Freundschaft: Briefe des
Verlegers an den Komponisten*, ed. Kurt
Stephenson (Hamburg, 1961), p. 50. For a
transcription of Brahms's hand-written
catalogue, see Alfred Orel, 'Ein eigenhändiges
Werkverzeichnis von Johannes Brahms: Ein
wichtiger Beitrag zur Brahmsforschung', *Die
Musik* 29 (1937), pp. 529–41. Notwithstanding
Brahms's rigorous self-criticism, Alwin Cranz's
recollection, as reported by Max Kalbeck, that
the composer claimed to have written 'more
than twenty string quartets' before publishing
his first two in 1873, seems highly exaggerated.
Max Kalbeck, *Johannes Brahms*, 4 vols. (Berlin,
1904–14; rpt of final edn of each vol. (1921,
1921, 1912–13, 1915), Tutzing, 1976), vol. II,
p. 440.
11 Brahms's calendar books (one each for the
years 1867–9 and 1871–97) are housed in
Vienna, Stadt- und Landesbibliothek, Ia
79.559). Two important studies of the quartets
may be found in Michael Musgrave, ed., *Brahms
2: Biographical, Documentary, and Analytical
Studies* (Cambridge, 1987): see Arnold Whittall,
'Two of a Kind? Brahms's Op. 51 Finales'
(pp. 145–64); and Allen Forte, 'Motivic Design
and Structural Levels in the First Movement of
Brahms's String Quartet in C Minor'
(pp. 165–96). See also Friedhelm Krummacher,
'Reception and Analysis: On the Brahms
Quartets, Op. 51, Nos. 1 and 2', *19th-Century
Music* 18 (1994/95), pp. 24–45.
12 James Webster, 'Schubert's Sonata Form and
Brahms's First Maturity', *19th-Century Music* 3
(1978/79), pp. 18–35; and 4 (1979/80),
pp. 52–71.
13 Donald Francis Tovey, 'Brahms's Chamber
Music' in his *The Main Stream of Music and
Other Essays* (New York, 1949), p. 244.
Significantly the work was conceived in 1862 as
a string quintet with two cellos (i.e. with the
same unusual disposition of instruments as
found in Schubert's quintet); it was first revised
in 1864 as a Sonata for Two Pianos, in which
form it was published as Op. 34bis.
14 Tovey, 'Brahms's Chamber Music', p. 244.
15 For an excellent account, see Walter Frisch,
*Brahms and the Principle of Developing
Variation* (Berkeley and Los Angeles, 1984),
pp. 83–6.
16 *Johannes Brahms Briefwechsel II: Johannes
Brahms im Briefwechsel mit Heinrich und
Elisabet von Herzogenberg*, vol. II, ed. Max

Kalbeck, 4th rev. edn (Berlin, 1921), p. 146.

17 Tovey, 'Brahms's Chamber Music', p. 243.

18 Letter of 29 July 1861 in *Clara Schumann – Johannes Brahms: Briefe aus den Jahren 1853–1896*, ed. Berthold Litzmann, 2 vols. (Leipzig, 1927; rpt Hildesheim and Wiesbaden, 1989), vol. I, p. 371.

19 Letter of 15 October 1861, in *Johannes Brahms Briefwechsel V: Johannes Brahms im Briefwechsel mit Joseph Joachim*, vol. I, ed. A. Moser, 3rd edn (Berlin, 1921), p. 313.

20 One other work with paired fifths that might figure into all this is Haydn's so-called *Quinten* Quartet Op. 76 No. 2, whose Menuetto, as Michael Musgrave has observed (*The Music of Brahms*, p. 101), offered a model for the fierce and weighty two-part canon in D minor with which Brahms's trio begins. At the same time, it seems quite possible that Brahms had noticed that Schumann's second theme, with its long-breathed melody (given out twice, taken up by the various instruments and all set over an off-the-beat accompaniment), derives from the second theme in the finale of Beethoven's String Quartet in F Op. 59 No. 1.

21 Hans Keller, 'The Classical Romantics: Schumann and Mendelssohn', *Of German Music* (London, 1976), p. 201.

22 Notably, appearing at the same time as the C major Trio was the String Quintet in F Op. 88, which in its gentle lyrical opening provides the trio with a 'feminine' contrast of its own.

23 As examples of this 'amplified binary form' Daverio cites the first movements of the Piano Quartet in G minor and Piano Trio in C minor, and the finales of, again, the Piano Quartet in G minor, Piano Quartet in A, Piano Quintet, First String Quartet, Violin Sonata in D minor, Piano Trio in B (revised version), Second String Quintet, Clarinet Trio, and First Clarinet Sonata. See John Daverio, 'From "Concertante Rondo" to "Lyric Sonata" ': A Commentary on Brahms's Reception of Mozart', in David Brodbeck, ed., *Brahms Studies*, vol. I (Lincoln, Nebr., 1994), pp. 111–36. Several of the same movements are discussed in Robert Pascall, 'Some Special Uses of Sonata Form by Brahms', *Soundings* 4 (1974), pp. 58–63. Although Daverio assigns the first movement of Op. 87 to the category of sonata form with both development and recapitulation beginning in the tonic – presumably because one of the themes of the second group is subjected to development – other aspects of this movement, as we shall see, are explained more satisfactorily in terms of a binary model.

24 The slow movements of the First, Third and Fourth symphonies are marked by similar 'digressive' allusions, in which, as Robert Bailey has put it, Brahms seems 'for a moment…to depart from the context of the movement, bringing in a short section apparently different from anything else in the movement, and then allowing the original context to resume' ('Musical Language and Structure in the Third Symphony' in George Bozarth, ed., *Brahms Studies: Analytical and Historical Perspectives*, (Oxford, 1990), p. 405). Bailey's concern is with the Third Symphony, in which the composer alludes to the 'Immolation Scene' at the end of Wagner's *Götterdämmerung*. In the slow movement of the First Symphony, the composer renews an allusion to Schumann's *Manfred* that had played a large role in the opening Allegro; see David Brodbeck, *Brahms: Symphony No. 1*, pp. 55–7. In the Fourth Symphony, allusion is made to the slow movement of Beethoven's Fifth Symphony; see Kenneth Hull, 'Allusive Irony in Brahms's Fourth Symphony' in David Brodbeck, ed., *Brahms Studies*, vol. II (Lincoln, Nebr., 1998), pp. 141–9.

25 Similar thematic transformations in the development section mark also the first movements of the G minor Piano Quartet (bars 303ff.), the A major Piano Quartet (bars 144ff.), the Piano Quintet (bars 208ff.), the Violin Sonata in A (bars 137ff.) and the Clarinet Quintet (bars 98ff.).

26 In addition to those instances that I discuss below, a few others can be cited here. In the tonally ambiguous opening of the Second String Quartet, for example, beginning with the notes A–F–A–E, Brahms revisits Joachim's motto 'Frei aber einsam' – and indeed in a far more explicit manner than he had done in the Scherzo in C minor from twenty years earlier. And in the secondary group of the opening movement of the Second Violin Sonata (one of several chamber works that Brahms composed on Lake Thun in the summer of 1886), Brahms alludes to his own songs 'Wie Melodien zieht es mir' Op. 105 No. 1 and 'Komm bald' Op. 97 No. 5, neither of which had yet appeared in print at the time when the sonata was written. Kalbeck concluded that the references indicated that the sonata had been written 'in Erwartung der Ankunft einer geliebten Freundin', that is, in anticipation of the arrival at the Swiss resort of the beautiful contralto Hermine Spies, with whom Brahms was smitten at the time (Kalbeck, *Johannes Brahms*, vol. IV, p. 16). At the same time, in the lyrical primary theme of the same work (beginning $\hat{3}$–$\hat{7}$–$\hat{1}$), Brahms makes a rather more 'public' allusion to the 'Preislied' from Wagner's *Die Meistersinger von Nürnberg*, as noted with disapproval in Eduard Hanslick's early review

of 'Brahms's Newest Instrumental Compositions' (1889) (reprinted in Frisch, *Brahms and His World*, pp.145–50).

27 *Clara Schumann – Johannes Brahms: Briefe*, vol. I, p. 75. In the summer of 1877 Brahms re-used the same theme as the subject of a canonic study; see my review of *Johannes Brahms: Thematisch-bibliographisches Werkverzeichnis*, by Margit L. McCorkle, *Journal of the American Musicological Society* 42 (1989), pp. 427–30.

28 *Briefwechsel VI*, p. 291.

29 Dillon Parmer, 'Brahms the Programmatic' (Ph.D. dissertation, University of Rochester, 1995), pp. 81–3.

30 Letter of June 1879, in *Billroth und Brahms im Briefwechsel*, ed. Otto Billroth (Berlin and Vienna, 1935), p. 293.

31 Dillon Parmer, 'Brahms, Song Quotation, and Secret Programs', *19th-Century Music* 19 (1995/96), pp. 167–77.

32 Quoted in Michael Struck, 'New Evidence on the Genesis of Brahms's G major Violin Sonata, Op. 78', *The American Brahms Society Newsletter* 9/1 (1991), p. 5.

33 James Webster, 'The C Sharp Minor Version of Brahms's Op. 60', *Musical Times* 121 (1980), pp. 89–93.

34 Quoted in Kalbeck, *Johannes Brahms*, vol. III, pp. 12–13; translated in Webster, 'The C Sharp Minor Version of Brahms's Op. 60', p. 91.

35 Hofmann, 'Johannes Brahms im Spiegel der Korrespondenz Clara Schumanns', p. 48; and 'Fragebogen für Herrn Hofkapellmeister Albert Dietrich', ed. Max Kalbeck, transcribed in *Katalog 100: Johannes Brahms*, Musikantiquariat Hans Schneider (Tutzing, 1964), p. 12. Webster ('The C Sharp Minor Version of Brahms's Op. 60'), who did not know of the existence of either Clara's letter to Joachim or Dietrich's recollection, incorrectly assumed that the work dated from 1856, when it entered Brahms's own correspondence with the violinist.

36 Letter from Clara to Joachim of 4 December 1856, quoted in Hofmann, 'Johannes Brahms im Spiegel der Korrespondenz Clara Schumanns', p. 48.

37 For Brahms's subsequent verbal allusions to *Werther* in connection to this quartet, see Kalbeck, *Johannes Brahms*, vol. III, p. 12; *Billroth und Brahms*, p. 211; *Johannes Brahms Briefwechsel IX: Johannes Brahms: Briefe an P. J. Simrock und Fritz Simrock*, vol. I, ed. Max Kalbeck (Berlin, 1917), pp. 200–1; and *Johannes Brahms Briefwechsel XIII: Johannes Brahms im Briefwechsel mit Th. Wilhelm Engelmann*, ed. Julius Röntgen (Berlin, 1918), pp. 22–5.

38 See Schumann's entry in the so-called marriage diaries from March 1841: 'With a dear gentle wife things go smoothly. Honestly, my next symphony shall be named "Clara" and I will portray her in it with flutes, oboes, and harps' (*The Marriage Diaries of Robert & Clara Schumann: From Their Wedding Day through the Russia Trip*, ed. Gerd Nauhaus, trans. Peter Ostwald (Boston, 1993), pp. 68–9). The reference here is to the first version of Schumann's Fourth Symphony, which dates from the spring of 1841.

39 Basil Smallman, *The Piano Quartet and Quintet: Style, Structure, and Scoring* (Oxford, 1994), pp. 94–5.

40 George Henschel, *Personal Recollections of Johannes Brahms* (Boston, 1907; rpt New York, 1978), p. 30; see also Ethel Smyth, *Impressions that Remained: Memoirs* (New York, 1946), p. 237.

41 *The Music of Brahms*, p. 117. See also Parmer, 'Brahms the Programmatic', pp. 206–7. As Musgrave notes (*The Music of Brahms*, p. 21), the main theme of the same finale by Mendelssohn had earlier served as a source of allusion in the scherzo of Brahms's Piano Sonata in F minor Op. 5.

42 Although in his hand-written catalogue of his own works Brahms dated this piece 'January 1854', it seems more likely to have been the product of the following spring, at which point it enters the composer's correspondence with Joachim. It was long thought that the public premiere of the trio had taken place in New York, in a performance given on 27 November 1855 by the pianist William Mason, the violinist Theodore Thomas, and the cellist Carl Bergmann. Michael Struck has recently established that the work was actually first heard six weeks earlier in a Trio-Soirée given in Danzig. See George S. Bozarth, 'Brahms's B major Trio: An American Premiere', *The American Brahms Society Newsletter* 8 (1990), pp. 1–4; and Michael Struck, 'Noch einmal Brahms's B major Trio: Where Was the Original Version First Performed?' *The American Brahms Society Newsletter* 92 (1991), pp. 8–9.

43 *Johannes Brahms Briefwechsel IV: Johannes Brahms im Briefwechsel mit J. O. Grimm*, ed. Richard Barth (Berlin, 1907), p. 150.

44 Among other comparative studies of the two versions, see Hans Gál, *Johannes Brahms: His Work and Personality*, trans. Joseph Stein (London, 1963; rpt Westport, Conn., 1977), pp. 155–82; Ivor Keys, *Brahms Chamber Music* (Seattle, 1974), pp. 41–50; Ernst Herttrich, 'Johannes Brahms – Klaviertrio H-dur Op. 8, Frühfassung und Spätfassung – ein analytischer Vergleich' in Martin Bente, ed., *Musik Edition Interpretation: Gedenkschrift Günter Henle* (Munich, 1980), pp. 218–36; and Franz

Zaunschirrn, *Der frühe und der späte Brahms*
(Hamburg, 1988). Both versions may be heard
in a recording by the Odeon Trio
(Quintessence, 2PMC-2716).
45 Eric Sams, 'Brahms and His Clara Themes',
Musical Times 112 (1971), p. 434.
46 Kalbeck, *Johannes Brahms*, vol. I, p. 153.
47 Kenneth Hull, 'Brahms the Allusive' (Ph.D.
dissertation, Princeton University, 1989),
pp. 236–9. Schumann's allusion was noted in
J. W. Wasielewski, *Robert Schumann: Eine
Biographie*, 3rd edn (Bonn, 1880); Brahms's
allusion was noted by Hermann Kretzschmar in
the essay 'Johannes Brahms' (1884), which was
reprinted in his *Gesammelte Aufsätze über
Musik und Anderes aus den Grenzboten* (Leipzig,
1910), p. 158. Brahms was, of course, familiar
with Schumann's own practice of eliminating
autobiographical references in the revised
editions that he issued of the
Davidsbündlertänze and other 'personal' works
from the 1830s.
48 Sams, 'Brahms and His Clara Themes',
p. 433. For a fuller discussion, see Parmer,
'Brahms the Programmatic', pp. 146–61.
49 On Brahms's ambivalent attitude towards
the relative merits of the two versions, see his
letters to Clara Schumann of 3 September 1889
(*Clara Schumann – Johannes Brahms: Briefe*,
vol. II, p. 393) and Simrock of 13 December
1889 and 29 December 1890 (*Briefwechsel XII*,
pp. 37, 39).
50 Peter Ostwald, *Schumann: The Inner
Voices of a Musical Genius* (Boston, 1985),
p. 127.
51 See Charles Rosen, *The Classical Style:
Haydn, Mozart, Beethoven*, exp. edn (New York,
1997), p. 513. In the finale of the Second
Symphony the allusion to *An die ferne Geliebte*
is achieved by means of a similar process of
thematic evolution.
52 The String Quintet was composed shortly
after the death in 1889 of Gisela von Arnim, to
whom Joachim had been briefly engaged in the
early 1850s, and whose evident decision to end
the engagement had inspired the violinist's
motto 'Frei aber einsam'. As Hans Kohlhase has
suggested, the main theme of the quintet's slow
movement begins with a 'double anagram'
consisting of a fusion of the notes of F–A–E
with a musical spelling of Gisela's name
(G♯–E–A = Gis–E–La); in this light, Brahms's
evident allusion in the third movement of the
quintet to Bach's setting of the words 'Ruhe
sanfte' ('rest gently') in the *St Matthew Passion*
seems all the more moving. See Hans Kohlhase,
'Brahms und Mendelssohn: Strukturelle
Parallelen in der Kammermusik für Streicher',
in *Brahms und seine Zeit*, pp. 65–7. On Brahms's

awareness of Joachim's own use of the mottoes
F–A–E and G♯–E–A, see David Brodbeck, 'The
Brahms–Joachim Counterpoint Exchange; or,
Robert, Clara, and "the Best Harmony between
Jos. and Joh."' in David Brodbeck, ed., *Brahms
Studies*, vol. I, pp. 43–7. It seems significant, too,
that these allusions should come in a work in
which Brahms returned for the first (and only)
time since his Second String Sextet to the
medium of strings alone in G major; it was in
the first movement of the sextet, after all, that
the composer had woven a reference to his own
erstwhile fiancée, Agathe von Siebold.
53 Frisch, *Brahms and the Principle of
Developing Variation*, p. 146.
54 The First Clarinet Sonata, in particular, has
drawn close analytical attention. See, for
example, Christian Martin Schmidt, *Verfahren
der motivisch-thematischen Vermittlung in der
Musik von Johannes Brahms dargestellt an der
Klarinettensonate f-moll, Op. 120, No. 1*
(Munich, 1971); Frisch, *Brahms and the
Principle of Developing Variation*, pp. 147–51;
and Peter H. Smith, 'Brahms and the
Neapolitan Complex: ♭II, ♭VI, and Their
Multiple Functions in the First Movement
of the F-Minor Clarinet Sonata' in Brodbeck,
ed., *Brahms Studies*, vol. II, pp. 169–208.
55 Following the initial triadic ascent (E–G–B),
this tune continues with a chain of descending
thirds and ascending sixths. If the opening
theme of the Fourth Symphony represents the
most famous instance of this fingerprint of the
Brahmsian style, the finale of the work at hand
offers the most extensive: bars 77–88 unfold a
chain of no fewer than thirty-two links (passing
from clarinet to piano), which is soon followed
by another chain, beginning in bar 97,
consisting of another fifteen links (passing from
cello to clarinet).
56 On 'axial melody', see Leonard B. Meyer,
Explaining Music: Essays and Explorations
(Berkeley and Los Angeles, 1973), pp. 183–91.
Better-known examples of this melodic type,
which consists of an 'axis-tone' embellished by
neighbour-notes above and below, are the first
theme of the finale of Dvořák's 'New World
Symphony' and the main theme of the slow
movement of Brahms's Fourth Symphony.
57 Malcolm MacDonald, *Brahms* (New York,
1990), p. 367.
58 Quoted in Walter Frisch, *The Early Works of
Arnold Schoenberg, 1893–1908* (Berkeley and
Los Angeles, 1993), p. 7.
59 Frisch (*Early Works of Schoenberg*, pp. 6–14)
offers the most sensitive account of Zemlinsky's
'Brahmsian' phase (though without much
consideration of the Clarinet Trio in D Minor).
For an assessment of Zemlinsky's handling of

the 'Brahmsian' style in Op. 3, see Alfred
Clayton, 'Brahms und Zemlinsky' in Susanne
Antonicek and Otto Biba, eds., *Brahms-
Kongress Wien 1983, Kongressbericht* (Tutzing,
1988), pp. 81–94.
60 Hugo Leichtentritt, 'German Chamber
Music' in *Cobbett's Cyclopaedic Survey of
Chamber Music*, 2nd edn, 3 vols. (Oxford,
1963), vol. I, p. 449.
61 Arthur Abell, *Talks with Great Composers*
(New York, 1955), pp. 148–9. Although Abell
might well have taken some liberty with Bruch's
remarks, there is no reason to doubt the general
accuracy of his representation of the
composer's ideas. (Abell's recollections of
Brahms himself have always been treated with
reserve by Brahms scholars, since he provides
information of a kind Brahms hardly ever
vouchsafed even to his intimate circle, and
because of the declared 'psychic' orientation of
the writer.)

6 **Formal perspectives on the symphonies**
1 For an introduction to the music of Brahms,
consult Michael Musgrave, *The Music of
Brahms*, rev. edn (Oxford, 1994) and Malcolm
MacDonald, *Brahms* (London, 1990). A concise
survey of critical and analytical issues raised by
the symphonies may be found in Siegfried
Kross, 'Brahms the Symphonist' in Robert
Pascall, ed., *Brahms: Biographical, Documentary
and Analytical Studies* (Cambridge, 1983),
pp. 125–45.
2 See the discussion of Brahms's chromaticism
in David Brodbeck, 'Brahms, the Third
Symphony, and the New German School' in
Walter Frisch, ed., *Brahms and His World*
(Princeton, 1990), pp. 65–80. Broader in scope
and more technical is Christopher Wintle, 'The
"Sceptred Pall": Brahms's Progressive
Harmony' in Michael Musgrave, ed., *Brahms 2:
Biographical, Documentary and Analytical
Studies* (Cambridge, 1987), pp. 197–222.
3 Carl Dahlhaus, *Between Romanticism and
Modernism: Four Studies in the Music of the
Later Nineteenth Century*, trans. Mary Whittall
(Berkeley, 1980), p. 47.
4 The phrase is Giorgio Pestelli's. See his *The
Age of Mozart and Beethoven* (Cambridge,
1984), p. 136.
5 Leon Botstein, 'Time and Memory: Concert
Life, Science, and Music in Brahms's Vienna', in
Frisch, ed., *Brahms and His World*, p. 19.
6 See Virginia L. Hancock, *Brahms's Choral
Music and His Library of Early Music* (Ann
Arbor, Mich., 1983).
7 See Walter Frisch, *Brahms and the Principle of
Developing Variation* (Berkeley, 1984).

8 See his *Late Idyll: The Second Symphony of
Johannes Brahms*, trans. Peter Palmer
(Cambridge, Mass., 1995), p. 118. Originally
published 1990.
9 For a detailed analysis of harmony and voice-
leading in this movement, see Carl Schachter,
'The First Movement of Brahms's Second
Symphony: The First Theme and its
Consequences', *Music Analysis* 2/1 (1983),
pp. 55–68.
10 For a more detailed analysis of this
movement, including the claim that thematic
variation is used to generate almost all
materials from a single source, see David
Osmond–Smith, 'The Retreat from Dynamism:
A Study of Brahms's Fourth Symphony' in
Pascall, ed., *Brahms: Biographical, Documentary
and Analytical Studies*, pp. 147–165.

7 **'Veiled symphonies'? The concertos**
1 Schumann's essay 'Neue Bahnen' ('New
paths') was published in the *Neue Zeitschrift für
Musik* 18 on 28 October 1853.
2 As is well known, the autograph of the C
major Sonata is inscribed 'Vierte Sonate'. If the
previously completed F♯ minor Sonata is the
'Dritte Sonate', there must have been at least
two other discarded examples of the form. The
G minor sonata Brahms is said to have played to
Louise Japha at the age of eleven may not have
belonged to this series.
3 Adolf Schubring, 'Schumanniana Nr. 8: die
Schumann'sche Schule IV: Johannes Brahms',
Neue Zeitschrift für Musik 56/12 (21 March
1862), p. 93. Cited here from the translation by
Walter Frisch in Walter Frisch, ed., *Brahms and
his World* (Princeton, 1990), p. 105.
4 Brahms's plans for the finale remain
unknown, though Christopher Reynolds has
suggested ('A Choral Symphony by Brahms?'
19th-Century Music 9/1 (1985), pp. 3–25) that
he may have contemplated a choral component
à la Beethoven's Ninth. For a recent and
comprehensive re-examination of the source
literature of the Piano Concerto's genesis see
George S. Bozarth, 'Brahms First Piano
Concerto Op. 15: Genesis and Meaning' in
R. Emans and M. Wendt, eds., *Beiträge zur
Geschichte des Konzerts* (Bonn, 1990),
pp. 211–47.
5 *Clara Schumann – Johannes Brahms: Briefe
aus den Jahren 1853–1896*, ed. Berthold
Litzmann, 2 vols. (Leipzig, 1927; rpt
Hildesheim and Wiesbaden, 1989), vol. I, p. 76.
6 Michael Musgrave, *The Music of Brahms*, rev.
edn (Oxford, 1994), p. 122. Although Brahms's
opening seems clearly to evoke that great
progenitor, the relationship may not be one of

direct inspiration. Brahms did not, in fact, hear Beethoven's symphony in performance until the end of March 1854, by which time the first movement of his two-piano sonata would appear to have been substantially drafted.

7 'In D minor in 6/4 – slow' is Brahms's description in his letter to Schumann of 30 January 1855: *Clara Schumann – Johannes Brahms: Briefe*, vol. I, p. 69.

8 *Letters to and from Joseph Joachim*, selected and translated by Nora Bickley (London, 1914), p. 160.

9 In a recent study – 'Contradictory Criteria in a Work of Brahms' in David Brodbeck, ed., *Brahms Studies*, vol. I (Lincoln, Nebr., 1994), pp. 81–110 – Joseph Dubiel suggests that this passage can be heard as 'an extraneous issue imposed upon a situation still awaiting completion' (p. 88).

10 D. F. Tovey, *Essays in Musical Analysis*, vol. III: *Concertos* (London, 1936), p. 108.

11 Tovey, *Essays in Musical Analysis*, vol. I: *Symphonies* (London, 1935), p. 216.

12 Walter Frisch usefully reprints Tovey's important essay on this work in Frisch, ed., *Brahms and His World*, pp. 151–9. The concerto was drafted by 1858, though revision occupied Joachim until early 1860. It was published in 1861. It has been most recently recorded by Elmar Oliveira, violin, with the London Philharmonic Orchestra conducted by Leon Botstein, CD IMP Masters MCD 27 DDD.

13 Tovey's essay errs, I suspect, in placing Joachim's concerto 'in direct line of descent' between Beethoven and Brahms. A detailed chronology of the Brahms and Joachim concertos would be fascinating and is sadly lacking; but it appears that they evolved almost concurrently, and that in its original sonata/symphony form, Brahms's was the earlier work.

14 Bozarth, 'Brahms's First Piano Concerto', p. 225 n. 55.

15 Siegfried Kross, 'Brahms and E. T. A. Hoffmann', *19th-Century Music* 5 (1981–82), pp. 193–200. Bozarth, pp. 230–8, offers a subtle reading of the parallels between Kreisler's situation in Hoffmann's novel and Brahms's in the mid-1850s.

16 *Clara Schumann – Johannes Brahms: Briefe*, vol. I, p. 198.

17 Bozarth, 'Brahms First Piano Concerto', pp. 226–9 notes the soloist's allusion, earlier in the movement, to Brahms's and Clara's joint cadenza to Mozart's Piano Concerto No. 20, K.466 – another potent D minor concerto that certainly occupies some place in the ancestry of Brahms's Op. 15.

18 The multicoloured facsimile of Brahms's

autograph, published in 1979 by the Library of Congress, bears eloquent testimony to this process (*Johannes Brahms: Concerto for Violin, Op. 77: A Facsimile of the Holograph Score with an Introduction by Yehudi Menuhin and a Foreword by Jon Newsom* (Washington, 1979)). It should be noted, however, that the neat red-ink revisions of the solo part, which were thought likely to be in Joachim's hand when the facsimile was published, have since been identified as the work of Simrock's editor Robert Keller, entrusted in June 1879 with putting the various sources for the work in order. See *The Brahms–Keller Correspondence*, ed. George S. Bozarth in collaboration with Wiltrud Martin (Lincoln, Nebr., 1996), p. 22 and n. 3. They thus represent Brahms's final thoughts on the relevant passages, not necessarily the acceptance of Joachim's suggestions.

19 Lalo's five-movement *Symphonie espagnole* for violin and orchestra (1875) is hardly likely to have figured in Brahms's thoughts. It may be more significant that as recently as 8 November 1874 he had conducted Berlioz's *Harold en Italie*, with its concertante viola, at a concert of the Geselleschaft der Musikfreunde.

20 Letter of 'June', 1878, *Clara Schumann – Johannes Brahms: Briefe*, vol. II, p. 145.

21 Michael Musgrave has drawn attention to the kinship of the main Adagio melody and the 'Sapphische Ode' from Brahms's Op. 94 *Lieder* (composed, apparently, some years later).

22 The veteran Ruggiero Ricci recorded Brahms's concerto with the Joachim cadenza plus fifteen others – by Busoni, Tovey, Ysaÿe, Kreisler, Singer, Hermann, Auer, Ondriček, Kneisel, Marteau, Kubelik, Busch, Heifetz, Milstein and himself. Curiously he omits the fine cadenza by Enescu, which retains some currency. The most recent cadenza known to me is by Joshua Bell, included on his 1996 Decca recording – testimony to a still-living tradition.

23 It is certainly possible to imagine passages on the violin, and a 'conjectural restoration' might be a fascinating exercise. But the scherzo's ideas seem naturally to require the greater power of the piano, and there is every reason to think that the movement was much altered for its eventual incarnation.

24 As noted by Constantin Floros in his liner notes to the recording of the B♭ Piano Concerto with Maurizio Pollini and the Vienna Philharmonic Orchestra conducted by Claudio Abbado, DG 419 471–2 (1977).

25 The F♯ tonality may also be considered a reference to Clara, by a tradition within Brahms's music that goes back to the *Schumann*

Variations Op. 9 dedicated to her, and the finale of the 1854 version of the B major Piano Trio, with its appeal to her couched in the F♯ major second theme.

26 These include the minor-third span of their respective head-motifs, and the hint of extension in each into Schumann's 'Clara-motif'.

27 Once again, Brahms did not necessarily accept all his suggestions. Joachim's florid emendation for bars 328ff. of the finale was published by Karl Geiringer in *Brahms: His Life and Work*, 2nd edn, trans. H. B. Weiner and Bernard Miall (London, 1948), p. 264.

28 One might spare a thought, in the circumstances, for Viotti's two Symphonies concertantes for two violins and orchestra, but I am unable to determine if, or how well, Brahms know these works. The interest of Joachim and Brahms in the Viotti A minor Concerto and its relationship to Brahms's Violin and Double Concertos are further discussed by Simon McVeigh in 'Brahms's Favourite Concerto: Viotti's Concerto No. 22', *The Strad* 105 (April 1994), pp. 343–7.

8 The scope and significance of the choral music

1 Robert Schumann, 'Neue Bahnen', *Neue Zeitschrift für Musik* 18 (28 March 1853), p. 1.

2 Hans Michael Beuerle, *Johannes Brahms: Untersuchungen zu den A-cappella-Kompositionen: ein Beitrag zur Geschichte der Chormusik* (Hamburg, 1987); Virginia Hancock, *Brahms's Choral Compositions and His Library of Early Music* (Ann Arbor, Mich., 1983); Siegfried Kross, *Die Chorwerke von Johannes Brahms* (Berlin, 1958).

3 On the changing status of instrumental and vocal music around 1850, see Leon Botstein, 'Listening through Reading: Musical Literacy and the Concert Audience', *19th-Century Music* 16 (1992), pp. 129–45.

4 Brahms's study of early music during these years is best reflected in the so-called 'counterpoint correspondence', which is considered comprehensively by David Brodbeck in 'The Brahms–Joachim Counterpoint Exchange; or, Robert, Clara, and "the Best Harmony between Jos. and. Joh."' in David Brodbeck, ed., *Brahms Studies*, vol. I (Lincoln, Nebr.,1994), pp. 30–80.

5 See Beuerle, *Johannes Brahms: Untersuchungen zu den A-cappella-Kompositionen*, especially chapter 3, 'Brahms' Verhältnis zum Chor und zur Chormusik', pp. 105, 107, 114–16.

6 For a list of Brahms's performances of early

music see Hancock, *Brahms's Choral Compositions*, pp. 209–11.

7 A distinction must be drawn between actual settings of folk-songs, as contained in the fourteen *Deutsche Volkslieder* WoO 34 that Brahms published in 1864 and dedicated to the Vienna Singakademie (for whom they were presumably composed), and folk-like choral settings such as the twelve *Lieder und Romanzen* for women's chorus Op. 44 (pub. 1866) which are primarily based on romantic poetry. None of the melodies in Op. 44 are based on folk-songs, and the only actual folk-lyrics in the set are German translations from Italian and Slovak (Nos. 3 and 4 respectively).

8 Sophie Drinker suggested that an early version of Op. 41 No. 1 ('Ich schwing mein Horn ins Jammertal') for men's chorus may have existed as early as 1847, when the fourteen-year-old Brahms conducted a men's chorus at Winsen, a country town near Hamburg (Sophie Drinker, *Brahms and his Women's Choruses* (Merion, Pa.), 1952), p. 95. On Brahms's stay in Winsen and his musical activities there (including the composition of two other short choral works) see Florence May, *The Life of Johannes Brahms*, 2nd edn, 2 vols. (London, 1948; rpt 1977), vol. I, pp. 72–81.

9 See Brodbeck, 'The Brahms–Joachim Counterpoint Exchange'.

10 Brahms had already mentioned the Benedictus in a letter to Clara Schumann on 26 February 1856 (*Clara Schumann – Johannes Brahms: Briefe aus den Jahren 1853–1896*, ed. Berthold Litzmann, 2 vols., (Leipzig, 1927; rpt Hildesheim and Wiesbaden, 1989), vol. I, p. 178). The eighteen-bar canon must have been a favourite of the composer, for in the ensuing months Brahms began to build his canonic mass around that item, and later he reset it for SSAA for performance by his Hamburg women's chorus. Finally, he re-used the canon in the form in which it is best known today, reset to two separate German biblical texts in the motet 'Warum ist das Licht gegeben' Op. 74 No. 1.

11 Brahms's inexperience in practical performance matters is related in the comments of his friend the Göttingen choral director Julius Otto Grimm, to whom Brahms sent a copy of his incomplete mass in 1857. Grimm labelled the mass virtually impossible to perform because of the alto tessitura, which was 'barbarously low', adding: 'I cannot imagine any chorus in Europe singing it the way you have in mind' (letter of 4 May 1857, as cited in Johannes Brahms, *Messe*, ed. Otto Biba (Vienna, 1984), p. 3).

12 Brahms constructed similar canons by fourths in two other choral works of this

period: verse 6 of 'Der englische Gruß' Op. 22 No. 1 (see below) and 'Adoramus Te' Op. 37 No. 2.

13 The Benedictus appears in the partbooks of the Völckers sisters; see Margit L. McCorkle, *Johannes Brahms: Thematisch-bibliographisches Werkverzeichnis* (Munich, 1984), pp. 534–5.

14 Kross, *Die Chorwerke von Johannes Brahms*, p.116.

15 For a broad overview of Brahms's folk-song settings see McCorkle, *Brahms Werkverzeichnis*, pp. 552ff. Therein, fifty-two folk-song arrangements among the repertoire of the Hamburger Frauenchor (see WoO 36–38) and the *Deutsche Volkslieder* WoO 34 can be securely listed among the folk-song settings that Brahms made for choruses he was directing. The twelve folk-song settings for mixed choir WoO 35 were also almost certainly intended for Brahms's Detmold and Vienna choirs.

16 The *locus classicus* for this characterisation of Renaissance music is E. T. A. Hoffmann's essay 'Alte und neue Kirchenmusik', *Allgemeine musikalische Zeitung* 16 (1814), pp. 577–84, 593–603, 611–19. For an English translation see David Charlton, ed., *E. T. A. Hoffmann's Musical Writings* (Cambridge, 1989), pp. 351–76.

17 The socio-political ramifications of choral music in nineteenth-century Germany are discussed in: George L. Mosse, *The Nationalization of the Masses: Political Symbolism and Mass Movements in Germany from the Napoleonic Wars through the Third Reich* (Ithaca, NY, 1975).

18 The first appearance of Op. 22 Nos. 1–2 and 4–7 stems from rehearsals by the Frauenchor between June and September of 1859. However, when Brahms offered the songs to the publisher Rieter Biedermann in 1861, he claimed to have begun them in 1858. See McCorkle, *Brahms Werkverzeichnis*, p. 77.

19 See Hancock, *Brahms's Choral Compositions*, pp. 114–15.

20 Brahms made further settings that include the original folk melodies (as transmitted in *Deutsche Volkslieder mit ihrer Original-Weisen*, Part I, ed. A. Kretzschmer (Berlin, 1840); Part II, collected [on the basis of Kretzchmer's work] by A. W. Zuccalmaglio (Berlin, 1840)) for three of the texts in Op. 22. A piano–vocal setting of 'Der englische Gruß' appears as No. 8 from WoO 32, thirty-two folk-song settings that Brahms sent in manuscript to Clara Schumann in 1858 and which were published posthumously in l 926. 'Maria ging aus Wandern' appears as No. 22 of that set and, with a slightly more developed accompaniment, as No. 14 in the *Deutsche Volkslieder* WoO 33, which Brahms published as

seven books of seven songs in 1894. In 1863–64 Brahms composed an alternative SATB setting of 'Es wollt' gut Jäger jagen' which was published in 1864 as the last in the set of fourteen *Deutsche Volkslieder für gemischten Chor* (WoO 34). See McCorkle, *Brahms Werkverzeichnis*, pp. 583–601.

21 Such chorale-like arch shapes can be found in other of Brahms's works as well, most notably No. 1 of the much later *Vier ernste Gesänge*, Op. 121 (1896). For a comparison of these melodies see Michael Musgrave, *Brahms: A German Requiem* (Cambridge, 1996), p. 34.

22 Although Dietrich's remarks are discussed throughout the Brahms literature, Musgrave's recent monograph explains their relevance most clearly and evenhandedly (*Brahms: A German Requiem*, p. 6).

23 Musgrave succinctly traces the many forms this 'Selig' motive takes in the piece (*Brahms: A German Requiem*, pp. 24–6). The most thorough (and perhaps overreaching) examination of the 'Selig' motive is undertaken by Walter Westafer in his dissertation 'Overall Unity and Contrast in Brahms's German Requiem' (University of North Carolina, 1973).

24 Christopher Reynolds, 'A Choral Symphony by Brahms?' *19th-Century Music* 9 (1985), pp. 3–25. See also Musgrave, *Brahms: A German Requiem*, pp. 26–34.

25 Brahms, however, was not beyond adding his own voice to the tradition: his musical settings often interpreted his borrowed texts quite freely, as is nowhere more apparent than in the instrumental reprise of the *Schicksalslied*, which suggests a reconciliation of sorts that is not implied by Hölderlin's text. See John Daverio, 'The *Wechsel der Töne* in Brahms's *Schicksalslied*', *Journal of the American Musicological Society* 46 (1993), pp. 84–113.

26 The personal background for the *Alto Rhapsody*, including Brahms's comments to Clara about Julie, are recounted in Kross, *Die Chorwerke von Johannes Brahms*, pp. 290–7.

27 Among the later choral works only the *Tafellied* Op. 93b calls for (piano) accompaniment. This brief setting of Eichendorff's 'Dank der Damen', which follows the text in its 'call and answer' format between the men's and women's voices, was composed for the Krefeld Singverein in recognition of a particularly fine performance of the *Gesang der Parzen* in the summer of 1884. See Max Kalbeck, *Johannes Brahms*, 4 vols. (Berlin, 1904–14; rpt of final edn of each vol. (1921, 1921, 1912–13, 1915), Tutzing, 1976), vol. III (2nd edn), p. 516.

28 On the history of the 'Missa Canonica' and its recomposition in Op. 74 No. 1, see Robert Pascall, 'Brahms's Missa Canonica and Its

Recomposition in His Motet "Warum" Op. 74
No. 1' in Michael Musgrave, ed., *Brahms 2:
Biographical, Documentary and Analytical
Studies* (Cambridge, 1985), pp. 111–36.
29 Brahms became familiar with the text, a
German translation of the Latin hymn 'Rorate
Coeli', by 1864, but did not mention the piece
until 1870 in a letter to Max Bruch. See George
Bozarth, 'Johannes Brahms und die geistlichen
Lieder aus David Gregor Corners Groß-
Catholischen Gesangbuch von 1631' in Susanne
Antonicek and Otto Biba, eds., *Brahms-Kongreß
Wien 1983, Kongreßbericht* (Tutzing, 1988), pp.
67–80, and Hancock, *Brahms's Choral
Compositions*, p. 82.
30 Hancock, *Brahms's Choral Compositions*,
p. 119.
31 As described by Heinrich Christoph Koch in
his *Musikalisches Lexikon* (Frankfurt am Main,
1802; rpt Hildeshem, 1985), p. 1271.
32 Siegfried Kross and Hans Michael Beuerle
have ably demonstrated the use of motivic
development in Op. 93 in analyses of Nos. 1–3:
see Kross, *Die Chorwerke von Johannes Brahms*,
pp. 407–14, and Beuerle, *Untersuchungen zu
den A-cappella-Kompositionen*, pp. 304–14,
324–30.
33 As recounted by Kalbeck, *Johannes Brahms*,
vol IV, p. 521.
34 Reinhold Brinkmann defines the mature
Brahms through these qualities in *Late Idyll:
The Second Symphony of Johannes Brahms*,
trans. Peter Palmer (Cambridge, Mass., 1995).
35 Whereas Beuerle and Kross also have made
this observation, Hancock has made the most
thorough study of the implications of Schütz's
music on Brahms's late choral style: see
Brahms's Choral Compositions, pp. 135ff.

**9 Words for music: the songs for solo voice
and piano**
1 Brahms wrote over 200 original songs and
upwards of 100 folk-song arrangements for
solo voice and piano; his original songs
appeared steadily throughout his life,
sometimes in a sequence of consecutive opus
numbers, as in Opp. 46–9, 94–7 and 104–7.
2 Max Kalbeck, *Johannes Brahms*, 4 vols.
(Berlin, 1904–14; rpt of final edition of each
vol. (1921, 1921, 1912–13, 1915), Tutzing,
1974), vol. I, p. 133. His own settings of Heine
came later. Op. 71 No. 1; Op. 85 No. 1; Op. 85
No. 2; Op. 96 No. 1; Op. 96 No. 3; Op. 96 No. 4.
3 'Mondnacht' WoO 21, composed in 1853;
published in *Johannes Brahms Sämtliche Werke*,
vol. VII, p. 62.
4 George Henschel, *Musings and Memories of a
Musician* (London, 1918), p. 113.

5 There are two settings of Goethe: the
dramatic ballad *Gesang der Parzen* ('The Song
of the Fates') Op. 89, and the fragment from
'Harzreise im Winter' known as the *Rhapsodie*
(Alto Rhapsody) for Alto Voice, Chorus and
Orchestra Op. 53; Schiller provides the text for
the setting of the dirge titled *Nänie*, Op. 82 and
Hölderlin a passage from the poem 'Hyperion'
set as the *Schicksalslied* ('Song of Destiny') Op.
54.
6 Henschel, *Musings and Memories of a
Musician*, p. 87.
7 Gustav Jenner, *Johannes Brahms als
Mensch, Lehrer und Künstler* (Marburg, 1905),
p, 30.
8 Jenner, *Johannes Brahms*, pp. 31, 35.
9 Letter of 10 November 1875 to Rieter
Biedermann: *Johannes Brahms Briefwechsel
XIV: Johannes Brahms im Briefwechsel mit
Breitkopf & Härtel, Bartholf Senff, J. Rieter
Biedermann u. A.* (Berlin, 1920), p. 256.
10 *Clara Schumann – Johannes Brahms: Briefe
aus den Jahren 1853–1896*, ed. Berthold
Litzmann, 2 vols. (Leipzig, 1927; rpt
Hildesheim and Wiesbaden, 1989), vol. I, p. 294.
11 The poem of 'Therese' is from Gottfried
Keller, *Neuere Gedichte* (Brunswick, 1851)
where it forms part of the cycle *Von Weibern:
Alte Lieder: 1846*.
12 The text of 'Es liebt sich so lieblich im
Lenze!' appears with the title 'Frühling' in the
section 'Romanzen 1839–42' in *Neue Gedichte*
(Hamburg, 1844). Brahms has slightly adapted
the second verse and made other changes.
13 The poem of 'Wie Melodien zieht es' is
taken from Klaus Groth's *Hundert Blätter,
Paralipomena zum Quickborn* (Hamburg, 1854)
in the section 'Klänge'.
14 Ludwig Hölty's poem 'Die Mainacht',
written in 1774, was first published in the
Musenalmanach (Göttingen) of 1775. Brahms
used J. H. Voss's 1804 edition, where the poem is
somewhat altered. He omitted the second
stanza of the poem, in which the poet praises
the 'Flötende Nachtigall'.
15 The poem of 'Wir wandelten' Op. 96 No. 2 is
a translation from the Hungarian and is taken
from Daumer's *Polydora, ein weltpoetisches
Liederbuch* (Frankfurt am Main, 1855). Brahms
made only minor changes.
16 'Feldeinsamkeit' is taken from Allmers's
Dichtungen (Bremen, 1860), with slight
variants. The author disliked Brahms's setting
as being too elaborate for his poem.
17 The poem of 'Wie bist du meine Königin' is
taken from G. F. Daumer, *Hafis* (Hamburg,
1846), a collection of Persian poems with
poetical additions of various nations and
countries. Brahms retained it intact with the

small exception of the original 'Rose Glanz' in verse 2.

18 Kalbeck, *Johannes Brahms*, vol. IV, p. 476.

10 Conducting Brahms

1 Symphony No. 1 and St Anthony Variations; EMI CD C 754286 2; Symphony No. 2 and Tragic Overture;: EMI CD: 0777 7 54875 2; Symphonies Nos. 3 and 4: EMI CD:7243 5 56118 2; *Ein deutsches Requiem* and *Begräbnisgesang* EMI CD: 0777 7 54658 2.

2 Joseph Joachim and Andreas Moser, *Violinschule*, 3 vols. (Berlin, 1902–5), trans. A. Moffat (Berlin, 1905).

3 Ibid., vol. II, p. 96 (quoted from Ludwig Spohr, *Violin-schule*, Vienna 1832).

4 Ibid.

5 Ibid., p. 96a.

6 Ibid., pp. 92, 95.

7 Pierre Marie François de Sales Baillot, *L'art du violon* (Paris, 1835); ed. and trans. Louise Goldberg as *The Art of the Violin* (Evanston, Ill., 1991), p. 239.

8 Article 'Bow', *The New Grove Dictionary of Music and Musicians* (London, 1980), vol. III, p. 133.

9 Letter of c. 20 May, 1879. *Johannes Brahms Briefwechsel VI: Johannes Brahms im Briefwechsel mit Joseph Joachim*, vol. II, ed. Andreas Moser, 2nd edn (Berlin, 1912), pp. 148–50.

10 Florence May, *The Life of Brahms*, 2nd edn, 2 vols. (London, 1948), vol. I, p. 19.

11 See the visual scheme given in Robert Pascall, *Playing Brahms: A Study in 19th-century Performance Practice* (Nottingham, 1990), p. 13.

12 Aspects of Henschel's professional life are recalled in George Henschel, *Musings and Memories of a Musician* (London, 1918).

13 The changes in the markings are detailed in Michael Musgrave, *Brahms: A German Requiem* (Cambridge, 1996), pp. 73, 91.

14 *Brahms in der Meininger Tradition: seine Sinfonien und Haydn Variationen in der Bezeichnung von Fritz Simrock*, ed. Walter Blume (Stuttgart, 1933).

15 Henschel, *Musings and Memories of a Musician*, p. 314.

16 Quoted and translated by Pascall from *Brahms in der Meininger Tradition* in Pascall, *Playing Brahms*, p. 16.

11 The editor's Brahms

1 Georg, later Sir George Henschel. See George Henschel, *Personal Recollections of Johannes Brahms* (Boston,1907), pp. 22–3. Max Kalbeck, *Johannes Brahms*, 4 vols. (Berlin, 1904–14; rpt

of final edn of each vol. (1921, 1921, 1912–13, 1915), Tutzing, 1976), vol. III, pp. 247–8.

2 Margit L. McCorkle, *Johannes Brahms: Thematisch-bibliographisches Werkverzeichnis* (Munich, 1984), pp. 812–13. On Brahms's friendship with Kupfer, see Kalbeck, *Johannes Brahms*, vol. IV, pp. 549–51.

3 *Johannes Brahms Briefwechsel IX: Johannes Brahms: Briefe an P. J. Simrock und Fritz Simrock*, vol.I, ed. Max Kalbeck (Berlin, 1917), p. 162.

4 *Johannes Brahms Briefwechsel X: Johannes Brahms: Briefe an P. J. Simrock und Fritz Simrock*, vol. II, ed. Max Kalbeck (Berlin, 1917), p. 80.

5 This is sometimes wrongly described in the Brahms literature as a postcard; in fact, it is a cropped piece of manuscript paper. It is illustrated in facsimile in *Johannes Brahms, Leben und Werk*, ed. Christiane Jacobsen (Wiesbaden, 1983), p. 117, as frontispiece of the current Eulenburg score of the symphony (No. 425) and in *Johannes Brahms; Symphony No. 1*, ed. Robert Pascall (= Neue Ausgabe sämtlichen Werke), series I, vol. I (Munich, 1996), p. 203.

6 *Deutscher Liederhort: Aus der vorzüglicheren Deutschen Volkslieder nach Wort und Weisen aus der Vorzeit und Gegenwart*, collected and elaborated by Ludwig Erk, newly arranged and presented by F. M. Böhme, 3 vols. (Leipzig 1893–4), vol. II, No. 575b. Brahms had already set the Eichendorff text in 1860 as 'Der Gärtner', *Gesänge für Frauenchor* Op. 17 No. 3.

7 *Briefwechsel X*, p. 37.

8 Kalbeck, *Johannes Brahms*, vol. III, p. 232.

9 *Brahms-Institut an der Musikhochschule Lübeck: 32 Stichvorlagen von Werken Johannes Brahms*, Patrimonia 107 (Berlin and Kiel, 1995) pp. 36–8.

10 My translation from the original in the Library of Congress, Washington DC. Brahms's correspondence with Robert Keller has recently been published: *The Brahms–Keller Correspondence*, ed. George S. Bozarth, in collaboration with Wiltrud Martin (Lincoln, Nebr., 1996): for this letter, see pp. 2–3.

11 Frithjof Haas, *Zwischen Brahms und Wagner: Der Dirigent Hermann Levi* (Zurich and Mainz, 1995), p. 106.

12 *Johannes Brahms Briefwechsel VI: Johannes Brahms im Briefwechsel mit Joseph Joachim*, vol. II, ed. Andreas Moser, 2nd edn (Berlin, 1912), p. 220 (my translation).

12 A photograph of Brahms

1 One only regrets that Brahms cut such a small *tranche* from the middle of this superb

poem, which ends with a magnificent peroration evoking the subject matter of the paintings of Caspar David Friedrich; and which begins with an arresting image:

Dem Geier gleich
Der auf schweren Morgenwolken
Mit sanftem Fittich ruhend
Nach Beute schaut,
Schwebe mein Lied.

How could he have resisted the vulture hovering . . .?

Brahms's own ending – the closing chorale – is, alas, the weakest section of the piece, attempting consolation and reconciliation but only achieving a certain sanctimoniousness.

2 Stated by Webern's pupil, Arnold Elston. See Hans Moldenhauer, *Anton Webern, A Chronicle of His Life and Work* (London, 1978), p. 481.

3 Interest has, however, been increasing latterly, and the centennial year bought some welcome performances. Claudio Abbado has recorded *Nänie*, the *Alto Rhapsody* and *Gesang der Parzen* with the Berlin Philharmonic Orchestra and the Berlin Radio Chorus, CD DG 435342-2 DDD.

4 The first Viennese performance of the Clarinet Quintet took place in the music room of the Palais Wittgenstein – much frequented by Brahms, who had his special chair near the door so he could slip in and out. The room had sculptures by Max Klinger but also panels by Gustav Klimt. Did Brahms avert his eyes? We shall never know. In any case, the room was destroyed during the Second World War. (Captions to illustrations between pp. 420 and 421 in Styra Avins, *Johannes Brahms: Life and Letters* (Oxford, 1997).

5 The visual tastes of the great composers are another matter entirely, perhaps better left to an article on Schoenberg's paintings (and Ingres's violin playing).

6 Peter Gay, 'Aimez-Vous Brahms? On Polarities in Modernism', in *Freud, Jews and Other Germans: Masters and Victims in Modernist Culture* (Oxford, 1978), pp. 231–56.

7 Michael Musgrave, 'The Cultural World of Brahms' in Robert Pascall, ed., *Brahms: Biographical, Documentary and Analytical Studies* (Cambridge, 1983), pp. 21–2.

8 If we are to pursue the comparison: Wagner said that composition was the art of transition. Yet some of Brahms's transitions are better – superior in subtlety and expedition – than the sometimes bumpy scene-shifting to which we are occasionally subjected in Wagner. Conversely, Brahms's subtlety would have gone for nothing in the theatre.

9 Virginia Hancock, articles in *Brahms, Biographical, Documentary and Analytical Studies*, pp. 27–40 and Michael Musgrave, ed., *Brahms 2: Biographical, Documentary and Analytical Studies* (Cambridge, 1987), pp. 95–110.

10 Brahms's comment to Hermann Levi, quoted in Max Kalbeck, *Johannes Brahms*, 4 vols. (Berlin, 1904–14; rpt 1976), vol. I, p. 165.

11 Charles Rosen, *The Classical Style: Haydn, Mozart, Beethoven*, exp. edn (New York, 1997), p. 460.

12 See 'Alexander von Zemlinsky and Karl Weigl: Brahms and the Newer Generation: Personal Reminiscences', trans. Walter Frisch in Walter Frisch, ed., *Brahms and His World* (Princeton, 1990), pp. 205–6.

13 See also Chapter 7, pp. 168–9 and note 28.

List of works

It is impossible to specify the working periods of Brahms's compositions consistently and with accuracy in view of their long gestation periods, which often spread over many years. Publication background is much better known from his correspondence, and the first editions of his works can be dated with accuracy.

Opus no.	Title	Date of publication
1	Sonata in C major (pno.)	1853
2	Sonata in F sharp minor (pno.)	1854
3	Six Songs (voice/pno.)	1853
4	Scherzo in E flat minor (pno.)	1854
5	Sonata in F minor (pno.)	1854
6	Six Songs (voice/pno.)	1853
7	Six Songs (voice/pno.)	1854
8	Trio in B major (pno./vl./vc.)	1854 (revised 1891)
9	*Variations on a Theme of Schumann* [Schumann Variations] (pno.)	1854
10	*Ballades* (pno.)	1856
11	Serenade in D (orch.)	1860
12	*Ave Maria*, female voices/orch. or org.)	1861
13	*Begräbnisgesang* [Funeral Hymn] (mixed choir/wind orch.)	1861
14	Eight Songs and Romances (voice/pno.)	1861
15	Concerto in D minor (pno./orch.)	1861
16	Serenade in A major ('for small orchestra')	1860
17	Songs (female voices/two horns/harp)	1861
18	Sextet in B flat (2 vl./2 va./2 vc.)	1862
19	Five Songs (voice/pno.)	1862
20	Three Duets (SA/pno.)	1862
21/1	*Variations on an Original Theme* (pno.)	1862
21/2	*Variations on a Hungarian Song* (pno.)	1862
22	*Marienlieder* (mixed choir, unaccomp.)	1862
23	*Variations on a Theme by Schumann* (pno. duet)	1866
24	*Variations and Fugue on a Theme of Handel* [Handel Variations] (pno.)	1862
25	Quartet in G minor (pno./vl./va./vc.)	1863
26	Quartet in A major (pno./vl./va./vc.)	1863
27	*Psalm 23* (3-part female choir/pno. or org. accomp.)	1864
28	Duets for Alto and Baritone (pno.)	1863
29	Two Motets (5-part mixed choir, unaccomp.)	1864
30	*Geistliches Lied* [Sacred Song] (mixed choir/org. or pno. accomp.)	1864
31	Three Quartets (S A T B/pno. accomp.)	1864
32	[9] Songs (solo voice/pno.)	1865
33	[15] Romances from Tieck's *Magelone* (solo voice/pno.)	1865 and 1869
34	Quintet in F minor (2 vl./va./vc./pno.)	1865
34b	Sonata (two pnos./'after Op. 34')	1872

35	*Variations on a Theme of Paganini (Studies)* (pno.) [2 books]	1866
36	Sextet in G (2 vl./2 va./2 vc.)	1866
37	*Drei Geistliche Chöre* [Three Sacred Choruses] (female voices, unaccomp.)	1865
38	Sonata in E minor (vc./pno.)	1866
39	[16] Waltzes (pno. duet)	1866
40	Trio in E flat (pno./vc./horn [or va.; or vc.])	1866
41	Five Songs (male choir, unaccomp.)	1867
42	Three Songs (6-part choir, unaccomp.)	1869
43	Four Songs (solo voice/pno.)	1868
44	Twelve Songs and Romances (female choir, unaccomp., or with optional pno. accomp.)	1866
45	*Ein deutsches Requiem* [A German Requiem] (S Bt soloists/choir and orchestra (org. ad lib.))	1869
46	Four Songs (voice/pno.)	1868
47	Five Songs (voice/pno.)	1868
48	Seven Songs (voice/pno.)	1868
49	Five Songs (voice/pno.)	1868
50	*Rinaldo* (T solo/male choir/orch.)	1869
51	Two Quartets (2 vl./va./vc.): No. 1 in C minor; No. 2 in A minor	1873
52	[18] *Liebeslieder* Waltzes (pno. 4 hands and voices [S A T B] 'ad lib.'	1869
52a	[18] *Liebeslieder* Waltzes (pno. 4 hands)	1869
53	*Alto Rhapsody* (A solo/male choir/orch.)	1870
54	*Schicksalslied* [Song of Destiny] (mixed choir/orch.)	1871
55	*Triumphlied* [Song of Triumph] (8-part choir/orch.)	1872
56a	*Variations on a Theme of Haydn* ['St Antony Chorale'] (orch.)	1874
56b	*Variations on a Theme of Haydn* ['St Antony Chorale'] (2 pnos.)	1874
57	Eight Songs (solo voice/pno.)	1871
58	[8] Songs (solo voice/pno.)	1871
59	[8] Songs (solo voice/pno.)	1873
60	Quartet in C minor (pno./vl./va./vc.)	1875
61	Four Duets (S A/pno.)	1874
62	Seven Songs (mixed choir, unaccomp.)	1874
63	[9] Songs (solo voice/pno.)	1874
64	[3)]Quartets (S A T B/pno.)	1874
65	*Neue Liebeslieder*. Waltzes (S A T B/pno. 4 hands)	1875
65b	*Neue Liebeslieder*. Waltzes (pno. 4 hands)	1875
66	Five Duets (S A/pno.)	1875
67	Quartet in B flat (2 vl./va./vc.)	1876
68	Symphony in C minor (orch.)	1877
69	Nine Songs (solo voice/pno.)	1877
70	Four Songs (solo voice/pno.)	1877
71	Five Songs (solo voice/pno.)	1877
72	Five Songs (solo voice/pno.)	1877
73	Symphony in D major (orch.)	1878
74	Two Motets (mixed choir, unaccomp.)	1878
75	[4] Ballades and Romances (S A/pno.)	1878
76	[8] *Klavierstücke* [Piano Pieces] (pno.)	1879
77	Concerto in D major (vl./orch.)	1879
78	Sonata in G major (vl./pno.)	1880
79	Two Rhapsodies (pno.)	1880
80	*Academic Festival Overture* (orch.)	1881
81	*Tragic Overture* (orch.)	1881

82	*Nänie* (mixed choir/orch.; harp ad lib.)	1881
83	Concerto in B flat (pno./orch.)	1882
84	[5] Romances and Songs (one or two voices/pno.)	1882
85	Six Songs (solo voice/pno.)	1882
86	Six Songs (solo voice/pno.)	1882
87	Trio in C major (pno./vl./vc.)	1882
88	Quintet in F major (2 vl./2 va./vc.)	1882
89	*Gesang der Parzen* [Song of the Fates] (6-part mixed choir/orch.)	1883
90	Symphony in F major (orch.)	1884
91	Two Songs (A/va./pno.)	1884
92	[4] Quartets (S A T B/pno.)	1884
93a	[6] Songs and Romances (mixed choir, unaccomp.)	1884
93b	*Tafellied* (6-part mixed choir/pno.accomp.)	1885
94	Five Songs (voice/pno.)	1884
95	Seven Songs (voice/pno.)	1884
96	Four Songs (voice/pno.)	1886
97	Six Songs (voice/pno.)	1886
98	Symphony in E minor (orch.)	1886
99	Sonata in F major (vc./pno.)	1887
100	Sonata in A major (vl./pno.)	1887
101	Trio in C minor (pno./vl./vc.)	1887
102	Concerto in A minor [Double Concerto] (vl./vc./orch.)	1888
103	[11] *Zigeunerlieder* [Gypsy Songs] (S A T B/pno.)	1888
104	Five Songs (mixed choir, unaccomp.)	1888
105	Five Songs (solo voice/pno.)	1888
106	Five Songs (solo voice/pno.)	1888
107	Five Songs (solo voice/pno.)	1888
108	Violin Sonata in D minor (vl./pno.)	1889
109	*Fest- und Gedenksprüche* [Festival and Memorial Sayings] (8-part mixed choir, unaccomp.)	1890
110	Three Motets (4- and 8-part mixed choir)	1890
111	Quintet in G major (2 vl./2 va./vc.)	1891
112	Six Quartets (S A T B/pno.)	1891
113	Thirteen Canons (female voices unaccomp.)	1891
114	Trio in A minor (pno./clarinet (or va.), vc.)	1892
115	Clarinet Quintet in B minor (clar./2 vl./va., vc.)	1892
116	[7] Fantasias (pno.)	1892
117	Three Intermezzos (pno.)	1892
118	Six *Klavierstücke* [Piano Pieces] (pno.)	1893
119	Four *Klavierstücke* [Piano Pieces] (pno.)	1893
120	Two Sonatas (clar./pno.; or va., or vl.): No. 1 in F minor; No. 2 in E flat major	1895
121	*Vier Ernste Gesänge* [Four Serious Songs] (solo voice/pno.)	1896
122	Eleven Chorale Preludes (org.)	published posthumously, 1902

Works without opus number

Fifty-One Exercises (pno.)	1893 (WoO 6)
[49] *Deutsche Volkslieder* [German Folksongs]	
(Books 1–VI: solo voice/pno. Book VII for a leader ('Vorsänger') and small choir)	1894 (WoO 12)

'Mondnacht' (solo voice/pno.)	1854 (WoO 21)
14 *Deutsche Volkslieder* [German Folksongs] (4-part choir S A T B, unaccomp.)	1864 (WoO 34)
Volkskinderlieder [Children's Folksongs] solo voice/pno.)	1858 (WoO 31)
Chorale Prelude and Fugue on 'O Traurigkeit, O Herzeleid' (org.)	1881 (WoO 7)
Fugue in A flat minor (org.)	1864 (WoO 8)
Study ('after Chopin') (pno.)	1869
Rondo ('after C. M von Weber') (pno.)	1869
Presto ('after J. S. Bach') (pno.)	1879
Presto ('after J. S. Bach') (pno.) [second version]	1879
Chaconne ('after J. S. Bach') (pno. left hand)	1879
Gavotte ('after C. W. von Gluck')	1871
[21] Hungarian Dances (pno., 4 hands) [4 Books]	1869, 1880 (WoO 1)
Hungarian Dances (pno., 2 hands) [Book 1]	1872
[3] Hungarian Dances (orch.) [Nos. 1, 3, 10 of above]	1874

Works published posthumously [without opus number; select list]

Two Gigues (pno.)	[1855] 1927 (WoO 4)
Two Sarabandes (pno.)	[1855] 1917 (WoO 5)
Two Gavottes (pno.)	[1854–5] 1979 (WoO 3)
Prelude and Fugue in A minor (org.)	[1856] 1927 (WoO 9)
Prelude and Fugue in G minor (org.)	[1857] 1927 (WoO 10)
Scherzo in C minor ['FAE' Sonata] (vl./pno.)	[1853] 1906 (WoO 2)
'Missa Canonica' [Canonic Mass] (4- 6-part mixed choir, unaccomp.	[1856] 1984 (WoO 18)

Other individual pieces, the many folk-song arrangements and canons, and further arrangements of other composers' works are listed in Michael Musgrave, *The Music of Brahms*, rev. edn (Oxford, 1994). For systematic and comprehensive details of the history of Brahms's works and of their publication, see Margit L. McCorkle, *Johannes Brahms: Thematisch-bibliographisches Werkverzeichnis* (Munich, 1984). See also Index, p. 319.

Bibliography

Abell, Arthur, *Talks with Great Composers* (New York, 1955).

Avins, Styra, *Johannes Brahms: Life and Letters* (Oxford, 1997).

Beuerle, Hans Michael, *Johannes Brahms: Untersuchungen zu den A-cappella-Kompositionen: ein Beitrag zur Geschichte der Chormusik* (Hamburg, 1987).

Biba, Otto, *Johannes Brahms in Wien* (Vienna, 1983).

  Mit den Gedanken in Wien (Vienna, 1984).

Billroth und Brahms im Briefwechsel, ed. Otto Billroth (Berlin and Vienna, 1935).

Botstein, Leon, 'Time and Memory: Concert Life, Science, and Music in Brahms's Vienna' in Walter Frisch, ed., *Brahms and His World* (Princeton, 1990), pp. 65–80.

  'Listening through Reading: Musical Literacy and the Concert Audience', *19th-Century Music* 16 (1992), pp. 129–45.

Bozarth, George S., 'Johannes Brahms und die geistlichen Lieder aus David Gregor Corners Groß-Catholischen Gesangbuch von 1631' in Susanne Antonicek and Otto Biba, eds., *Brahms-Kongreß Wien 1983, Kongreßbericht* (Tutzing, 1988), pp. 67–80.

  'Brahms's B major Trio: An American Premiere', *The American Brahms Society Newsletter* 8 (1990), pp. 1–4.

Bozarth, George S., ed., *Brahms Studies: Analytical and Historical Perspectives* (Oxford, 1990).

  The Brahms–Keller Correspondence, in collaboration with Wiltrud Martin (Lincoln, Nebr., 1996).

Johannes Brahms Briefwechsel I und II: Johannes Brahms im Briefwechsel mit Heinrich und Elisabet von Herzogenberg, ed. Max Kalbeck, 4th rev. edn (Berlin, 1921).

Johannes Brahms Briefwechsel IV: Johannes Brahms im Briefwechsel mit J. O. Grimm, ed. Richard Barth (Berlin, 1907).

Johannes Brahms Briefwechsel V und VI: Johannes Brahms im Briefwechsel mit Joseph Joachim, vols. I and II, ed. Andreas Moser (Berlin, 1921, 1912).

Johannes Brahms Briefwechsel IX und X: Johannes Brahms: Briefe an P. J. Simrock und Fritz Simrock, vols. I and II, ed. Max Kalbeck (Berlin, 1917).

Johannes Brahms Briefwechsel XI und XII: Johannes Brahms: Briefe an Fritz Simrock, vols. I and II, ed. Max Kalbeck (Berlin, 1919).

Johannes Brahms Briefwechsel XIII: Johannes Brahms im Briefwechsel mit Th. Wilhelm Engelmann, ed. Julius Röntgen (Berlin, 1918).

Johannes Brahms Briefwechsel XIV: Johannes Brahms im Briefwechsel mit Breitkopf und Härtel, Bartholf Senff, Johann Melchior Rieter Biedermann u. A. (Berlin, 1920), p. 183.

Johannes Brahms Briefwechsel XVIII n.s.: Johannes Brahms im Briefwechsel mit Julius Stockhausen, ed. Renate Hofmann (Tutzing, 1993).

Brahms-Institut an der Musikhochschule Lübeck: 32 Stichvorlagen von Werken Johannes Brahms, Patrimonia 107 (Berlin and Kiel, 1995).

Johannes Brahms, *Messe*, ed. Otto Biba (Vienna, 1984).

Johannes Brahms: Concerto for Violin, Op. 77: A Facsimile of the Holograph Score with an Introduction by Yehudi Menuhin and a Foreword by Jon Newsom (Washington, 1979).

Brinkmann, Reinhold, *Late Idyll: The Second Symphony of Johannes Brahms*, trans. Peter Palmer (Cambridge, Mass., 1995).

Brodbeck, David, 'Brahms, the Third Symphony, and the New German School' in Walter Frisch, ed., *Brahms and His World* (Princeton, 1990), pp. 65–80.

'The Brahms–Joachim Counterpoint Exchange; or, Robert, Clara, and "the Best Harmony between Jos. and Joh."' in David Brodbeck, ed., *Brahms Studies* (Lincoln, Nebr., 1994), pp. 30–80.

Brahms: Symphony No. 1 (Cambridge, 1997).

Clayton, Alfred, 'Brahms und Zemlinsky' in Susanne Antonicek and Otto Biba, eds., *Brahms-Kongreß Wien 1983, Kongreßbericht* (Tutzing, 1988), pp. 81–94.

Cone, Edward T., 'Three Ways of Reading a Detective Story or a Brahms Intermezzo' in Robert P. Morgan, ed., *Music: A View from Delft* (Chicago and London, 1989), pp. 77–93.

Curtis, Robert Lee, *Ludwig Bischoff: A Mid-Nineteenth Century Music Critic* (Cologne, 1979).

Dahlhaus, Carl, *Between Romanticism and Modernism: Four Studies in the Music of the Later Nineteenth Century*, trans. Mary Whittall (Berkeley, 1980).

Nineteenth-Century Music, trans. J. Bradford Robinson (Berkeley and Los Angeles, 1989).

Daverio, John, 'The *Wechsel der Töne* in Brahms's *Schicksalslied*', *Journal of the American Musicological Society* 46 (1993), pp. 84–113.

Dietrich, Albert, *Erinnerungen an Johannes Brahms* (Leipzig, 1898).

Drinker, Sophie, *Brahms and his Women's Choruses* (Merion, Pa., 1952).

Dubiel, Joseph, 'Contradictory Criteria in a Work of Brahms' in David Brodbeck, ed., *Brahms Studies* (Lincoln, Nebr., 1994), pp. 81–110.

Dunsby, Jonathan, *Structural Ambiguity in Brahms: Analytical Approaches to Four Works* (Ann Arbor, Mich., 1981).

Ehrmann, Alfred von, *Johannes Brahms* (Leipzig, 1933).

Forte, Allen, 'Motivic Design and Structural Levels in the First Movement of Brahms's String Quartet in C Minor' in Michael Musgrave, ed., *Brahms 2: Biographical, Documentary, and Analytical Studies* (Cambridge, 1987), pp. 165–96.

Friedländer, Max, *Brahms Lieder*, trans. C. L. Leese (Oxford, 1928).

Frisch, Walter, *Brahms and the Principle of Developing Variation* (Berkeley and Los Angeles, 1984).

'Brahms: From Classical to Modern' in R. Larry Todd, ed., *Nineteenth-Century Piano Music* (New York, 1990), pp. 31–54.

Brahms: The Four Symphonies (New York, 1996).

Gál, Hans, *Johannes Brahms: His Work and Personality*, trans. Joseph Stein (London, 1963).

Gay, Peter, 'Aimez-Vous Brahms? On Polarities in Modernism' in *Freud, Jews and Other Germans: Masters and Victims in Modernist Culture* (Oxford, 1978).

Geiringer, Karl, *Brahms: His Life and Work,* 2nd edn, trans. H. B. Weiner and Bernard Miall (London, 1948).

Haas, Frithjof, *Zwischen Brahms und Wagner: Der Dirigent Hermann Levi* (Zurich and Mainz,1995).

Hancock, Virginia L., *Brahms's Choral Compositions and His Library of Early Music* (Ann Arbor, Mich., 1983).

Hanslick, Eduard, *Music Criticisms 1846–99,* trans. and ed. Henry Pleasants (Baltimore, 1950).

Henschel, George, *Personal Recollections of Johannes Brahms* (Boston, 1907; rpt New York, 1978).

Musings and Memories of a Musician (London, 1918).

Herttrich, Ernst, 'Johannes Brahms – Klaviertrio H-dur Op. 8, Frühfassung und Spätfassung ein analytischer Vergleich' in Martin Bente, ed., *Musik Edition Interpretation: Gedenkschrift Günter Henle* (Munich, 1980), pp. 218–36.

Heuberger, Richard, *Erinnerungen an Johannes Brahms,* ed. K. Hofmann, 2nd edn (Tutzing, 1976).

Hofmann, Kurt, *Johannes Brahms und Hamburg,* 2nd edn (Hamburg, 1986).

Hofmann, Renate, 'Johannes Brahms im Spiegel der Korrespondenz Clara Schumanns' in Constantin Floros, Hans Joachim Marx and Peter Petersen, eds., *Brahms und seine Zeit: Symposion Hamburg 1983* (Hamburg, 1984).

Hull, Kenneth, 'Brahms the Allusive' (Ph.D. dissertation, Princeton University, 1989).

Hübbe, Walter, *Brahms in Hamburg* (Hamburg, 1905).

Joseph Joachim's Briefe an Gisela von Arnim 1852–59, ed. Johannes Joachim (Göttingen, 1911).

Letters to and from Joseph Joachim, selected and translated by Nora Bickley (London, 1914), p. 160.

Kalbeck, Max, *Johannes Brahms,* 4 vols. (Berlin, 1904–14; rpt of final edn of each vol. (1921, 1921, 1912–13, 1915), Tutzing, 1976).

Kalbeck, Max, ed., 'Fragebogen für Herrn Hofkapellmeister Albert Dietrich', transcribed in *Katalog 100: Johannes Brahms, Musikantiquariat Hans Schneider* (Tutzing, 1964).

Keys, Ivor, *Brahms Chamber Music* (Seattle, 1974).

Kraus, Antje, *Die Unterschichten Hamburgs in der ersten Hälfte des 19. Jahrhunderts* (Stuttgart, 1965).

Kraus, Detlef, 'Des Andante aus der Sonate Op. 5 von Brahms', in *Brahms Studien* III, ed. Helmut Wirth (Hamburg, 1979).

Kretzschmar, Hermann, 'Johannes Brahms' (1884), in *Gesammelte Aufsätze über Musik und Anderes aus den Grenzboten* (Leipzig, 1910).

Kross, Siegfried, 'Brahms the Symphonist' in Robert Pascall, ed., *Brahms: Biographical, Documentary and Analytical Studies* (Cambridge, 1983), pp. 125–45.

Johannes Brahms: Versuch einer kritischen Dokumentar-Biographie, 2 vols. (Bonn, 1997).

Krummacher, Friedhelm, 'Reception and Analysis: On the Brahms Quartets, Op. 51, Nos. 1 and 2', *19th-Century Music* 18 (1994/95), pp. 24–45.

Leichtentritt, Hugo, 'German Chamber Music' in *Cobbett's Cyclopaedic Survey of Chamber Music*, 2nd edn, 3 vols. (Oxford, 1963).

Litzmann, Berthold, *Clara Schumann: Ein Künstlerleben*, 3 vols. (Leipzig, 1906–9).

MacDonald, Malcolm, *Brahms* (London, 1990).

Matthews, Denis, *Brahms Piano Music* (London, 1978).

May, Florence, *Johannes Brahms*, trans. Ludmille Kirschbaum, 2 vols. in 1 (Leipzig, 1911).

The Life of Brahms, 2nd edn, 2 vols. (London, 1948).

McCorkle, Margit L., *Johannes Brahms: Thematisch-bibliographisches Werkverzeichnis* (Munich, 1984).

Meurs, Norbert, *Neue Bahnen? Aspekte der Brahms-Rezeption 1853–1868, Musik und Anschauung im 19. Jahrhundert*, vol. III (Cologne, 1996).

Moldenhauer, Hans, *Anton Webern, A Chronicle of His Life and Work* (London 1978).

Musgrave, Michael, 'The Cultural World of Brahms' in Robert Pascall, ed., *Brahms, Biographical, Documentary and Analytical Studies* (Cambridge, 1983), pp. 1–26.

'Brahms First Symphony: Thematic Coherence and Its Secret Origin', *Music Analysis* 2/2 (July 1983), pp. 117–34.

The Music of Brahms (London, 1985; rev. edn, Oxford, 1994).

Brahms: A German Requiem (Cambridge, 1996).

Musgrave, Michael, ed., *Brahms 2: Biographical, Documentary, and Analytical Studies* (Cambridge, 1987).

Mosse, George L., *The Nationalization of the Masses: Political Symbolism and Mass Movements in Germany from the Napoleonic Wars through the Third Reich* (Ithaca, NY, 1975).

Notley, Margaret, 'Brahms as Liberal: Genre, Style, and Politics in Late-19th-Century Vienna', *19th-Century Music* 17 (1993/94), pp. 107–23.

Ochs, Siegfried, *Geschehenes, Gesehenes* (Leipzig and Zurich, 1922).

Orel, Alfred, 'Ein eigenhändiges Werkverzeichnis von Johannes Brahms: Ein wichtiger Beitrag zur Brahmsforschung', *Die Musik* 29 (1937), pp. 529–41.

Osmond-Smith, David, 'The Retreat from Dynamism: A Study of Brahms's Fourth Symphony' in Robert Pascall, ed., *Brahms: Biographical, Documentary and Analytical Studies* (Cambridge, 1983), pp. 147–65.

Ostwald, Peter, *Schumann: The Inner Voices of a Musical Genius* (Boston, 1985).

Parmer, Dillon, 'Brahms the Programmatic' (Ph.D. dissertation, University of Rochester, 1995).

'Brahms, Song Quotation, and Secret Programs', *19th-Century Music* 19 (1995/96), pp. 161–90.

Pascall, Robert, 'Brahms's Missa Canonica and Its Recomposition in His Motet "Warum" Op. 74 No. 1' in Michael Musgrave, ed., *Brahms 2: Biographical, Documentary and Analytical Studies* (Cambridge, 1985), pp. 111–36.

Playing Brahms: A Study in 19th-century Performing Practice (Nottingham, 1990).

Brahms's First Symphony Andante – the Initial Performing Version. Commentary and Realization (Nottingham, 1992)

Pascall, Robert, ed., *Brahms: Biographical, Documentary and Analytical Studies* (Cambridge, 1983).

Reimann, Heinrich, *Johannes Brahms, Berühmte Musiker*: Lebens- und

Charakterbild nebst Einführung in die Werke der Meister, 5th edn (Berlin, n.d. [c. 1919]).

Reynolds, Christopher, 'A Choral Symphony by Brahms?' *19th-Century Music* 9 (1985), pp. 3–15.

Rink, John, 'Playing in Time: Rhythm, Metre and Tempo in Brahms's *Fantasien* Op. 116' in John Rink, ed., *The Practice of Performance*, (Cambridge, 1995).

Rosen, Charles, *The Classical Style: Haydn, Mozart, Beethoven*, exp. edn (New York, 1997).

'Hedwig von Salomons Tagebuchblatt, Leipzig, 5.12.1853', in *Katalog 100: Johannes Brahms, Musikantiquariat Hans Schneider* (Tutzing, 1964).

Sams, Eric, 'Brahms and His Clara Themes', *Musical Times* 112 (1971).

Schachter, Carl, 'The First Movement of Brahms's Second Symphony: The First Theme and its Consequences', *Music Analysis* 2/1 (1983), pp. 55–68.

Schenker, Heinrich, 'Brahms: Variationen und Fuge über ein Thema von Handel, op. 24', *Der Tonwille* 4/2–3 (1924), pp. 3–48.

Schoenberg, Arnold, 'Brahms the Progressive' in Leonard Stern, ed., *Style and Idea* (Berkeley and Los Angeles, 1975), pp. 398–441.

Schubring, Adolf, 'Five Early Works by Brahms', trans. Walter Frisch in Walter Frisch, ed., *Brahms and His World* (Princeton, 1990), pp. 113, 116.

'Schumanniana Nr. 8: die Schumann'sche Schule IV: Johannes Brahms', *Neue Zeitschrift für Musik* 65/12–16 (21 March –18 April 1862); trans.Walter Frisch in Walter Frisch, ed., *Brahms and his World* (Princeton, 1990), pp. 103–22.

Clara Schumann – Johannes Brahms: Briefe aus den Jahren 1853–1896, ed. Berthold Litzmann, 2 vols. (Leipzig, 1927;rpt Hildesheim and Wiesbaden, 1989).

Schumann, Robert, *On Music and Musicians*, ed. Konrad Wolff, trans. Paul Rosenfeld (Berkeley and Los Angeles, 1946).

The Marriage Diaries of Robert & Clara Schumann: From Their Wedding Day through the Russia Trip, ed. Gerd Nauhaus, trans. Peter Ostwald (Boston, 1993).

Sisman, Elaine, 'Brahms's Slow Movements: Reinventing the "Closed" Forms' in G. Bozarth, ed., *Brahms Studies: Analytical and Historical Perspectives* (Oxford, 1990), pp. 79–103.

Smallman, Basil, *The Piano Quartet and Quintet: Style, Structure, and Scoring* (Oxford, 1994).

Smyth, Ethel, *Impressions that Remained: Memoirs* (New York, 1946).

Specht, Richard, *Johannes Brahms*, trans. E. Blom (London, 1928).

Spengel, Julius, *Johannes Brahms, Characterstudie* (Hamburg, 1898).

Steiner, Adolf, *Johannes Brahms*, 1. Teil, *86.Neujahrsblatt der Allgemeinen Musikgesellschaft Zürich* (Zurich, 1898).

Stephenson, Kurt, *Johannes Brahms's Heimatbekenntnis* (Hamburg, 1933).
Johannes Brahms in seiner Familie: Der Briefwechsel (Hamburg, 1973).

Stephenson, Kurt, ed., *Johannes Brahms und Fritz Simrock: Weg einer Freundschaft: Briefe des Verlegers an den Komponisten* (Hamburg, 1961).

Struck, Michael, 'New Evidence on the Genesis of Brahms's G major Violin Sonata, Op. 78', *The American Brahms Society Newsletter* 9/1 (1991), p. 5.

'Noch einmal Brahms's B major Trio: Where Was the Original Version First Performed?' *The American Brahms Society Newsletter* 9/2 (1991), pp. 8–9.

Swafford, Jan, *Johannes Brahms: A Biography* (New York, 1997).

Tovey, Donald Francis, *Essays in Musical Analysis: Chamber Music* (London, 1944).
'Brahms's Chamber Music', *The Main Stream of Music and Other Essays* (New York, 1949).

Webster, James, 'Schubert's Sonata Form and Brahms's First Maturity', *19th-Century Music* 3 (1978/79), pp. 18–35; and 4 (1979/80), pp. 52–71.
'The C Sharp Minor Version of Brahms's Op. 60', *Musical Times* 121 (1980), pp. 89–93.

Widmann, Josef Viktor, *Johannes Brahms in Erinnerungen* (Berlin, 1898).

Whittall, Arnold, 'Two of a Kind? Brahms's Op. 51 Finales' in Michael Musgrave, ed., *Brahms 2: Biographical, Documentary and Analytical Studies* (Cambridge, 1987), pp. 145–64.

Wintle, Christopher, 'The "Sceptred Pall": Brahms's Progressive Harmony' in Michael Musgrave, ed., *Brahms 2: Biographical, Documentary and Analytical Studies* (Cambridge, 1987), pp. 197-222.

Zaunschirrn, Franz, *Der frühe und der späte Brahms* (Hamburg, 1988).

Index